Flames Across the Border

Flames the

Honour pricks me on. Yea, but how if honour prick me off when I come on? how then? Can honour set-to a leg? No. Or an arm? No. Or take away the grief of a wound? No. Honour hath no skill in surgery, then? No. What is honour? A word. What is that word, honour? Air. A trim reckoning! Who hath it? He that died o' Wednesday. Doth he feel it? No. Doth he hear it? No. 'Tis insensible, then? Yea, to the dead. But will it not live with the living? No. Why? Detraction will not suffer it. Therefore I'll none of it: honour is a mere scutcheon: and so ends my catechism.

Falstaff, in Shakespeare's
Henry IV, Part I, act 5, sc. 1.

Pierre Berton

Across Border

1813~1814

Anchor Canada

National Library of Canada Cataloguing in Publication Data

Berton, Pierre, 1920-
  Flames across the border, 1813–1814

Includes index.
ISBN 0-385-65838-9

1. Canada – History – War of 1812.* 2. United States – History –
War of 1812. I. Title.

FC442.B468 2001   971.03'4   C2001-930599-0
E355.B468 2001

Cover photo: Tecumseh, courtesy The Field Museum (A93851c)
Cover design: CS Richardson
Printed and bound in Canada

Published in Canada by
Anchor Canada, a division of
Random House of Canada Limited

Visit Random House of Canada Limited's website:
www.randomhouse.ca

FRI 10 9 8 7 6 5 4 3 2

Books by Pierre Berton

The Royal Family
The Mysterious North
Klondike
Just Add Water and Stir
Adventures of a Columnist
Fast Fast Fast Relief
The Big Sell
The Comfortable Pew
The Cool, Crazy, Committed
    World of the Sixties
The Smug Minority
The National Dream
The Last Spike
Drifting Home
Hollywood's Canada
My Country
The Dionne Years
The Wild Frontier
The Invasion of Canada
Flames Across the Border
Why We Act Like Canadians
The Promised Land
Vimy
Starting Out
The Arctic Grail
The Great Depression
Niagara: A History of the Falls
My Times: Living with History
1967, The Last Good Year

Picture Books
The New City (with Henri Rossier)
Remember Yesterday
The Great Railway
The Klondike Quest
Pierre Berton's Picture Book
    of Niagara Falls
Winter
The Great Lakes
Seacoasts
Pierre Berton's Canada

Anthologies
Great Canadians
Pierre and Janet Berton's
    Canadian Food Guide
Historic Headlines
Farewell to the Twentieth Century
Worth Repeating
Welcome to the Twenty-first
    Century

Fiction
Masquerade (pseudonym
    Lisa Kroniuk)

Books for Young Readers
The Golden Trail
The Secret World of Og
Adventures in Canadian History
    (22 volumes)

CONTENTS

Maps

Drawn by Geoffrey Matthews

Cast of Major Characters

Henry Goulburn, British politician; commissioner at Ghent peace talks, 1814.

George Gleig, Lieutenant, 85th Regiment, attack on Washington, 1814.

John Harvey, Lieutenant-Colonel; deputy adjutant-general, British forces in Canada.

Lord Liverpool, Prime Minister, 1812–27.

George Macdonell, Lieutenant-Colonel, 2nd Battalion, Select Embodied Militia.

Robert McDouall, Lieutenant-Colonel, Royal Newfoundland Regiment; aide to Sir George Prevost, 1813; commander at Michilimackinac, 1814.

William Hamilton Merritt, Captain; commander, Provincial Dragoons.

Sir George Prevost, Governor General and Commander-in-Chief of His Majesty's forces in Canada, the Atlantic Colonies, and Bermuda.

Henry Procter, Major-General; commander, Right Division, Detroit frontier, 1813.

Phineas Riall, Major-General; commander, Right Division, Niagara frontier, 1814.

John Richardson, gentleman volunteer, 1st Battalion, 41st Regiment.

John Beverley Robinson, Acting Attorney General, Upper Canada.

Robert Ross, Major-General; commander of army attacking Washington, August, 1814.

Sir Roger Hale Sheaffe, Major-General; Commander-in-Chief and Administrator, Upper Canada, October 1812 – June 1813.

John Strachan, Anglican minister; chaplain of Fort York.

Tecumseh, Shawnee war chief; leader of the Indian confederacy.

John Vincent, Major-General; commander, Centre Division, Niagara frontier, 1813.

James Lucas Yeo, Commodore; commander-in-chief, naval forces on the Great Lakes.

On the American side

John Quincy Adams, American ambassador to Russia; commissioner at Ghent peace talks, 1814.

John Armstrong, Secretary of War, 1813–14.

James Bayard, Senator; commissioner at Ghent peace talks, 1814.

John Boyd, Brigadier-General; succeeded Morgan Lewis as commander at Fort George, 1813; commanded at Battle of Crysler's Farm.

Jacob Brown, Major-General; commander on Niagara frontier, 1814, succeeding James Wilkinson.

Cyrenius Chapin, Buffalo surgeon; commander of partisan irregulars, Niagara frontier, 1813.

Isaac Chauncey, Commodore; commander of naval forces on the Great Lakes.

Henry Clay, Speaker of the House; commissioner at Ghent peace talks, 1814.

George Croghan, Major, later Lieutenant-Colonel; commander at Fort Stephenson, 1813; led attack on Michilimackinac, 1814.

Henry Dearborn, Major-General; commander of Army of the North to July, 1813.

David Bates Douglass, 2nd-Lieutenant, artillery, Fort Erie.

Jesse Elliott, Lieutenant; second-in-command, naval forces, Lake Erie.

Edmund Gaines, Brigadier-General and Adjutant General; commander at Fort Erie, summer, 1814.

Albert Gallatin, Secretary of the Treasury; commissioner at Ghent peace talks, 1814.

William Henry Harrison, Major-General; former governor of Indiana Territory; commander of the Army of the Northwest.

Wade Hampton, Major-General; commander of the army on Lake Champlain, 1813.

Jarvis Hanks, drummer boy, 11th Infantry.

George Izard, Major-General; operated on Lake Champlain and Niagara frontier, 1814.

Thomas Jesup, Major, 19th Infantry, at Chippawa and Lundy's Lane.

Richard Johnson, Congressman; Colonel, Kentucky regiment of mounted rifles, Battle of the Thames, 1813.

Morgan Lewis, Major-General, Niagara frontier, succeeding Zebulon Pike as Dearborn's second-in-command to June 1813; second-in-command to James Wilkinson, autumn, 1813.

George McClure, Brigadier-General, New York Militia; commander at Fort George, late autumn, 1813.

Thomas Macdonough, Commodore, naval forces, Lake Champlain, 1814.

Alexander Macomb, Brigadier-General; commander of army at Plattsburgh, September, 1814.

James Madison, President, 1809–17.

Benajah Mallory, Major, Canadian Volunteers; former member Upper Canadian legislature; traitor. Succeeded Joseph Willcocks in command.

Abraham Markle, Major, Canadian Volunteers; former member Upper Canadian legislature; traitor.

James Monroe, Secretary of State, 1811–15. Replaced John Armstrong as Secretary of War, autumn, 1814.

Oliver Hazard Perry, Commodore, naval forces, Lake Erie, 1813.

Zebulon Montgomery Pike, Brigadier-General; second-in-command to Dearborn at York, 1813.

Peter Buell Porter, Congressman; Quartermaster General, later Major-General, New York Militia, Niagara frontier, 1813–14.

Eleazar Ripley, Brigadier-General under Jacob Brown, Niagara frontier, 1814.

Jonathan Russell, American ambassador to Sweden; commissioner at Ghent peace talks, 1814.

Winfield Scott, Colonel and Adjutant-General, Niagara frontier, 1813; Brigadier-General under Jacob Brown, Niagara frontier, 1814.

Tobias Stansbury, Brigadier-General; commander of Maryland Militia, Bladensburg, August, 1814.

James Wilkinson, Major-General; commander, Army of the North, 1813, succeeding General Dearborn.

Joseph Willcocks, Lieutenant-Colonel, Canadian Volunteers; former member Upper Canadian legislature; traitor.

William Winder, Brigadier-General; captured at Stoney Creek, 1813; commander of Washington defences, 1814.

Eleazer Wood, Captain, Engineers, siege of Fort Meigs, 1813; Colonel and aide to Jacob Brown, Niagara frontier, 1814.

PRELUDE: New Brunswick Goes to War

MADAWASKA RIVER, LOWER CANADA, March 5, 1813

The cold has become unbearable. The temperature stands at twenty-seven below, Fahrenheit. A northeaster, sweeping down the frozen expanse of Lake Temiscouata, cuts like a scythe through the greatcoats of the soldiers, bent double in the teeth of the gale. The snow is frozen hard as sand. Only the squeak of the toboggans, the rasp of the snowshoes, and the whine of the wind breaks the white silence. It has been like this for the best part of a fortnight, ever since the regiment left Saint John, and it is growing worse.

The light company of the 104th – the New Brunswick Regiment – shuffles forward, single file, following the winding course of the Madawaska. This is the rearguard, the last of six companies, each spread out a day apart, trudging through the Canadian winter toward Lower Canada to help resist the next American invasion. In this silent, hostile forest there is no sign of settlement, no tinkle of sleighbells, no welcoming pillar of smoke – only the sullen pines, half crushed beneath their burden of snow. Even the birds are silent; it is too cold for song.

Lieutenant John Le Couteur gasps forward on his snowshoes, the wind cutting off his breath. In spite of layers of flannel and fur, the cold seems to reach to the very core of his body. He is temporarily in charge, for his captain has taken a party on ahead to prepare huts and firewood. Perhaps there will be shelter at the day's end, but Le Couteur remembers the previous evening when the men's hands were so numb they could scarcely work, let alone singe a piece of salt pork over a sputtering flame.

As he leads his squad around a bend in the river, he is alarmed to see that the forward elements have stopped, causing the centre and rear to bunch up. In this weather it is death to halt. He steps out of the line, flounders through the deep snow beside the track, and moves up the column, noting that every man he passes is rubbing snow into frostbitten cheeks. His own nose is frozen, but he cannot attend to that. He must get Private Reuben Rogers onto a toboggan and under a pile of blankets: the soldier's entire body is an ulcerated mass from frostbite, as if he had been plunged into a vat of boiling water. That done, he gets the column moving again.

It is slow going. Le Couteur knows that the men in the lead suffer most and must be replaced every four or five minutes if they are to survive. By the time the company reaches the huddle of huts, 90 men out of 105 are suffering from frostbite. The roughly constructed quarters are over-crowded — jammed with shivering troops because the company ahead has been forced back across the lake by the gale. That night Le Couteur finds it impossible to keep warm. One man who tries gets too close to the fire and burns his feet.

The next morning, both companies set off across the Grand Portage between Lake Temiscouata and Rivière du Loup (leaving poor Rogers behind with a corporal). They force their way through a spectral land-scape — burned country, where the skeleton pines rise out of the twelve-foot drifts like ghosts. Here are weary hills to climb and dangerous, ice-sheathed slopes down which to manoeuvre runaway toboggans. Sleep that night is not possible, for a high wind turns the pine thatch on one hut to tinder dryness. When it catches fire, officers and men turn out, thigh deep in the snow, freezing their feet as they struggle to put out the flames.

After these adversities, all that follows is anticlimax. As the men trudge off, dragging their toboggans, Le Couteur realizes with a sense of relief that the wilderness is almost behind them. Presently he hears the music of distant sleighbells breaking the interminable silence. A horse and cutter appears, loaded with rum and provisions from the commissariat in Quebec. The village of St. André is not far off, and here the men from New Brunswick and Nova Scotia — sons of Loyalists and British sol-diers — view for the first time the great sweep of the St. Lawrence. A road of beaten snow leads upriver to the capital; on this hard surface it is not difficult to march twenty miles in a day.

A fortnight later, the entire regiment is in Quebec City, basking in the praise of the Governor General. But the march is not over. Now the New Brunswickers set off for Montreal with Le Couteur pushing on ahead to report their speedy arrival to Major-General Francis De Rottenburg. Are the troops in good wind? the General asks. In excellent wind, replies the proud lieutenant. Then, says the General, they can push on another two hundred miles to Kingston.

"They think we are like the children of Israel," one of the soldiers cries when he hears that news. "We must march forty years before we halt!"

On they go, sweating now in the spring sun, wading to their hips in icy freshets, but never faltering until, on April 12, an extraordinary spectacle greets them. The town of Kingston lies before them and beyond, a familiar sight to any Maritimer: the masts and spars of tall ships.

16

"The sea! The sea!" the men cry out. "The ships! The ships!"

A flood of sensations overcomes Le Couteur: astonishment...delight... wonder. Here is an entire squadron of warships frozen on the bosom of the lake! He had not expected to find men-of-war so far inland.

The date is April 12. In just fifty-two days, close to six hundred troops have marched more than seven hundred miles, most of it on snowshoes, under the worst possible conditions without losing a man (for the frost-bitten Private Rogers is about to rejoin his company). This remarkable trek has helped to tip the scales of war. Directly across the lake, at Sackets Harbor, an American army, poised to invade Canada, waits for the ice to break. Its target was Kingston. But now, with reinforcements pouring in — their numbers blown out of all proportion by rumour — that target has been changed. The Americans will attack York instead. The lifeline that links the two Canadas will not be severed.

OVERVIEW
The All-Canadian War

THE BORDER WAR OF 1812 was a singular conflict. Geography, climate, weather, language, and propinquity combined to make it distinctively Canadian. It was a seasonal war: campaigns were timed with one eye on the calendar, the other on the thermometer. It was a stop-and-go war: seeding and harvest often took priority over siege and attack. It was a neighbours' war (but no less vicious for that): men fought their own kin; others refused to fight; trade between enemies was frowned on but never successfully suppressed. It was a pinch-penny war: in 1813, the Americans actually tried to run it on a budget of $1,480,000 a month – a parsimony that greatly frustrated the campaign of that year. It was a long-distance war, fought on a thousand-mile front from the Upper Mississippi to Lake Champlain; yet the total number of combatants never exceeded the combined casualties in the greatest of the Napoleonic battles. Finally, it was an incendiary war in which private homes as well as public buildings and military fortifications went up in flames, fuelling a desire for revenge that transcended strategy and politics.

It was also the last war fought on Canadian soil. By the end of the first campaign in January, 1813, Canada had successfully resisted all attempts at invasion. As a result, the morale of the United States was at its lowest ebb. The government of James Madison, which had hurled its armies at the Canadian border to chastise Great Britain for her arrogance on the high seas, had learned that the conquest of British North America was not, after all, "a mere matter of marching."

Thomas Jefferson's thoughtless phrase left a sour taste in the mouths of those who had survived the triple disasters of Detroit, Queenston Heights, and Frenchtown. These prisoners of war were the only Americans left in Canada when the campaign begun in 1812 ended in massacre at Frenchtown in the wilderness of Michigan territory.

Three armies captured! Outbluffed in August by the British general Isaac Brock, the Americans at Detroit gave up without firing a shot, their commander doomed to face a court martial for cowardice. At Queenston, in October, Canada lost her hero-general but won a resounding victory when the New York militia refused to cross the river or hid in the underbrush waiting to surrender. And at French-town, in January, on the frozen banks of the River Raisin, when the flower of Kentucky fell to the scalping knives of the Potawatomi, the remnants of another army were herded across the border to captivity.

Now it was too cold to fight, especially for those southerners who marched blithely north in their thin linsey-woolsey blouses, expecting to be home before the leaves deserted the maples. In Europe, the remnants of Napoleon's Grande Armée on its winter retreat from Moscow continued to skirmish with Cossack guerrillas, but on the Canadian border the combatants simply sat it out. Except for Frenchtown, campaigns ended in December not to resume until spring.

In the defence of British North America, the weather was as important an ally as the Indians and the British regulars, who bore the brunt of the fighting. The invaders could not move until the ice left the lakes. A forward thrust late in the season could mean, if not disaster, at least stalemate. No American was prepared to sit out the winter on hostile ground in hastily built huts or thin tents. Even on friendly soil, conditions were such that officers deserted their own troops.

This was a wilderness war, much of it fought in such isolation that the combatants had no idea of events in the outer world. On the western flank in the first months of 1813, the soldiers and fur traders who formed the militia would have had no clear picture of the war in Europe: the decimation of the Grande Armée in its retreat from Moscow; the defection of Prussia from the Napoleonic cause; the resurgence of an anti-French coalition, which was already signalling the downfall of Bonaparte. In wintertime, the news could take four months or longer to reach the captured bastion of Michilimackinac Island at the western end of Lake Huron.

There were further anomalies. The War of 1812 was not the only war in which both sides spoke the same language, but it was one of the few in which tens of thousands on both sides violently opposed it, sat it out, or maintained both friendly and commercial relations with the so-called enemy. The absence of a language barrier made desertion attractive, espionage easy, subterfuge possible. In the dark it was difficult to distinguish friend from foe. Spies and planted decoys crossed and re-crossed the border with information for opposing generals, some of it authentic, some of it intended to deceive.

The Atlantic provinces took little part in the war, having made a pact with their American neighbours to continue business as usual. The New England states, especially Vermont and Massachusetts, were so opposed to "Mr. Madison's war" that they refused to send troops or lend money to the government. In 1814, they even considered secession.

Thousands of state militia, especially those from New York and Pennsylvania, thought so little of the conflict that they stood on their constitutional rights and refused to cross the border at crucial moments during the campaign. America's Founding Fathers had never contemplated an offensive war; the state militia, in the law's strictest interpretation, could be used only in the defence of the Union.

In Upper Canada, where three out of five settlers were recent arrivals from the United States, there was at best apathy, at worst treason. The Loyalists, who made up a fifth of the population, were keen to fight, as were the sons of British immigrants, army officers, upper-class merchants, and civil servants. But the farmers, desperate to harvest their crops, scorned by the ruling elite, virtually disenfranchised by the colonial autocracy, felt no such compunction. Much of the despair felt at the beginning of the conflict had been wiped out by Brock's successes. But most yeomen (as they were officially called) simply wanted to be left alone.

If propinquity encouraged understanding, distance exaggerated differences. Kentucky was hawkish from the beginning, but by February, 1813, its zeal had turned to rage. Henry Procter, the victor at Frenchtown on the River Raisin, had recrossed the Detroit River hurriedly, expecting a counter-attack and leaving his wounded prisoners, Kentuckians all, to the savagery of his Indian allies. The resultant massacre brought the state to the boiling point. *"Remember the Raisin!"* became a recruiting cry. Few of the new soldiers, thirsting for revenge, knew what a Canadian looked like. Many lumped them with the Indians. As for the Canadians, they thought of Kentuckians as wild beasts.

Although President Madison had disavowed any territorial ambitions at the war's outset, most Kentuckians and not a few others saw the invasion of Canada as a war of conquest. That was not the war's original purpose. America only wanted to teach the British a lesson by attacking their North American colonies. The Napoleonic war had strained British-American relations to the breaking point. Determined to throttle Bonaparte, Great Britain thought nothing of enforcing her blockade of European ports by stopping and searching American ships in mid-ocean. Desperately short of seamen, she insisted that every man born an Englishman must serve as one. By impressing from U.S. ships any sailor she considered British – and at cannon point if necessary – she succeeded in enraging all Americans.

"Honour" was a word much used in 1812. The British were still treating the United States as a colony. The Americans, in honour, could not accept that. The British, in honour, could not back down. The War of 1812 was to be called, with some truth, the Second War of Independence. Britain finally gave in on the matter of the blockade, but the news did not reach Washington before war was declared. By then it was too late; the war fever, once whipped up, would not subside. Madison announced that hostilities would continue as long as the British insisted on impressing seamen from American vessels. "Impressment" became a war cry. The Americans, Madison insisted, would *never* give in on impressment. Nor would Great Britain, mistress of the seas. Honour would not allow it.

Because the United States could not carry the war to the heart of Britain, she did the next best thing and attacked Canada. And so this war for maritime rights was fought mainly on land and on fresh water by men who were largely untrained and often reluctant, led by officers who were often incompetent and usually myopic.

As the campaign of 1813 approached, the American regular forces outnumbered the British seventeen thousand to seven thousand. This was illusory; many of the so-called regulars in the U.S. armies were untrained recruits. In addition, the British had an additional force of at least two thousand Indians at Detroit and on the Niagara frontier, the best and most constant under the command of the brilliant Shawnee war chief, Tecumseh. The Americans had not, as yet, used Indians in battle.

Both sides could also call upon large reserves of citizen soldiers – the militia, always an uncertain factor in battle. The American militia draftees and volunteers were generally called up for short terms – as little as sixty days, as much as a year. With the exception of the Kentuckians, most refused to continue in service beyond their designated term.

In Canada, the Sedentary Militia, largely untrained and incompetent, was available as an auxiliary arm in time of crisis. All fit males between eighteen and sixty were obliged to serve in it when circumstances required. The Incorporated Militia of Upper Canada consisted of volunteers serving for the duration and made up of young men attracted by patriotism, a sense of adventure, or the bounty of eight dollars paid to every man on enlistment. In Lower Canada, a similar body, the Select Embodied Militia, composed of men from eighteen to twenty-five, was drawn by lot to serve for a maximum of two years. These were paid and trained as regulars. There were, in addition, regular units recruited in Canada such as the Glengarry Light Infantry (or Fencibles) and the Provincial Corps of Light Infantry, better known as Canadian Voltigeurs. When properly trained, these men fought as bravely and as efficiently as the British regulars. At Châteauguay they stood off an entire American army, unaided.

At the senior levels, on both sides of the border, there was extraordinary incompetence. Many of the British regular officers were

Wellington's cast-offs, who had reached their rank through the indefensible practice of purchasing promotion. In British military eyes, the Canadian war had a low priority. As a British Army surgeon, William "Tiger" Dunlop observed, "any man whom The Duke deemed unfit for the Peninsula was considered quite good enough for the Canadian market."

As for the American army, at the start of the war Winfield Scott, a future commanding general, remembered that "the old officers had, very generally, sunk into either sloth, ignorance, or habits of intemperate drinking." Regimental leaders were chosen for their political influence.

Federalists, who opposed the government, were excluded from command and "the selection from those communities consisted mostly of coarse and ignorant men," while in others, educated men were passed over in favour of "swaggerers, dependants, decayed gentlemen... utterly unfit for any military purpose whatever." Although some of the worst of these choices had been put out to pasture after the disasters of 1812 and eight new brigadier-generals created, Scott's blunt critique still held true in 1813.

To a visitor from another milieu, the European style of battle transferred to Canada must have seemed incongruous, even comic. Such a one was the celebrated Sauk chief, Black Hawk, who was contemptuous of the white man's mode of fighting. As he explained it to his astonished comrades: "Instead of stealing upon each other and taking every advantage to *kill the enemy* and *save our own people*, as we do (which, with us, is considered good policy in a war chief), they march out, in open daylight, and fight regardless of the number of warriors they may lose." The observant Black Hawk then gave a witty account of the self-serving dispatches and General Orders that opposing commanders used to justify their blunders and make defeat seem like victory:

After the battle is over, they retire to feast and drink wine, as if nothing had happened; after which, they make a *statement in writing* of what they have done — *each party claiming the victory!* and neither giving an account of half the number that have been killed

26

on their own side. They all fought like braves, but would not do to *lead a war party* with us.... Those chiefs would do to *paddle* a canoe, but not *steer* it....

The regular troops on both sides were trained to fight the kind of European set-piece battle that raised Black Hawk's eyebrows. In 1812, parade-ground drill and army tactics were identical. The basic infantry weapon was the awkward, muzzle-loading Brown Bess musket, a notoriously inaccurate weapon scarcely able to hit a barn door at one hundred feet—and not meant to. The little one-ounce ball, wobbling down the unrifled barrel, could fly off in any direction. This did not matter, for the soldier did not aim his musket; he pointed it in the direction of the enemy line, fired it only when ordered. The effect of several hundred men, marching in line, shoulders touching, each firing in unison, reloading, and advancing behind a spray of shot—the file closers filling the gaps as soon as a man dropped—could disconcert all but the best-trained troops. The noise alone was terrifying, for the musket's roar makes the crack of a modern rifle sound like a popgun. And, in those days before smokeless powder, the battlefield was obscured by thick greyish white clouds shortly after the first volleys were loosed.

A well-trained soldier could fire off five rounds in a minute if on his own, or two or three a minute if firing in unison—a singular tribute to the persistence of the drill sergeants, for the loading of the Brown Bess was an awkward business, although the army drill manual reduced it to eighteen swift, economical motions. The weapon was fired when the firelock struck the flint, in the fashion of a modern cigarette lighter. (The larger locks on heavy cannon worked on the identical principle.) In practice, since the musket was a short-range weapon, an advancing line rarely fired more than two or three volleys; after that the bayonet was used—the British, especially, considered it the basic infantry weapon. The rifle was slower firing but more accurate and probably more effective in bush warfare.

The regulars who fought in line were not the neat-looking soldiers of the war paintings. Their uniforms were patched, tattered, sometimes hanging in shreds. Some had no uniforms. The phrase "literally naked" appears again and again in the official correspondence of both

27

armies from commanders complaining that their men have neither shoes, tunics, nor pantaloons. Sanitation was primitive, sickness widespread. Men sometimes went a year without being paid, and hundreds deserted for that reason alone.

In battle after battle, the combatants on both sides were at least half drunk. Physicians believed that a daily issue of spirits was essential to the good health of the troops who, in spite of it, suffered and often died from measles, malaria, typhus, typhoid, influenza, and a variety of diseases that went under the vague collective names of "ague" or "lake fever." The British were given a daily glass of strong Jamaica rum. The Americans were fed a quarter-pint of raw whiskey. Many a teen-aged farm boy got his first taste of spirits in the army, and many were corrupted by it. An era of drunkenness, which led to the temperance movement in mid-century, was surely a legacy of the war. Much of the looting in the wake of battle was initiated by men seeking hard liquor.

The lack of hospital supplies and proper food helped to bolster the sick list. In Canada, almost every item the army needed, from rum to new uniforms, came by ship from overseas. Every scrap of canvas, every yard of rope, every anchor, cannonball, bolt, cable, rivet came across the ocean by sail to Montreal. From there it was trundled by sleigh in winter or flatboat in summer to Kingston, York, Fort George, or Amherstburg. Troops on the Niagara peninsula, a thousand miles from the sea, were fed on pork from Ireland, flour from England, grog from the West Indies. Upper Canada was joined to the lower province by the most tenuous of supply lines – the St. Lawrence route. If the Americans could cut that lifeline at Kingston, the upper province would certainly wither and fall. That was the basic American strategy in 1812 – a strategy foiled by Brock and Tecumseh. With the new campaign awaiting only the opening of the lakes, it remained the American strategy in 1813.

Three new armies threatened Canada. The Army of the North at Plattsburgh on Lake Champlain, only fifty miles south of Montreal, forced the British to keep the bulk of their troops in Lower Canada to meet the threat. The Army of the Center, at Sackets Harbor, Oswego, and the Niagara River, threatened Kingston, Fort George, and York. The Army of the Northwest, under William Henry Harrison, secure behind the ramparts of Fort Meigs on the Maumee, was poised to retake Detroit, cross the river, and threaten Fort Amherstburg and the valley of the Thames.

John Armstrong, the new American Secretary of War, worked out the strategy. In order to field enough men to cut the Canadian lifeline he planned to move the Plattsburgh army secretly to Sackets Harbor. There, the combined forces under Major-General Henry Dearborn would, with the co-operation of the newly built American fleet, sweep across the lake and capture Kingston. Harrison, on the American left flank, was ordered to create enough diversions to prevent British reinforcements being sent east to resist the American thrust. But he was told not to attack Canada until a second American fleet, under construction on Lake Erie, was ready to seize control of the waters. The Americans had learned an expensive lesson in 1812: he who controls the lakes controls the war.

On both Lake Erie and Lake Ontario, the two sides were engaged all winter in a frantic shipbuilding contest. The British were hammering together two big frigates for Lake Ontario, one at Kingston, another at York. The Americans were rushing their Lake Ontario fleet to completion at Sackets Harbor. The British had another big ship on the ways at Amherstburg, preparing for the coming struggle for Lake Erie. The Americans, who had had no vessels on Erie in 1812, were building an entire fleet at Black Rock and at Presque Isle.

Time was of the essence. The side that got its ships into the water first could control the lake. So delicate was the balance of power that whoever managed to destroy one or more enemy vessels might easily gain naval superiority.

If Kingston were to be captured, the British supply line to Upper Canada cut, and the fleet in the harbour destroyed, the war was as good as over. With undisputed control of Lake Ontario, the Americans could easily invade the upper province, then mount an attack down the St. Lawrence to seize Montreal. And yet, as spring approached both Commodore Isaac Chauncey and Major-General Dearborn began to have second thoughts about the projected attack on Kingston. Dearborn became convinced that between six and eight thou-

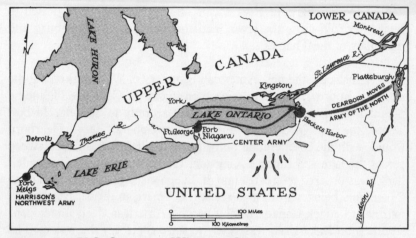

Changing U.S. Strategy, Winter, 1813

sand troops were guarding the Canadian stronghold, including three thousand regulars. This was a monumental overestimate. The regulars did not exceed nine hundred and were supported by only a handful of militia. Yet such was Dearborn's apprehension that he daily expected an attack on his base at Sackets Harbor. Chauncey, while disputing Dearborn's figures, believed that the British knew of the American plans and would be prepared for any attack. This extraordinary failure of nerve set the tone for the campaign to follow.

Somehow, the two cautious commanders managed to persuade themselves that an attack on York would be just as effective and more certain of success. In short, they decided to lop off a branch of the tree rather than attack the trunk – a total reversal of the original American plan, which had insisted on the capture of Kingston before any assault on York or Fort George.

Still, there was *something* to be gained at York, for the Americans had no corner on myopia. Instead of concentrating their activities at Kingston, the British had foolishly decided to build one of their big ships at York's unprotected harbour. That ship, *Isaac Brock*, and one or two smaller vessels, would be the object of the combined naval and military assault on the Upper Canadian capital. If the ships at York could be captured intact and transferred to the American navy, Chauncey would have control of the lake. After that, the main British bastion on

30

the Niagara – Fort George – could be seized, the peninsula rolled up, and, finally, Kingston invaded.

Both commanders succeeded in convincing the Secretary of War and each other that this strategy would be the most effective for the spring of 1813. Both waited impatiently for the ice to break in the lakes. On April 18, Sackets Harbor was open, freeing the fleet, but a week went by before the ships set sail. Finally, on the evening of April 26, after a rough passage, the invasion force appeared off the Scarborough bluffs not far from Little York. The campaign of 1813 was under way.

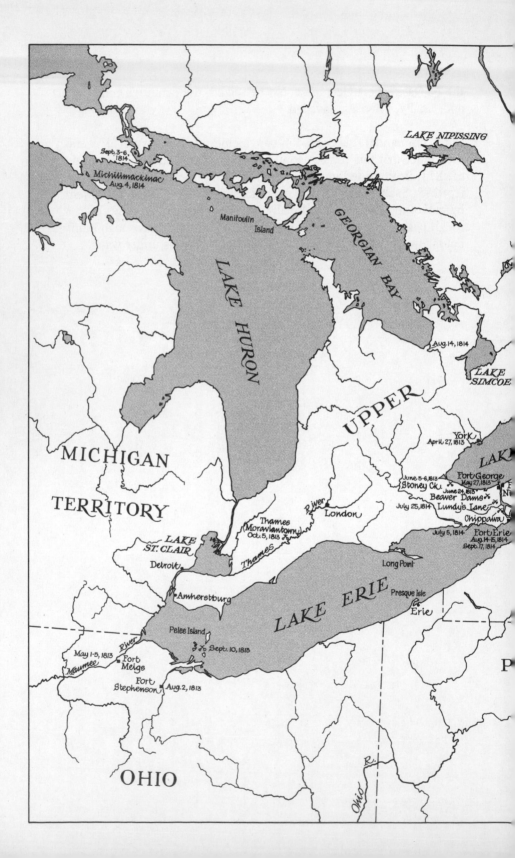

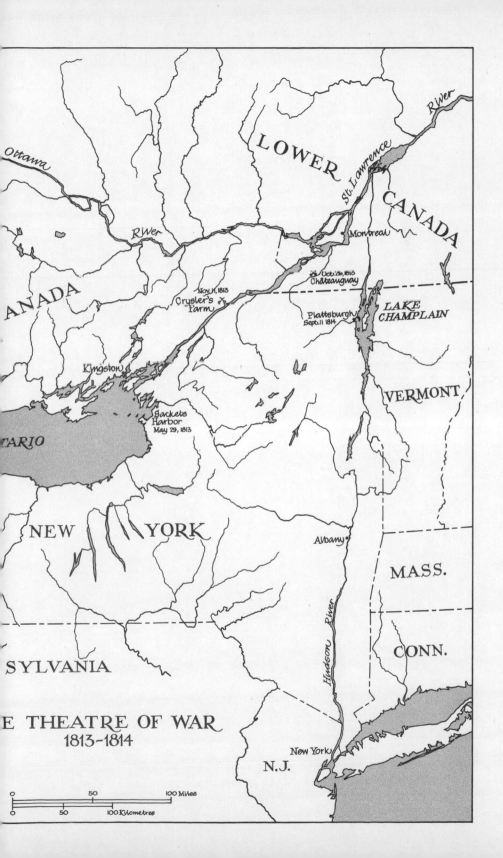

Ottawa

LOWER

River

St. Lawrence *River*

CANADA

Montreal

ANADA

Oct. 26, 1813
Chateauguay

Nov. 11, 1813
Crysler's
Farm

Plattsburgh
Sept. 11 1814

LAKE
CHAMPLAIN

Kingston

VERMONT

Sackets
Harbor
May 29, 1813

TARIO

NEW   YORK

Albany

MASS.

Hudson River

SYLVANIA

CONN.

E THEATRE OF WAR
1813–1814

New York

N.J.

0   50   100 Miles
0   50   100 Kilometres

I

THE CAPTURE OF
LITTLE YORK
April 26 – May 2, 1813

While its left wing holds fast on the Lake Erie front, the main American army, under Major-General Dearborn, embarks at Sackets Harbor to attack York, the capital of Upper Canada. Its purpose is twofold: to seize the two large warships in Toronto harbour, add them to its fleet, and thus gain naval superiority on Lake Ontario; and to destroy the garrison troops. That accomplished, the American command is convinced that Fort George, and later Kingston, will fall before a combined land and water attack, and Upper Canada will be out of the war.

YORK, UPPER CANADA, April 26, 1813

The Reverend Dr. John Strachan, schoolmaster, missionary, and chaplain of the York garrison, is in the act of drafting a letter to his mentor, the Reverend James Brown, professor at Glasgow University.

"I have just received a letter from my Brother sealed with black," Strachan has written. "My mother...is no more.... My mind is strong to bear misfortune tho it sometimes recoils upon itself. My heart would break before a Spectator knew I was much affected. I think that I can bear calamity better than others...."

Calamity of another kind is lying just beyond the eastern bluffs, but the stoical clergyman is not aware of it. Having unburdened himself, he changes the subject, suggests publication of a joint volume of sermons, then suddenly breaks off, blotting the paper, as an express rider, galloping through the muddy streets, shouts out his news.

"...I am interrupted," Strachan writes. "An express has come in to tell us that the enemy's Flotilla is within a few miles steering for this place all is hurry, and confusion, and I do not know, when I shall be able to finish this...."

But finish it he will, some six weeks later, making a fair copy of the blotted draft, which he carefully saves, as he saves everything – his letters, first and final copies, poems, manuscripts, journals, sermons, and polemics – for the Reverend Doctor rejoices in the conviction that he is marked for posterity. In that he is right, for coming events will help propel him into a position of leadership. John Strachan will shortly become the most powerful man in Upper Canada aside from the Governor himself, the acknowledged leader of the ruling elite soon to be known as the Family Compact.

Before he puts his pen aside, Strachan adds one more sentence: "I am not afraid, but our Commandant is weak."

It is a revealing remark by a man who prides himself on having conquered all emotions, or at least their outward manifestations – fear, passion, grief – and who sees himself also as a military expert, an armchair general. He has pronounced views on almost everything, thinks nothing of dispatching long letters of military advice to professional soldiers. An amateur tactician, he is an opponent of the defensive strategy prescribed by the British war office and carried out by the cautious and conciliatory commander-in-chief, Sir George Prevost, Governor General of Canada.

"Defensive warfare will ruin the country," declares Strachan. Did not Isaac Brock, his dead hero, believe that offence was the best defence? In the pugnacious clergyman's view, Major-General Sir Roger Hale Sheaffe, Brock's successor in charge of the forces of Upper Canada, is weak and vacillating. As for the navy, its officers are "the greatest cowards who ever lived." Strachan reserves his praise for the civilian soldiers who make up the militia, especially the York Volunteers, who number among their officers a commendable sprinkling of his own protégés. In Strachan's view, the militia "are capable of doing more than the bravest Veterans."

This is bunkum. The militia fought bravely enough at Queenston Heights; but many are badly trained – in many cases not trained at all – and have a dismaying habit of quitting their duty for the harvest fields.

Yet such are Strachan's persuasive powers that he will one day convince the country, against all evidence, that these civilians are the saviours of Upper Canada. It is an attractive myth, powerful enough to unite a province. A century after the war, it will still be believed.

Strachan, then, is the catalyst that will make this grubby little war appear as a great national enterprise, in which an aroused and loyal populace almost single-handedly repulses a corrupt and despotic invader. Even before war threatened, he understood his duty: to save Upper Canada from the Americans. For in Strachan's eyes they are "vain and rapacious and without honor," obsessed with "licentious liberty."

That is also the view of the Loyalists, those American Tories who moved into Canada after the Revolution and who must continue to justify that decision by rejecting all republican and democratic values. Strachan believes as implicitly in the British colonial system as he believes in the Church of England. A cornerstone of his faith is the partnership of Church and State, especially in matters of education – a useful tool to combat republicanism. He both despises and fears the incursion of Methodism, an alien cult from below the border, "filling the country with the most deplorable fanaticism." He is equally aghast at the number of American settlers pouring into the province from the border states, bringing with them – in his view – an irreligious and materialistic way of life.

He is a man of many convictions. If the stocky figure in clergyman's black, moving across the mud-spattered cobbles of Little York seeking more news of the Yankee fleet, is subject to doubts, he keeps them concealed behind a dour mask. At thirty-five he is not unhandsome – a black Scot with a straight nose, a firm cleft chin, and drooping eyes – a little sad, a little haughty. He is beyond argument the most energetic man in town, if not in the province, and, as events are about to prove, one of the most courageous. He teaches the chosen in his own grammar school, runs his parish, presides at weddings, funerals, christenings, and military parades, pokes his nose regularly into government, and manages a prodigious literary output: textbooks, newspaper articles, sermons, an emigrant's guide, moral essays, and an effusion of indifferent poetry – sonnets, quatrains, lyrics, odes – even an autobiography, set down at the age of twenty-two.

The war has hardened his attitudes. To him it is a just war, one that Christians can prosecute with vigour and a clear conscience: "The justice of our cause is...indeed half the victory."

He is not alone in this conviction. Aboard the tall ships lurking outside the harbour, bristling with cannon, other men, equally purposeful, are preparing for bloody combat; and their leaders are as certain as John Strachan that their cause is just and that the God of battles stands resolutely in their ranks.

•

ABOARD U.S.S. MADISON, off York, Upper Canada, April 26, 1813

In his cabin on the American flagship, Zebulon Montgomery Pike, the American army's newest brigadier-general, scratches out a letter to his wife, knowing it may be his last.

"We are now standing on and off the harbor of York which we shall attack at daylight in the morning: I shall dedicate these last moments to you, my love.... I have no new injunction, no new charge to give you, nor no new idea to communicate.... Should I fall, defend my memory and only believe, had I lived, I would have aspired to deeds worthy of your husband...."

Throughout his military life Pike has aspired to deeds of glory that will bring him everlasting renown. Yet, in spite of a flaming ambition, the laurel has eluded him. Although he has been a soldier for nineteen of his thirty-four years, his only action has been an inglorious skirmish on the Canadian border the previous November, stumbling about in the dark through unknown country, his troops shooting at their own men.

He yearns for his nation's accolade. If he cannot get it in life, he is perfectly prepared to accept a hero's death. He has already written to his father, another old soldier, that he hopes to be "the happy mortal destined to turn the scale of war." If not, "may my fall be like Wolfe's – to sleep in the arms of victory."

Although he is a good officer he is better known as an explorer, in spite of the fact that his explorations have been inept and his published journals badly written, unrevealing, and inaccurate to the point of dishonesty. Twice hopelessly lost, captured and held prisoner by the Spanish, he has achieved a certain notoriety for a peak in the Rockies which bears his name, even though he did not discover it, did not climb it, did not come within fifteen miles of it. Even that dubious expedition was overshadowed by the journey of Lewis and Clark, of whom Brigadier-General Pike is more than a little jealous.

Qualities that in a civilian might be considered flaws have made him an effective commander. He is bold, even impulsive. Having eloped with his cousin, to the fury of her wealthy father, he dramatically declared, "Whilst I have breath I will never be the slave to any." Serenely confident in his own ability, he feels destined for greatness. Almost pathologically patriotic, he is a stickler for discipline and morality, lecturing his soldiers on the evils of drink and debauchery.

He is loyal to his friends and heroes, notably his long-time patron, Major-General James Wilkinson, undoubtedly the greatest rogue ever to wear two stars, a man despised and distrusted by almost every other officer save Pike. This commendable if foolhardy fealty has frustrated Pike's ambitions. In spite of years of politicking, promotion has been maddeningly slow. The war is his opportunity. "If we go into

Canada," he wrote to Wilkinson, "you will hear of my fame or of my death. For I am determined to seek the 'Bubble' even in the cannon's mouth."

Who knows what the morrow may hold? Further promotion, perhaps. Pike has been chosen to lead the troops in the attack on York, for his commanding general, Henry Dearborn, is ill, or pretends to be. An indecisive, grotesque pudding of a man, who looks and acts far older than his sixty years, Dearborn longs for retirement. He scarcely inspires confidence in his troops, who call him Granny. At 250 pounds, he is so gross that he has trouble getting about and must be trundled in a two-wheeled device, later to be copied by midwestern farmers and dubbed a "dearborn."

The fleet stands off the bluffs to the east of the Don River – fourteen sail in all, jammed with fourteen hundred troops. Six hundred are crowded aboard *Madison*, many seasick, all weary of close quarters. Now, after four days of fits and starts, the troops learn that the attack will be made on the Upper Canadian capital and not, as some believed, on Fort George, at the Niagara's mouth, or on Kingston.

Pike's orders to his officers are explicit: any man who fires his musket or quits his post is to be instantly put to death. The bayonet is to be used in preference to the bullet. Plunderers of private property will be shot, but public stores may be looted with impunity. The honour of the American army is at stake; the country cannot suffer another defeat; "the disgraces which have recently tarnished our arms" must be wiped clean. Honour – that most precious of all human commodities – must finally be satisfied.

●

LITTLE YORK, April 26, 1813

As General Pike seals the letter to his wife, Mrs. Grant Powell, dressed in her finest gown, waits nervously in her drawing room on Front Street for the guests she has invited to supper. They are more than fashionably late. The clock ticks off the minutes; finally, one woman arrives; nobody else. What can it all mean? Is Mrs. Powell being snubbed? No; the news is not quite that bad. Her father-in-law, Mr. Justice William Dummer Powell, arrives breathlessly with the explanation: the American fleet has been sighted; he and all other able-bodied men have been called on to bear arms – everyone between the ages of sixteen and sixty, and even some outside that span. Young Allan MacNab, a mere fourteen but big for his age, has shouldered a musket; so has John Basil, the ancient doorkeeper of the Legislative Council.

Justice Powell, in common with John Strachan, most government officials, British officers, and common soldiers, is convinced that the attack can be repulsed. Major-General Sheaffe may be a weak commander in Strachan's belief, but at least he is in town, having postponed his departure for Fort George because of a hunch that the Americans are coming. Also, by good fortune, two companies of the British 8th Regiment, known as the King's, just happen to be passing through York.

Now, as John Strachan leaves his house to seek more details and Mrs. Powell ruefully cancels her supper party, the farmers begin to straggle in, weapons on their shoulders. Some have had militia training. Lieutenant Ely Playter has just reached his farmhouse on Yonge Street after a day at the garrison when he is routed out again, with his brother George, by Major William Allan, a leading merchant now second-in-command of the York Volunteers. Wartime speculation in flour, pork, and rum will make Allan wealthy. The events of this week will help make him powerful as well.

York is a community of fewer than a thousand souls. Now it is abuzz. People rush about, hiding valuables, burying treasure, exchanging news, gawking at soldiers.

Donald McLean, Clerk of the House of Assembly, who has exchanged gown for musket, hurries to the home of the absent inspector general and squirrels away all of the public papers.

The Chief Justice, Thomas Scott, and his fellow jurist, Powell, both members of the province's executive council, hurry to the home of Prideaux Selby, the Receiver General. Selby is on his deathbed, insensible to all the events of this and future nights. He is beyond help, but the three thousand pounds of public money in his keeping is not. The pair convinces Selby's daughter that this fund must be concealed. She hides most of it in an iron chest but secretes a small sum in another container with some public documents, which she takes to Donald McLean's. The Americans, it is reckoned, will not credit the Clerk of the Assembly with having so much cash.

Major-General Sir Roger Sheaffe cannot be sure where the main attack will come. To resist the invaders he has three hundred regulars, three hundred militia, perhaps one hundred Indians. Most are in the main garrison, close to the Governor's house commanding the entrance to the harbour west of the town. But Sheaffe cannot be certain the enemy will land there. He has had to divide his force, quartering a company of regulars and some militia at the eastern end of the settlement. Until he has a clearer idea of the enemy's intention he must protect both entrances to Toronto harbour, hoping to move swiftly to repulse the landing. He will need resolute troops, but the militia are not all as eager as John Strachan believes. Some have been murmuring their discontent for days, planning to go back to their farms as soon as their pay arrives.

When Ely Playter reaches the garrison he finds a whirlwind of activity. Patrols and pickets are being dispatched in all directions for the security of the community. Playter is given a job at once: he is to take two men and search out Major James Givins of the Indian Department. The tribesmen – Chippewa and Mississauga – will be needed on the morrow.

Playter finds Givins with General Sheaffe at the Governor's house. Here there is no sense of panic. Some will affect to remember the Major-General's forthright remark on this night – that "it would be a breakfast spell to drive every damned Yankee into the lake." Now Sheaffe tells Playter that nothing can be done until dawn. At first light, Playter is to take some Indians and patrol eastward to try to spot a possible enemy landing at that end of the town. Until then, Sheaffe says, he might as well snatch some sleep. At that the lieutenant-farmer gratefully stretches out on the floor of the Governor's dining room and slumbers peacefully until cockcrow.

●

YORK, UPPER CANADA, April 27, 1813

John Strachan is up at four and astride his horse, galloping westward toward the garrison. The American fleet has come into view, and Strachan cannot stand to be on the perimeter of the action. He must be at the centre, for it is power he seeks – he makes no bones about that – and as the events of the next few days will show, he knows how to seize it. Not for nothing has he educated the sons of the elite, first in Cornwall, now at York. His avowed plan is to place these young men in positions of influence. The weak lower house – the House of Assembly – the only elected body in the province, is composed, in his view, of "ignorant clowns." He blames that on "the spirit of levelling that seems to pervade the province," a dangerous Yankee idea. But when he gets his pupils into the assembly, then "I shall have more in my power." Already his chief protégé, John Beverley Robinson, a solemn twenty-one-year-old of good Loyalist stock who fought at Queenston, has been named acting attorney general.

Strachan understands the road to power, knows how to cultivate the aristocracy, how to make the most of opportunity. He has married into power: his pretty little wife, Ann, is the widow of Andrew McGill, brother of James, one of Montreal's leading fur merchants whose name will one day be enshrined on a famous university. The McGill connection has opened doors to Montreal's ruling merchant class. A Doctor of Divinity degree, for which Strachan has actively lobbied, adds to his stature. Strachan, the elitist, knows how to make the most of his fellow elitists, for although "there are no distinctions of rank in this country no people are so fond of them. If a fellow gets a commission in the militia however low he will not speak to you under the title of Captain." But everybody speaks to the Reverend Doctor Strachan.

The Reverend Doctor gazes out onto the lake. He counts fourteen sail, the ships in line, flagship in the van, others behind towing assault craft. As he gallops to the water's edge, he sees the fleet drop anchor. He raises his spyglass, observes the decks thickly covered with troops, some already clambering into the boats. A question forms on the lips of the amateur tactician: Where are *our* men? Why are there no troops rushing to the invasion point to repel them? It is a question that Dr. Strachan, protector of York, will ask again when the battle is done, for he has set his sights on the Major-General himself. Roger Sheaffe's days as Administrator of Upper Canada are numbered.

The whole town has watched the fleet round Gibraltar Point, hesitate, then move on, the morning clear and sunny, no trace of haze, a brisk east wind filling the sails. Ely Playter has already seen it. Rising from the dining-room floor of the Governor's house, he is off with his Indian scouts, galloping seven miles toward the east to make sure no Americans have landed on the far borders of the town. Satisfied, he and his men double back toward the garrison. As they do, they hear the guns start to fire.

Major-General Sheaffe faces a dilemma, though his features do not betray it. Even his detractors – and he has many – will remark on his absolute coolness in the events that follow. He is a bulky man, a little ponderous, less impulsive than his former commander, Brock, in whose shadow he languishes. It grates on Sheaffe that the dead hero should get the credit for the victory at Queenston. After all, Brock was losing the battle when he incautiously dashed up the heights to his death. The day was saved by Sheaffe's careful flanking movement, but men like Strachan have made Brock the symbol of Canadian resistance to the invader.

Yet Sheaffe admired, indeed loved, Brock, who once saved him from demotion. Years before, Sheaffe was so hated by his men for his harsh discipline that they plotted to kill him. As Brock put it, "he possesses little knowledge of Mankind." The mutiny was nipped, and Sheaffe, at Brock's urging, was kept in his post at Fort George – a good officer if not a great one who, as his superior predicted, learned from his experience.

He has no wish to fight the Americans, has, in fact, asked to be posted elsewhere, for they are his former countrymen. The Revolution split his family: Roger Hale Sheaffe stayed loyal to the Crown, but his sister remained in Boston until her death. Though New England wants no part of this war, it does not sit easily with Sheaffe that he may be responsible for the deaths of men who know his family.

But he has no time for reflection as the American fleet glides past the garrison. Where do they intend to land? His force is so thin he cannot guess or gamble. The only men he can depend on are his three hundred regulars – the two companies of the King's (one at the far end of town), a few members of the Newfoundland Fencibles, and a handful of Glengarry Light Infantry. The Indians are unpredictable, most of the militia useless.

One mile to the west of the garrison, opposite a small clearing – the site of an old French fort – the enemy ships attempt to anchor. This is the intended landing place. It is a military axiom that an amphibious landing must be halted at the water's edge before the enemy can establish a beachhead. The Americans will have to come ashore in waves, sending the boats back for more troops after the first have leaped over the side. In the initial minutes, then, Sheaffe's force will outnumber the invaders. Now is the time to rush every available man through the woods that separate the garrison from the landing point, with orders to hurl the Americans back.

Sheaffe will not gamble. Already he has waited overlong. Now he dispatches his troops piecemeal: Major Givins and the Indians first, to oppose the landing, then a company of Glengarries to support them. He would like to send the militia, but not being disciplined they are still straggling in and have yet to form up in the ravine near the garrison. In their place he sends the grenadier company of the King's,

45

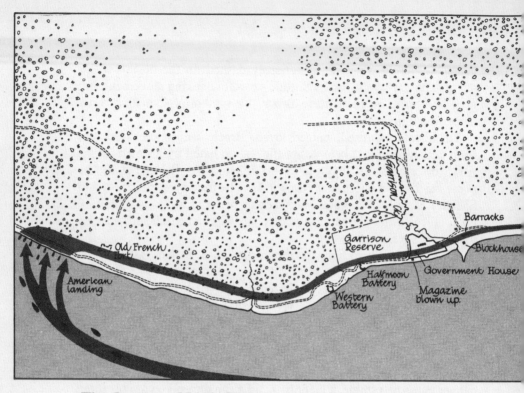

Labels on the map: American landing · Old French fort · Garrison Cr. · Garrison Reserve · Halfmoon Battery · Western Battery · Magazine blown up. · Government House · Blockhouse · Barracks

The Capture of Little York

under its elegant captain, Neal McNeale, and the Newfoundland Fencibles. He sends for the second company of the King's, beyond the eastern end of town. Then, when the militia is finally formed, he dispatches them under their adjutant general, Aeneas Shaw, to protect his right flank along the Dundas road. Sheaffe also has two six-pounders at his disposal, but he does not believe these can be trundled through the woods and so does not commit them.

At this point, things begin to go wrong for Roger Sheaffe. Shaw is supposed to know every foot of the ground between the garrison and the old fort, but somehow – nobody can explain how – he takes the Glengarries with him on his flanking movement. They lose their way, retrace their steps along a maze of paths, and arrive late at the landing. By this time the American advance troops are ashore, the green-clad riflemen threading their way into the woods, cutting down the tardy defenders.

•

GENERAL PIKE cannot stand the inaction. From his position on the foredeck of *Madison* he can see Captain Benjamin Forsyth's rifle

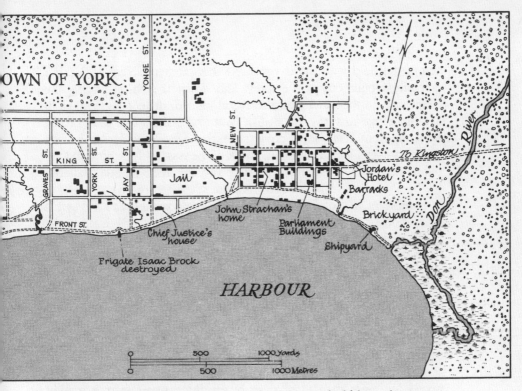

Map of the Town of York showing YONGE ST., KING ST., GRAVES ST., YORK ST., BAY ST., NEW ST., FRONT ST., Jail, Jordan's Hotel, Barracks, John Strachan's home, Parliament Buildings, Chief Justice's house, Brickyard, Shipyard, Frigate Isaac Brock destroyed, HARBOUR, Don River, To Kingston. Scale: 500, 1000 Yards / 500, 1000 Metres.

corps pulling for the Canadian shore. A stiff east wind blows them past the chosen landing place and, as the soldiers struggle with the oars, the painted forms of Givins's Indians emerge from the woods and open fire.

"Rest on your oars," says Forsyth in a low voice as the musket balls rattle into the boats. "Prime!"

His men shake black powder from horn to pan, ram in their cartridges, return the fire.

This is Pike's moment. The glory he seeks lies directly ahead; the Indians are already scattering into the woods.

"By God!" cries the General, "I can't stand here any longer."

Turns to his staff: "Come, jump into the boat."

Off he goes, surrounded by his suite, directly toward the centre of the fray, a square, serene figure in blue and an obvious target for the balls that whistle around his head but leave him untouched.

Forsyth's men are ashore, seeking the protection of the woods, the natural habitat of American sharpshooters, hiding behind trees and logs, covering the main landing of the infantry, skirmishing with the redcoats.

Pike wades ashore with his men, forms the infantry into platoons under the high bank, orders them to scale the incline and charge across the field with the bayonet. At this moment, Neal McNeale's grenadiers pour out of the forest and down the bank, forcing the Americans to the water's edge. Several light-draft schooners move in at close range to spray the British with grape-shot. The heavy balls, bursting from their sacs, do terrible damage. Neal McNeale falls dead; so does Donald McLean, Clerk of the Assembly, who saved the public accounts the night before. The Indians, their morale shattered by the shower of grape, vanish from the scene.

Caught in a crossfire between the naval barrage and Forsyth's sharpshooters, the regulars stumble back into the woods. Used to the broad plains and open warfare of Europe, they are unaccustomed to frontier skirmishing; in their scarlet jackets they make easy targets for the riflemen concealed between logs and trees.

"Show us our enemy! Show us our enemy!" they cry, but disciplined for a different kind of battle, they disdain the natural protection of the forest and drop like grouse on a highland shoot. Of 119 grenadiers, only 30 survive the ordeal. Two, it is believed, fall through the rotting ice of a deep pond, which will be known to future generations as Grenadier Pond. Another, both legs shattered, survives in the woods for more than three days by drinking water from a muddy pool, only to expire as he is rescued.

Yet it does not occur to the grenadiers to retreat, any more than it occurs to them to seek cover until, after a futile attempt to dislodge the Americans, their surviving officers lead them back toward the Western Battery that guards the lake road. By now the din in the woods is deafening – the shouts of the combatants, the warwhoops of the Indians, the roar of cannon and musket, and above all this the piercing notes of Forsyth's bugler indicating success.

The naval guns continue to pour a hail of grape and canister shot into the woods as Pike forms his men into columns and, with the fife and drum corps playing "Yankee Doodle," marches them toward York through the woods along the road that hugs the lake.

Ely Playter, back from his reconnaissance at the eastern end of town, arrives just as the first of the retreating British stagger out of the woods. Above the sound of music he can hear the cheers of the American sailors as six ships, beating against a brisk east wind, move up toward the Western Battery. Here Sheaffe intends to make a stand. It will not be easy, for the battery is already jammed with men, all jostling each other and harassing the gunners who are doing their best to return the fire from the lake. The six American vessels can throw more than two hundred pounds of iron at the battery in a single volley. The twelve British gunners, working largely with old, condemned cannon whose trunnions have broken off, have scarcely one-third the firepower. Pike's men have managed to haul two field guns through the woods – a feat that Sheaffe believed impossible. Now they advance upon the battery, arms at the trail.

Before the Americans can fling themselves at the battery, a dreadful accident brutally shatters the defenders' morale. In the cramped quarters, somebody jostles one of the gunners. Behind him is a portable wooden magazine, crammed with cartridges and powder. A spark from a gunner's slow match falls into the box, causing an explosion, killing more than a dozen men, scorching others horribly, and tearing away the gun platform.

A twelve-year-old boy, Patrick Finan, standing at the garrison gate, sees the maimed and burned men emerge, faces coal black, hair frizzled, clothing charred. He will never forget the spectacle or the unbearable odour of roasting flesh. One man is brought out in a wheelbarrow, so badly battered that Finan thinks every bone in his body must be broken. He lies in a heap, shaking with every movement, his legs dangling from his body as if held by the merest thread, his shrieks adding to the hullabaloo.

John Strachan has not been still all this time. He has galloped back to town, left his horse at home to prevent its capture, hastened back to the garrison on foot, encountered the stream of wounded emerging from the woods, and helped some of them reach medical aid. Now he experiences the shock of the explosion and thinks an enemy ship has been blown up. A glance at the carnage of the battery and the fleeing militiamen disabuses him. He decides to head back to town to see to the safety of his wife and the other women.

The regulars, meanwhile, are struggling to remount the big gun. The militia are fleeing. Nobody seems to know exactly what is to be done. The General himself is not at the battery. Outnumbered, he has decided that the town cannot be defended and is laying plans to save his regulars and deny the public stores to the enemy.

Pike's force advances with little opposition, seizes the Western Battery, moves on to the so-called Halfmoon Battery, which, being unarmed, is no battery at all, and pushes on along the lake toward Government House and the garrison.

The retreating militia have lost all semblance of order. Many are already across the creek that separates Government House from the blockhouse and barracks on the eastern bank. But Ely Playter and several others cling to the right bank, having exchanged their officer's swords for muskets. Up comes Major Allan, who orders them to rally the militia and make a stand, but the fire from the ships is so hot that all seek the protection of the garrison battery. A further attempt is made to form the militia in a small hollow, but when the citizen soldiers see the beaten regulars retreating they refuse orders.

Playter realizes that the garrison is about to be evacuated. He does not know that Sheaffe and his officers have already decided to pull out and blow up the main magazine on the waterfront below Government House. Within this underground fort are at least two hundred barrels of gunpowder – perhaps five hundred – together with a vast quantity of cartridges, shells, round shot. Sheaffe, concerned only with saving his regulars, gives little attention to the straggling militia, several dozen of whom are within a whisper of the magazine.

The fuse is burning. Playter and his men have already been ordered to march off. But the young farmer has left his coat in his quarters. He runs to retrieve it, warning another straggler, a cook named Mrs. Chapman, to make haste away as the Americans are coming. Somebody else is inside the post – Matthias Saunders, struggling to remove a portable magazine from behind one of the twelve-pound guns. He, too, is unaware that the magazine is about to blow.

Zebulon Montgomery Pike is within four hundred yards of the garrison, having halted his column and ordered his men to hug the ground while he brings up the six-pounder and the howitzer which his gunners have dragged through the mud and stumps. He is on the verge of victory and knows it. At any moment he expects to see a white flag rise from the blockhouse ahead. When that happens he will have the honour of receiving the sword of the ranking British general and accepting the surrender of close to a thousand men. It will be the first victory of American arms after ten months of bitter defeat. For lesser exploits in this disappointing war men of lower rank have received ceremonial swords and the thanks of Congress, their names toasted the breadth of the land, their profiles engraved on medals of solid gold. How sweet the prospect!

He sits down on a stump, awaiting the final attack. One of his men has captured a Canadian militia sergeant, and the Brigadier-General with his two aides, Lieutenant Donald Fraser and Captain John Nicholson, prepares to question him.

At this instant the ground shakes and the world turns dazzling white. A prodigious roar splits the ears of the attackers as a gigantic cloud spurts from the blazing magazine to blossom in the sky. From this vast canopy there bursts in all directions an eruption of debris – great chunks of masonry, broken beams, gigantic boulders, rocks and stones of every size. This terrifying hail pours down upon the attackers, covering the ground for a thousand feet in every direction, killing or maiming more than a hundred men, striking off arms and legs, crushing chests, decapitating bodies.

Ely Playter, who has retrieved his coat and reached the barrack gate, has an appalling close-up view. Miraculously, he is untouched. He sees huge boulders dropping all around him, some skipping across the ground, others burying themselves in the mud. He sees Matthias Saunders's leg smashed to a pulp. He sees a boulder kill the horse of Sheaffe's aide, Captain Robert Loring. He sees the oldest volunteer of all, the doorkeeper of the legislature, John Basil, struck twice in head and knee. The British casualties run to forty, most of them militia. But the Americans suffer more than five times that number. Their General is among the dying.

Zebulon Pike lies prostrate among his mangled followers. A huge boulder has crushed his ribs, torn a large hole in his back. His aide and pupil, Nicholson, is dead. So is the unfortunate Canadian sergeant.

Pike's wounds are mortal and he knows it. How ignominious – to be killed by a falling rock! Not for him the gallant death, waving his sword in the teeth of the fray, achieving the instant martyrdom of a Nelson or a Brock. Time only for a few gasping phrases for the history books: "Push on, my brave fellows, and avenge your general!"

As the surgeons carry him from the field, the troops give a sudden huzza. The General turns his head at that. Someone tells him that the Union Jack has been hauled down from the shattered fort and the Stars and Stripes is going up. He manages a wan smile. The Americans have won the battle of Little York, yet somehow, in spite of the cheering, Pike's victory is not quite the triumph that Washington hoped for. The two warships in the harbour will not bolster the American fleet on Lake Ontario. One is in flames; the other has got away. And the British regulars, who ought to have surrendered, have slipped out of the bag before the noose can be pulled tight. The British army escapes to fight another day, and Brigadier-General Zebulon Montgomery Pike, expiring aboard *Madison*, his head pillowed on the captured British flag, will go down in history not as a military hero but only as one who accidentally gave his name to a mountain that somebody before him discovered and somebody after him climbed.

•

JOHN STRACHAN, en route from the garrison to his home, hears the explosion of the magazine just as he enters the town. He hastens to his house, finds his wife in a state of terror, bundles her and the children off to a friend's home some distance out of town, then rushes back toward the garrison. In a ravine he finds Sheaffe and the regular troops preparing to leave. Later, Strachan will demand to know why the Major-General did not seize this moment to counter-attack. But Sheaffe, a good half mile from the scene, has no way of knowing the havoc the explosion has wreaked on the enemy. With his cause lost, the most sensible thing he can do is burn the naval stores and the big vessel *Isaac Brock*, under construction in the harbour, and retire with his men to reinforce Kingston.

Young Patrick Finan, still dazed by the spectacle of two magazine explosions, has joined in the retreat with his family. The two-week journey by foot, horseback, and finally canoe is no pleasure trip. The spring snows have just melted; a heavy rain pelts down; the Kingston road is a river of mud; and the settlers en route are hostile. On the way out of town, the Finans meet several recent arrivals from below the border who are cheered by the American success. Young Finan is shocked, but the atmosphere does not dissipate as the troops move eastward. Believing the Americans have won the war, many a settler does not hesitate to avow his disloyalty. And when the Finan family begs for transport, the farmers, who have purposely concealed their horses and wagons in the woods, insist they have none.

In York, the command of the militia devolves upon Lieutenant-Colonel William Chewett, the sixty-year-old surveyor general, and his second-in-command, Major William Allan, the merchant. This pair has been detailed by Sheaffe to deal with the enemy. But Strachan, who turns up just as the arrangements are completed, has no intention of being left out. He volunteers his services, and in the days to come, the clergyman and not the officers will be chief negotiator for the people of Little York.

Ely Playter, meanwhile, struggles to catch up to the bands of militia retreating from the shattered garrison. Breathless after escaping from the explosion, he looks over his shoulder to see the first American skirmishers breaching the line of wooden pickets on the edge of the ditch protecting the Governor's house. A few spent musket balls sizzle his way, to no effect. Now, as the militia are halted, Playter watches while a small group heads back toward the garrison with a white flag. A few moments later the negotiators return; they have been told to come back in fifteen minutes.

Playter marches toward town with the militia. An infantry captain gallops up, asks for help to fire the marine stores and the brig *Isaac Brock*. (The *Duke of Gloucester* was, by good fortune, out of the harbour when the attack came.) When the dockyard is safely ablaze they repair to Jordan's Tavern, where some of Playter's friends are surprised to find him alive.

Though grateful to be in one piece, the young farmer is exhausted by the day's events. He heads up Yonge Street to the family farmhouse, plagued by fears of the unknown, apprehensive of the enemy's intentions. How will the Americans treat him and his friends? He is almost too tired to care. When he reaches his home he flops on his cot and sleeps like a dead man.

•

AT THE HOME of the Commissary, George Crookshank, on Front Street near the western edge of the town, an acrimonious argument is taking place between the Americans and the militia negotiators. The invaders are furious at the burning of one vessel and the escape of another. The major object of the expedition – to change the delicate balance of naval power on the lake – has been frustrated in the most dishonourable fashion, *after* the white flag of surrender has gone up. The Americans, who expected to deal with Sheaffe and his regulars, are mortified to find that the real army is out of reach and they must treat with amateur soldiers and a clergyman.

Strachan, who is rapidly assuming the leadership of the York negotiators, replies with spirit to the American representatives – Colonel George Mitchell of the 3rd Artillery and Major William King of the 15th Infantry. He and his associates knew nothing of the burning of the ship, he argues, and cannot be held responsible. He puts the blame on the retreating regulars. When the Americans castigate

Sheaffe, the Canadians, who will never forgive the General for deserting them, agree. At last a surrender document is worked out. Strachan is not happy with it but must accept it, having no bargaining power.

Under its terms, all arms and public stores are to be given up to the Americans; the militia will not be made prisoners but will be paroled and thus neutralized for the remainder of the war unless exchanged. The officers are to be imprisoned. Private property will be respected.

King and Mitchell go back to the American lines to have the document ratified. They do not return. A junior officer arrives in their stead, arrests Major Allan, takes his sword, marches him off in the centre of a column of soldiers.

But now a black-clad figure dashes into the heart of the column, protesting this breach of the traditional white flag. It is Strachan. He catches up with Allan and marches proudly with him through town. Strachan the martyr? Not entirely; his clerical habit gives him a certain invulnerability. Yet it is an act of considerable courage, and the people of York will not forget it. In standing up to the enemy, John Strachan has given them back a little of their bruised pride.

Allan is held, but Strachan is not. With the terms of surrender still unsigned, those of the militia who can be found are imprisoned in the garrison. Their officers are freed under parole until the morning. Benjamin Forsyth's riflemen are appointed to patrol the town, a decision that strikes fear into the inhabitants, for this is the corps which, in Strachan's view, "bears the worst character in the American army."

Yet the looting on this night is comparatively light. Some Americans invade the House of Assembly and plunder the office of the late clerk, Donald McLean. Houses vacated by terrified women fleeing to the open country are also a target. With her husband absent, Mrs. James Givins, the wife of the Indian Department leader, and her seven children are driven from her home by plunderers who strip it of all valuables – furniture, curtains, bedsheets, liquor, everything from a silver toast rack to an English saddle. And when Judge Powell takes the distressed woman to General Dearborn to complain, the American commander replies that he cannot protect her. To the Americans, the officers of the British Indian Department are pariahs; the scalps taken at Frenchtown earlier in the year have not been forgotten.

The home of Powell's son, Grant, acting superintendent of the Marine Department, is also looted. Mrs. Powell, his American-born wife, her supper party aborted on the previous evening, had fled to a neighbour's. Now she returns to discover Americans in her house, one of them munching on a piece of loaf sugar. A spirited argument follows, with the soldier, a six-footer, getting much the worst of it.

Go home, says Mrs. Powell, *and mind your own business*.

"I guess I wish I could," replies the soldier, miserably.

Mrs. Powell relents a little, asks where he lives.

"Down to Stillwater, New York," he tells her. "I've one of Major Bleecker's farms."

At which Mrs. Powell bursts into laughter, for Major Bleecker is her father.

As the night deepens, silence falls over the occupied town. Only in the garrison hospital, guarded by five hundred American soldiers, is there activity. Here, scores of desperately wounded men from both sides scream without let-up into the darkness. An American surgeon's mate, Dr. William Beaumont, records their cries:

Oh Dear! Oh Dear! Oh, my God, my God! Do, Doctor! Doctor! Do cut off my leg, my arm, my head to relieve me from misery! I can't live! I can't live!

Beaumont has seen death, but this macabre scene rends his heart — the men groaning and screaming, the surgeons, "wading in blood," severing limbs with knife and saw or trepanning shattered skulls. The most hardened assassin, the cruellest savage, thinks Beaumont, would be shocked at the spectacle. For forty-eight hours, without food or sleep, the young doctor cuts and slashes, sickened by the carnage of war.

In his eyes these mashed and mangled men are no longer friends or enemies, only fellow creatures. Nobody, he thinks, can view such a spectacle without the blood chilling in his veins; none can behold it without agonizing sympathy.

•

LITTLE YORK, April 28, 1812

John Strachan is in a state of high dudgeon. The indignity suffered by William Allan is too much; worse, the terms of capitulation have yet to be ratified.

At the home of Prideaux Selby, the dying receiver general, the outraged clergyman encounters William King, the American infantry major who prepared the surrender document the previous day. Strachan goes for King, charges him with breaking his promise to have the document ratified, cries *Deception!* The American retreats a little before this blast, apologizes, urges Strachan to see his superior officer, Colonel Cromwell Pearce who, with Pike dead and Dearborn still aboard *Madison*, is the ranking American officer on shore.

Strachan hurries to the garrison, tackles Pearce in his quarters, demands action. Pearce says he can do nothing but agrees to order rations for the militia, who have been held all night in the blockhouse without food or medicine. Now the militant clergyman demands to be taken out to meet Dearborn himself; but before a boat can be arranged the General lands, accompanied by the Commodore of the fleet, the corpulent Isaac Chauncey.

Dearborn is in a bad humour, clearly nonplussed by the presumption of this cleric badgering him over minor details of a surrender the General considers a *fait accompli*. Strachan brandishes the articles of capitulation; Dearborn glances at the document without comment. Strachan persists: when will Dearborn parole the officers and men of the militia? When will he allow the townspeople to care for their own sick and wounded? Dearborn's irritation grows. Who are the conquered here? Who the conqueror? Who is this strange civilian with the thick Scots burr who seems to think he can deal with generals? He tells Strachan, harshly, that the Americans have been given a false return of the captured officers, then warns him away. *Keep off*, he orders Strachan; *don't follow me around*. He has more important business to attend.

Strachan will not be diverted. He turns to Chauncey, looses a diatribe at him: this is a new mode of treating people in a public character, he says. He, Strachan, has transacted business with greater men than Dearborn without being insulted. Perhaps the delay in signing the surrender document is intentional: to give the riflemen a chance to loot with impunity before the pledges regarding private property are signed. Well, he, Strachan, will not be duped or insulted. Either the document is signed at once or it will not be signed at all: there will be *no* capitulation! Let the Americans do their worst!

With that he turns on his heel and walks back to the garrison, where the other members of the surrender committee await him.

These brusque tactics are successful. Dearborn, in a better humour, appears, rereads the surrender terms, and ratifies them. The militia are paroled. The community begins to return to something resembling normality. But the public funds so carefully concealed must be given up; if not, the Americans threaten to burn the town.

The Americans get the paper money from the home of Donald McLean, but not the gold. Major Allan's wife and Mrs. Prideaux Selby have worked out a plan to save it. They persuade Selby's chief clerk, Billy Roe, to dress up as an old market woman, complete with sunbonnet and voluminous skirts. The gold goes into a keg, is loaded onto a one-horse wagon and covered with vegetables. Roe in his disguise drives slowly out toward the Don River, crosses it, passes the American guards without incident, and buries the treasure.

In the farmhouse on Yonge Street, Ely Playter is awakened by a friend, Joel Beman, who, believing him killed, has arrived to look after the Playter family. Playter dispatches his wife and children to Newmarket in Beman's wagon, then with his brother George walks back toward town, picking up fragments of news from passersby and friends. He has no intention of giving his parole to the Americans and the following day packs up his valuables and hides them. He and his brother take refuge in the woods and watch helplessly as looters break down his door and pillage his possessions – his sword, a set of razors, a powder horn, a shot pouch, a box of jewellery, clothing.

The next day – Friday, April 30 – on William Allan's advice he agrees at last to go to the garrison, sign his parole, and get a pass from the enemy.

The town is pillaged – "dismal" is Playter's word. The garrison buildings are shattered. The Council Office is stripped bare, every window broken. The legislative building, a low, one-storey brick structure with two wings, one for each house, is ablaze. Nobody knows who set the fire. The Americans are blamed but without any hard evidence. The best guess is that the culprits are individual American sailors, who wear no military uniform; they have discovered a human scalp in the building and have, presumably, used this example of British infamy as an excuse to fire the entire structure.

The scalp (it may be only a wig) is presented to Commodore Chauncey, who sends it on to the Secretary of the Navy with the undocumented charge that it was found hanging over the Speaker's mace in the main chamber. The following day the Americans burn what remains of the Governor's house and other buildings at the fort. These are the only fires, but the myth that "the Americans burned the capital" gathers credence in the years that follow.

Little York is scarcely a cohesive community. The upper class is united in its opposition to the American invasion, but scores of ordinary citizens welcome it, or at least accept it. For every man concealing himself to escape parole there seems to be another eager to sign a paper that will take him out of the war. A number openly join the enemy; some are actually aboard *Madison* or at the garrison giving information to Dearborn. When it becomes clear that the Americans intend to evacuate the town, panic seizes the disaffected, some of whom urge the American officers to hold on to York and give them protection, promising to help the invaders and complaining of "the further exposure to the fury and persecution of the royalists."

Suspicion and sedition go hand in hand, as neighbour breaks with neighbour over idle remarks or disloyal outbursts. In Michael Dye's tavern in Markham Township, Alfred Barrett offers a toast: "Success to the American fleet!" His cronies, John Lyon and Simeon Morton, raise their glasses in agreement. George Cutter overhears them and notes as well a conversation between two others who agree that it is foolish to support the government of Upper Canada – the country, they say, really belongs to the United States, and they both hope the Americans will win. On Cutter's evidence, and that of others, all four men will find themselves in the York jail, charged with sedition.

Elijah Bentley, an Anabaptist preacher who has pleaded with Dearborn to arrange a parole for his son, tells a friend that he has seen more liberty during those few hours with Dearborn than he had seen in the whole of the province: why, the men in the American army were allowed to answer their own officers back! For these remarks and others, Bentley too will be jailed.

The Americans also make themselves popular with many of the farmers by distributing a quantity of farm implements, which had been sent out from Britain intended for the settlers but as a result of bureaucratic inertia had never been distributed.

John Finch, who has been given some iron and ploughshares, encounters a fellow farmer, Henry Mulholland, and upbraids him for taking part in the attempt to repulse the invaders. Finch grows bolder: the British government, he declares, is austere and tyrannical. He would rather see his sons serve in hell than in a British garrison. He hopes the American fleet will destroy York "and all the damned crew." Henry Mulholland stores all this in his mind and, when the time comes, informs upon Finch who, with more than two dozen others, finds himself under indictment.

But one does not need to be disaffected to applaud the distribution of farm equipment. Many are convinced that the ruling class was reserving all this largesse for its friends. Before the fleet departs, the

American soldiers also distribute to destitute families all the peas, flour, and bread they cannot load on board the ships.

Dr. Strachan is not to be seduced by this generosity. His church has been looted; anarchy of a sort prevails. Once again the resolute clergyman goes after the hard-pressed Dearborn. All the American general wants to do now, as April gives way to May, is to get out of York. There is no advantage in holding the town. The brig in the harbour is destroyed. More significantly, all the public stores destined for the Detroit frontier have been captured. All the armament and equipment for the British squadron on Lake Erie and the new ship under construction at Amherstburg – cables, cordage, canvas, tools, guns, ammunition – have been seized and cannot be replaced. This is a considerable loss and will badly cripple the British Right Division, which holds Detroit and most of Michigan Territory, for it can affect the balance of naval power on Lake Erie where the Americans are constructing a fleet of their own. If the Americans can win Lake Erie, Detroit will be regained and the entire right wing of the British Army will be in peril.

Dearborn is embarrassed by the continued looting, which makes a mockery of the terms of surrender (but not so embarrassed that he can resist the offer of a private soldier to purchase for one hundred dollars the gold snuff box, set with diamonds, looted from the effects of Major-General Sheaffe). He realizes that he cannot control his own troops and wants nothing more than to leave as soon as the fleet is ready. He is only too happy to turn the civilian control of the town back to the magistrates and rid himself of the importunate Dr. Strachan and his friends.

Control does not return easily. On May 1, as the fleet makes ready to sail, Strachan surprises two looters, rushes impetuously at them demanding that they cease, and almost receives a bullet for his pains. An officer appears and forestalls Strachan's murder. That night, most of the Americans board their ships, leaving the town to deal with its own disaffected.

Commodore Chauncey, riding out a storm that keeps the American troops trapped and seasick on board the fleet for the best part of the week, is convinced that "we may consider the upper province as conquered." Although the troops that attacked York are now reduced through injury, illness, and death to one thousand effectives, reinforcements are on the way. Dearborn expects six hundred men to join him at Oswego. More are expected from Buffalo. Another thousand troops are waiting at Sackets Harbor, ready to go on board. "With this force," Chauncey believes, "Fort George and the whole Niagara frontier must fall without great sacrifice of lives."

The Commodore has reason to feel elated. His handling of the fleet during the attack cannot be faulted. Dearborn, old, ill, worn out by his exertions at York, is less certain of an accolade. He himself took no part in an action that cost three hundred casualties – more than twice those of the British. Worse, in the view of the Secretary of War, John Armstrong, Sheaffe has outwitted him by preferring the preservation of his troops to that of his post and "thus carrying off the kernel leaves us only the shell." Armstrong is already planning to replace his ailing general.

For the people of York, the invasion marks a watershed. Nothing can ever be quite the same again. Those who fought the good fight, with weapons or with words, will occupy a special place in the community. The heroes of the day – Allan, for one, and especially Strachan – will become the leaders of the morrow. The lines are drawn; those who aided the Americans, by word as much as by deed, are held to be traitors.

The militia, who saw little action in the battle of York, sustaining no more than ten casualties, are the darlings of the community. The regulars, who bore the brunt of the fighting, are castigated as men who care only about saving their own skins. This is wholly unfair, as is the memorandum that Strachan prepares for Sir George Prevost, the Governor General. The document, running to ten pages and signed by seven eminent citizens, berates Sheaffe, whose name "is odious to all ranks of people." Strachan writes that the citizens of York "are indignant rather than dispirited and while they feel the disgrace of their defeat they console themselves with the conviction that it was owing entirely to their commander."

Sheaffe is attacked for taking the very action that his enemy, Dearborn, is criticized for allowing: getting his troops out of town and destroying the ship in the harbour, an act that Strachan claims "incensed the enemy to such a degree as to expose the town to indiscriminate pillage and conflagration."

Strachan's message to Prevost is blunt: Sheaffe must go. "Without a new commander and more troops this Province must soon be overpowered." At least some members of York's minor aristocracy agree. Mrs. Powell, for one, is planning to draw off all her wine and pack the bottles in sawdust in the event of precipitate flight, for "a miracle alone can save us."

Sir George Prevost cannot agree with Strachan's armchair assessment of his general's conduct, especially as neither the chaplain of York nor any of his colleagues can suggest what *they* might have done in the circumstances. But Sir George is a practical politician and diplomat as well as a general of armies. Clearly Sheaffe has outlived his usefulness in Upper Canada. He will not be sent back as administrator; eventually, a phlegmatic Swiss-born major-general, Francis De Rottenburg, will be sent in his stead; but that is two months in the future. In the meantime, without title or stipend, but with all the power he needs, John Strachan reigns supreme.

2

STALEMATE ON THE NIAGARA PENINSULA
May 27 – August 1, 1813

Following the attack on York, American strategy calls for an immediate amphibious landing at the mouth of the Niagara River to seize Fort George and Fort Erie, destroy the defending army, and roll up the peninsula. For this task the Americans have sixteen warships and seven thousand men. The British have eighteen hundred regulars dispersed along the Niagara frontier; most of the militia have returned to their farms. Ill and indecisive, Major-General Dearborn dallies for a fortnight before launching the invasion. It comes at last on May 27, 1813.

NEWARK, UPPER CANADA, May 27, 1813

Dawn. Brigadier-General John Vincent, commander of the British Centre Division, stands with his staff near the lighthouse overlooking Lake Ontario at the Niagara's mouth, trying to peer through the blanket of fog that masks the water. He is almost certain there are ships out there, but he cannot be sure. He expects invasion, for a rocket has already flared up from the American side, but he can only guess where it will come. Nor can he know whether there will be one landing or several.

He is, however, painfully aware that he is badly outclassed. The guns from Fort Niagara across the river have already shattered his imperfect defences, and his own troops, spread out thinly all along the frontier from Newark to the falls, are exhausted from night watches. Vincent himself has had no sleep.

Young William Hamilton Merritt of the Provincial Dragoons, standing beside him, spyglass to eye, points suddenly out into the lake. The curtain of fog lifts, as in a theatre, and there is now revealed to Vincent and his staff a spectacle they will never forget – sixteen ships standing out from the lakeshore, sweeping toward them in a two-mile arc. Behind, on towlines, 134 open boats, scows, and bateaux, crowded with men and artillery, move steadily toward the Canadian side.

Even as Vincent and the others put spurs to their horses and gallop upriver toward Fort George, the cannon begin to thunder – fifty-one guns in action on the lake, another twenty from Fort Niagara, pouring a hail of iron and exploding shells across the fields and roads. The barrage is so powerful that Ely Playter, forty miles away at York, distinctly hears the rumble of the guns. A cannonball tears through the wall of the Carrol house in Newark. Mrs. Carrol, whose husband is a British gunner, hastily wraps her two small boys in bedding and rushes into a neighbouring wheatfield. Another ball ploughs into the ground beside the terrified trio. They leap up and join the throng of refugees heading for Four Mile Creek.

The enemy ships are manoeuvring to catch the British batteries in a cross-fire. The effect is shattering. The battery at the lighthouse manages to fire off a single shot before it is destroyed. Another at Two Mile Creek has to be abandoned. As the fleet continues its majestic movement forward, three schooners move close to shore to cover the landing at Crookstown, a huddle of farmhouses near the mouth of Two Mile Creek. In a thicket overlooking this potential invasion point Vincent has hidden a guard of fifty Mohawk under their celebrated Scottish chief, John Norton. A hail of missiles fired at point-blank range pierces the covert, killing two Indians and wounding several before the main body flees.

On board the American flagship *Madison*, Major-General Dearborn, too ill to lead the attack himself, watches nervously as the assault boats move toward the shore. He sees a young naval officer, Oliver Hazard Perry, directing the fire of the schooners from an open boat, standing tall in the stern in full uniform, oblivious to enemy musket fire. Perry is rowed from vessel to vessel, telling each where to anchor to achieve the best field of fire. That done, he boards *Madison*, determined to have nothing further to do with an invasion he believes to be badly planned and ineptly mounted.

Gazing at the churning waters below, Perry falls prey to conflicting emotions. He chafes for action, has come all the way from Lake Erie to take charge of the sailors and marines in the assault – rowing for weary hours under the threat of British cannon, then galloping bareback through dense forests in a driving storm – only to find his advice ignored. He has no intention of taking the blame for any disaster that results.

But Perry has a sudden change of heart. The one man he admires, Colonel Winfield Scott, Dearborn's adjutant-general, is in danger. Scott stands in the leading flatboat with Benjamin Forsyth's green-clad riflemen, the same sharpshooters who led the attack on York, but

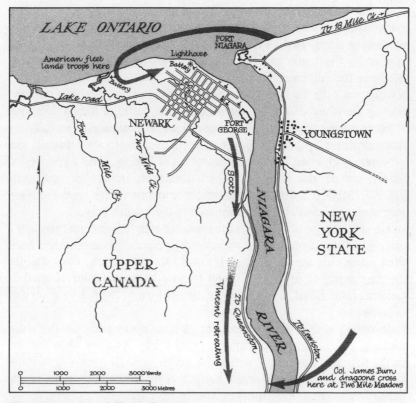

The map shows the area around Fort George with the following labels: LAKE ONTARIO, American fleet lands troops here, Battery, Lighthouse, FORT NIAGARA, To 18 Mile Ck., Lake road, NEWARK, FORT GEORGE, YOUNGSTOWN, Four Mile Ck., Two Mile Ck., Scott, Vincent retreating, To Queenston, NIAGARA RIVER, UPPER CANADA, NEW YORK STATE, To Lewiston, Col. James Burn and dragoons cross here at Five Mile Meadows, N, 1000 2000 3000 Yards, 1000 2000 3000 Metres

The Capture of Fort George

Perry sees that he is being blown off course and is about to miss the landing point. If Scott and the entire advance guard are not ordered immediately to pull to the windward, they will lose the protection of the covering schooners.

Gone, suddenly, are all Perry's scruples. He begs to be allowed to avert the disaster. Dearborn assents, and Perry leaps back into his gig, picks up Scott, and with his help herds the scattered assault craft back on course.

As the advance guard pulls for the bank, Perry rows swiftly over to *Hamilton*, the closest schooner to shore. He is no sooner alongside than a lookout on the mast shouts that the whole British army is advancing on the double to thwart the landing.

Most of the American officers do not believe the British will make a stand. This view is reinforced by the presence of a high bank, which conceals the defending troops. But Perry senses danger, sets off to warn Scott, rows hard past *Hamilton*, and slips in and out between the advancing ships. Just as he reaches the lead assault boat, the British appear on the bank and fire a volley, most of which goes over the heads of the riflemen. Confusion follows. Some of the oarsmen stop rowing while the soldiers begin firing wildly in every direction. Perry, fearing that they will shoot each other, yells to them to row to shore.

Scott echoes the order. The big colonel has planned carefully for this moment. Captured at Queenston and exchanged after months as a prisoner in Quebec, he has no intention of letting a less experienced officer bungle the landing. When Dearborn made him adjutant-general, Scott insisted on retaining command of his 2nd Artillery Regiment, insisted also on commanding the assault wave.

He is in charge of twenty boats containing eight hundred men and a three-pounder cannon. His orders are specific: advance three hundred paces only across the beach toward the high bank, then wait for the first wave of infantry – fifteen hundred troops under Brigadier-General John Boyd, a one-time soldier of fortune with a long service in India.

Into the water go Scott's men, through the spray and onto the sand, forming swiftly into line, cannon on the left. As they dash for the bank, the next wave approaches the beach in such a torrent of musketry that Boyd sees the entire surface of the water turn to foam; he himself will count three musket balls in his cloak.

As Boyd's men hit the beach, some of Scott's assault force have already reached the crest of the twelve-foot clay bank. The British and Canadian militia, bursting out of the shelter of a ravine two hundred yards away, hurl them back down the cliff. Scott – a gigantic figure, six feet five inches tall – is unmistakable. One of the Glengarries attacks him with a bayonet. Scott dodges, loses his footing, tumbles back down the bank.

On board *Madison*, Dearborn sees his adjutant-general fall and utters an agonizing cry:

"He is lost! He is killed!"

But Scott has already picked himself up and is leading a second charge up the bank.

The schooners have slackened their covering fire for fear of hitting their own men. Perry, realizing this, pulls over to *Hamilton* and directs its nine guns to pour grape and canister onto the crest. The British retreat to the cover of the ravine, where more troops are forming. Lieutenant-Colonel Christopher Myers, Vincent's acting quarter-master general, now leads a second attack on the men clawing their way up the bank. Once again Scott is forced back.

A scene of singular carnage follows. Two lines of men face each other at a distance of no more than ten yards and for the next fifteen minutes fire away at point-blank range. On the British side, every field officer and most junior officers are casualties. Myers falls early, bleeding from three wounds. The British, fighting against odds of four to one, are forced back, leaving more than one hundred corpses piled on the bank. An American surgeon, James Mann, who lands after the battle is over, counts four hundred dead and wounded men, strewn over a plot no longer than two hundred yards, no broader than fifteen.

Lieutenant-Colonel John Harvey, Vincent's deputy adjutant-general who has arrived with reinforcements, now steps into the wounded Myers's command and leads his shattered force in a stubborn retreat from ravine to ravine back toward the little town of Newark, scarred by shellfire and totally deserted.

Chauncey, meanwhile, has brought his flagship, *Madison*, into the river opposite the British fort. At the same time comes news of another American column massing at Youngstown farther upriver, apparently intent on crossing and cutting off the British retreat. As more troops land on the beach, the Americans form into three columns with the riflemen and light infantry flitting through the woods on the right to get past Harvey's forces and threaten his rear.

Vincent realizes that nothing can save the fort. Tears glisten in his eyes as he dispatches a one-sentence note to Colonel William Claus of the Indian Department, in charge of the garrison, ordering him to blow up the magazine, evacuate the fort, and join the retreating army on the Queenston road.

At the fort, Colonel Claus orders his men to leave, sets several long fuses on the three magazines, tries to chop down the flagpole to retrieve the Union Jack. The axe is blunt, the work only half done when the American advance troops are heard outside the fort. Claus drops his axe, makes a hurried escape.

The American columns move cautiously on the fort, their advance rendered ponderous by the lack of draught animals: the heavy artillery must be manhandled. Winfield Scott, impatient to pursue the British, seizes the riderless horse of the wounded Myers and dashes off at the head of his skirmishers, galloping down the empty streets of Newark and on to the fort, half a mile beyond, in time to capture two

British stragglers. From them he learns that the guns are spiked, the magazines about to blow.

Off he gallops, trying to save the ammunition. He is under the wall of the fort when the main magazine goes up, hurling a cloud of debris into the air. A piece of timber falls on Scott, throwing him from his horse, breaking his collarbone. Two officers pull him to his feet and he presses on, forces the gate, stamps out the lighted train leading to the smaller magazines. Then he turns his attention to the flagstaff, partly cut through by Claus. In spite of his injury, he topples it with the blunt axe, claims the flag as a souvenir.

In dashes Moses Porter, the artillery colonel, who has also spotted the British standard flying and wants it for himself.

"Damn you, Scott!" he cries. "Those cursed long legs of yours have got you here ahead of me."

Meanwhile Vincent and his division are retreating swiftly and silently toward the village of St. Davids, the infantry retiring through the woods, the artillery and baggage along the road. Their ultimate goal is Burlington Heights at the head of the lake. The Americans are in danger of winning another hollow victory, and Scott knows it. Painfully, he hoists his big frame back onto his injured horse and gallops off once more in the wake of his own light troops who are already picking up stragglers from the British column.

The original American plan called for Colonel James Burn and his dragoons to cross the river from Youngstown to cut off the British retreat, but this attack has been delayed by the threatening fire of a British battery. Now, with the whole of the Niagara frontier being evacuated, Burn is able at last to land his fresh troops within musket shot of the enemy stragglers.

When he arrives on the Canadian shore, Burn asks Scott to wait fifteen minutes while he forms up his men; then their combined forces can proceed to harry the British retreat.

It is a fatal delay, for neither officer has reckoned on the timidity of the high command. Dearborn, who can scarcely stand and has to be helped about by two men, is incapable of decision; he will claim afterwards that the troops were too exhausted to engage in pursuit, ignoring all evidence that Burn's dragoons are fresh and Scott's skirmishers eager for the fray. Dearborn has turned direct command over to Major-General Morgan Lewis, who finally lands after the battle on the beach is over. Lewis is a politician, not a soldier, a former chief justice and governor of New York State, a brother-in-law of the Secretary of

War, and a boyhood friend of the President. He loves playing at commander, revels in pomp and ceremony, and once, in a memorable speech to the New York militia, made a remark that has become a persistent source of ridicule: the drum, General Lewis purports to believe, is "all important in the day of battle."

Lewis is terrified of making a mistake – a bad quality in a commanding officer. He remembers the follies of overconfidence that destroyed Van Rensselaer's army at Queenston and Winchester's at Frenchtown the previous year and decides to play it safe.

He sends two messengers forward to restrain Scott from any further advance. Scott disregards the order.

"Your general does not know that I have the enemy within my power," he tells them. "In seventy minutes I shall bag their whole force, now the dragoons are with me."

But, as Scott waits for the rest of Burn's boats to land, Brigadier-General Boyd himself rides up and gives him a direct order to withdraw to Fort George. Disgusted, Scott abandons his plans. He can see the rearguard of Vincent's army disappearing into the woods. The defeated columns are marching off in perfect order, with much of their equipment intact, a circumstance that lessens the American triumph. Once again the invaders have cracked the shell of the nut but lost the kernel. Trapped all year in the enclave of Fort George, unable to break out for long because of Vincent's raiders lurking on the outskirts, an entire American army will be reduced to illness, idleness, and frustration.

Scott controls his disgust. In spite of a natural impulsiveness, he has learned to curb his tongue in the interests of his career, for he is nothing if not ambitious. But he cannot forgive Boyd, the man who ordered him back to Fort George just as he was about to destroy an army.

In Scott's later assessment, this blustering soldier of fortune is serviceable enough in a subordinate position but "vacillating and imbecile beyond all endurance as a chief under high responsibilities." Notwithstanding this harsh appraisal, Boyd is soon to take charge of all the American forces occupying the Niagara frontier.

Dearborn's immediate inclination is to move his troops to the head of the lake by water and cut off the British retreat. For that venture he needs the enthusiastic co-operation of the fleet and its commodore, Isaac Chauncey. That is not forthcoming. Chauncey, at forty-one, has gone to flesh – a pear-shaped figure with a pear-shaped head, double-chinned and sleepy-eyed. The navy has been his life. He earned his reputation during the attack on Tripoli in 1804 but is better known as a consummate organizer. In command on both lakes, he is really concerned with Ontario, where he is determined to achieve naval superiority. This obsesses him to the exclusion of all else. His task, as he sees it, is to build as many ships as possible, to preserve them from attack, and to destroy the enemy's fleet. But his fear of losing a contest – and thus losing the lake – makes him wary and overcautious. Chauncey will not dare; before he will attack his adversary's flotilla everything must be right: wind, weather, naval superiority. But, since nothing can ever be quite right for Chauncey, this war will be a series of frustrations in which he, and his equally cautious opposite number, Sir James Yeo, flit about the lake avoiding decisive action, fleeing as much from their own irresolution as from the opposing guns, always waiting for the right moment, which never comes.

Now comes word that a British fleet is at the other end of the lake threatening Sackets Harbor. The attack fails, but the Americans panic, briefly setting fire to the partially built warship *General Pike*, thus delaying its launch date. That is enough for Chauncey, who leaves the Niagara frontier, taking all his ships and two thousand troops, a defection that allows Vincent's army to reach the protection of the heights above Burlington Bay. If the Americans are to dislodge them, they must now proceed by land.

•

STONEY CREEK, UPPER CANADA, June 5, 1813

To young Billy Green and his brother Levi, the war is a lark. The older settlers may be in a state of panic, believing with some reason that the British are about to desert them, but when the Green brothers hear that the Americans are only a few miles away they cannot restrain their excitement. Nothing will do but that they have a good look at the advancing army.

With the fall of Fort George, the greater part of the Niagara peninsula has been evacuated by the British army. The Americans have taken Fort Erie and are pushing up the peninsula – have already reached Forty Mile Creek, some thirty-one miles from Newark. General Vincent's army has retired to Burlington Heights and dug in, but there is not much hope that his seven hundred regular troops can hold the position against three thousand of the enemy. The militia

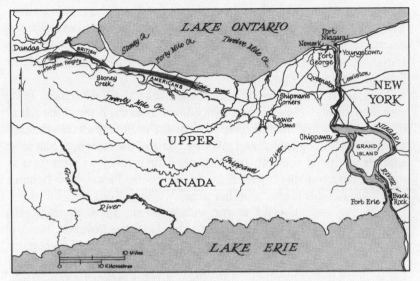

The Niagara Peninsula, 1813

have been disbanded and sent home – deserted by the British, in the opinion of Captain William Hamilton Merritt, whose volunteer horsemen still continue to harass the forward scouts of the advancing enemy. Like many others, Merritt is convinced that the army will retreat to Kingston, leaving all of the western province in the hands of the invaders.

None of this concerns young Billy, a high-spirited youth of nineteen, youngest of Adam Green's seven children. Left motherless almost at birth, shortly after the family moved up from New Jersey, he is known as a loner and a woodsman who can shinny up any tree and swing from branch to branch like a monkey. Now, at six o'clock on a humid spring morning, the two brothers clamber up the Niagara escarpment and make their way south until they reach a point above the American camp at the mouth of Forty Mile Creek.

At noon, hidden from view, they watch the Americans marching by, wait until almost all have passed, then begin to yell like Indians – a sound that sends a chill through the stragglers. "I tell you those simple fellows did run," is the way Billy describes it.

Back along the ridge the brothers scamper, then scramble back down to the road the soldiers have just passed over. Here they run into a lone American, one boot off, tying a rag onto his blistered foot.

As he grabs for his musket, Levi Green belabours him with a stick. The resultant yells of pain draw a rattle of musket fire from the rearguard, whereupon the brothers dash back up the slope, whooping Indian-style, until they reach Levi's cabin on a piece of bench land halfway up the escarpment.

The sound of warwhoops and gunfire draws several settlers from their homes, and a small crowd looks down from the brow of the hill at the Americans marching through the village of Stoney Creek – a scattered huddle of log cabins and taverns. Some of the marchers halt long enough to fire at the hill, one musket ball coming so close that it strikes a fence rail directly in front of Levi's wife, Tina, who is holding their oldest child, Hannah, in her arms.

Now the two descend to the village where their sister, Kezia Corman, reports that the Americans have taken her husband, Isaac, a prisoner. Billy starts off at a dead run across Stoney Creek, whistling for his brother-in-law. A few moments later he hears an owl hoot and knows it is Isaac. The missing man has made his escape by pretending to be friendly to the American cause – a plausible enough pretence in this province.

Isaac simply told the major who captured him that he is a Kentuckian and first cousin to William Henry Harrison. It is true; his mother is Harrison's father's sister. The major promptly released him and when Corman explained that he could not get through the American lines, cheerfully gave him the countersign of the day which, appropriately enough, is made up of the first syllables of Harrison's name: *Wil-Hen-Har*.

Billy Green is now in possession of a vital piece of information. He knows what he must do – get a message to the British at Burlington Heights. Back he goes to Levi's farm, borrows his brother's horse, Tip, rides him as far as he can, ties him to a fence, and makes his way to the British lines on foot.

At this very hour, the British are planning to gamble on a night attack against the American camp. Lieutenant-Colonel Harvey has already reconnoitred the enemy position and believes it to be vulnerable. Harvey is by far the most experienced officer in the division. At thirty-four, he is thirteen years younger than his commander, Vincent, but has spent more than half his life on active service in Holland, France, Ceylon, Egypt, India, and the Cape of Good Hope. The illegitimate son of a peer, Lord Paget (so it is whispered), he is married to the daughter of another, Lord Lake.

In an army that has its fair complement of laggards, the hawk-faced Harvey stands out. Landing at Halifax in the dead of the previous winter, he pushed on to Quebec on snowshoes. He has served in enough campaigns to hew to two basic military principles. He is a firm believer first in "the accurate intelligence of the designs and movements of the enemy, to be procured at any price," and second, in "a series of bold, active, offensive operations by which the enemy, however superior in numbers, would himself be thrown upon the defensive."

Harvey now puts these twin precepts into operation. He has not only reconnoitred the enemy himself, but also one of his subalterns, James FitzGibbon of the 49th, an especially bold and enterprising officer, has apparently disguised himself as a butter pedlar and actually entered the American camp and noted the dispositions of troops and guns.

Harvey is able to report to Vincent that the Americans are badly scattered, that their cannon are poorly placed, that their cavalry is too far in the rear to be useful. He urges an immediate surprise attack by night at bayonet point. It is, in fact, their only chance. Ammunition is low; the American fleet may arrive at any moment. If that happens the army must retreat quickly or face annihilation. Vincent agrees and bowing to Harvey's greater experience and knowledge of the ground sensibly puts him in charge of the assault.

Now, thanks to Billy Green, Harvey has the countersign. He asks Billy if he knows the way to the American camp.

"Every inch of it," replies Billy proudly.

Harvey gives him a corporal's sword, which Billy will keep for the rest of his long life, and tells him to take the lead. It is eleven-thirty. The troops, sleeping on the grass, are aroused, and the column sets off on a seven-mile march through the Stygian night. It is so dark the men can scarcely see each other, the moon masked by heavy clouds, the tall pines adding to the gloom, a soft mist blurring the trails. Only the occasional flash of heat lightning alleviates the blackness.

Their footfalls muffled by the mud of the trail, the troops plod forward in silence. Harvey has cautioned all against uttering so much as a whisper and has also taken care to order all flints removed from firelocks to prevent the accidental firing of a musket. Billy Green, loping on ahead, finds he has left the column behind and must retrace his steps to urge more speed; otherwise it will be daylight before the quarry is flushed. Well, someone in the ranks is heard to mutter, that will be soon enough to be killed.

By three, on this sultry Sunday morning, Harvey's force has reached the first American sentry post. After it is over nobody can quite remember the order of events. Someone fires a musket. At least one sentry is quietly bayoneted. ("Run him through," whispers Harvey to Billy Green.) Another demands the countersign and Billy gives it to him, at the same time seizing his gun with one hand and dispatching him with his new sword held in the other. An American advance party of fifty men, quartered in a church, is overpowered and taken prisoner.

The Americans are camped on James Gage's field, a low, grassy meadow through which a branch of Stoney Creek trickles. The main road, down which the British are advancing, runs over the creek and ascends a ridge, the crest marked by a tangle of trees and roots behind which most of the American infantry and guns are located, their position secured by hills on one side, a swamp on the other.

Directly ahead, in a flat meadow below the ridge, the British can see the glow of American campfires. Moving forward to bayonet the sleeping enemy, they discover to their chagrin that the meadow is empty. The Americans have left their cooking fires earlier to take up a stronger position on the ridge.

In the flickering light of the abandoned fires the attackers fix flints; but by now all hope of surprise has been lost, for the attackers are easily spotted in the campfire glow. As they dash forward, whooping like Indians to terrify the enemy (who believe, and will continue to believe, that they have been attacked by tribesmen), they are met by a sheet of flame. In an instant all is confusion, the musket smoke adding to the thickness of the night, the howls of the British mingling with the sinister *click-click-click* of muskets being reloaded. All sense of formation is lost as some retire, others advance, and friend has difficulty distinguishing foe in the darkness.

The enterprising FitzGibbon, seeing men retreating on the left, runs along the line to restore order. The left holds, and five hundred Americans are put to flight; but the British on the right are being pushed back by more than two thousand. The guns on the ridge above are doing heavy damage. Yet, as Harvey has surmised, the American centre is weak, for the guns do not have close infantry support.

Major Charles Plenderleath of the 49th, a veteran of the battle of Queenston Heights, realizes that his men have no chance unless the guns are captured. He calls for volunteers. Alexander Fraser, a huge sergeant, only nineteen, gathers twenty men and with Plenderleath

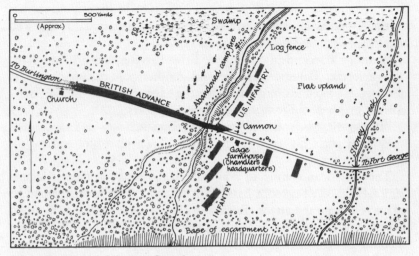

The Battle of Stoney Creek

sprints up the road to rush the guns. Two volleys roar over their heads, but before the gunners can reload they are bayoneted. Plenderleath and Fraser cut right through, driving all before them, stabbing horses and men with crazy abandon. Fraser alone stabs seven, his younger brother four. The American line is cut, four of the six guns captured, one hundred prisoners seized.

The American commander, Brigadier-General John Chandler, a former blacksmith, tavernkeeper and congressman, owes his appointment to political influence rather than military experience, of which he has none. He will spend the rest of his life defending his actions this night. As an associate remarks, "the march from the anvil and the dram shop in the wane of life to the dearest actions of the tented field is not to be achieved in a single campaign."

The General is up at the first musket shot, galloping about on his horse, shouting orders, trying to rally his badly dispersed troops. He can see the British outlined against the cooking fires but not much more. On the crest of the hill, pocked by unexpected depressions and interspersed with stumps, brushwood, fence rails and slash, his horse stumbles, throws him to the ground, knocking him senseless. When he recovers, all is confusion. Badly crippled, he hobbles about in the darkness crying, "Where is the line? Where is the line?" until he sees a group of men by the guns, which to his dismay do not seem to be firing. He rushes forward, mistaking the men of the British 49th for his own 23rd, realizes his error too late, tries to hide under a gun carriage, and is ignominiously hauled out by Sergeant Fraser, who takes his sword and makes him prisoner.

Chandler's second-in-command, Brigadier-General William Winder – a former Baltimore lawyer and another political appointee – is also lost. He too finds himself among the enemy, pulls a pistol from its holster, and is about to fire when Fraser appears.

"If you stir, Sir, you die," says the sergeant.

Winder takes his word for it, throws down his pistol and sword, and surrenders.

The American command now falls to the cavalry officer, Colonel James Burn, whose troops have been placed too far in the rear to be effective during the attack. Burn and his horsemen roar down on the British, cut through the lines, and open fire, only to find that they are shooting at their comrades in the 16th Infantry, who, with their commander lost, are wandering about firing at one another. Friend and foe are now intertangled, both sides taking prisoners, neither knowing how the battle is going. General Vincent himself, knocked from his horse and separated from the British staff, is lost somewhere in the woods, stumbling about in the wrong direction.

Each force leaves the field believing the other victorious. Heavily outnumbered from the start, with a quarter of his force killed, wounded, or captured, Harvey decides to withdraw without Vincent, before the Americans can recover from their confusion. He takes with him three captured cannon, a brass howitzer, two American generals, and more than one hundred prisoners.

The Americans are also preparing to flee, as William Hamilton Merritt, the leader of the volunteer dragoons, discovers when he rides back to the field shortly after dawn, seeking the missing Vincent. An armed sentry at the Gage farmhouse orders him to halt, but the resourceful horseman decides on a bluff, raps out a query.

"Who placed you there?" Merritt barks.

The sentry, seeing the blue coat of a dragoon, takes him for one of his own officers. Before he can catch his breath, Merritt makes him a prisoner, then, using the same subterfuge, captures a second sentry.

He cannot find Vincent, but he is able to report that the Americans are in a panic, destroying everything that cannot be removed – provisions, carriages, arms, blankets. In their haste, they do not even stop to bury their dead but are gone before noon, littering the road with a stream of discarded baggage and the occasional corpse.

The British return to the Stoney Creek battlefield that afternoon to find guns, stores, and baggage still scattered about the field among the litter of the dead. Some of the American tents are still standing. Vincent turns up at last, exhausted, half-famished, his sword, hat, and horse all missing. Lost in the woods, convinced that his army had been annihilated, he has blundered about for seven miles, expecting at any moment to be captured. This embarrassing footnote to the action has no part in the report that Harvey makes to Sir George Prevost. Nor does the signal contribution of Billy Green, who will for the remainder of his eighty-four years be known locally as Billy Green, the Scout.

The American retreat continues. From Fort George, Dearborn orders Major-General Morgan Lewis, his deputy commander, to make haste to Stoney Creek to attack the British. Lewis, who allowed the British to slip out of his grasp during the capture of Fort George, postpones the advance for half a day – because of a rainstorm! The old politician is not held in great esteem by his fellows. Peter B. Porter, Congressman, War Hawk, and Quartermaster General of New York, comments that Lewis "could not go sixteen miles to fight the enemy, not because his force was too small, but because he had not waggons to carry tents and camp kettles for his army." Porter claims that Lewis's own baggage moves "in two stately wagons – one drawn by two, the other by four horses, carrying the various furniture of a Secretary of State's office, a lady's dressing chamber, an alderman's dining room and the contents of a grocer's shop."

All this ponderous accoutrement is now threatened as the British fleet under Sir James Yeo appears outside the mouth of the Niagara, apparently threatening Fort George. Dearborn, whose physical condition is aggravated by mental stress, nervously dispatches a series of notes urging Lewis to send back all his dragoons and eight hundred foot-soldiers to defend the fort.

Yeo moves his vessels up to Forty Mile Creek, where the Americans are camped. Lewis, who has just arrived on the scene, resolves to retire at once, abandoning his supplies in such haste that the occupying British seize 600 tents, 200 camp kettles, 140 barrels of flour, 150 stands of arms, and a baggage train of twenty boats for which the Americans have neglected to supply an escort.

Within three days of the Battle of Stoney Creek, the situation along the Niagara frontier has been reversed. The Americans had been in full possession of the peninsula, outnumbering the British defenders at least three to one. The command at Montreal was prepared to evacuate most of the province, to sacrifice the militia and pull back the regulars to Kingston. But as the result of a single unequal contest, hastily planned at the last minute and fought in absolute darkness by confused and disorganized men, the invaders have lost control. On June 9, they burn Fort Erie and evacuate all the defence posts along the Niagara River, retiring in a body behind the log palisades of Fort George. Except for a few brief forays, it will be their prison until winter forces them across the river to American soil.

•

NEAR BEAVER DAMS, Upper Canada, June 21, 1813

Lieutenant James FitzGibbon and his Bloody Boys are hot in pursuit of Dr. Cyrenius Chapin, an American surgeon from Buffalo whose band of mounted volunteers has been plundering the homes of Canadian settlers along the Niagara River. Leaving his men hidden near Lundy's Lane, FitzGibbon moves up the road seeking information about Chapin's movements. Ahead he spots a fluttering handkerchief: Mrs. James Kerby, wife of a local militia captain, is trying to get his attention. She runs to him, urges him to flee: Chapin has just passed through at the head of two hundred men.

But FitzGibbon does not retire. Up ahead he has spotted an enemy dragoon's horse hitched to a post in front of Deffield's Inn. He rides up, dismounts, bursts into the inn. An American rifleman covers him, but FitzGibbon, who is wearing a grey-green fustian overall covering his uniform as a disguise, clasps him by the hand, claims an old acquaintance, and having thus thrown the enemy off guard, seizes his rifle barrel and orders him to surrender. The man refuses, clings to his weapon, tries to fire it while his comrade levels his own piece at FitzGibbon. FitzGibbon turns about and, keeping the first rifle clamped in his right hand, catches the other's with his left and forces it down until it points at his comrade. Now FitzGibbon exercises his great strength to drag both men out of the tavern, all three swearing and calling on one another to surrender.

Up runs Mrs. Kerby, begging and threatening. Up scampers a small boy who throws rocks at the Americans. The trio continues to struggle until one of the dragoons manages to pull FitzGibbon's sword from its sheath with his left hand. He is about to thrust it into his opponent's chest when Mrs. Deffield, the tavernkeeper's wife, who has been standing in the doorway all this time, a small child in her arms, kicks the weapon out of his hand. As he stoops to recover it, she drops the infant, wrenches the sword away from the American, and runs off.

FitzGibbon throws one of his assailants against the steps and disarms him. The other is attacked by Deffield, the tavernkeeper, who knocks the flint out of his weapon, rendering it useless. FitzGibbon mounts his horse and, driving his two prisoners before him, makes his escape two minutes before Chapin's main force arrives.

The incident adds to FitzGibbon's reputation as a bold and enterprising guerrilla leader. The Niagara peninsula at this moment is a no-man's land, the populace split between those loyal to the British cause and others who flock to the American side. It is not always possible to distinguish between friend and foe in this heterogeneous society of old soldiers, English and Scots immigrants, fervent Loyalists, and rootless new arrivals from America. Old feuds and personal grudges play their own role in the growing schism that sets family against family and alarms the high command.

The two most notorious defectors are Joseph Willcocks, a disgruntled newspaper editor and member of the House of Assembly, and his colleague, Benajah Mallory. The pair are in the act of forming a body of mounted "Canadian Volunteers" to aid the Americans and terrify the Loyalists. Willcocks has some grudges to settle.

For much of the populace the best policy is to lie low and try to keep out of trouble. There are some, however, who are prepared to risk their lives to harass the Americans. It is FitzGibbon's task to aid these partisans – to keep the enemy off balance and penned up in Fort George by a series of ambuscades and skirmishes. With Harvey's blessing he has organized some fifty volunteers from the 49th, provided them with grey-green coveralls as disguises, and trained them in guerrilla warfare. They gallop about the frontier, never sleeping in the same place twice, signalling each other by means of cow bells, which excite no suspicion in this pastoral lowland. They call themselves the Bloody Boys.

FitzGibbon – the man who entered the American camp at Stoney Creek disguised as a butter pedlar – is the perfect leader for such a force. He is a popular officer, unconventional, immensely strong and lithe. The semi-literate son of an Irish cottager, he entered the service too poor to advance himself by the successive purchase of rank. But he was fortunate that Isaac Brock was his commanding officer, for he was Brock's kind of soldier. Fiercely ambitious, almost entirely self-educated, an omnivorous reader in spite of his meagre schooling, FitzGibbon soon came to Brock's attention. Under Brock, he learned grammar, spelling, manners. His patron lent him books, corrected his pronunciation. FitzGibbon can never forget the day when, as adjutant taking dictation from his commander, he mispronounced the word "ascertain" and felt so ashamed that he immediately purchased a spelling book, a dictionary, and a grammar. The three volumes made him so amazed at his own ignorance that he determined to better himself. The orderly room, he has remarked more than once, was his high school, the mess room his university.

He learned also, under Brock, how to handle men. He treats them "as a lady would her piano – that is put them in tune (good humour) before I played upon them." As a result, his men have such faith in him that, as one of them puts it, "if he had told any one of them to jump into the river, he would have obeyed."

On June 22 FitzGibbon, having narrowly escaped Cyrenius Chapin's marauders, takes his men to the two-storey stone house owned by a militia captain, John De Cew, not far from Beaver Dams on Twelve Mile Creek, about seventeen miles from Fort George.

The De Cew house, which FitzGibbon has appropriated as headquarters, forms the apex of a triangle of defence that the British have thrown out to contain Fort George. At the left base of the triangle, seven miles away at the mouth of Twelve Mile Creek, Major Peter De Haren is stationed with three companies of regulars. At the right base, farther up the lake on the heights above Twenty Mile Creek, Lieutenant-Colonel Cecil Bisshopp is posted with a small brigade of light infantry. William Hamilton Merritt's Provincial Dragoons, FitzGibbon's Bloody Boys, John Norton's Mohawks, and Captain Dominique Ducharme's band of Caughnawaga Indians patrol the intervening countryside, forcing back the American pickets and harassing the enemy's own marauders.

It is all very romantic – men on horseback, often in disguise, riding through the night, cutting and thrusting, taking prisoners, making hairbreadth escapes. For those whose homes are plundered and whose menfolk are wounded or killed it is also tragic, but by European standards it is not war. At the very moment when FitzGibbon is struggling with Chapin's dragoons, the Duke of Wellington is hurling 87,000 men against Napoleon's brother Joseph, King of Naples, on the Spanish plain of Vitoria. Wellington's victory costs him five thousand casualties; the French lose eight thousand and are driven back across the Pyrenees. Napoleon's cause is clearly doomed, though not finished, and a wild bacchanalia ensues that makes the looting and burning on the Niagara peninsula seem like very small potatoes indeed.

The following evening, just after sunset, while Wellington's army is recovering from its victory orgy in far-off Spain, a slight and delicate little Loyalist woman in a gingham dress stained with mud makes her appearance at the De Cew house to announce that she has an important message for FitzGibbon. She is Mrs. James Secord, aged thirty-eight, mother of five, wife of a militiaman badly wounded at Queenston Heights. She tells FitzGibbon that she has heard from Americans in Queenston that an attack is being planned on the De Cew headquarters the following day. To carry her warning, she has made her way on foot through the dreaded Black Swamp that lies between Queenston and De Cew's, staying clear of the main roads in order to avoid capture. She is exhausted but game, triumphant after her long journey, which has apparently taken her, at some risk, through the camp of the Caughnawagas.

Laura Secord's adventure, which is destined to become an imperishable Canadian legend, causes FitzGibbon to alert Norton's Mohawks and to keep men posted all night to warn of impending attack. None comes. Is her story, then, a fabrication? Scarcely. She is the daughter of a Loyalist family; her husband is still crippled from wounds inflicted by American soldiers. She has not struggled nineteen miles in the boiling sun from Queenston, through St. Davids and across a treacherous morass on a whim.

In all her long life, Laura Secord will tell her story many times, embellishing it here and there, muddying it more than a little. The Prince of Wales himself will hear of it. Others will add to it: a cow will become part of the legend.

Laura's story will be used to underline the growing myth that the War of 1812 was won by true-blue Canadians – in this case a brave Loyalist housewife who single-handedly saved the British Army from defeat. It dovetails neatly with John Strachan's own conviction that the Canadian militia, and not the British regulars or the Indians, were the real heroes.

But one mystery remains: Laura will never make clear exactly how she heard the rumour of an impending attack on the afternoon or evening of June 21. On this detail she is vague and contradictory, telling FitzGibbon that her husband learned of it from an American officer; telling her granddaughter, years later, that she herself over-heard it from enemy soldiers who forced her to give them dinner in Queenston.

Her exhausting odyssey is even more baffling because it is undertaken on the most tenuous of evidence – an unsubstantiated rumour, flimsy as gossamer, nothing more. On June 21 the Americans have made no firm plans to attack De Cew's. Even Lieutenant-Colonel Charles Boerstler, the man chosen to lead the eventual assault, does not know of it until the afternoon of June 23.

Who are these Americans in Queenston on June 21? They must be Chapin's guerrillas, for the regular troops have been called back to Fort George for fear of being cut off. Yet Chapin, by his own statement, knows nothing of any attack on De Cew's – will not hear of it until orders are issued on June 23.

Yet *something* is in the wind. Has someone whispered a warning in Mrs. Secord's ear? Who? It is not in her interest to give her source. News travels on wings here on the Niagara frontier. Who knows what damage might be done if Laura revealed what she knew? Her invalid husband and children could easily be the subject of revenge in this peninsula of tangled loyalties.

Like everybody else who has lived along the border, the Secords have friends on both sides of the line. Before the war people moved freely between the two countries, buying and selling, owning land, operating businesses without regard to national affiliations. Chapin himself was a surgeon in Fort Erie before he helped to found the town of Buffalo. His men are virtual neighbours; the Secords would know most of them. It may be that in later years, when the past becomes fuzzy, Mrs. Secord simply cannot remember the details of her source, though she seems to remember everything else. It is equally possible that she refuses to identify her informant to save him and his descendants from the harsh whispers and bitter scandal of treason.

•

FORT GEORGE, UPPER CANADA, June 23, 1813

Henry Dearborn is in a bad way. Cooped up in Fort George by a numerically weaker adversary and, in his own words, "so reduced in strength as to be incapable of any command," he has been humiliated by the continuing assaults on the outskirts of his position. Dominique Ducharme's Caughnawagas have just attacked a barque on the Niagara within sight of the fort, killing four American soldiers, wounding seven more, and escaping into the maze of trails that veins the forests along the frontier. It is too much. He has tried to excuse the reverse at Stoney Creek as a "strange fatality," a pomposity which so exasperates the Secretary of War that he hurls the remark back at him in an acid letter that deplores *"the two escapes of a beaten enemy."* Armstrong rubs Dearborn's nose in it by underlining the words.

The ailing general knows he must do something to restore his shattered reputation. Why not a massive excursion to wipe out the Bloody Boys? He has only just learned that FitzGibbon has made his headquarters at the De Cew house. Five hundred men and two guns guided by Chapin and his marauders ought to do the job.

The details are handled by his new second-in-command, Brigadier-General John Boyd, who has replaced the ponderous politician Morgan Lewis but is no more popular than his predecessor. Winfield Scott has little use for this former soldier of fortune, while Lewis, who is not unbiased, believes him to be a bully and a posturer. Lewis has cautioned against just the sort of attack that Boyd and Dearborn now contemplate.

The command at Fort George is, in fact, rife with petty jealousies. There is little love lost between Dr. Chapin, who will guide the expedition, and the officer chosen to lead it, Lieutenant-Colonel Charles Boerstler, a thirty-five-year-old regular from Maryland who clearly despises the self-appointed civilian guerrilla. Yet of the two, the surgeon appears to be the more warlike. The sallow-faced Boerstler is uncommonly sensitive to imagined slights. Chapin, a lithe six-footer with a great beak of a nose, piercing blue eyes, and a long face bronzed by the sun, was once bitterly opposed to war with Britain – he still belongs to the Federalist opposition – but has since become an enthusiastic and unorthodox belligerent, known for his boldness as well as his ego. He cannot stand Boerstler, calls him "a broken down Methodist preacher." Boerstler, on his part, has no use for Chapin, thinks him "a vain and boasting liar."

Chapin is so put off by Boerstler's appointment that he tries to get the high command to replace him, but Dearborn and Boyd decide to go with Boerstler, who has been embarrassingly touchy at being passed over on previous occasions and who has for days been pleading for a chance to lead an attack against the British.

Boerstler does not like Boyd and he does not like Winfield Scott, both of whom have been involved in what he considers slights to his abilities. Originally detailed by Lewis to lead the attack on Fort George, he was passed over at the last moment in favour of Scott. Just four days ago, Boyd replaced him on another assignment, again at the last moment – a decision that produced a heated scene between the two commanders. Chapin's remonstrances are in vain. Neither Boyd nor Dearborn is prepared to slight the sensitive Boerstler a third time.

The expedition is hastily and imperfectly planned. No attempt is made to divert the posts at the other two corners of the defensive triangle while De Cew's is being attacked. Nor is there any reserve on which Boerstler can fall back in case of disaster. The problem is a lack of men: half the army is too sick to fight. The shortage is so serious that officers are forced to turn out on night patrol, shouldering muskets like privates. Boerstler has been promised a body of riflemen – essential in the kind of bush fighting that is certain to take place – but these sharpshooters, having been placed on guard, cannot be relieved. He marches off without them.

Captain Isaac Roach, so sick he can scarcely draw his sword, volunteers to go on the expedition with his company in place of an exhausted friend, but he has grave doubts about the mission. He hands his pocketbook to an old comrade, Major Jacob Hindman.

"I have no doubt we shall get broken heads before my return," says Roach, "and if so send my trunk and pocketbook to my family."

His closest cronies, all members of Winfield Scott's family of artillery officers, see him off. None has confidence in Boerstler. He is, in Roach's opinion, "totally unfit to command."

The column reaches Queenston an hour before midnight in absolute silence. Boerstler dispatches patrols to prevent any citizen escaping with news of the troops' advance. (Laura Secord has now been at FitzGibbon's headquarters for more than twenty-four hours.) Lighted candles are prohibited, the men ordered to sleep on their arms. At daybreak the detachment moves on to St. Davids, where it surprises two of Dominique Ducharme's Caughnawaga skirmishers. One is shot; the other escapes to warn Ducharme and his superior, Major De Haren, of the American advance.

Meanwhile the Americans are moving in column up the side of the Niagara escarpment, which the local settlers insist on calling a mountain. They halt at the top, move on for about a mile past an open field and into a defile bordered on both sides by thick woods. It is here that the Battle of Beaver Dams begins.

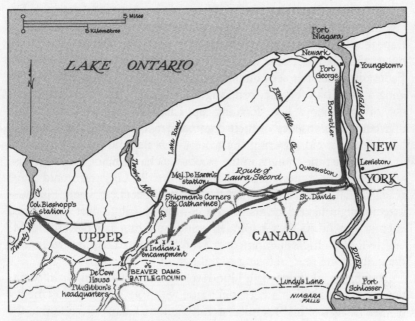

The Battle of Beaver Dams

Each of the leading actors in the tangled drama that follows sees it in retrospect through the distorted lens of his own ego. Some three hours later, when it is all over and men lie dead, wounded, or captive, none can have a clear idea of exactly what happened. Yet each persuades himself that he alone is possessed of the truth.

François Dominique Ducharme sees it as a straightforward victory. He is forty-eight, a veteran of twenty-five years' service in the western fur country – a small, agile, incredibly tough skirmisher who now finds himself detailed to Upper Canada in charge of a band of Caughnawagas from the lower province. In his view, the decisions, the tactics, the victory are totally his – and those of his Indians. It is he, Ducharme, who persuades Major De Haren to allow him to move out of his original position in order to ambush the Americans in the woods. It is his Indians who kill every single one of Chapin's advance guard at the outset of the battle. His allies, the Mohawks, who are on the far side of the road, flee at the first musket volley while Ducharme and his followers drive the Americans back to a coulee, surround them, and force a surrender. Or so Ducharme will remember and believe.

To Charles Boerstler, the architect of the American defeat is Dr. Cyrenius Chapin. Boerstler believes that Chapin has led him into a trap, that he knows nothing about the country, has never been within miles of De Cew's, and may well be a traitor since he *is* a former Federalist. Boerstler sees himself as a beleaguered commander, struggling against bad fortune, ordering his wagons and horses to the rear out of the enemy fire, forming up Chapin's men himself in the unaccountable absence of their commander, concealing the wound in his thigh to avoid lowering the troops' morale, and leading a gallant charge against the Indians in the woods – a charge made futile because of his lack of experienced sharpshooters. If only he could have reached that open field beyond the copse of beeches, where his musketeers might have used their parade-ground drill to oust the painted enemy! *If only!* As for Chapin, Boerstler sees him as a coward, reluctant to follow orders, taking cover with his men among the wagons in the gully at the rear, refusing to fight at all.

To Chapin, Boerstler is a blunderer who leans on him for information, boasts of seeking a personal battle with FitzGibbon ("Let me lay my sword against his"), and gratefully follows Chapin's lead up to the pass in the escarpment. Chapin foresees the Indian ambush, warns his commander, and is in the act of driving five hundred natives through the woods when he is called back, against his will, by the timid and hesitant Boerstler who finally orders him to the rear to select gun positions, with clear instructions not to pursue the enemy. Chapin must stand with his men at the guns and take fearful punishment while Boerstler and his troops move farther to the rear. Or so Chapin will come to believe.

One thing is clear: by noon the troops are exhausted. Boerstler, feeling hemmed in by the woods and the hidden Indians, has made the mistake of leading his men forward and keeping them too long exposed to heavy fire. The fault is not entirely his; the detachment was too small, the plans imperfect and hurried. The troops have been up since dawn, have marched eleven miles without refreshment, have fought for three hours under a blazing sun, have exhausted their ammunition. What is to be done?

Time will blur the memories of all the participants, but it does not matter, for at this moment James FitzGibbon appears on the scene carrying a white flag and demanding an American surrender.

FitzGibbon has actually been in the area for some time, having been alerted earlier in the morning by Ducharme's scouts to the presence of an enemy column advancing toward his post. He has reconnoitred the battlefield and sent for his men, but the chances of capturing the Americans do not look good. He cannot depend on the Indians, who are coming and going on whim, some running off, others returning to the struggle; none is capable of forcing a surrender, and their leader, Ducharme, cannot speak English. At best, he thinks, the Americans will manage to untangle themselves and retire to Fort George. At worst, he and his small detachment of forty-four Bloody Boys may themselves be made prisoners. Finally, FitzGibbon decides upon a bluff, strides forward, white flag in hand.

Boerstler sends his artillery captain, McDowell, to meet him. The two parley. FitzGibbon resorts to the tried and true threat: he has been dispatched by Major De Haren to inform the Americans that they are surrounded by a superior force of British, that they cannot escape, and that the Indians, having met with severe losses, are infuriated to the point of massacre – a tragedy that can only be averted if Boerstler surrenders. Boerstler refuses. He is not accustomed, he says, to surrender to an army he has not seen.

FitzGibbon's bluff has been called. There is no unseen army – only Ducharme and his Caughnawagas. Nonetheless, FitzGibbon boldly proposes that the Americans send an officer to examine De Haren's force: that will convince them that the odds against them are overwhelming. Boerstler agrees but declares there will be no surrender unless he finds he is badly outnumbered. FitzGibbon then retires on the pretence that he must consult with De Haren who is, of course, nowhere near the scene. Instead, FitzGibbon runs into Captain John Hall, who has just ridden up with a dozen Provincial Dragoons. Hall agrees, if necessary, to impersonate the absent major.

Back goes FitzGibbon to report that De Haren will receive one of the American officers. Boerstler sends a subaltern who encounters Hall, believing him to be De Haren. Hall, thinking quickly, declares that it would be humiliating to display his force but insists it is quite large enough to compel surrender.

Boerstler, weak from loss of blood, asks for time to decide. FitzGibbon gives him five minutes, explaining that he cannot control the Indians much longer.

"For God's sake," cries Boerstler, "keep the Indians from us!" and, with the spectre of the River Raisin never far from his mind, agrees to surrender.

FitzGibbon faces a problem. How can his tiny force disarm five hundred of the enemy without his subterfuge being discovered—especially when the real Major De Haren is nowhere to be found? Fortunately, a more senior officer, Lieutenant-Colonel John Clark, arrives, followed shortly after by De Haren himself with a body of troops.

FitzGibbon has a further problem: he must explain his deception to De Haren before the Major unwittingly reveals it to the enemy. Moreover, he wants credit for the surrender and fears that De Haren will rob him of it. To his discomfiture, De Haren brushes him aside. Clearly, he is about to offer surrender conditions of his own to Boerstler.

FitzGibbon is not Brock's disciple for nothing. Impulsive action is called for. He steps up quickly, lays his hand on the neck of the Major's horse, speaks in a low, firm voice:

"Not another word, sir; these are my prisoners."

Steps back and cries loudly:

"Shall I proceed to disarm the American troops?"

De Haren cannot but agree.

FitzGibbon is still afraid that the Major will, by some remark, ruin everything. The Americans can easily overwhelm them if the deception is revealed. He quickly orders the troops into file, and as soon as some are formed raps out an order to the men to march, thus driving Boerstler and De Haren forward to prevent further conversation between them.

The marching Americans, still armed, are rapidly approaching FitzGibbon's small force of Bloody Boys. He suggests to De Haren that the captives ground arms at once.

"No," says De Haren harshly, "let them march through between our men and ground their arms on the other side."

What folly! thinks FitzGibbon. *When they see our handful will they really ground their weapons?*

Turns to De Haren: "Do you think it prudent to march them through with arms in their hands in the presence of the Indians?"

At the mention of the dreaded word *Indians*, Boerstler throws up a hand:

"For God's sake, sir, do what this officer bids you."

De Haren agrees, and as the prisoners drop their weapons, the tribesmen appear from behind trees and bushes and rush toward them. Some of Boerstler's men, terrified, seize their weapons once more, whereupon FitzGibbon, springing up on a stump, shouts that no one will be hurt. The Indians are allowed to plunder muskets, knives, swords, and other equipment, but the chiefs, having promised they will not injure their captives, hold their men in check. Ducharme and his Caughnawagas are displeased; they are not allowed to scalp the dead, and much of the plunder goes to the Mohawks, who did little fighting. As Norton, the Mohawk chief, puts it in a long-to-be-remembered aside: "The Caughnawaga Indians fought the battle, the Mohawks got the plunder and FitzGibbon got the credit."

The Battle of Beaver Dams confirms the inability of the invaders to break out of their enclave at Fort George. Boerstler has lost more than five hundred men, including Chapin and twenty-one of his mounted corps. The big doctor is not a prisoner for long. About three weeks later, while being conveyed to Kingston by boat, he succeeds in over-powering his captors and escaping with two boatloads of prisoners. For the United States it is the only bright spot in an otherwise sorry picture.

Dearborn is stunned by the disaster. He describes the Battle of Beaver Dams as "an unfortunate and unaccountable event." But generals must be accountable, and when the news reaches Washington there is an immediate demand for the sick old soldier's removal. Congress is in session when this "climax of continual mismanagement and misfortune" (to quote Congressman Charles Ingersoll) reaches the capital. By this time Dearborn is too sick to care. His officers – those who have not been killed, wounded, captured, or driven to their beds by the fever raging within the fort – urge him to move the army back to American soil at once. A council of war finally agrees to hold fast. Dearborn is removed at last, as much to his own relief as to that of his officers. Only when his replacement is named are eyebrows raised. The new commander, James Wilkinson – Pike's hero – is perhaps the most despised general officer in the army. Before the year is over and Fort George finally returns to British hands, many will long for Dearborn's return.

•

NEAR FORT ERIE, Upper Canada, July 10, 1813

James FitzGibbon, concealed behind the willows that fringe the Niagara's high bank, peers through his glass at the American community of Black Rock, directly across the gorge. Here, for the taking, are vast quantities of stores as well as extensive military and naval barracks. FitzGibbon, whose Bloody Boys are hidden in nearby barns, is convinced that a lightning attack against the settlement, if managed with complete surprise, can deal the enemy a serious blow and also serve to stretch the dwindling supplies of the British.

The troops are in a bad way. The commissariat is out of salt, the necessary item to preserve meat. The Green Tigers, as the 49th are dubbed, are in the words of one officer "literally naked." The 41st on the Detroit frontier is in rags and without shoes. A stream of urgent, almost frantic pleas from Major-General Henry Procter at Amherstburg makes it clear that the Right Division is in a bad way.

FitzGibbon lowers his glass to discover that two lieutenant-colonels, Cecil Bisshopp, a regular officer, and Thomas Clark of the 2nd Lincoln militia, have happened upon his hiding place. Both are in uniform, the former resplendent in scarlet and gold braid, and both are walking about in full view of the enemy. FitzGibbon is aghast. The success of his plan depends on keeping the Americans ignorant of the British return to the frontier.

Bisshopp tells FitzGibbon that he has already proposed an attack on Black Rock and has asked the new commander, De Rottenburg (Sheaffe's replacement), for three hundred men to do the job. De Rottenburg has allowed him two hundred. Does FitzGibbon think the barracks can be taken and the stores destroyed or captured with such a small force?

FitzGibbon can barely resist a smile. He has been planning to attack Black Rock with his forty-four Bloody Boys! When Bisshopp hears this, he laughs: "Oh, then! I need ask you no more questions but go and bring the two hundred men."

He orders the impetuous FitzGibbon to wait until the following morning when he and his boys will lead the advance across the river and, if necessary, cover the retreat.

The boats, brought up from their hiding place at Chippawa Creek, push off at two the following morning in a thick mist. A strong current forces FitzGibbon's party well below the landing place. The main party is drifting even farther downriver and FitzGibbon realizes that they will land half an hour later than planned. Nonetheless, he follows orders – to advance immediately upon landing – and leads his men on a concealed march through the woods toward the marine barracks and blockhouse half a mile downriver from Black Rock.

So complete is the surprise that an eight-man picket, all raw militia, is captured before it can give any alarm. FitzGibbon fires the blockhouse and barracks, then, moving rapidly through the town, reaches the army camp at Fort Gibson, guarded by 150 militia.

Peter B. Porter, Quartermaster General for the state of New York, in charge of the militia at Black Rock, has been on watch for most of the night and has just managed to get to sleep in his big stone house on the main street when FitzGibbon's advance guard dashes by. Porter leaps up and, clad only in a linen nightshirt, climbs out of a window at the back, finds a horse, mounts it with some difficulty, and dashes off toward Buffalo to rouse the militia. Five minutes later, Bisshopp's advancing troops seize his house.

In Hawley's Tavern on the river bank a small drama is being enacted. James Sloan, an itinerant pedlar of goods and groceries, is asleep when the sound of FitzGibbon's bugle causes him to jump out of bed. To his astonishment, the tavern is empty; all have fled at the sight of Bisshopp's approaching troops. A luckless baker named Wright, who also tried to escape into the woods, lies dead in the street below.

Sloan decides that bed is the safest place for him and climbs back under the covers. A few moments later he sees a strange Irish face peering at him through the window.

"Sergeant Kelly!" says the face. "Here is a man in bed."

The door bursts open as two Green Tigers enter the room and order Sloan out of bed.

Can't get out of bed, says Sloan, cowering under the covers. *I'm sick*.

The remark enrages the two Irishmen, who swear they'll skivver him where he lies.

At that Sloan jumps up and pulls on his clothes. Sergeant Kelly in a more kindly tone asks if he has any liquor. The pedlar produces a demijohn of cherry bounce, the two soldiers fill their canteens, and all three take several hearty pulls on the jug.

The trio are soon on the best of terms. Sloan's new friends suggest that he return to bed: it is the safest place to be in Black Rock at the moment. Sloan agrees, leaps back under the covers, and the two tipsy Irishmen depart.

But Sloan's curiosity gets the better of him. What is happening out there? Emboldened by cherry bounce, he climbs out of bed, peers through the window at the drama in the street. He can see the naval and military barracks and the fifty-ton schooner *Zephyr* all in flames. British troops are stripping Porter's warehouse and an adjoining store of army property. An officer in a red coat rides up and down the street.

It dawns on the pedlar that he can be an instant hero: he can slip unobserved through the front door of the tavern and capture that officer! His fears vanish as glory beckons. But first he will need a gun; surely, somewhere in this tavern there must be a weapon! He rummages about vainly until he is halted by a cry from the river. Unhappily for him, the boats that brought the British across the Niagara are being poled up to the rendezvous point and are at this very moment passing the tavern. Somebody spots him through a window on the river side and shouts a warning. A cordon of troops surrounds the house and batters at the hall door. Sloan opens it, and two officers, who look more like peasants to him, announce that he is their prisoner. Sloan falls back on an old excuse, says he is too sick to move. It does not work.

They take him to Bisshopp, the officer on the horse whom Sloan thought to capture.

"Young man," says Bisshopp, breaking in on his protestations, "you must go to Canada."

Well, that is all right with James Sloan. The idea, in fact, rather appeals to him. He will see something of a new country and of the famous British Army. When his curiosity is satisfied he will simply nail two or three rails together with strips of bark and, being a strong swimmer, propel himself back across the Niagara.

Sloan cannot help liking Lieutenant-Colonel Bisshopp. He considers him a mild and humane-looking man and guesses his age at about thirty-six. Actually Bisshopp is barely thirty, but his years of service in the guards, as military attaché in St. Petersburg, as aide to Wellington in Portugal, as an infantry officer in Holland, have matured him. The oldest surviving son of a baronet, a one-time Member of Parliament, he is heir to an ancient title and a considerable fortune. Duty and duty alone keeps him in Canada. Service in this coarse colonial backwater is "complete banishment," and "were it not for the extensive command I have and the quantity of business I have to do, I should hang myself." His men adore him; he thinks more of their welfare than he does of his own. To FitzGibbon, he is "a man of most gentle and generous nature," more beloved by the militia than anyone else.

But FitzGibbon also believes that Bisshopp is lacking in judgement. The events that follow underline the accuracy of that assessment. Having dealt Black Rock a heavy blow, the leader of the Bloody Boys wants to be off before the Americans can rush reinforcements from

94

Buffalo. The British have not lost a man. The boats, brought up from the landing place, are ready to take off the troops. But Bisshopp insists on waiting until eighty or ninety barrels of salt, so precious to the army, are brought out of Porter's warehouse and rolled to the water's edge. That is his undoing.

The owner of the salt, Peter B. Porter, is at this moment galloping about in the woods between Buffalo and Black Rock in his nightshirt, seeking to rally the militia. This war is partially of his making; as chairman of the House Foreign Relations Committee and a key member of Henry Clay's determined little group of War Hawks, he pushed for declaration in the spring of 1812. The war has brought him a measure of wealth, for he is a provisioner to the militia as well as quartermaster, ordering from himself and selling to himself the contents of the warehouse being looted by the British. Now in the Two Mile Woods he encounters a troop of dragoons en route to Black Rock from Buffalo. He orders them to fall back and wait in a field while he proceeds to collect the scattered citizen soldiers.

By seven o'clock, Porter has 250 men formed up in some sort of order, to whose ranks are added thirty Indians, mainly Senecas, under two chiefs, Farmer's Brother and Young King. This is the first time in the war that the Americans have employed Indians as combatants – the first time, in fact, that any large group of natives has wanted to fight on the side of the Long Knives. But these tribesmen feel that their own territory is under attack and so attach themselves to Porter's advancing forces.

Half of Bisshopp's force has already been sent back across the river. The remainder is engaged in loading the boats with salt and other stores when the attack comes. The American militia and the Indians burst from the woods on either flank, catching Bisshopp off guard.

Bisshopp is shaken. As he will ruefully remark, a body of Cossacks could not have surprised him more. He orders the main body of his men to make for the boats, then with FitzGibbon at his side leads a small detachment up a hill to meet the attackers and cover the withdrawal. As he rushes forward, a bullet from an Indian rifle shatters his left thigh. Some of his men turn back and rush to the prostrate figure of their commander.

"Oh, my lads," cries Bisshopp, "dead or alive don't leave me here."

Several assure him that they will lose their own lives rather than see him taken. They carry him down to the boats on the dead run, but before they reach them, he is hit by a second ball in the right wrist. Other members of the rescue party drop around him as he is hoisted into a boat overloaded with escaping soldiers. As the oarsmen pull away, the Americans pour a deadly fire into the little flotilla. Twenty-seven British are killed or wounded, among them Sloan's drinking companion, Sergeant Kelly, who will not recover. And Bisshopp is struck for a third time, high up in the right arm.

His physical wounds are not serious; his mental sufferings are. He cannot forgive himself for the loss of his men, cannot accept the idea that a single soldier should be shot while trying to rescue him. The surgeon who attends him has no fears for his recovery, yet Bisshopp daily grows worse, even when his commanding general, Francis De Rottenburg, pays him a visit and tries to ease his conscience. All he can talk about as his condition worsens is the loss of his men, until one evening, still blaming himself for the tragedy, he expires "without a struggle, nay, without a groan."

●

YORK, UPPER CANADA, July 31, 1813

Panic! Square sails on the lake...white jibs...red stripes and blue stars flying from the sterns. With the half-charred *General Pike* finally launched at Sackets Harbor, the naval balance on Lake Ontario has changed again. The Americans are back in force on this humid mid-summer morning – at least a dozen vessels standing for the harbour.

By the time the leading vessels anchor off the garrison, the town is all but emptied of men. William Allan, merchant and militia major, leads the exodus, the memory of his earlier imprisonment still seared into his mind. It is true that he and the others have given their parole, but they do not trust the Americans. Along the Niagara frontier other paroled militia officers have been bundled up and taken across the border to captivity on foreign soil. Allan is taking no chances.

He reaches the Playter farmhouse on north Yonge Street. With the help of the two Playter brothers, Allan conceals a boatload of five thousand cartridges and another crammed with baggage in a marsh near the Don River. He himself moves north and hides out in the woods.

Through the silent streets of the empty town, two men make their way to the garrison. Grant Powell has elected to stay and so, of course, has the Reverend Dr. Strachan. (Who would dare imprison *him*?) They reach the garrison about two o'clock and wait developments.

They watch the largest vessels come to anchor at three. The wind is so light that the schooners, trailing behind, must use their sweeps. At four, they see the boats put off. Two hundred and fifty men land without opposition. All available British troops have retired to defend Burlington Heights.

White flag in hand, Strachan tackles the first officer to reach the shore and demands to be taken to the Commodore. Chauncey, with Winfield Scott at his elbow, is cordial enough. Indeed, he expresses regret at the theft of books from the library the previous April, says he has made a search of the fleet for the books, has found several and will return them. Strachan demands to know his intentions, points out that the present inhabitants are only women and children. Does he mean to destroy the community? If so, will he allow the removal of these non-combatants?

Chauncey reassures him: no looting is contemplated, only the seizure of the public stores and the burning of all fortifications. The major purpose of the expedition is retaliation for British attacks on the far side of the lake, especially a recent hit-and-run assault on the little community of Sodus. He does not say it, but the real reason for the expedition, surely, is the need to do *something*. Cooped up in Sackets Harbor and Fort George, denied a naval confrontation by the elusive James Yeo, stalemated in their attempts to seize the Niagara peninsula, the Americans need to simulate action.

Chauncey asks where the public stores are located. Strachan and Powell will not tell him. It does not matter, because Chauncey already knows or soon finds out – knows the state of York's defences, knows the position of the army on Burlington Heights, knows every single transaction that has taken place in York. As he remarks later to Strachan, he "never heard of any place that contained half the Number of persons, Publickly known & avowadly to be Enemys to the Government & Country to be allowed to remain at rest...."

Chauncey knows that some of the public stores are secreted in William Allan's store and that Allan himself, a militia officer under parole, has been collecting and sending information to the British army and aiding in the forwarding of troops. Winfield Scott offers a five-hundred-dollar reward for Allan's capture and sends his men to break into the store. They seize everything, break open several officers' trunks, give away the contents, and burn a large quantity of hemp. Others open the jail and release all the prisoners. When Strachan attempts to protest to Winfield Scott, the American colonel brushes him off, declares he'll seize all the provisions he can find.

In this he has the aid and comfort of a group of disaffected Canadians. John Lyon, one of the ringleaders, brings his wagon down Yonge Street to help the Americans move the captured flour to the boats. His crony Calvin Wood, jailed for sedition, is one of those released from the York jail. Wood and several others go aboard the American ships to give the enemy information; in gratitude, his new-found friends present him with seven barrels of flour.

From these informants Chauncey learns that boatloads of arms, baggage, and ammunition have been hauled up the Don River. It is late in the evening; a half-hearted attempt to storm Burlington Heights has been called off; the fleet is about to leave. Now, however, the Commodore postpones his departure. The following morning the troops disembark, and three armed boats move up the Don seeking the hidden supplies. But Ely Playter and his brother have already squirreled most of them away, and the searchers return disappointed.

The troops evacuate the town, burn the barracks, blockhouses, and all other buildings at Gibraltar Point, and return to the ships, which weigh anchor the following dawn and set sail for Sackets Harbor. Again, unaccountably, the Americans have declined to occupy the capital and cut the line between Kingston and the British forces on the Niagara.

The town breathes more freely. Though the inhabitants do not know it, this is the last time a hostile flotilla will anchor in Toronto Bay. The new centre of action is on Lake Erie, more than two hundred miles to the southwest. Even as Chauncey's fleet sails out of the harbour, a mixed force of British regulars, Canadian militia, and Indians is launching a bloody attack on Fort Stephenson, the American outpost on Sandusky Bay. Farther along the shoreline to the east, Oliver Hazard Perry is about to give his adversary the slip, manoeuvre his brand new fleet out of its prison at Presque Isle, and challenge British naval authority on the lake.

The war has passed York by, but its effects will linger on, long after hostilities end. John Lyon, Calvin Wood, and a clutch of other dissidents will soon find themselves in jail. Charges of sedition, taunts of treason, will be thrown at any who, by deed, word, or even gesture, appeared to espouse the American cause. It will no longer be prudent to praise the American way of life, as Timothy Wheeler, among others, has done in the hearing of his neighbours, or even to attack "the old Tories," as Edward Phillips has done.

A "committee of information" is about to come into being to take depositions from all loyal subjects who wish to inform on their neighbours. Its members are men of impeccable loyalty and substance: the core of the future Family Compact – Strachan, Allan, Thomas Ridout, and the acting attorney general's brother, Captain Peter Robinson, whose name will one day be immortalized by the town of Peterborough. The acting attorney general, John Beverley Robinson, cannot participate in person since the committee's actions, strictly speaking, are illegal. But he is with them in spirit, for "the country must not be lost by a too scrupulous attention to forms." In Upper Canada, during an emergency, individual civil liberties are not a matter of pressing concern. Individualism, after all, is an American concept, "liberty" a Yankee word.

3

The Northwest Campaign: 1
THE SIEGE OF FORT MEIGS
April 12 – May 8, 1813

While the British Centre Division prepares to defend the Niagara peninsula, the Right Division, with Indian help, plans to attack the American base at Fort Meigs on the Maumee River, near the west end of Lake Erie. The time is propitious. The British, who have captured most of Michigan Territory, control the lake. Most of the American defenders are leaving the garrison, their term of service at an end. If Fort Meigs falls, the American left wing will collapse and the land north of the Ohio is likely to revert to the Indians who fight on the British side under the Shawnee war chief, Tecumseh.

FORT MEIGS, OHIO, April 12, 1813

Major-General William Henry Harrison, commander of the American Army of the Northwest, returning to his headquarters here on the swirling Maumee, looks up at his fortified camp and senses that something is not quite right.

The eight-acre stockade, one hundred feet above the river, is encircled by a fence of fifteen-foot pickets driven deep into the ground for permanence. Permanence? What are those gaps in the fence line? Why are the eight blockhouses unfinished? The British are only a few miles away at Amherstburg across the Detroit River. Hostile Indians are already lurking among the oaks and beeches. Has nothing been done in his absence?

Very little, it seems. Harrison, drumming up reinforcements in the wilderness, left the strengthening of the fort in charge of a brigadier-general of the Virginia militia – Joel B. Leftwich. But Leftwich is not to be found, has in fact taken off with all his men, their six months' tour of duty having ended the previous week. This "phlegmatic, stupid old granny," as a captain of the engineers calls him, stopped all work on the defences, announcing that he could not make the militia do anything – and therefore they might as well stay in their tents out of the mud and the water. Instead of improving the works, they have been permitted to burn the timber intended for the blockhouses and to pull up the pickets for fuel.

The quality of the militiamen assigned to Harrison does not inspire much confidence. Some of the senior officers cannot read or write; many more cannot spell. The reports of the general officers often read like the contents of a six-year-old's exercise book. Harrison, the scholar who reads Latin and Greek, is dismayed to discover that one field officer who has been given a day to fill out a form is unable to manage the task. Few know anything about military customs, drill or discipline. Two Ohio captains after two months in the service still labour under the belief that sergeants of the regular army outrank them; while serving as officers of the guard they meekly ask the NCO's permission to go to dinner!

All this must gall Harrison, the one-time governor of Indiana whose passion is military history. But his brooding features do not betray it. His is an ascetic's face, aquiline, stretched long like pull-toffee. The hollow cheeks, the thin nose, the sombre eyes give him a mediaeval look that masks his feelings.

At the moment he is frustrated over the orders of the new Secretary of War, John Armstrong, who has forbidden him to go on the attack until the ships that the naval commander, Oliver Hazard Perry, is building can control Lake Erie. Harrison is used to having his own way, has enjoyed *carte blanche* until this month. Now he is being hedged in, ordered to economize. Governor Isaac Shelby of Kentucky is itching to raise fifteen thousand troops to help Harrison avenge last January's massacre at Frenchtown, but Armstrong demurs. The government, he declares, can afford to spend only $1,400,000 a month on this war. Harrison is allotted twenty thousand.

Economy or not, Harrison has been forced to bribe some of the six-month men to hang on at Fort Meigs until reinforcements arrive. He has about twelve hundred troops in camp but only 850 are fit for duty – half of them untrained – against an estimated three thousand British, Canadians, and Indians.

Dismayed by the lack of public spirit among the militia, he has overstepped his authority and urged Governor Shelby to send him an additional fifteen hundred Kentuckians. Shelby, invoking a new Kentucky law, complies at once, and even now these men are on the march down the Maumee Valley. But will they arrive in time? Harrison has offered a bonus of seven dollars a month to any man who will offer to remain on duty until the new recruits appear. Two hundred Pennsylvanians agree to stay for fifteen days. The Kentucky troops in camp are hawkish: if the General will lead them against the

The Northwest Frontier

men who massacred their fellow soldiers at Frenchtown they will follow him without any bribe.

Upon Harrison's return to the fort, the troops are plunged into a whirlwind of activity. The chief engineer has booked sick, but his replacement, Captain Eleazer D. Wood, throws himself into the task of reinforcing the stockade. Harrison, who seems to be everywhere at once, orders his officers to conduct daily drills of the raw recruits to prepare them for the coming siege. It is not easy. Most of the officers need drilling as badly as their men.

They are much better at felling trees, digging trenches, splitting logs and raising bulwarks – an activity that proceeds under Eleazer Wood's direction. Work parties haul in fuel for the garrison and timber to fill breeches in the walls. Others dig wells in preparation for a lengthy siege.

Harrison has known since early April that the British, aware of his reduced state, are preparing an attack and expect a swift and easy contest. His old adversary, Tecumseh, has fifteen hundred tribesmen under his command at Fort Amherstburg on the Canadian side of the Detroit River. Fortunately for Harrison, the British commander, Major-General Henry Procter, has moved tardily, allowing the Americans a breathing space. But now the British have landed in full force at the mouth of the Maumee and are moving up the left bank. One of Harrison's scouting parties discovers them on the twenty-eighth, camped on the site of the old British Fort Miami, and estimates their strength at between fifteen hundred and two thousand. Tecumseh's Indians have already crossed the river and surrounded the American camp, picking off those soldiers foolhardy enough to leave the stockade for water. Fort Meigs is all but cut off, its garrison outnumbered two to one. Harrison's only hope lies in the reinforcements from Kentucky, somewhere on the Upper Maumee, nobody yet knows exactly where.

●

MÉTOSS, HEAD CHIEF of the Sauks, lies belly down in a thicket close by the walls of the fort, waiting for any thirsty American soldier who attempts to steal down to the river. Like his fellow chief, Black Hawk, he has become a bitter enemy of the Americans – and with reason, for they have managed to squeeze fifty million acres of good Mississippi Valley land out of his people. He has come here to fight the Long Knives at the behest of Robert Dickson the fur trader, now an official of the British Indian Department, whom the Sioux call *Mascotopah*, the Red-Haired Man. Each night Métoss crosses the river from his tepee near the British camp to pick off one of the enemy or take a prisoner. The woods are alive with his fellow tribesmen, creeping behind the stumps and logs that litter the clearing around the fort or clambering into the elms to fire down upon the men within the walls.

He is an imposing figure, Métoss – six feet tall, with classic Roman features, his torso, arms, and thighs daubed with war paint, a circlet of feathers ornamenting his head. To the Americans behind the tall pickets, the encroaching Indians are only shadows, featureless and unreal. To the frontiersmen of Ohio and Kentucky they are no better than animals, without human feelings, to be shot on sight, war or no war. No American jury will convict a white man for murdering an Indian any more than it will censure him for slaughtering buffalo.

Métoss's thirteen-year-old son crouches beside his father, peering into the darkness, playing at being a man. He is his father's favourite. Métoss can deny him nothing, even this moment of danger. He has urged him not to come; but the boy is here.

They are very close to the fort, their temerity fuelled by the Americans' inability to locate them in the gloom. Does Métoss catch the glint of a telescope, flickering in the moonlight, behind the palisade? For once the enemy has him spotted. A moment later comes a flash, a coarse roar, and the whistle of grape-shot – scores of heavy balls released from their skin of canvas, whirling in the air, ripping the bark from the trees, shredding the new leaves of spring, tearing into the bowels of the child beside him, who dies, writhing, in his arms.

Revenge! Back at his tepee, securely pinioned, is Métoss's captive, a young American soldier taken the night before. Wild with grief, the father picks up the small mangled body, carries it to his canoe, slips across the river. All of his terrible despair is funnelled into an implacable purpose: he will purge his sorrow with a stroke of the tomahawk.

The red-headed Dickson, who seems to know everything that transpires in his camp, is there ahead of him. *Do not do this thing*, says Dickson. *Do not destroy this man. Surrender him instead to me – otherwise your father, the King, will look on you with sorrow.*

No other white man and few other native chiefs have Dickson's power over the western tribes. He is the master of the fur country, the protector of his people, their unquestioned champion, spokesman, general. To save them from starvation he has been prepared to beggar himself, and he has never betrayed their trust. Métoss cannot refuse him.

The chief tears off his headdress, struggles with his emotions, goes at last to his tepee. There he pulls a knife from his belt, severs his captive's thongs, takes him by the hand, leads him to Dickson, speaks in a mournful voice:

"You tell me that my Great Father wishes it – take him!"

Then, no longer able to control his emotions, he weeps like a baby.

The boy is buried next day with full military honours. The body is laid out first in Métoss's tent, a small rifle beside it with a quantity of ammunition and provisions for the journey that must follow. A dozen warriors painted black perform a solemn ritual dance. Suddenly, the chief rushes into the midst of the group, frantic with sorrow, his grief violent, ungovernable. They lead him, at last, from the body of his son, and the funeral procession moves off toward the newly dug grave on the river bank under the command of Lieutenant Richard Bullock of the 41st.

The red-coated firing party discharges the customary three rounds. The black-painted warriors follow with volley after volley. And still Métoss cannot control his grief. In the months that follow he becomes attached to Bullock, the officer who headed the firing party, makes him a chief of the Sauks, asks him to exchange names, treats him as a blood relative as if to replace his missing son. But he cannot staunch his tears, and it is the better part of a year before anybody sees him smile.

●

FORT MEIGS, OHIO, April 28, 1813

Rain drenches the besieged American camp. The flash of lightning competes with the blaze of cannon; the crack of thunder with the roar of musketry. Indian warwhoops add to the cacophony.

Into this hellish night – into the mud, into the unseen tangle of stumps and broken logs, into hidden thickets and lurking shadows – goes a young captain, William Oliver, protected briefly by an escort of dragoons and by the thickness of the night itself. He carries a two-sentence message from Harrison to Brigadier-General Green Clay, in command of the Kentucky reinforcements somewhere on the upper reaches of the Maumee:

Dear Sir: I send Mr. Oliver to you, to give you an account of what is passing here. You may rely implicitly on him.

The note reveals nothing, for Oliver's chances of getting through are minimal. The real message will be oral. Harrison can only wait and hope while he strengthens his defences. Meanwhile, to raise morale, he composes one of those eloquent general orders for which he is famous:

Can the citizens of a free country who have taken arms to defend its rights, think of submitting to an army composed of mercenary soldiers, reluctant Canadians goaded to the field by the bayonet, and of wretched, naked savages? Can the breast of an American soldier, when he casts his eye on the opposite shore, the scene of his country's triumphs over the same foe, be influenced by any other feelings than the hope of glory? Is not this army composed of the same materials with that which fought and conquered under the immortal Wayne? Yes, fellow soldiers, your General sees your countenances beam with the same fire which he witnessed on that glorious occasion; and although it would be the height of presumption to compare himself with that hero, he boasts of being that hero's pupil. To your posts, then, fellow citizens, and remember that the eyes of your country are upon you.

Harrison's order contains all the proper ingredients. It reinforces the American attitude that this war is a fight for freedom, that the British regulars are really mercenaries without a cause, that the Canadians are enslaved and must be goaded to fight. It conjures up the savagery of a so-called civilized nation that fights its colonial wars with unrestrained natives. Finally, it recalls past glories; directly across from Fort Meigs is the site of the Battle of Fallen Timbers, where General "Mad Anthony" Wayne humbled the combined Indian armies.

Harrison's order is also a statement of America's military philosophy. It reminds the young recruits from Ohio and Kentucky that they are citizens first and soldiers second (a truth with which the regulars would wryly agree) and that their commander is a citizen, too, and an equal. This approach, which springs out of the Revolution, is at odds with that of the British, who believe in disciplined professional soldiers following orders without question within the perimeters of a rigid caste system. No British general would ever refer to his men as "fellow citizens" – nor would a Canadian, for that matter.

But Harrison must inspire his artillery with more than words. The British are building gun emplacements on a ridge directly across from the fort, on the north side of the Maumee, concealing their own gunners in a hollow at the rear. A second battery has been moved across the river and is about to bear down on his position. The General sees at once that his own entrenchments will be ineffective against these massed cannon. He must drastically alter his own defensive plan. With Eleazer Wood's engineering help he will criss-cross the camp with a series of traverses – great embankments of earth, buttressed against cannon fire, with caves scooped out at the base in which the half-buried troops can eat and sleep.

The largest of these embankments is planned to run the entire length of the fort. Because it must be constructed in secrecy, Harrison has his second line of tents taken down to leave an open avenue but keeps the first line standing to mask the work of construction. Now the entire camp is employed throwing up this vast wall of earth, three hundred yards long, fifteen feet high, twenty feet thick at the base. The troops work in three-hour shifts, urged on by Wood who is heartened and astonished by their energy and courage.

This is work the raw recruits understand, for they have toiled with pick and shovel on frontier farms for most of their lives. Driven to almost superhuman exertions by the British activity across the river and by the musket balls of the Indians raining down into the camp, they are remarkably cheerful, singing as they work:

> *Freemen, no longer bear such slaughter,*
> *Avenge your country's cruel woe!*
> *Arouse, and save your wives and daughters,*
> *Arouse, and expel the faithless foe.*

The heavy rains turn the camp into a swamp, filling the trenches with water and slowing the work, which must be finished before the British get their cannon into position. But the British, too, are hampered by weather. Their gun emplacements are completed on April 29. Now they must secretly move up their two big twenty-four-pounders. At nine that evening, under cover of darkness, two hundred men straining on drag ropes with several teams of oxen start to haul the heavy ordnance along the river road through mud that reaches to the wagons' axles. It takes six hours to move the guns one mile; the first streaks of dawn are lighting the sky before they are finally in place.

All this ponderous preparation weighs on Tecumseh. It is Harrison he wants—Harrison, the former governor of Indiana who has stolen the Indians' land; Harrison, whose troops have wantonly burned the villages of the Miami, Kickapoo, Potawatomi, and Ottawa; Harrison, who has sworn to destroy the Indian confederacy, which the Shawnee war chief and his mystic brother, the Prophet, forged on the banks of the Tippecanoe.

Now Harrison is hiding from him, his men burrowing into the earth like frightened animals. Why cannot the so-called victor of Tippecanoe come out into the open and fight like a man? Tecumseh dispatches a blunt challenge to his old enemy:

"I have with me 800 braves. You have an equal number in your hiding place. Come out with them and give me battle. You talked like a brave man when we met at Vincennes and I respected you, but now you hide behind logs and earth like a ground hog. Give me your answer."

There is no reply. The former governor must see once again in the mirror of his memory that swarthy, hazel-eyed figure in unadorned deerskin who upset so many of his plans, frustrated his attempts to buy native territory for a pittance, dared to face him down on his own estate at Vincennes; who has through the magic of his personality, the eloquence of his oratory, and the quickness of his intelligence managed to rally the tribes of the American northwest and bring them over to the British side. It is Tecumseh who is at the root of America's disgrace; his presence at Detroit tipped the scales to give the British a bloodless victory and control of most of Michigan Territory. His example has brought others swarming to the British cause – Sioux, Sauk, Chippewa, and Menominee from the far reaches of the Upper Mississippi; Mohawk from the Grand Valley of Upper Canada; Caughnawaga from the St. Lawrence; and a horde of American Indians from the Old Northwest.

A rumour has spread through the American lines that Major-General Procter has promised Tecumseh all of Michigan Territory and Harrison's head as well, should the British be victorious at Fort Meigs. More than any other enemy leader, Tecumseh is both feared and admired by the Americans. Harrison has no intention of responding to his taunt.

He will not sleep this long night until he has made a full tour of the camp to make certain every man is at his post. His adjutant of the day, who will accompany him, is one Ohio militiaman he can trust – a wiry, twenty-six-year-old draftee named Alexander Bourne. Bourne does not need to be here, one hundred miles from civilization, drenched by the chill rain, living in a muddy cave, preyed on by hostile Indians. The law allows substitutes, and Bourne could easily have afforded to pay a neighbour ninety dollars to serve six months in his place. But, in spite of the pleading of his friends, Bourne refused. Not all of his fellow militiamen were as steadfast. In the first draft of three men from his unit, Bourne's name was seventeenth on the roll. He was taken anyway because the first fourteen ran off to the woods and were hidden by cronies. Now he is an instant officer, promoted of necessity from private to lieutenant because the company sergeant is so drunk he cannot call the roll.

Bourne's first task this night is to inform Major Alexander that he is duty field officer. He finds him drinking brandy in an officers' marquee, protesting he is unfit for duty. Bourne takes him by the arm, and the two stumble through the lines, the Major lamenting his situation, the adjutant doing his best to cheer him up. The General, it develops, is far too occupied to notice the Major's state. Off they all go on their rounds, General and staff, the drunk and the sober, tumbling into ditches, sometimes two or three on top of one another as the

British round shot hurtles harmlessly into the river bank below. It is the first time that Bourne, or indeed Harrison himself, has been exposed to the British artillery fire, but Bourne is not dismayed. He and his comrades are determined now to defend the fort to the last, for they are convinced that surrender will mean massacre at the Indians' hands.

As for Harrison, he can only hope that Brigadier-General Green Clay's reinforcements are within striking distance of his besieged garrison.

•

FORT MEIGS, OHIO, May 1, 1813

The artillery barrage, which the British believe will shatter Harrison's strong point, begins at 11 a.m., but before the red flag goes up signalling the first shot, Major-General Procter and his gunners are faced with a frustrating spectacle. Suddenly, as if pulled by an invisible cord, the masking line of tents goes down revealing an immense shield of earth that screens every tent, horse, and man. Behind it, the men lie in trenches and caves hollowed out in the earthen bulwark, awaiting the inevitable.

The first ball has no sooner sped across the river and buried itself in the mud than Harrison turns to his acting quartermaster, a twenty-two-year-old named William Christie.

"Sir," says the General, "go and nail a banner on every battery, where they shall wave as long as the enemy is in view." Christie hurries off to obey.

The British seem to have unlimited ammunition – huge twenty-four-pound balls of solid pig iron, smaller shot weighing twelve pounds, and bombs – heavy iron shells full of black powder, fused to explode directly above the heads of the defenders, spewing jagged bits of shrapnel in all directions.

They are crack shots, these British gunners. John Richardson, a gentleman volunteer with the British 41st, and, at the age of sixteen, a veteran of two previous battles, notes that the big cannon are aimed as accurately as rifles. As a member of the covering party protecting one battery, he asks the bombardier's permission to charge and point one of the pieces and experiences a sense of delight and power to see the ball land exactly where it is aimed.

But although the British send more than 250 missiles crashing into the fort, these do little damage, most burying themselves in the clay of the traverse, now rendered mushy by the incessant rain. Only a handful of men are wounded and only one killed.

Because Harrison is short of ammunition, his own gunners cannot afford the British extravagance. They have 360 shot only for their eighteen-pound cannon, about the same number for their twelves. As the British are also firing twelve-pound balls into the camp, the Major-General sees no reason why these cannot be returned. He offers a gill of whiskey to every man who delivers an enemy ball to the magazine keeper. Before the siege is over, more than one thousand gills have gone down the throats of the resourceful soldiers. To them, it is a happy substitute for water, which is difficult to come by. The well being dug behind the traverse is not finished, and the men are reduced to scooping up the muddy contents of rainwater pools.

The cannonade lasts until eleven at night, commences with redoubled fury the following dawn. In the next two days the British pour close to one thousand shot into the fort. One militia man, acting on his own, stands on the embankment, warning his comrades of every shot, becoming so skilful that he can predict exactly where each will fall. As he watches the smoke erupt from a British muzzle he calls out "bomb" or "shot," adding a phrase to indicate its destination – a blockhouse, the main battery, the commissary. His friends urge him to take cover, but he refuses until one shot defies his calculations. The smoke from the cannon has moved neither to right nor to left; he cannot gauge the target. He stands motionless, perplexed, silent, until the great ball strikes him full in the chest, tearing him apart.

Now the British gunners concentrate their fire on the magazine. It has been moved out of the traverse for fear that an exploding bomb may fire it and is now within a small blockhouse, which must be covered with earth for full protection.

"Boys," says an officer, "who will volunteer to cover the magazine?"

Nobody moves. The British are hurling red-hot cannonballs, which hiss sickeningly as they sink into the mud, sending up clouds of acrid smoke; one would be enough to blow up the building. Finally a few men hesitantly step forward. The gunners have not yet got the range. Perhaps if they move quickly they can get the job done.

They no sooner reach the blockhouse than a cannonball slices off one man's head. Like men possessed the survivors fling earth on top of the building. Then, to their horror, a bomb falls on the roof, lodges on a brace, spins about like a top. All but one throw themselves face down into the mud, expecting to be blown to pieces. The holdout reasons that since death is inevitable if the bomb bursts, he might as well take a chance. He seizes a boat hook, pulls the sputtering missile to the ground, and jerks the fuse from its socket. His comrades rise and complete their job.

Not far away, Lieutenant Alexander Bourne and a fatigue party of Ohio militia men are struggling to complete an entrenchment. Red-hot cannonballs, aimed at the magazine, whiz past the work party, boiling up the mud until the soldiers can stand it no longer. Bourne reports to Eleazer Wood that he cannot keep his men at this danger-ous work. The engineer gives him an unlimited order on the commis-sary for whiskey, telling him to issue it every half-hour and make the men drink it until they become insensible to fear – but not so drunk, he warns, that they cannot complete the job. Thus fortified, the men reel about, drunkenly curse the British, and ply their shovels until the task is finished.

Bourne, the patriot, is a man fascinated by human nature, and here, during the heat of the barrage, he has an opportunity to examine it under stress. As the cannon thunder and the ground shakes and the rain pelts down he notes examples of indifference, courage, foolhardi-ness, and cowardice – the four human characteristics that are intensi-fied by war.

One man, he observes, a saddler from Philadelphia named Isaac Burkelon, seems totally insensible to fear. He is that oddity found in every army, the man who volunteers for everything – having for a price replaced a wealthy Chillicothe citizen in the draft. Bourne comes out of his blockhouse one morning to find a huge bombshell hurtling toward him. He calls to Burkelon to lie down, but the saddler refuses to muddy his clothes. When the bomb bursts four feet away, hurling him to the ground and covering him with filth, he rises, shakes him-self, and laughs as if he had just indulged in a bit of spirited horseplay.

Another in Bourne's company, a sixty-year-old German named Bolenstein, watches another bomb fall outside the blockhouse. It strikes a stump, bounces off it, skips across the ground. Nothing will do but that Bolenstein should go after it, like a youth chasing a foot-ball. In vain Bourne calls him to come back; he is already outside the enclosure, and the sentinels, who are under orders to shoot any man who leaves without permission, are cocking their guns and shouting warnings. Bolenstein tells them to fire away – he means to retrieve the bomb and pull out the fuse. Fortunately it fizzles out, and he returns, laughing, with his prize.

By contrast, Bourne's quartermaster, Sutton, is a coward, so afraid of death that he can neither eat nor sleep. He crouches behind a pile of flour barrels, and while his comrades stand laughing at him, a twenty-four-pound ball crashes through the floor above his head, throwing staves and hoops in every direction and covering him with flour. He jumps up, hurls himself into a wet ditch, screaming "Oh Lord! Oh Lord!" to emerge plastered with paste.

To protect themselves from the bombshells, the men dig holes behind the traverse, covering each with a plank on top of which they shovel a protective mantle of earth. At the warning cry "Bomb!" each runs for his mole hole; but as the rain continues and the hollows fill with water they are forced back into the tents to emerge, half-awake, at each warning cry until, exhausted and indifferent to danger, they ignore the alarms, determined not to be disturbed, as one puts it, "if ten thousand bombs burst around them."

By May 3, four British batteries are hammering the fort. Frustrated by Captain Wood's earthen wall, Procter that night sends a force across the river to establish another. These cannon and mortars, hidden in a thicket only 250 yards from the fort, catch the defenders in a brief crossfire. But Wood has already anticipated the move and a new traverse, hastily thrown up at right angles to the old one, renders the fire ineffective.

The following day – the fourth of the siege – the British fire slackens as if the heart had gone out of the gunners. The defenders, in spite of their exhaustion, are in the habit of waving their hats and giving three cheers whenever the guns are silent, receiving each time an echoing yell from Tecumseh's followers in the woods. Now, as the cheering dies, a white flag is seen. Captain Peter Latouche Chambers of the 41st arrives under its protection to ask for a parley with Harrison on behalf of his commander.

Says Chambers: "General Procter has directed me to demand the surrender of this post. He wishes to spare the effusion of blood."

To which Harrison responds with some warmth: "The demand under the present circumstances, is an extraordinary one. As General Procter did not send me a summons to surrender on his first arrival, I had supposed that he believed me determined to do my duty. His present message indicates an opinion of me that I am at a loss to account for."

Generals, in this war, may fire cannon at one another, but insults are odious. Captain Chambers hastens to correct any impression of incivility:

"General Procter could never think of saying anything to wound your feelings, sir. The character of General Harrison, as an officer, is well known. General Procter's force is very respectable, and there is with him a larger body of Indians than has ever before been embodied."

There it is: the veiled threat that if the fort is taken, the Indians cannot be prevented from massacring the survivors. The threat worked at Michilimackinac early in the war and it worked again at Detroit, when Isaac Brock and Tecumseh terrified William Hull into surrendering not only an army but also most of Michigan. It does not work with Harrison.

"Assure the General," Harrison responds in his stilted fashion, "that he will never have this post surrendered to him upon any terms. Should it fall into his hands, it will be in a manner calculated to do him more honor, and to give him larger claims upon the gratitude of his government, than any capitulation could possibly do."

In short, Harrison is prepared to fight to the last man. He does not like Procter and in this chilly exchange makes little attempt to hide his disdain for the man who every American believes (and with truth) abandoned defenceless and wounded Kentucky troops to the hatchets of the Potawatomi after the battle of the River Raisin in January.

Nonetheless he knows his situation is critical. The fort cannot hold out forever. Once its ammunition is gone, Harrison's men will be at the mercy of an immeasurably stronger and better-trained army of seasoned British regulars and enraged natives.

Midnight comes. The bombardment ceases. Men sleep exhausted in their muddy shelters. And then, out of the blackness comes Captain William Oliver, Harrison's emissary. He has slipped through the Indian lines, guarded by fifteen dragoons, all virtually invisible on this foggy, moonless night.

Captain Oliver brings heartening news: General Clay and his reinforcements are only two hours away. Harrison realizes he must act at once. He knows that the bulk of the British force is two miles downriver at the old British Fort Miami, that most of Tecumseh's Indians are on the right bank, investing his position. This means that the big guns across the river, harassing his stockade, are lightly manned.

He forms his plan swiftly: he will strike simultaneous blows on both sides of the river. Part of Clay's advancing force will spike the guns on the opposite shore. The remainder will attack the Indians on the near bank. Once the battle is joined, the Americans will burst out of the fort, attack the British battery in their rear, and defeat the British and Indians on the American-held side of the river.

The plan depends on surprise, discipline, and perfect timing. Harrison is only too well aware that Clay's Kentuckians are green, having seen no more than thirty days' service. Nonetheless, it is a gamble he must take. He dispatches his aide, Captain Hamilton, and a subaltern under cover of the black night to carry his orders to General Clay.

•

BELOW THE MAUMEE RAPIDS, Ohio, May 5, 1813

Lieutenant Joseph Underwood lies shivering in the stern of the leading American flatboat in General Clay's flotilla as it sweeps down the Maumee in the wan light of daybreak. Underwood is recovering from a severe attack of measles; his single blanket, wrapped tightly around him, is not enough to protect him from the raw drizzle that beats across the valley. Behind him, swirling in the curves of the river, are seventeen similar craft, each carrying one hundred Kentuckians protected from the arrows of marauding Indians by heavy shields of timber nailed to the bulwarks.

Underwood can hear the rumble of the big guns downriver. As the little fleet courses on, the rumble grows louder, becomes a deafening roar. The sound seems to well up from the bottom of the flatboat until the atmosphere dances with it and the world vibrates with every volley.

It is Underwood's first experience of cannon fire. He will never forget it. He is only twenty, an ardent Kentucky volunteer, recruited as a private but elected lieutenant in the democratic fashion of the American militia, which will have no truck with the military authoritarianism of Europe. The words of his general still ring in his ears:

"Kentuckians stand high in the estimation of our common country. Our brothers in arms who have gone before us to the scene of action have acquired a fame which should never be forgotten by you – a fame worthy of your emulation – Should we encounter the enemy, *remember the fate of your butchered brothers at the River Raisin – that British treachery produced their slaughter!*"

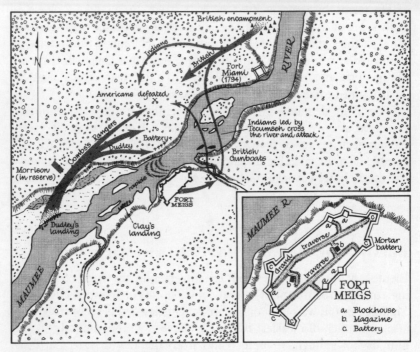

The Battle of Fort Meigs

The devil Procter is up ahead: the moment for revenge has arrived at last.

On the right bank of the river, Underwood spots two men waving at the flotilla. Lieutenant-Colonel William Dudley, in command of the lead boat, dispatches a canoe to pick them up. These are Harrison's emissaries: they have a message for General Clay. Dudley sends them back to Boat Number Thirteen. Underwood watches them go, wondering what their message is. Alas, he and his comrades will never be told the details.

Like most American militia commanders, Green Clay is more politician than soldier. His roots go back to America's beginnings: his great-grandfather first came to Virginia with Sir Walter Raleigh. The Speaker of the House is a cousin; Clay himself has served as a member of both houses of the Kentucky legislature. At fifty-five he is wealthy from land speculation. He is also something of a classical scholar, has named his son (a future ambassador) Cassius Marcellus

Clay, a name that will be adopted by succeeding generations of blacks on his tobacco plantation, one of whose descendants will become heavyweight boxing champion of the world.

Harrison's emissary, Hamilton, has memorized a succinct message for Clay:

"You must detach about eight hundred men from your brigade, who will land at a point I will show, about one or one and a half miles above the fort, and I will conduct them to the British batteries on the left side of the river. They must take possession of the enemy's cannon, spike them, cut down the carriages, and return to the boats. The balance of the men under your command will land on the right bank, opposite to the first landing, and will fight their way through the Indians to the fort."

Clay makes his plans: Lieutenant-Colonel William Dudley, the senior officer, now in the lead boat, will land the first twelve craft on the left bank to carry the assault on the cannon. Clay will lead the remaining six boats to the right bank to harass Tecumseh's force.

Hamilton goes off downstream to convey Clay's orders to Dudley. Underwood, lying in the stern of the lead boat, watches him climb aboard and converse with his commander. Dudley is a heavy, fleshy man, "weak and obstinate but brave" in Harrison's assessment, "ignorant and rash" in the later, rueful opinion of Eleazer Wood, the engineer. Like Underwood, Dudley has never heard a hostile gun until this morning. In common with so many other citizen commanders he also suffers from a fatal flaw: he does not bother to explain to his subordinates the full purpose of Harrison's plan – to spike the cannon and get out fast. Lieutenant Underwood, who is second-in-command of Captain John Morrison's company, is told only that the troops will land on the left bank and storm the enemy batteries. And then? Nobody tells him.

Suddenly – gunfire! On the right bank muskets flash as a group of Indians appear. One of the captains is wounded in the head. The troops fire back and the Indians flee, no doubt to warn the British.

It comes home to Underwood that he is about to fight and perhaps to die, and with that realization everything takes on a different hue. The morning may be grey, the wind raw, the rain chill, the brooding woods oppressive, yet the world has never looked brighter or more attractive. He gazes about him at ordinary objects and realizes that for him they may soon disappear forever. His thoughts go back to home, to old friends, and in his mind he bids them farewell. He finds that he is neither frightened nor alarmed but strangely calm with the calmness of melancholy.

His daydream is interrupted as the boats nose into the bank and the troops leap off and form up in three columns, one hundred yards apart. The left column is to swing around on the flank and get behind the British guns while Dudley on the extreme right attacks the batteries from the river side. The centre column, led by Underwood's captain, Morrison, will come up in reserve. Captain Leslie Combs will lead his company of thirty riflemen as an advance party to protect the flank.

Silently, the Kentuckians creep forward. Suddenly Combs's rangers flush a small party of Indians, who after a brief skirmish flee toward the British encampment. At this the troops break their silence and with a tremendous yell fall upon the enemy batteries. The British gunners flee in disorder, and Dudley's men, without bothering to wait for the spikes that are being sent by Harrison to hammer into the powder holes, use ramrods from their muskets to render the cannon powerless.

At this point, everything that Harrison had hoped for has been achieved. The guns have been silenced before Procter's reinforcements can be brought forward or the Indians on the opposite bank can cross the river. It is time to retire, but Dudley's men do not know this. They loiter around the useless guns, confused and disorganized, cheering themselves hoarse. In vain, Harrison, watching from the fort, signals them to return. The troops believe the General is cheering them on and so cheer back.

As the minutes tick by, more Indians appear at the fringe of the woods bordering the open plain on which the British guns are placed. *Indians!* Caution cannot compete with ancestral memories, folk tales, gaudy stories handed down by uncles and grandfathers who have, since the days of Daniel Boone, battled the redskins on the old frontier. Flushed with victory, oblivious to the entreaties of Dudley, who flails about him with a half-pike, the Kentuckians tear after the painted enemy. The slowly retreating tribesmen draw their quarry farther and farther away from the protection of the plain, where the fort's cannon can give them cover, and deeper into a wooded labyrinth, creased by ravines and encumbered by stumps and logs.

Harrison is in anguish.

"They are lost! They are lost!" he cries from his vantage point across the river. "Can I never get men to obey my orders?"

He offers one thousand dollars to any volunteer who will cross over and warn Dudley. A young lieutenant instantly accepts, rushes to the bank, struggles to launch a pirogue, finally gets it into midstream only to realize he is too late. British reinforcements have arrived. The smell of defeat is in the air.

●

OLD FORT MIAMI, OHIO, May 5, 1813

John Richardson, the teen-aged gentleman volunteer with the British 41st, is just sitting down to breakfast in a wet shelter made of evergreen boughs when a rabble of gunners dashes into camp crying out that the Americans have seized the batteries.

Richardson looks ruefully at the scanty meal he will never eat – a tough steak of half-cooked beef, a piece of dry bread, a mug of tea made from sassafras root, sweetened with sap from the sugar maple. It is not much of a meal, but here in this sodden camp it is a banquet. Richardson, who has not yet attained his full growth, is perennially ravenous, a condition aggravated by the fact that, being a junior, he is the last to reach the cooking pot. On the forced march that follows, the future novelist thinks more of the uneaten meal and what will happen to it than he does of the approaching conflict.

The sound of musket fire on the left snaps him out of his reverie. The Americans are in possession of the guns: Richardson can see them milling about the batteries. The Scotch mist of dawn has turned to driving rain, rendering the mud knee deep. In this soft pudding the men flounder forward in an attempt to retrieve their losses. One of the 41st falls dead. Captain Peter Chambers – the same officer who dealt with Harrison the day before – seizes the dead man's musket, throws away his own sword, and shouts:

"Who will follow me and retake that battery?"

"I will!" cries little John Richardson. Two other officers and a dozen men push forward with him against the American right flank.

Richardson, who believes this tiny attacking force will be wiped out, is astonished when the Americans give way. He does not yet know that Tecumseh and his Indians have swum the river and sucked the American left flank into the maze of the forest. As the Kentuckians stumble forward, mauled by the elusive native sharpshooters withdrawing behind logs and stumps, Tecumseh circles around behind them. Caught in an ambush, the green troops are driven back toward the advancing British, trapped between two fires.

Captain Morrison's reserve column has hastened to the rescue of his fellow Americans – too late. Joseph Underwood gets a brief glimpse of Lieutenant-Colonel Dudley, who rails at him for not keeping his men in better line; but the ground is so uneven, the bush so thick that any sort of parade-ground manoeuvre is impossible, especially for raw troops. It is the last time Underwood will see Dudley alive.

Morrison falls, shot through the temple, his optic nerve severed by a musket ball. Underwood does what he can for his sightless captain, then takes command of the company, already falling back under Tecumseh's ambush.

The retreat becomes a rout. The Kentuckians rush back through the woods toward the batteries, where Underwood confidently expects they can re-form and repel the Indians. Men are dropping all around him as he runs. Suddenly he feels something slam into his back – a stunning, deadening blow that pitches him forward onto his hands and knees. He pulls himself to his feet, throws open his waistcoat to see if the ball has passed through his body. There is no sign of it. He stumbles on, emerging at last from the woods onto the open ground where the batteries stand. Somebody seizes his sword: a British soldier.

"Sir," cries his captor, "you are my prisoner!"

Underwood is astonished, looks about, sees the ground littered with discarded muskets.

Says his captor: "Your army has surrendered."

He has difficulty understanding this, stumbles forward to a line of captives, recognizes one of his men, Daniel Smith.

"Good Lord, Lieutenant," says Smith, his eyes brimming with tears, "what does all this mean?"

Underwood tells him what he has himself only just discovered: they have been defeated. Of Dudley's force of 800, fewer than 150 have escaped. The rest are either captured or dead, including the Colonel himself, whose corpse, already scalped, lies somewhere in the forest.

The prisoners are marched downriver toward the old British fort, now not much more than a crumbling ruin. As they are driven forward, the Indians loot them of clothes and possessions. Underwood loses all his outer clothing but manages to hide his watch. Because he has read somewhere that the Indians treat best those who show no fear, he stares sternly at his native captors until one strikes him full in the face with a stick. Underwood decides that humility is a better policy.

On reaching the fort, the prisoners face a hideous ordeal. On their left, some twenty paces back from the river bank, stands a line of armed Indians reaching to the gate of the enclosure. Each man must run this gauntlet, already slippery with blood and flanked by a hedgerow of naked, scalped corpses. Some of the British escorts attempt to prevent the Indians from belabouring the column with tomahawks, war clubs, and rifles, but when one British regular from the 41st is shot through the heart, these attempts cease.

Underwood notices that the men nearest the river bank, and thus farthest from the line of warriors, suffer the most as they try to reach the fort. He determines to run as close as possible to the Indians, who will not be able to shoot him in the curve of the laneway without killing their own people. He dashes forward, feeling the blows of ramrods on his back. The man ahead drops dead. Underwood stumbles across his corpse, but others fall on it, blocking the passageway. In the end he reaches the safety of the fort, badly bruised and bleeding from the wound in his back but still alive.

Within the ruined walls of the old fort, hundreds of Kentucky prisoners mill about. Underwood, exhausted, rests on the ground, his head in the lap of a fellow soldier. But the terror has not ended. A gigantic rawboned brave, face and body painted jet black, climbs on an earthen embankment and harangues the crowd in an angry voice. Some of the British who understand the Potawatomi tongue attempt to reason with him.

"Oh, *Nichee wah!*" they cry, again and again. "Oh, brother, don't do it!"

It is useless. The Indian raises his rifle, shoots a man at the foot of the embankment, reloads, shoots another dead. Panic ripples through the crowd. The big Potawatomi leaps down, draws his tomahawk, sinks it into the head of another victim. Those closest to the attacker scramble to get away, trampling their own comrades including Underwood, who, face down and half smothered by his own gore, can hear the cracking of skulls around him. When he extricates himself, he counts four corpses on the floor, their scalps already dangling from the Potawatomi's belt.

A general massacre seems inevitable. The Indians are already throwing the covers off their rifle locks. Suddenly a tall warrior in fringed deerskin gallops into the fort, makes his way to the heart of the throng, climbs onto the embankment, shouting over the din. The crowd grows quiet, the Indians begin to grunt as the stranger points directly at the murderer and delivers what is clearly a dressing-down. The Potawatomi warrior scowls, shakes his head, turns on his heel, leaves. Only later do the prisoners realize that their deliverer is the celebrated Tecumseh.

Nobody can be sure what the Shawnee war chief has said for none can understand his tongue. It is well known that he abhors torture and the slaying of prisoners – has been opposed to it since his boyhood when he watched a white man slowly roasted at the stake and swore he would never again countenance such savagery. Later the story of his intervention at Fort Miami will take on the trappings of legend, for this is a man who, being larger than life, inspires myth. Some will pretend to recall that he buried his tomahawk in the head of the murderer, but that is fancy. The Shawnee does not need to indulge in violent gestures; his tongue is enough to subdue his followers.

He is Tecumseh and he is unique. After a year of warfare he has managed to hold together the fragile alliance of tribesmen entirely through the iron force of his personality. There are some this day who fancy they see in those dark features omens of despair. Some profess to see tears in the hazel eyes. Others claim that he cries out in passion, "Oh! What will become of my Indians?" – that he seeks out Procter and asks why he has not intervened, that he attacks the British general, sneering, "Begone, you are unfit to command; go and put on petticoats."

It is possible. He has little love for Procter, whom he considers a weak commander. But none can really know what transpires between them, for, apart from Matthew Elliott of the British Indian Department, no one speaks Shawnee – and Elliott is unlikely to tell. Elliott has seen massacres before, has in fact taken part in several; in that sense he is as savage as the Indians.

The prisoners, secure at last from further attack, are formed up in four lines to be counted. One of the Kentucky men strips off Underwood's mud-streaked bloody garments and offers him his hunting jacket, saved from the looters. As the Indians begin to select prisoners to be taken to the villages for ransom or adoption, the younger men, who are most wanted, try to crowd into the centre of the mob, beyond reach.

Unable to struggle, the wounded Underwood is thrust to the outside. An Indian hands him a piece of meat, and the soldier is certain he intends to carry him off. He decides to act boldly, borrows the Indian's knife, cuts the meat into pieces, offers it to his friends, saving a small bit for himself mostly as a show of politeness, for he has little appetite. When he returns the knife the Indian leaves – he was only being friendly – and Underwood sighs in relief. Shortly he will be paroled to his home in Kentucky. For him the war is over, and he can return to his fledgling law practice. Some day he will be a United States senator, a judge, a presidential elector. And always he will carry in the flesh of his back the leaden musket ball discharged from an Indian gun during the bloody battle of Fort Meigs.

•

OLD FORT MIAMI, OHIO, May 6, 1813

The day after the battle, as dusk descends, John Richardson accompanies Major Adam Muir of the British 41st on a stroll through the Indian encampment, a few hundred yards from the British tents.

A grotesque sight meets his eyes. Here are Chippewa and Menominee warriors decked out in the blue-and-gold uniforms of American officers, strutting about in unaccustomed high leather boots which force them into awkward postures. Here are others – Sioux, Winnebago, Potawatomi – wearing ruffled shirts that contrast with their dusky bodies. Behind them are tepees ornamented with saddles, bridles, rifles, daggers, swords, pistols, many intricately wrought and exquisitely designed. Mingled with these trophies are the scalps of the Americans, half dried, dyed with vermilion, suspended from poles, swinging gently in the night breeze. Interspersed with these grisly trophies are hoops upon which portions of human skin have been stretched – a hand here, a foot there, with the nails still clinging to it – while strewn about the camp are the flayed limbs, half gnawed by packs of wild dogs that roam among the tents.

On the face of it, the plunder suggests a stupendous British victory. Here, for instance, parcelled among the tribesmen, is the personal baggage of Brigadier-General Green Clay, captured after he left his boat in the shadow of the American fort the previous morning. A general officer does not travel light. Clay's camp kit includes a trunk, a portmanteau, flat iron, coffee mill, razor strop and box, inkstand and quills, reams of paper, three halters, shoebrushes, blacking, saddle and bridle, tortoise-shell comb and case, a box of mercurial ointment, silver spoons, mattresses and pillows, three blankets, three sheets, two towels, linen for a cot, two volumes of *M'Kenzie's Travels*, two maps, spyglass, gold watch, brace of silver-mounted pistols, umbrella, sword, two pairs of spurs (one silver), a pair of shoes, bottle-green coat, scarlet waistcoat, blue cashmere and buff cashmere waistcoats, striped jean waistcoat, cotton pantaloons, bottle-green pantaloons, cord pantaloons, short breeches, flannel waistcoat and shirt, five white linen shirts, two check shirts, nine cravats, six chamois, two pairs of thread stockings, three pairs of thread socks, hunting shirt, hat, two pairs of gloves – all in the hands of the Indians.

Yet all this loot is deceptive. While Dudley was attacking the British batteries, Clay himself with six boatloads of Kentucky soldiers was successfully fighting his way into Fort Meigs. And though he lost his personal kit he managed to bring in all the cannonballs and ammunition. Harrison's two sorties, timed to coincide with the attack on the guns, have both been successful. The British battery on the American side of the river has been destroyed, the Indians driven off.

Moreover, under pretence of a prisoner exchange Harrison has been able to take advantage of a brief armistice to bring in the rest of the ammunition the defenders need so badly. A message from Procter, calling on him to surrender, is treated with disdain.

Both sides have reached a stalemate. Harrison is so exhausted from lack of sleep, so miserable from the cold and the driving rain that he has not the strength to compose a detailed account of the affair for the Secretary of War. His men, too, are worn out. The wounded lie untended in the trenches, supported on rails that barely keep their bodies above water. But the fort still stands. Procter has not been able to capture it.

Nor can he. The Indians, loaded with plunder, are drifting back to their villages with their wounded to display their prisoners and their trophies. A deputation of chiefs waits upon the British general to explain that they cannot prevent this exodus; it is the custom after every battle. Only Tecumseh and a handful of followers remain.

The citizen soldiers cannot be relied on either. Another deputation of eight officers from the 1st and 2nd Regiments of the Essex and Kent militia makes it clear that if the men are not allowed to return to their farms to sow their spring wheat and corn, "the consequence must be famine next winter." Indeed, half the militiamen have already taken off; it is beyond the power of any commander to hold on to the rest.

The regulars are in a bad state, suffering from dysentery, ague, and fatigue as a result of wretched weather, poor food, and exhausting fighting. On top of this comes the news that Little York has fallen to the enemy – a piece of intelligence not calculated to lift the army's morale. Procter has no choice but to raise the siege and return to Amherstburg.

Both commanders in their official reports put the best possible face on the battle, overestimating their adversary's strength as well as his losses and minimizing their own.

Procter writes to Sir George Prevost that he believes the enemy's casualties to have been between one thousand and twelve hundred. Harrison assures Armstrong that no more than fifty Kentuckians have been killed and that he has reason to believe that many have escaped up the river to Fort Defiance.

As a result of Procter's report, Prevost's General Order announces "the brilliant result of an action which took place on the banks of the Miami river...which terminated in the complete defeat of the Enemy and the capture, dispersion or destruction of 1300 Men by the Gallant division of the Army under the Command of Brig. General Procter...."

Harrison in a similar General Order, issued about the same time, "congratulates the troops upon having completely foiled their foes and put a stop to their career of victory which has hitherto attended their Arms. He cannot find words to express his sence [*sic*] of the good conduct of the Troops of every description and of every corpse [*sic*]."

Only at the end does he temporize:

"It rarely occurs that a General has to complain of the excessive ardor of his men yet such appears always to be the case whenever the Kentucky Militia are engaged. It is indeed the sorce [*sic*] of all their misfortunes. They appear to think that valor alone can accomplish anything.... Such temerity although not so disgraceful is scarcely less fatal than Cowardice...."

4

The Northwest Campaign: 2
THE CONTEST FOR
LAKE ERIE
June – September, 1813

American strategy in the Northwest is to destroy the British-Indian alliance. That will secure their left flank and free thousands of troops for the main struggle farther to the east. But the Americans cannot move their army out of Fort Meigs until they control Lake Erie and the Detroit River, at present British waterways. The spring and summer of 1813 find both sides engaged in a shipbuilding contest for supremacy on the lake – the Americans at Presque Isle, the British at Amherstburg.

ABOARD THE BRIG CALEDONIA, en route from Buffalo, New York, to Presque Isle, June 13, 1813

Oliver Hazard Perry, the American commodore, returning to Lake Erie after his part in the capture of Fort George, lies tossing in his bunk, a victim of what the doctors call "bilious fever." It is a recurring malady. The invalid looks the picture of health – a tall robust naval commander, his plump cheeks framed by dark, curly sideburns. Those who encounter him are struck by the symmetry of his figure, the grace of his movements. Yet with Perry appearances are deceptive: in moments of stress he falls prey to what is virtually a chronic complaint.

For the past several weeks, the stress has been almost constant: the responsibility of constructing a new fleet from scratch, the long horseback ride along the Niagara followed by the attack on Fort George, and, most recently, a struggle to warp a small flotilla of five vessels out of their haven near Black Rock on the Niagara and on to Presque Isle on Lake Erie, where the major American warships are under construction.

It has not been easy. On Perry's arrival at Black Rock a strong west wind made any movement impossible for a week. Finally, with the help of two hundred soldiers and several teams of oxen, his men managed to haul the boats upstream for three miles in the teeth of the gale. Now at last he is on his way, leading the flotilla in the prize brig *Caledonia*, seized from the British the preceding summer by Lieutenant Jesse Elliott.

Elliott, though junior in rank to Perry, is far better known to the American public, a national hero, awarded a sword by Congress for that daring escapade – the only victory in a string of scandalous defeats. A veteran, also, of the recent attack on York, chosen originally to command on Lake Erie, he finds himself, at thirty-one, superseded by a late arrival four years younger than himself and with less battle experience. In such circumstances only a man devoid of human flaws – and Elliott has his share – could fail to be a little jealous. And Elliott is vain, given to boasting, and not always generous with subordinates, for he likes to retain the credit for any accomplishment.

A bit of a troublemaker (he has already fought one duel, will fight more), he has piqued Perry's right-hand man, Daniel Dobbins, by sneering at his choice of the sheltered harbour of Presque Isle as a shipyard. A shallow sandbar blocks the entrance; Elliott, who has never visited Lake Erie, claims that Perry's big ships cannot get across it. He much prefers his own choice of Black Rock, in spite of the fact that the harbour there is a *cul de sac*, within easy range of British guns at Fort Erie and within striking distance of the British army.

Fortunately, the British have been forced, briefly, to abandon Fort Erie in their scramble up the peninsula. Perry takes advantage of their absence to manoeuvre the five vessels out of their potential trap and, under cover of fog, up the Niagara River into Lake Erie.

The two young naval officers, who as a result of this summer's events will be pitted against each other in bitter controversy, are a study in contrasts. Both are brave men who joined the navy in their teens as midshipmen and fought the Barbary pirates in the Tripolitan wars at the start of the century. There the similarities end. Elliott comes from a long line of black Donegal Irishmen; his kinsman and enemy is that same Matthew Elliott of the British Indian Department who is Tecumseh's friend, Harrison's *bête noire*. Fatherless since the age of nine (the elder Elliott having been slain by Indians), he is hot tempered, brooding, quick to take offence at any imagined slight.

Perry's people are Quakers, his father a retired naval captain. He comes from a family of eight – a brother, Matthew, will one day gain fame by opening Japan to the West. Like Elliott, he has a quick temper but has learned to keep it under control. Most of his colleagues find him quiet, unemotional, sedate, courteous, a little humourless. Dr. Usher Parsons, his surgeon, finds him to be the most remarkable

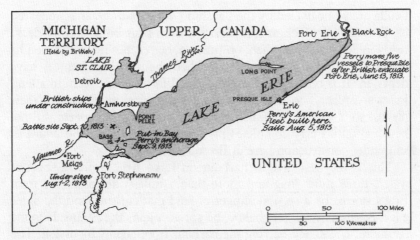

Action on Lake Erie, Summer, 1813

officer he has known for impressing his subordinates with almost reverential awe, inculcating in them a dread of giving their commander offence. He is well read, plays the flute, is a capable fencer, a student of both history and drama, and a fearless and elegant horseman.

He is also a man of considerable moral rectitude. He disdains to indulge in naval profanity and, although it is customary to allow any fleet commander a percentage of construction costs, Perry has refused to take a penny, in sharp contrast to his superior, Chauncey, who is reaping a fortune at Sackets Harbor. "It might influence my judgement," says Perry, "and cause people to question my good faith."

Does this paragon have no chinks in his armour? There is one reassuring imperfection. It is said that Perry, who does not give a hang for musket ball or grape-shot, has an almost pathological fear of cows, will trudge through mud to avoid one if he hears so much as a moo. That, and a tendency to succumb to fever after periods of strain, appear to be his only frailties.

The wind, which has bedevilled Perry with its moodiness for the past week, now drops, and the squadron is forced to return to its anchorage at Buffalo. The following morning it sets off again, crawling along the shoreline, sails drooping in a wan breeze. In the first twenty-four hours it moves no more than twenty-five miles.

That night Perry anchors close to shore to escape detection. A man signals from the bank and comes aboard to warn that the British flotilla of five boats, led by the flagship *Queen Charlotte*, has appeared off Presque Isle. Sick or not, Perry is out of his bunk and on deck, ready to do battle. But when, on June 19, he reaches his destination he learns that the British, having finished their reconnaissance, have departed. It is one of the strokes of good fortune that seem to attend Perry's career. The British clearly outgun him, even without their biggest ship, *Detroit*, unfinished at Amherstburg. The fleets will not be equal until Perry completes his two brigs, *Lawrence* and *Niagara*, still under construction here at Presque Isle Bay.

This is the best natural harbour on Lake Erie, a placid sheet of water, three miles long and more than a mile wide, protected from Erie's storms by a six-mile finger of land that curls around the outer edge. A sandbar, six feet below the surface, joins the peninsula to the far shore, effectively barring the harbour from enemy incursion. The advantage is two-edged. Jesse Elliott is not the only one who is convinced that the big brigs under construction will draw too much water to cross the bar, especially with the British fleet lurking just outside.

Now, as the pilots manoeuvre the five light vessels through the narrow channel that splits the sandbar, Perry's men can see the village of Erie crowded along the shoreline – some fifty frame houses, a blacksmith shop, tannery, and court house, the last serving as a sail loft.

The shipbuilders have been here most of the winter, Perry since March. As a result of this season's labours, three of his staff will go into the history books: Noah Brown, his building superintendent, a carpenter since the age of fifteen and the owner of the most flourishing shipyard in New York; Henry Eckford, his architect and designer, a Scottish-born genius, whose own shipyard is next door to Brown's; and the indispensable Daniel Dobbins, organizer and troubleshooter, a seasoned lake captain whose home is here in Erie. Dobbins has seen more of the war than his colleagues, for he was captured by the British in the summer of 1812 and escaped to bring to Washington the early news of Detroit's surrender.

These are young, energetic men – average age, thirty-five. They need to be, for the problems of building sophisticated fighting vessels hundreds of miles from the centre of civilization seem almost insurmountable. Presque Isle's sole resource is timber. Everything else must be hauled in by keel boat and then ox cart, over roads that are no more than tracks wriggling through the forests, punctuated by mudholes, blocked by stumps and deadfalls. Dobbins and Perry have

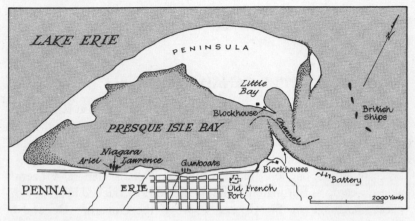

Presque Isle

had to travel to Meadville to scrape up steel to make axes. Iron comes from Bellefonte, spike rods from Buffalo, cables and hawsers from Pittsburgh, canvas from Philadelphia. Oakum is non-existent; the gunboats and brigs are caulked with old rope. Dobbins has to plunder his old schooner *Salina* for scrap iron, rigging, and shot.

Brown's army of axemen, choppers, and sawyers have partially denuded the surrounding forest, working from dawn to dusk, hacking down cucumber, oak, poplar, and ash for ribs, white pine for decks and bulwarks, black oak for planking and frames, red cedar and walnut for stanchions. It is all handwork; there are no sawmills within easy reach of the shipyard. So swift has the race been that a tree on the outskirts of the settlement can be growing one day and part of a ship the next.

Eckford, who outfitted all five of the vessels brought from Black Rock, has also designed four of the six being built at Presque Isle, including the two great brigs. Since no conventional craft of those sizes could get across the sandbar blocking the harbour's mouth, Eckford has had to design fighting vessels with extremely shallow drafts.

It is trying work. Unavoidable food shortages have caused more than one strike. Delays have been maddening. Anchors ordered for May 1 have not yet arrived. Yet, in spite of it all, the ships are in the water, nearing completion. Perry confidently expects that his fleet of eleven vessels will be ready by mid-July. He has, however, two problems: he does not have enough seamen to man them, and he still faces the difficult task of getting his biggest ships across the sandbar, beyond which the British are again lurking, ready to tear them to pieces before they can make sail.

•

SANDWICH, UPPER CANADA, July 4, 1813

Major-General Henry Procter, commander of the British Right Division, has never felt so frustrated. On this Independence Day, as his enemies fire rockets into the sky and sound church bells in celebration of their original victory over his countrymen, he vents his spleen in a brace of letters, one to Captain Robert McDouall, General Vincent's aide-de-camp at Burlington Heights, the other – couched in more temperate language – to Sir George Prevost, the Governor General of Canada.

Procter feels abandoned. His naval colleague, the one-armed Captain Robert Heriot Barclay, newly in command on Lake Erie, has returned from his reconnaissance of Presque Isle full of gloom. The new American brigs are already in the water while the British ship *Detroit* is still on the ways at Amherstburg. Procter knows what he should do: he should attack Erie at once and destroy Perry's fleet before it can be fitted; but he has neither men nor supplies for that task.

He is especially piqued at De Rottenburg, Sheaffe's replacement as commander of the forces in Upper Canada. Prevost has promised to dispatch the remainder of the first battalion of the 41st to Fort Amherstburg, but De Rottenburg, faced with the need to invest Fort George, has been dragging his feet. Procter does not believe that the commanding general has any intention of sending him a single man. He is short of gunners, clerks, servants, artificers, as well as fighting men. He is also short of food for his men and of money to pay them. Things are so bad that "we have scarcely the Means of constructing even a Blockhouse."

Captain Barclay is equally desperate for seamen. He has arrived with the merest handful, most of them incompetent, only a few able to speak English. He needs three hundred trained sailors and marines to man his fleet, but Sir James Lucas Yeo, his superior at Kingston, will not even send him a shipwright. A super-cautious commander, Yeo wants to hold on to every man and scrap of material to meet the threat of Chauncey's fleet on Lake Ontario.

It must be obvious to Procter that Prevost, De Rottenburg, and Yeo consider Lake Erie expendable. Indeed, it has been British strategy since the start of the war to defend Montreal and Quebec at any cost, even if it means abandoning Upper Canada. Now, with the Americans threatening the Niagara peninsula and Chauncey's fleet menacing the St. Lawrence lifeline, Procter's superiors are more reluctant than ever to weaken their own thin forces at Kingston and Burlington Heights. De Rottenburg says as much, bluntly, to Procter: he "must first secure Command of the lower Lake; after which there will be no Difficulty in recovering the Command of the Upper one."

Procter disagrees. On July 11, he ruefully writes to Prevost to point out that had he received the promised men and supplies, he could probably have destroyed all of Perry's vessels at Presque Isle, thus securing command of the lake and making a powerful diversion in favour of General Vincent's embattled Centre Division.

Across the water, Perry's fleet is rapidly approaching fighting trim. Barclay's new ship, *Detroit*, along with two gunboats under construction at Amherstburg, will even the odds on Lake Erie, but *Detroit* will not be launched until July 20, let alone rigged. Perry's shipbuilding problems are minor compared with those of the British. Canada has no steel or iron mills, no Pittsburghs or Philadelphias, no manufacturing worthy of the name. Everything but timber – nails, bolts, pulleys, lead, copper, glass, paint, resin, cordage, sails – must come from caches in Montreal and Quebec and ultimately from England. Cannon intended for Barclay's ship have been expropriated by Yeo at Kingston; new ones must be ordered and shipped across the Atlantic, up the St. Lawrence, across Lake Ontario (where Chauncey's fleet lies waiting) and, with the Niagara peninsula in flames, by a long land route through the forests of Upper Canada to Amherstburg.

Now the significance of the American attack on York comes into focus. It was, Chauncey said at the time, a blow from which the British could not recover. Certainly the loss of fifty thousand dollars' worth of stores – guns, ammunition, cables, cordage, canvas, tools, all destined for Barclay's fleet – is making itself felt. Prevost's only solution, which is no solution at all, is to urge Procter to make up his deficiencies by seizing guns and stores from the enemy "whose resources on Lake Erie must become yours." But Procter does not believe his force strong enough to attack Presque Isle with its blockhouses and redoubts.

Yet he must do *something*, for the Indians are becoming restless. Supplies are so short that they are living mainly on bread; the traditional presents, by which the tribesmen are mollified, have not arrived. They chafe for action; without it even the best efforts of Tecumseh cannot keep them in line. Without a battle to fight, without glory and excitement, without the prospect of loot, scalps, or prisoners to ransom, the Indians will drift away to their villages and Procter's army will be irretrievably weakened.

Procter is made uncomfortably aware that he does not command the Indians. If anything, the Indians command him; they far outnumber his own force. To a very large degree his movements are "subject to their Caprices and Prejudices." One group is loyal to Tecumseh and his brother, the Shawnee Prophet, the other – recently arrived from the Far West – to Robert Dickson, the Red-Haired Man. Even Dickson cannot control his followers for long.

Tecumseh and the others insist on mounting a second attack on Fort Meigs. Procter believes, with good reason, that Harrison's stronghold is too tough a nut to crack. Yet he has no choice: if he does not go on the attack he will lose his Indian allies. So Fort Meigs it must be.

Tecumseh has worked out an ingenious plan to take the fort by deception, for he, too, realizes that it cannot be captured without heavy artillery. The trick is to lure the Americans *out* of the fort and fall upon them from an ambush. To that end he proposes to stage a sham battle at some distance from the palisade. Hearing the sounds of conflict, the Americans will believe that reinforcements are on their way to relieve the fort but are being attacked. Tecumseh's hope is that the enemy will burst out of the fort to aid their comrades, whereupon Procter's superior force will cut them up.

Within Fort Meigs, Brigadier-General Green Clay has been preparing for trouble. Spies and deserters have already informed him that the Indians are eager to resume the siege. He himself is bedridden with one of the several fevers that no surgeon can properly diagnose, but he keeps one-third of his force on duty at all times and orders the rest to sleep on their arms. Meanwhile he sends word to Harrison, at Lower Sandusky, that he will presently need reinforcements. If worse comes to worst, he has a suicidal plan: he will fire the magazine and blow up the fort and its occupants rather than face the hatchets and scalping knives of the tribesmen.

Procter's army, five thousand strong, reaches the mouth of the Maumee on July 20. Clay informs Harrison at once. Harrison, who does not yet know the British intentions, responds that he will send reinforcements if needed; meanwhile, Clay is to beware of surprise. Harrison moves his own headquarters nine miles up the Sandusky to

Seneca Town. From that point he can co-operate with either Fort Meigs or Fort Stephenson near Sandusky Bay, in case the attack should come at the latter point.

Procter moves up the Maumee, reaches Fort Meigs on the twenty-fifth, places his troops in a ravine on the right bank just below the fort. His cavalry is concealed in a neighbouring thicket. At the same time Tecumseh and his Indians circle around and lurk in the forest close to the road that leads to Lower Sandusky. It is along this road that Harrison's reinforcements must come. If Clay believes they are being attacked he will surely order his men out of the cover of the stockade, expecting to catch the Indians in a trap. At least that is the Shawnee's reasoning.

With his comrades in the 41st back on familiar ground, John Richardson waits impatiently in the concealing skirt of wood, half soaked in the clammy drizzle. Hours pass. Will the sham battle never begin? And when it does begin, will Tecumseh's ruse work?

Finally, from the southeast comes an explosion of musket fire, desultory at first, accompanied by savage yells, then increasing in volume until, approaching the fort, it becomes one incessant roar.

Within the fort, Clay's men hear it too, and are eager to be off to rescue their comrades. The wounded throw away their crutches, the sick abandon their bunks; but Clay restrains them. Harrison's message about reinforcements has arrived only a short time before. Clay simply does not believe that any relief could have come so quickly – especially as Harrison was awaiting word from the fort before committing his men. Clay is convinced that the musket fire is part of a grand deception. But he has difficulty in convincing his officers and restraining his troops, who are indignant at being held back. The fortunate advent of a thunderstorm forestalls what might have been a difficult situation.

Tecumseh has failed, but the Indians are still full of fight. If they cannot take Fort Meigs they are determined to seize Fort Stephenson, the lightly held bastion just upriver from Sandusky Bay. Procter has no choice but to follow where they lead.

●

SENECA TOWN on the Sandusky, Ohio, July 29, 1813

William Henry Harrison calls a council of his officers, here at his new headquarters, nine miles up the Sandusky. The General has just learned from Clay that Procter has abandoned the attempt on Fort Meigs and may be advancing on Fort Winchester, farther up the Maumee. Harrison does not believe it; the British have nothing to gain there. He assumes, correctly, that Procter will attack Fort Stephenson.

The council of nine is unanimous. The fort, a mile or so upriver from Sandusky Bay, with its weak garrison of 160 soldiers and its huddle of wooden buildings, cannot be held against an army of five thousand. Harrison scribbles an order to the fort's young commander, Major George Croghan:

> Immediately on receiving this letter you will abandon Fort Stephenson, set fire to it and repair with your command this night to headquarters. . . .

It is 10 P.M. Harrison's messenger, John Conner, accompanied by two Indians, sets off in the dark, only to find the swamp and thickets teeming with Tecumseh's tribesmen, who have come overland from the Maumee while Procter's force moves by water toward Sandusky Bay. Conner loses his way and arrives at Fort Stephenson tardily, just before noon.

Croghan reads Harrison's note and curses roundly. He has already written to a friend that he will "defend this post to the last extremity." Now he swears that he will fight the British even though he may be the first man killed in the attack. The lateness of Harrison's messenger gives him an excuse. He calls a council of his officers and pens an immediate reply:

> Sir: I have just received yours of yesterday, 10 o'clock P.M., ordering me to destroy this place and make good my retreat, which was received too late to be carried into execution. We have determined to maintain this place and by heavens we can.

He hands the letter to Moses Wright, a veteran of Tippecanoe and Fort Meigs and the best rider in the garrison. Tecumseh's men seem to be lurking behind every tree as Wright gallops through a hail of bullets. A ball goes through his cap, another clips his heel, his horse is mortally wounded. When he finally arrives at Harrison's tent, his clothes are in tatters from forcing his way through the heavy brush. The General puts down his morning coffee, reads the note in anger, swears that Croghan ought to be shot immediately for insubordination, and orders him removed from command. Colonel Sam Wells with an escort of dragoons is sent to relieve him.

Wells and his escort run into an Indian ambush, fight their way out, and deliver Harrison's blunt note, written by an assistant, to Croghan:

Sir: The General has just received your letter of this date informing him that you had thought it proper to disobey the order...delivered to you this morning. It appears that the information which dictated this order was incorrect, and as you did not receive it in the night, as was expected, it might have been proper that you should have reported the circumstance and your situation before you proceeded to its execution. This might have been passed over; but I am directed to say to you that an officer who presumes to aver, that he has made his resolution, and that he will act in direct opposition to the orders of his General, cannot longer be entrusted with a separate command. Colonel Wells is sent to relieve you. You will deliver the command to him and repair with Colonel Ball's squadron to this place.

Young George Croghan is not in the least abashed. He is only twenty-one, handsome and debonair, with a long aristocratic face, high forehead, and Roman nose. He comes from a line of fighting Irish. His family is both affluent and distinguished. His father has an enviable record as a Revolutionary officer. Two of his uncles on his mother's side are famous. One, William Clark, Governor of Missouri Territory, became, with Meriwether Lewis, the first white American to cross the continent to the Pacific. The other, General George Rogers Clark, is known as the Hannibal of the West for his conquest of the country northwest of Vincennes. Croghan himself is a veteran of the Battle of Tippecanoe under Harrison who, in recommending him for a commission in the regulars, wrote that he "possesses all the courage and fire which are so necessary to form a good officer."

Has that courage and fire caused Croghan to overstep the mark? By the time the dragoons escort him to Seneca Town, he has an ingenious explanation for his apparent flouting of orders. He has written the letter, he insists, in such a way as to deceive the enemy should it be captured – for any attempt to withdraw in daylight "would be more hazardous than to remain in the fort under all its disadvantages."

Harrison is mollified and also half convinced by Croghan that the fort can be held. The young major has constructed two new blockhouses and topped the sixteen-foot palisade with heavy logs, calculated to fall on the attackers. He has surrounded the entire stronghold with a ditch eight feet deep and eight feet wide. On the northwest angle of this formidable moat he has placed his only cannon, a six-pounder, and he has evacuated all the women, children, and invalids.

Croghan's enthusiasm is catching. Harrison returns him to his command, warning that if attack seems imminent Croghan is to burn the fort and retire upriver. But Harrison, one suspects, is well aware by now that his young subordinate is reluctant to leave without a fight.

●

FORT STEPHENSON, OHIO, August 1, 1813

Major-General Procter's gunboats sweep up Sandusky Bay and enter the river, pushed forward by a spanking breeze. By mid-afternoon they have landed in a cove, about a mile from the fort. Procter has Croghan outgunned. He will storm the palisades with three six-pounders and two 5½ inch howitzers. Croghan has "Old Betsey," an ancient six-pounder left over from the Revolution – nothing more.

Procter has five hundred regulars from the 41st light infantry and some seven hundred Indians – Winnebago, Menominee, Sioux – under the legendary Robert Dickson and Matthew Elliott, the aging superintendent of the British Indian Department. Hidden in the woods between Fort Meigs and Seneca Town are Tecumseh's followers, perhaps two thousand strong. Their presence makes retreat impossible – or so George Croghan will claim.

Harrison does not believe the fort can be held; the British outnumber the defenders seven to one. Procter, on the other hand, does not believe the fort can be taken – or so *he* will claim. Yet he has no choice but to attack. Hundreds of his native allies, disappointed by the failure to seize Fort Meigs, have already deserted him. Tecumseh has trouble holding on to his own people, many of whom are off chasing after cattle. Now Matthew Elliott, Tecumseh's long-time comrade, ailing and so infirm he can hardly sit a horse, issues what amounts to an ultimatum on behalf of the tribesmen: unless the fort is stormed, the British will never be able to bring another Indian into the field of battle.

Procter feels his command slipping away. He does not like the Indians nor their leaders, has never liked them. To him they have become a nuisance and a burden, consuming vast quantities of rations, refusing to take direction from their own chiefs, coming and going as they please. Yet he recognizes their proven value. Without the Indians in 1812, the British could not have held Upper Canada. Procter knows he cannot dispense with them and so agrees to Elliott's plan. If Procter's regulars will storm one face of the fort, Elliott promises, the Indians will storm the other.

But first, Procter decides to use a time-tested tactic: he will attempt to frighten Croghan into surrender by threatening an Indian massacre. Elliott, accompanied by Major Peter Chambers of the 41st approaches the fort under a flag of truce and is met by a young Kentucky sub-altern, Edmund Shipp. The British major points out that his commander has a large number of cannon, a sizeable body of troops, and so many Indians that it will be impossible to control them once the fort is captured.

Shipp has already been told what to reply: "My commandant and the garrison are determined to defend the post to the last extremity, and bury themselves in its ruins rather than surrender it to any force whatever."

Elliott intervenes: "You are a fine young man. I pity your situation; for God's sake, surrender and prevent the dreadful slaughter that must follow resistance."

"When the fort shall be taken," Shipp retorts, "there will be none to massacre."

As Shipp turns away, an Indian springs forward, seizes him by the coat, tries to take his sword. Elliott makes a show of aiding Shipp, expressing anxiety for his safety, perhaps to demonstrate that he cannot control his followers.

All this is too much for Croghan, watching from the ramparts.

"What does that mean?" shouts the Major. "Shipp, come in, and we will blow them all to hell."

No sooner is Shipp back inside the palisade than Procter's artillery opens up on the fort. Croghan replies with Old Betsey, but sparingly, to husband his ammunition, moving the six-pounder from place to place to make Procter believe he has more than one piece. Most of the British fire seems to be directed toward the pickets at the northwest angle of the fort. Croghan guesses that the main attack will come at that point. Late that night, he orders his second-in-command to move Old Betsey into a blockhouse where it can rake that portion of the ditch from behind a concealed porthole.

By dawn, Procter has moved his three cannon within 250 yards of the fort. During the day he hurls five hundred balls and shells at the embattled Americans. Now Croghan is certain the attack will come at the northwest angle; anything else will be a feint. He strengthens the pickets with bags of sand and flour, stuffs Old Betsey to the muzzle with half a charge of powder plus grape-shot, double slugs, and even old pieces of pottery, puts his Kentucky sharpshooters in place, and waits for the attack.

Croghan is correct about the British intentions. Procter plans a feint at the south end, sends his second-in-command, Lieutenant-Colonel Augustus Warburton, in a wide circle around the fort to effect the deception. Meanwhile, his main force, led by Lieutenant-Colonel William Shortt and Lieutenant J.G. Gordon, attacks from the north. The assault commences at four, the troops moving forward at the double to the sound of distant thunder, Shortt whistling away, Gordon swearing under his breath, storm clouds gathering on the horizon.

But why this haste? Procter's men are not prepared for a frontal assault on a fortified position. They have no scaling ladders to launch at the sixteen-foot pickets, and their axes are dulled from weeks of misuse. Procter is a flawed commander who tends to panic in circumstances that require steadfastness and resolve. Following his victory at the River Raisin he rushed away, leaving his prisoners to be massacred by the Indians because he feared (wrongly) that Harrison would send reinforcements to attack him. Now the same fear forces him to another hasty decision. He does not know that three days earlier Harrison himself considered withdrawing from Seneca Town and even now half expects Croghan to retire. So Procter, who will later insist that he did not want to attack Fort Stephenson, attacks it half-heartedly and in haste.

The Indians, who had urged the attack in the first place, turn out to be useless. Siege warfare and frontal assaults in the face of cannon fire are not their mode of fighting. They retreat early into a nearby wood and remain as spectators in the battle that follows. As for Warburton's feint against the south wall, it comes too late to be of any use.

Shortt and Gordon lead their men out of the cannon smoke some twenty paces from the ditch that encircles the fort and form them into line for the assault, as the Kentucky sharpshooters open up. The picket fence is higher, the ditch deeper than the attackers had expected. The troops hesitate. Private Shadrach Byfield sees one man about to flee; his neighbour cries that if he doesn't turn around and face the enemy he'll run him through with a bayonet. The two leaders rally the troops with shouts and slogans.

"Cut away at the pickets, my brave boys and give the damn Yankees no quarter," cries Shortt, as he clambers over the bank and leaps into the ditch. He claws his way up the far side to reach the palisade at the northwest corner – the first man to do so – but is thrown back. At this moment, Lieutenant Shipp unmasks Old Betsey, and a dreadful hail of musket balls, grape-shot, and jagged missiles is hurled the full length of the ditch, now filled with struggling men.

Shortt, a slug in his body, twists a handkerchief around his sword and raises it in surrender, but his enemies have already heard his cry for no quarter. A second volley from Shipp's six-pounder cuts him down. Gordon takes over, leaps up at the fence, hacking at the pickets with his sword until a ball strikes him full in the breast, killing him too.

More than fifty men lie dead in the ditch, the victims of Old Betsey's raking fire. Shadrach Byfield is still alive, advancing in the second line. He sees the man directly in front of him fall dead. Then the sergeant on his right drops, and the man on his left receives six balls in his body.

Procter's bugle is sounding the retreat; the attack has failed. The troops fall back under a withering fire to the shelter of a ravine that runs parallel to the ditch. The Americans have lost but one man – a drunkard who climbed to the top of the palisade.

Croghan's men continue to fire at anything that moves in the ditch or the ravine. Byfield, out of ammunition, crawling past his dead and wounded comrades seeking more powder and shot, spots an old friend, bleeding from a wound.

"Bill, how bee'st?" Byfield inquires.

"One of the Americans keeps firing at us, out of one of those loopholes," his comrade replies.

He points to the loophole. Byfield ventures a shot at it, and almost at the same moment his friend falls back.

"Bill, what's the matter?"

"They've shot me again!"

Dark falls. The rising moon casts a wan light in the ditch and ravine where men are groaning and dying, some complaining that Procter has deserted them. The order to retreat has already been passed from company to company in whispers and in Indian language to prevent the enemy hearing.

An American officer cries from the fort that when the British are gone "I will come out and take you in and use you well."

"Why don't you come out now," shouts Byfield, "and we will fight you five to one."

But he knows that he must escape, not fight. As he climbs to the top of the ravine, the flash of a gun catches his eye, and he flings himself forward as a shower of shot falls near him. Then he is up and running toward the British batteries.

As he leaps into a familiar entrenchment he runs into Procter.

"Where are all the rest of the men?" the Major-General asks.

"I don't think there are any more to come," Byfield replies. "They are all killed and wounded."

"Good God," Procter exclaims, with tears in his eyes.

John Richardson, meanwhile, is trying to convince the men in his platoon that they must quit the ravine. It is now half-past nine; the troops have been lying in the ankle-deep mud for four hours. Richardson's men are separated from the other companies by piles of brushwood. As a result the orders to retire have not reached them. But Richardson can tell from the indistinct sounds beyond that the troops are moving back.

He whispers to his followers that they must move out at once, but the men are fearful they will be spotted in the moonlight. Richardson, piqued, decides to leave them, climbs out of the ravine, and immediately stumbles over a corpse. That sound alerts the garrison, and the entire front of the fort lights up with gunfire. Balls whistle past his head and hiss through the long grass, but in spite of a second volley, the young gentleman volunteer makes his escape – and not a moment too soon, for the troops are already moving to the boats.

In his provision basket Richardson discovers several bottles of port wine, a gift from his family in Amherstburg. Exhausted, starving, and thirsty he proceeds to drain an entire bottle. The effect is instantaneous. Pleasantly inebriated, he settles down in the bottom of one of the boats, enjoying the most delicious moments of repose he has ever experienced. When he awakens, the sun is high in the sky, the lake is glassy, and the men around him are singing and joking, forgetful of the comrades whose dying groans racked their ears only a few hours before.

At the fort, those British still alive are already prisoners. Some have been saved during the night by the defenders, who lowered buckets of water to the wounded, half dead with thirst. Croghan himself, after thirty-six hours of continuous exertion, is too exhausted to send Harrison a detailed report of the battle. No matter. That cautious general is elated by the defeat of the one British officer for whom he has no respect. "It will not be amongst the least of General Procter's mortifications to find he has been baffled by a youth who has just passed his twenty-first year," he writes in a jubilant report to the Secretary of War.

Croghan's victory is the signal for a national celebration and the kind of adulation the American public, desperately short of heroes in this depressing conflict, is prepared to shower on any victor. The young major receives the thanks of Congress and, ultimately, a gold medal, not to mention an elegant sword from the ladies of Chillicothe, Ohio.

The benefits to America of this minor skirmish are more psychological than physical. Procter has lost the respect of his troops, whose resultant low morale will have serious consequences in the days to come. And the Indians are deserting the British. Even Tecumseh, that great optimist, has become disillusioned. He will continue to fight the Long Knives, desperately, hopelessly, but he must know that the long battle for his people and their land is coming to its tragic close.

•

PRESQUE ISLE BAY, Lake Erie, August 1, 1813

As George Croghan's small force prepares to defend Fort Stephenson, Oliver Hazard Perry rises once more from a sick-bed, inspirited by another stroke of good fortune – "Perry's Luck" it will come to be called. He learns that the British fleet, which has been hovering just outside the bay since July 19, effectively blockading his own flotilla, has unaccountably vanished. His own ships are ready to sail. The moment has come to take them over the sandbar that blocks the entrance.

He shakes off the "bilious" fever that seems to strike him after long periods of stress and fatigue. These have not been easy weeks. He still has not enough experienced seamen or officers to man his ships, and his entreaties to Chauncey, his plump superior on Lake Ontario, have been all but fruitless. Like his opposite number, Yeo, Chauncey wants to keep everything for himself; yet having everything, he does nothing. The two rival commanders, though physical opposites, are psychological counterparts. The slender, rawboned Yeo is ten years younger than his forty-one-year-old adversary, but each fears to tangle decisively with the other. The two fleets continue to slip furtively about the lake, engaging in minor skirmishes, cautiously avoiding all-out action, fleeing when necessary to their respective shelters at Kingston and Sackets Harbor, neither quite sure who has command of the waters, each awaiting the moment when he can outbuild the other, a moment that will never come. Each is convinced, not without reason, that a decisive naval battle on Lake Ontario would cripple one side; and since sailing ships are subject as much to the caprices of wind and weather as to human command, each fears the outcome of such a contest. If Yeo loses the lake, Canada falls; if Chauncey loses, America is humbled. Meanwhile, the two opposing fleets on Erie suffer from a lack of trained seamen.

Perry has no such qualms. He is eager to attack Barclay, even with ships that are only partially manned.

"I long to have at him," he tells Chauncey, and in the same breath pleads, "for God's sake…send me men and officers."

He is mortified when Harrison, reporting the second siege of Fort Meigs, asks for naval co-operation, which Perry cannot supply. Chauncey has finally sent him a handful of men, the dregs of his fleet, "a motley set, blacks, soldiers and boys," in Perry's description. A second detachment of sixty is even worse, many worn down by disease, one-fifth suffering from fever and dysentery, one a Russian who speaks no English. The two hundred soldiers who accompanied him from Black Rock have long since been ordered back to Sackets Harbor, and his only defence force is a comic opera regiment of Pennsylvania militia who are too afraid of the dark to stand watch at night. When Perry inquires about these unsoldierly qualms he receives a jarring reply from their commander: "I told the boys to go, Captain, but the boys won't go."

It is clear that Procter, after his failure in May, is wary of attacking any defensive position. But Perry is less concerned about his own defence than he is about his ability to attack. At the moment, his force is clearly superior to Barclay's and will be as long as the British ship *Detroit* remains unfinished.

"What a golden opportunity if we had men," he writes to Chauncey. Yet he is "obliged to bite [his] fingers in vexation" for want of them.

With the enemy out of the way Perry can at last get his new ships into the open lake without fear of molestation. Or is it a ruse? No matter; he must try. Now a new frustration bedevils him. The water has dropped to a depth of only four feet. The two brigs, *Lawrence* and *Niagara*, draw nine. Fortunately, Noah Brown has foreseen just such a calamity and devised a solution – four gargantuan box-like scows, known as camels, which can be floated or sunk at will. By placing a camel on each side of a ship and sinking each of them below the surface, the vessel can be raised by means of ropes and windlasses and set on a series of wooden beams resting on the camels. The scows are then plugged, pumped out, and brought to the surface. With the big ship resting on the supports, the entire ungainly contraption can be floated easily over the bar.

As Perry discovers, the process is more easily described than accomplished. The smaller vessels are lightened and warped over first to act as a protective screen in case Barclay's squadron should reappear. But more armament is needed to meet this threat; *Niagara* is kedged up close to the bar, her port broadside facing the open lake. If the British return, she will act as a floating battery. On shore, batteries support this formidable armament.

Now *Niagara*'s twin, *Lawrence*, a fully rigged brig pierced for twenty guns, is hauled forward on her kedge anchors under Dobbins's direction. For three hours, Dobbins's sweating men strip her of armament and ballast. The camels are brought alongside and the brig hoisted two feet; it is not enough. She still draws too much water. The process must be repeated. It is mid-morning, August 4, after "renewed and unparalleled exertions" when she finally floats free.

Officers and men have spent two sleepless nights, but the work is not over. *Lawrence* must be refitted, a task that takes until midnight. Now *Niagara* must be floated over the bar under *Lawrence*'s protecting guns. This is an easier operation, for the men have mastered the technique.

But before *Niagara* is free of the bar, trouble appears in the shape of two sails, seen through the haze, on the horizon. Barclay is back.

If there is such a thing as Perry's Luck, there is an antithetical adversity that might be dubbed Barclay's Mischance. The British commodore simply cannot believe Perry can get his big ships over the bar. He had gone off, apparently, to attend a dinner in his honour at Port Dover, where, in reply to a toast, he announced that he expected to return "to find the Yankee brigs hard and fast aground on the bar at Erie...in which predicament it would be but a small job to destroy them."

He has returned at a most inopportune moment for the Americans.

But Perry's Luck holds as nature conspires to deceive the British. The wind casts such a haze across the mouth of the bay that Barclay is misled into believing that all of Perry's fleet has successfully entered the open lake. Perry dispatches two of his smaller vessels to keep Barclay at bay. A few shots are exchanged, whereupon the British captain, believing himself outgunned, retires. By midnight, August 5, Perry's fleet of eleven, all fully armed, heads out into the lake for a two-day trial run, vainly seeking the elusive British.

Perry's worries are not over. On the evening of August 8, he takes dinner ashore with his only confidant, the purser, Samuel Hambleton, a one-time Maryland merchant, who at thirty-six is closer to Perry than any of the other junior officers, whose average age is less than twenty years.

To Hambleton, Perry unburdens himself. He is at a loss what to do. He has had to pay off a number of volunteers and is left with only those men who signed articles for four months' service. Now he has less than half the crew needed to man the fleet; of these, less than a quarter are regular naval personnel; and his officers have little experience. He knows delay is dangerous yet feels himself ill-prepared to encounter the enemy.

He is still suffering from fever and fatigue. The struggle to get *Lawrence* over the bar has worn him down; for two days he went without food or sleep. And he has just received a caustic letter from Chauncey that has put him in a dark mood. That officer has seized upon his remarks about black reinforcements to read him a lecture on race relations: "I have yet to learn that the colour of the skin, or the cut and trimmings of the coat, can affect a man's qualifications or usefulness."

Chauncey is especially offended because Perry has gone over his head, writing to the Secretary of the Navy directly, on the ground that the distance between Sackets Harbor and Erie is too great to make communication effective. That sounds very much as if Perry were suggesting a separate command on Lake Erie, an idea which, though sensible, annoys and mortifies the senior commander.

Chauncey cannot resist a further taunt:

As you have assured the secretary that you should conceive yourself equal or superior to the enemy with a force of men so much less than I had deemed necessary, there will be a great deal expected from you by your country, and I trust they will not be disappointed in the high expectation formed of your gallantry and judgement. I will barely make an observation which was impressed on my mind by an old soldier, that is "Never despise your enemy"....

It is too much. In a white heat Perry has just dictated a letter to the Secretary of the Navy requesting that he be removed from his station because he "cannot serve longer under an officer who has been so totally regardless of my feelings."

Does he really mean it? Probably not; the Secretary does not take it seriously, and Chauncey himself will respond at month's end with a mollifying note that will restore relations between the two officers. More important to Perry, the letter has scarcely been dispatched when another arrives. Perry is electrified: Chauncey is sending reinforcements after all! Jesse Elliott is on his way with several officers and eighty-nine seamen. Perry exclaims to his friend Hambleton that this is the happiest moment he has known since his arrival at Erie.

Elliott reaches Presque Isle on August 10. The men he brings are of a better calibre than their predecessors. Perry, whose flagship will be *Lawrence*, gives Elliott command of *Niagara* and allows him to choose his own crew. The ambitious Elliott selects the pick of the crop. *Lawrence*'s sailing master, William Taylor, complains that the vessels of the fleet are unequally manned – the best men are on *Niagara*. But Perry, in his new euphoria, lets Elliott's marked discourtesy pass.

He is more concerned about *Detroit*, nearing completion at Amherstburg and larger than any of his own vessels. He takes care to cruise the lake in battle formation and, since he has only forty seamen who know anything about guns, seizes the opportunity to drill his force. Off Sandusky, he fires a signal shot which on the nineteenth brings General Harrison, his staff, and a crowd of American Indian chiefs on board for a conference. The Indians explore the ship, clamber up the masts, perform a war dance on deck, gawk at the big guns while the two officers settle future strategy. Perry's plan is to force Barclay out of his harbour at Amherstburg. If that fails, he will transport Harrison's army across the lake to attack Procter. His fleet will hold at Put-in Bay, a safe anchorage in the Bass Islands not far from Sandusky Bay.

Here, sickness strikes again. Perry falls dangerously ill once more with fever. His thirteen-year-old brother, Alexander, who has insisted on coming to Erie with him, is also sick. The chief surgeon is too ill to work; his assistant, Usher Parsons, must be carried from ship to ship to minister to the ailing, flat on his back on a cot.

On August 31, with the Commodore still in his bunk, a welcome and unexpected reinforcement of one hundred Kentucky riflemen arrives from General Harrison. Most have never seen a ship before and cannot conceal their astonishment and curiosity. Like the Indians, they scale the masts, plunge into the holds, trot about each vessel from sick bay to captain's cabin, exclaiming over the smallest details. In their linsey-woolsey hunting shirts and pants they are themselves a curiosity to Perry's seamen. He indulges them for a time, then lectures them on ship's etiquette and discipline. They are to act as marines and sharpshooters in the battle to come.

The following day, Perry is well enough to put his squadron into motion toward Amherstburg, hovering outside the harbour as Barclay once blockaded him. *Detroit*, he observes, is now fully rigged. But Barclay declines to come out.

A few days later, three prisoners escape from Fort Amherstburg to warn him that Barclay is preparing for battle. He now has a fairly accurate account of his adversary's strength but overestimates his manpower, which is no greater than his own. In firepower, he outguns Barclay, two to one.

Sickness again strikes him, and he is forced back to his bunk. All his officers are ill with "lake fever." Sick or not, on the evening of September 9 Perry calls a council in the cabin of his flagship. Of his 490 men, almost a quarter are ill; some of the invalids, however, will still be able to fight. All three surgeons are ill, but Usher Parsons manages to stagger in for the meeting.

A long discussion follows. Each commander is given his instructions. Perry, in *Lawrence*, will attack Barclay's flagship, *Detroit*. Elliott, in *Niagara*, will attack the next largest British vessel, *Queen Charlotte*, and so on down the line. Because the British ships are armed chiefly with long guns and the American vessels carry the shorter, more powerful carronades, it is essential for Perry that the fight take place at close quarters. Otherwise his ships will be too far from the British, who with their longer range can batter him to pieces.

Perry leaves nothing to chance. He has already devised a series of signals for the day of action. Now he hands every officer written instructions, each containing one specific admonition: "Engage each designated adversary in close action, at half cable's length." He is wary of those long guns. If he has his way, his powerful short-range carronades will batter Barclay's vessels at point-blank range of one hundred yards.

After an hour's discussion, Perry rises, opens his sea chest, pulls out a strange flag. He has named his flagship *Lawrence* after the newest American naval hero, James Lawrence, who, mortally wounded on the deck of *Chesapeake*, uttered a dying plea: "Don't give up the ship!" Hambleton has had the ladies of Erie sew this slogan in letters of white muslin onto a dark blue flag. Perry exhibits it, tells his officers that when it is hoisted to his masthead it will be the signal for action. It is a curiously negative slogan, especially since Lawrence's men *did* give up the ship. But nobody comments on that.

The officers rise, but Perry is still not satisfied. He calls them back from the deck, goes over his plan once more. He wants to make absolutely sure that they will bring the British fleet into close action. Finally he dismisses them, echoing a phrase of Nelson's: "If you lay the enemy close alongside you cannot be out of your place."

But it is still not enough. As the officers' boats pull away from *Lawrence* to their own ships, Perry stands on deck and repeats Nelson's phrase. He cannot get those long British guns out of his mind. Barclay can easily stand out of range – especially if the wind is right – and reduce his fleet to matchwood before a single American shot strikes him.

It is ten o'clock of a lovely September evening. The moon is full, the lake like black glass, tinselled with silver. From the shore comes the hum of voices around campfires, the *peep-peep* of frogs in Squaw Harbor; from the quarterdecks of the anchored vessels the low murmur of officers, discussing the coming battle; from the fo'c's'les the crackle of laughter – sailors telling jokes, discussing the prospect of prize money.

Perry returns to his cabin; he has letters to write. If battle should come on the morrow and he is victorious, they need not be sent. If he should fall and die, these will be his final messages.

•

AMHERSTBURG, UPPER CANADA, September 9, 1813

Ill-prepared as he is, Robert Heriot Barclay knows he must lead his squadron into Lake Erie and fight the Americans. He realizes the odds are against him, that only a miracle can bring him victory. But he has no choice: Amherstburg is on the verge of starvation; his own crews are on half rations; they do not have a barrel of flour left. Procter's fourteen thousand followers, most of them Indians with wives and children, are reduced to a few barrels of pork, some cattle, and a little unground wheat. Barclay has held off until the last moment, hoping for promised reinforcements, guns, and equipment for his new ship, *Detroit*. He can hold out no longer. He must attempt a run to bring provisions from Long Point. But he knows that Perry's fleet awaits him at Put-in Bay, thirty miles to the southeast. He does not intend to shirk the encounter.

Like Perry, he is badly undermanned, in far worse condition than his adversary. The officers do not know their men; the men do not know their ships. He has been pleading for weeks for reinforcements, but the merest handful has arrived, most of them untrained. The troops have not been paid for months and the civilian artificers have refused to do further work on the ships without wages. Procter has warned Prevost that "there are not in the Fleet more than four and twenty *seamen*." Barclay has echoed these remarks to Yeo: "I am sure, Sir James, if you saw my Canadians, you would condemn every one (with perhaps two or three exceptions) as a poor devil not worth his Salt...."

Prevost has contented himself with penning fatuous letters likely to infuriate both commanders. On reaching the Niagara frontier on August 22, the Governor General ignored all his subordinates' misgivings. Their situation, he agreed, "may be one of some difficulty," but "you cannot fail in honourably surmounting it, notwithstanding the numerical superiority of the enemy's force, which I cannot consider as overbalanced by the excellent description of your troops and seamen: valerous [*sic*] and well disciplined." To which he added (as if mere words could win a battle): "Captain Barclay...has only to dare, and the enemy is discomfited."

Procter could not let that pass: "Your Excellency speaks of seamen valorous and well disciplined. Except, I believe, the 25 Captain Barclay brought with him, there are none of that description on this lake...."

Barclay is also short of cannon and equipment because of the spring attack on York. To outfit his new ship, he has been forced to borrow a motley collection of cannon from the ramparts of Fort Amherstburg. The big guns come in half a dozen sizes, each requiring its own ammunition, so that confusion will reign among the untrained gunners in the heat of battle. Nor can they be fired efficiently; the matches and tubes are spoiled or corroded. To set one off, an officer must snap his pistol over the touch-hole, an awkward procedure that slows the rate of fire. Everything on *Detroit* is makeshift: some of the sails, cables, and blocks have been borrowed from *Queen Charlotte* and other vessels, there being no others available in Amherstburg.

Prevost keeps promising that ordnance and men are on their way. On September 1, the reluctant James Yeo landed a dozen twenty-four-pound carronades, destined for Detroit, at Burlington on Lake Ontario, together with two lieutenants, two gunners, and forty-five seamen. The guns have moved no farther, but the seamen have just turned up and are, in Barclay's opinion, "totally inadequate." Sixteen are mere boys.

Prevost assures him that more are on the way; but Barclay cannot wait. At ten o'clock on this calm, moonlit night, as Perry paces his own deck a few leagues away, Barclay's fleet of six warships slips its moorings and moves out of the Detroit River onto the shining waters of the shallow lake.

In Europe, the noose is tightening around Napoleon. Austria has joined the Allied cause. The Prussian marshal, Gebhard Von Blücher, has already dealt the French a stunning setback at Katzbach. In St. Petersburg, three distinguished American diplomats have been cooling their heels since July, attempting, with limited success, to launch peace talks with Britain through the mediation of the Tsar. But none of this can have the slightest effect on the contest being waged here on a silent lake in the heart of a continental wilderness.

What is Barclay thinking as he walks the quarterdeck of his untried ship? Undoubtedly he has examined the odds, which are against him. Perry has ten vessels – three brigs, six schooners, and a sloop (one of which, however, will not get into action). Barclay has six: two ships, a brig, two schooners, and a sloop. Ships and brigs are square rigged, the former with three masts, the latter with two. It is largely on these that the contest will depend.

Barclay's flagship, *Detroit*, is the largest craft on the lake – 126 feet in length – at least fifteen feet longer than either of Perry's twin brigs, *Niagara* and *Lawrence*. But firepower counts more than size, and here Perry has the advantage, especially at close quarters. Long guns are most effective at eight hundred yards. At three hundred yards, the stubby carronades can do greater damage. Here, Perry's ships can shatter the British fleet with a combined broadside of 664 pounds. The British, who prefer the longer range, can reply with ony 264 pounds of metal. Barclay is also short of trained gunners and seamen. Of his total crew of 440, at least 300 are soldiers, not sailors. But three of every five men in Perry's crews are seamen.

Barclay has one advantage only. Perry's two largest vessels, *Lawrence* and *Niagara*, are inferior to him in long-range firepower. At long range, for instance, the American flagship faces nine times its own firepower. No wonder Perry is desperate to fight at close quarters.

Barclay may not have statistics, but he does have a rough idea of the two fleets' comparative strength. He has carefully taken the measure of the opposing squadron off Amherstburg, climbing to the highest house in the village to examine the vessels through his glass. His strategy is the opposite of Perry's. He must use his long guns to batter the Americans before they can come within range with their stubby carronades. It must be frustrating to realize that so much depends on forces over which he has no control. If he has the "weather gauge" – that is, if the wind is behind him, giving him manoeuvrability – then Perry will be in trouble. But if Perry has the gauge, the wind will drive him directly into the heart of the British fleet.

Tomorrow will tell the tale. For all Barclay knows, it may be his last day on earth. He may emerge a hero, honoured, promoted, decorated. More likely, he will have to shoulder the blame for defeat.

But Barclay is not the kind of man to consider defeat, for he was cast in the mould that has made Britain master of the seas. He is only twenty-eight, but like his contemporaries he has spent more than half his life – sixteen years – in the service of the British navy. Perhaps now his mind harks back to that soft May day in 1798 when at the age of twelve – a small, plump child with rosy cheeks and dark eyes – he took leave of his family and boarded a coach to join a British frigate at Greenock, weeping bitterly because, as he told a sympathetic innkeeper's wife, "I am on my way to sea and will never see father, mother, brothers and sisters again." It is a scene that Barclay cannot put out of his mind. The life of a teen-aged midshipman in the British navy is no feather bed. Young Barclay was "ill used," to quote a scribbled remark in an old family register.

It has not been an easy life or a particularly distinguished one. Barclay is a run-of-the-mill officer, no better, certainly no worse, than hundreds of others in the navy that Nelson shaped. "Ill used" fits his career – a wound at Trafalgar, an escape from drowning when a boat capsized, an arm lost in an engagement with the French. He carries with him a combination knife and fork with which to cut and eat his meat, one-handed. His rank is low; he is called a captain because he commands a ship on Lake Erie; officially he is only a commander. Compared with the big three-decked ships of the line, which are the navy's pride, this crude vessel *Detroit*, hammered together from green lumber and awkwardly rigged, must seem pitifully inadequate. Yet it is a command. He is painfully aware that he is second choice: the post was first offered by Yeo to William Howe Mulcaster, who promptly refused it, believing, quite rightly, that there is no honour in a badly equipped, undermanned fleet on a lake that the high command clearly views as a backwater. So the command has devolved on Robert Heriot Barclay, His Majesty's humble, obedient, and sometimes ill-used servant. How will fate, fortune, wind, and circumstance use him in the approaching conflict? Tomorrow will tell.

●

PUT-IN BAY, LAKE ERIE, September 10, 1813

Sunrise. High up on the mast of *Lawrence*, Perry's lookout spies a distant silhouette beyond the cluster of islands and cries out, "Sail, ho!"

Perry is out of his bunk in an instant, the cry acting as a tonic to his fever. Up the masthead goes his signal: *Get under way*. Within fifteen minutes his men have hauled in sixty fathoms of cable, hoisted the anchors, raised the sails, and steered the nine vessels for a gap between the islands that shield the harbour.

The wind is against him. He can gain the weather gauge by beating around to the windward of some of the islands; but that will require too much time, and Perry is impatient to fight.

"Run to the lee side," he tells his sailing master, William Taylor.

"Then you will have to engage the enemy to the leeward, sir," Taylor reminds him. That will give the British the advantage of the wind.

"I don't care," says Perry. "To windward or leeward, they shall fight today." Taylor gives the signal to wear ship.

The fleet is abustle. The decks must be cleared for action so that nothing will impede the recoil of the guns. Seamen are hammering in flints, lighting rope matches, placing shot in racks or in circular grummets of rope next to the guns. Besides round shot, to pierce the enemy ships, the gunners will also fire canister and grape – one a formidable cluster of iron balls encased in a cylindrical tin covering, the other a similar collection arranged around a central core in a canvas or quilted bag. Perry's favourite black spaniel is running about the deck in excitement; his master orders him confined in a china closet where he will no longer be underfoot. As the commander collects the ship's papers and signals in a weighted bag for swift disposal in case of surrender, his men are getting out stacks of pikes and cutlasses to repel boarders and sprinkling sand on the decks to prevent slipping when the blood begins to flow.

Usher Parsons is setting up a makeshift hospital in *Lawrence*'s wardroom. The brig is so shallow that there is no secure place for the wounded, who must be confined to a ten-foot-square patch of floor, level with the waterline, as much at the mercy of the British cannon-balls as are the men on the deck above.

Suddenly, just before ten, the wind shifts to the southeast – Perry's Luck again. The Commodore now has the weather gauge. Slipping past Rattlesnake Island, he bears down on the British fleet, five miles away. Barclay has turned his flotilla into the southwest. The sun bathes his line in a soft morning glow, shining on the spanking new paint, the red ensigns, and the white sails limned against a cloudless sky.

Staring at the fleet through his glass, Perry realizes that Barclay's line of battle is not as he expected. A small schooner, *Chippawa*, armed with a single long eighteen-pounder at the bow, leads the van, followed by a big three-master, which must certainly be *Detroit*. Perry had expected the British lead vessel to be the seventeen-gun *Queen Charlotte*, designated as Elliott's target.

He signals Elliott, up ahead on *Niagara*, to hold up while he draws abreast to question Captain Henry Brevoort, Elliott's acting marine officer, who, being a resident of Detroit, is familiar with the British squadron. Brevoort points out the small brig *Hunter*, standing directly behind *Detroit*, and *Queen Charlotte* behind her, followed by the schooner *Lady Prevost* and a small sloop, *Little Belt*.

Perry changes his battle order at once in order to bring his heaviest vessels against those of the enemy. The ambitious Elliott, who had originally asked to be in the forefront, "believing from the frequent opportunities I had of encouraging the enemy, that I could success-fully lead the van," is moved farther back, much to his chagrin; Perry himself intends to take on Barclay. Two American gunboats, *Scorpion* and *Ariel*, will operate off Perry's bow to act as dispatch vessels.

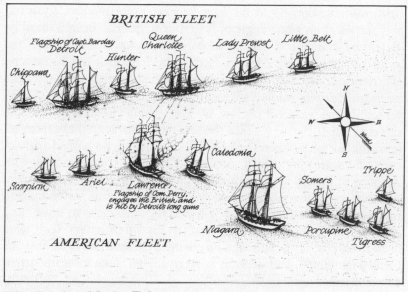

The Battle of Lake Erie: 12:15 p.m.

Caledonia, now in line behind *Lawrence*, will engage the British brig *Hunter*. Elliott in *Niagara* will follow to take on the larger *Queen Charlotte*. The four smaller vessels will bring up the rear.

Perry has all hands piped to quarters. Out come tubs of rations, bread bags, and the standard issue of grog; and out comes the flag that Perry has prepared for this moment.

"My brave lads," he cries, "this flag contains the last words of Captain Lawrence! Shall I hoist it?"

A cheer goes up. Even the sick — those who can walk — come out as Perry, moving from battery to battery, examining each gun, murmurs words of encouragement, exchanges a joke or two with those Kentuckians he knows best, and saves a special greeting for the men from his home state of Rhode Island, who make up a quarter of his fleet:

"Ah, here are the Newport boys! *They* will do their duty, I warrant!"

And to a group of old hands who, with the experience of earlier contests, have removed their cumbersome headgear and tied handkerchiefs around their brows:

"I need not say anything to you: *you* know how to beat those fellows."

A silence has descended on the lake. The British line, closed up tight, waits motionless in the light breeze. The American squadron approaches at an acute angle of fifteen degrees. The hush is deathly. To David Bunnell, a seaman aboard *Lawrence*, it resembles "the awful silence that precedes an earthquake." Bunnell has had a long experience at sea, has served, indeed, in both navies, but now finds his heart beating wildly; all nature seems "wrapped in awful suspense." In the wardroom below, its single hatch closed tight, the lone surgeon, Usher Parsons, sits in the half-light, unable to shake from his mind the horror he knows will shortly be visited upon him. He cannot curb his imagination, which conjures up dreadful scenes mingled with the hope of victory and the prospect of safe return to friends and kin.

At the guns, the men murmur to each other, giving instructions to comrades in case they should fall, relaying messages to wives and sweethearts. In his cabin, Perry rereads his wife's letters, then tears them to shreds, remarking that no enemy shall read them, turns to his friend Hambleton, and declares soberly: "This is the most important day of my life."

Slowly the distance between the two fleets narrows. Minutes drag by; both sides hold their breath. Perry has little control over the speed of his vessels – the gunboats at the rear, being slower, are already lagging badly behind.

One mile now separates the two flagships. Suddenly a British bugle breaks the silence, followed by cheering. A cannon explodes. To Dr. Parsons in the wardroom below, the sound, after the long silence, is electrifying. A twenty-four-pound ball splashes into the water ahead; the British are still out of range.

The American fleet continues to slip forward under the light breeze. Five minutes go by, then – another explosion, and a cannonball tears its way through *Lawrence*'s bulwarks. A seaman falls dead, killed by a flying splinter. The British have found the range. "Steady, boys, steady," says Perry.

An odd whimpering and howling echoes up from below. It is Perry's spaniel. The British cannonball has torn its way through the planking of the china closet, knocking down all the dishes and terrifying the animal, who will bark continually during the battle.

Perry calls out to John Yarnell, his first-lieutenant, to hail the little *Scorpion*, off his windward bow, by trumpet. He wants her to open up on the British with her single long thirty-two. He himself orders his gunners to fire *Lawrence*'s long twelves, but without effect: the British are still out of range.

Barclay's strategy is now apparent. Ignoring the other vessels in Perry's line, *Hunter*, *Queen Charlotte*, and the other British ships will concentrate their combined fire on *Lawrence* – a total of thirty-four guns. Barclay intends to batter Perry's flagship to pieces before she can get into range, then attack the others piecemeal. The British vessels are in a tight line, no more than half a cable's length (one hundred yards) apart. At this point, Perry's superior numbers have little significance, for, as he pulls abreast of the British, his gunboats are too far in the rear to do any damage. He signals all his vessels to close up and for each to engage her opponent. At 12:15 he finally brings *Lawrence* into carronade range of *Detroit*, so close that the British believe he is about to board.

Now, as the thirty-two-pound canisters spray the decks of his flagship, Robert Barclay suffers a serious stroke of ill fortune. His seasoned second-in-command, Captain Finnis, in charge of *Queen Charlotte*, has been unable to reach his designated opponent, partly because the wind has dropped and partly because Elliott, in *Niagara*, has remained out of range. Finnis, under heavy fire from the American *Caledonia*, determines to move up the British line, ahead of *Hunter*, and punish *Lawrence* at close quarters with a broadside from his carronades. But just as his ship shifts position, he is felled by a cannonball and dies instantly. His first officer dies with him. A few minutes later the ship's second officer is knocked senseless by a shell splinter. It is now 12:30. *Queen Charlotte*, the second most powerful ship in the British squadron, falls under the command of young Robert Irvine, a lieutenant in the Provincial Marine who has already shown daring in two earlier battles. But daring must take a back seat to experience. Irvine is no replacement for the expert Finnis, and all he has to support him is a master's mate of the Royal Navy, two boy midshipmen from his own service, a gunner, and a bo'sun. Barclay has lost his main support.

But *Lawrence* is reeling under the British hammer blows. The tumult aboard the American flagship is appalling. Above the shrieks of the wounded and the dying and the rumblings of the gun carriages come the explosion of cannon and the crash of round shot splintering masts, tearing through bulwarks, ripping guns from carriages. Soon the decks are a rubble of broken spars, tangled rigging, shredded sails, dying men. And over all there hangs a thick pall of smoke, blotting out the sun, turning the bright September noon to gloomy twilight.

Lieutenant John Brooks, head of Perry's marines, the handsomest officer at sea this day, a figure of "manly beauty, polished manners and elegant appearance," turns, smiling, to pass a remark to Perry when a cannonball tears into his hip, rips off a leg, hurls him across the deck. In terrible agony, Brooks screams for a pistol to end his life. Perry orders the marines to take him below. As they bend over him, Brooks's little black servant boy, twelve years old, bringing cartridges to a nearby gun, sees his fallen master and flings himself, sobbing, to the deck. Usher Parsons can do nothing for Brooks, who asks in his pain how long he has to live. A few hours at most, the doctor tells him.

Perry's first-lieutenant, John Yarnell, presents a grotesque appearance. His nose, perforated by a splinter, has swollen to twice its normal size. Blood from a scalp wound threatens to blind him. Parsons binds it with a bandanna, and Yarnell, returning to the deck, walks into a cloud of cattail down, torn from a pile of hammocks by round shot. Wounded a third time, he comes down once more for medical aid, his bloody face covered with down, looking like some gigantic owl. At this bizarre spectacle the wounded men cannot help laughing. "The devil has come for us!" they cry.

Perry seems to bear a charmed life. Men are dropping all around him; he suffers not a scratch. As he stops to give aid to one of his veteran gun captains, the man, drawing himself up, is torn in two by a twenty-four-pound ball. His second-lieutenant, Dulaney Forrest, is standing close to him when a shower of grape strikes him in the chest, knocking him to the deck. It is, fortunately, spent. As Perry asks Forrest if he is badly hurt, the stunned officer regains consciousness and cries, "I am not hurt, sir, but this is my shot!" and pulling out a handful from his waistcoat, pockets it as a souvenir.

The Commodore's little brother, acting as a messenger during the din of battle, is also knocked senseless by a splinter but is otherwise unhurt. Still the Commodore remains untouched. For the next century, American naval men will speak in awe of Perry's Luck. He is not, however, above helping that luck along. Not for Oliver Hazard Perry the glittering full-dress uniform of a Nelson or a Brock. He has no intention of being an easy target and has donned the plain blue jacket of a common sailor.

By 1:30, *Lawrence*'s sails are so badly shredded that the brig can no longer be controlled. In spite of the sand, the decks are slippery with blood, which seeps through the seams and drips on the faces of the wounded in the wardroom below. These soon include Perry's closest friend, the purser, Samuel Hambleton, whose shoulder blade has been fractured by a spent cannonball bouncing off a mast. Hambleton lies beside the dying Brooks, who makes a verbal will and asks him to look after his affairs.

The wounded are being taken down the hatch so quickly that Parsons can do little more than secure bleeding arteries and tie a few splints to shattered limbs. There is not time now for the amputations that must follow; only when a leg or arm hangs by a shred does the ailing surgeon stop to sever it.

Nor is there any protection from the battle raging above. At least five cannonballs rip through the walls of Parson's makeshift hospital. The doctor has just finished applying a tourniquet to the mangled arm of a young midshipman, Henry Lamb, when a ball passes through the room, tears the boy out of the surgeon's arms, and throws him against the wall, his body half severed. A seaman brought down with both arms fractured is scarcely in splints before another ball tears off his legs.

On the deck above, the carnage is dreadful as the gun crews are felled by the British grape. Perry calls down through the skylight to Parsons, asking him to send up one of his assistants to man a gun. The call is renewed every few minutes until the doctor has no help left.

Bizarre scenes and unlikely incidents punctuate the action, to remain in the minds of the survivors for years and to form part of the mythology of the battle. Two cannonballs pass through the powder magazine – without igniting it. Another enters the light room, knocks the snuff from a candle into a magazine; a gunner puts it out with his fingers before disaster can strike. One shot punctures a pot of peas boiling on deck and scatters them. David Bunnell, working his gun, notices that a pig has got loose and is greedily eating the peas even though both hind legs have been shot away. Another shot strikes a nearby gun, showering its crew with tiny pieces of gunmetal; one man is riddled from knees to chin with bits of cast iron, some as small as a pinhead, none larger than buckshot. He recovers.

Bunnell is one of the few gunners left who has not been killed or wounded. A shot takes off the head of the man beside him, blowing his brains so thickly into Bunnell's face that he is temporarily blinded. All marines have been ordered down from the masts to replace the gunners, and when the marines are put out of action Perry again calls down the hatch, "Can any of the wounded pull a rope?" Two or three manage to crawl on deck and lend a feeble hand. Wilson May, one of the sick, insists on relieving the men at the pumps so that they can help with the guns. He is not well and must sit down to do the job. At the battle's end he is still sitting there, a bullet through his heart.

The major battle is between *Lawrence* on one side and the two largest British vessels – *Detroit* and *Queen Charlotte* – on the other. Elsewhere, things are going badly for the British. *Hunter*, unable to cope with the American carronades (her own shot is falling short) runs up to the head of the line to assist *Chippawa*. At the rear of the line, the four smaller American craft are battering their two opponents, *Lady Prevost* and *Little Belt*. A ball carries away the former's rudder and she drifts helplessly out of action. Her commander, Lieutenant Edward Buchan, has been driven temporarily insane by a wound in the head. *Little Belt* also loses her commander; she runs to the head of the line and is out of the fight.

But where is Jesse Elliott and the new brig *Niagara*? To the fury of Perry's officers and men, she is standing well off, using her long guns to little effect, too far out of range to bring her carronades into action. Elliott's original orders were to attack *Queen Charlotte*, which is hammering away at Perry's flagship. He has not done so. *Niagara*, twin to *Lawrence*, lurks behind the slower *Caledonia*, every spar in place, her crew scarcely scratched, her bulwarks unscarred.

What has got into Elliott? In the bitter controversy that follows, his supporters will give several explanations and his detractors will make as many charges. Is it a matter of cowardice? Few will believe that. Elliott has shown himself a brave and daring officer and will demonstrate that quality again before the battle is done. Is he merely obeying orders to keep in line behind *Caledonia*? That is scarcely credible (though Elliott will argue it), for Perry's other order – to engage *Queen Charlotte* – was unequivocal. Has the lightness of the wind made it impossible to move closer? If so, how have other ships been able to manoeuvre? And why, if he needs the wind, is his topsail backed and his jib brailed?

None of these alibis make sense. There is, however, one explanation that fits the circumstances. It devolves on Elliott's known character, his ambitions, his mild paranoia. He is nettled at being superseded by a younger man, piqued at being taken out of the van at the last moment, is stubbornly hewing to the letter of Perry's instructions (but only part of them) to stay a cable's length from the vessel ahead. There is, perhaps, more than that. Elliott undoubtedly sees himself as the saviour of the day; when Perry is driven to strike his flag, he, Elliott, will move in.

On *Lawrence*, even the wounded are cursing Elliott.

"Why don't they come and help us?" young Dulaney Forrest asks his superior, the bleeding Yarnell.

"We can expect nothing from that ship," comes the bitter reply.

It is now past two. Perry's flagship is a shambles. Most of her guns are useless, dismounted by the enemy's shot, their breeches torn away, their carriages knocked to pieces. A handful of gunners stick to their posts, firing as quickly as they can. In his haste, David Bunnell sticks a crowbar down the muzzle of his cannon and fires that, too. The gun grows so hot from constant use that it jumps from its carriage. By now five of Bunnell's crew of eight are casualties. He moves to the next gun, finds only one man left, brings up his surviving crew members and tries to get the weapon into action. As he does so he looks down the deck and is shocked by the spectacle – a tangle of bodies, some dead, some dying, the deck a welter of clotted blood, brains, human hair, and fragments of bones sticking to the rigging and planking. Of 137 officers and men aboard *Lawrence*, only 54 have escaped injury or death.

One by one, *Lawrence*'s guns fall silent until she lies like a log in the water. Suddenly *Niagara* gets under way. Elliott, apparently believing Perry is dead, takes over and shouts an order to *Caledonia*, directly ahead, to move out of the line and let him pass – ostensibly to go to the aid of the disabled flagship. He does not do so. Instead, he passes *Lawrence* on the windward side, leaving that beleaguered vessel to the mercies of the British.

It is half-past two. Aboard *Detroit*, Barclay has been forced to go below to be treated for a bad wound in the thigh, secure in the belief that he has triumphed. His ship, too, has taken a fearful pummelling, its first officer dead, its spars and yards shattered, many of its guns out of action. The deck is clear of corpses, for the British do not share the American reverence for the dead and throw all bodies, except those of officers, immediately overboard. Here, too, is a bizarre spectacle: a pet bear, roaming the deck unhurt, licking up the blood.

Barclay's optimism is premature. Perry has no intention of giving up. Whatever Elliott's motives may be for staying out of the battle, he has at least left Perry a seaworthy brig, the equal of *Lawrence*, to continue the contest. Perry calls for a boat, takes four men, turns to Yarnell.

"I leave you to surrender the vessel to the enemy," says Perry, and orders his men to pull for *Niagara*. Then he remembers his special flag and calls for it. Hosea Sergeant, the last survivor of Gun Crew Nine, hauls it down, rolls it into a tight wad, tosses it down to the boat.

"If victory is to be gained, I'll gain it," says Perry.

He cannot control his excitement, refuses to sit down until his men, fearful for his life, threaten to ship their oars. On *Detroit*, the British catch glimpses of the craft, half hidden by the gunsmoke. Musket balls whistle past Perry's head, oars are shattered, round shot sends columns of spray into the boat, but Perry's Luck holds. When a twenty-four-pound ball hits the side of the rowboat, Perry tears off his jacket to plug the hole.

On *Lawrence*, some of the wounded are attempting to talk the surviving officers into fighting on.

"Sink the ship!" they cry, and "Let us sink with her!"

But Yarnell has no intention of indulging in further sacrifice. As he reaches *Niagara*, Perry, with "unspeakable pain," sees *Lawrence*'s flag come down. But the British cannot take the prize; all of *Detroit*'s boats have been shattered.

The American commodore is a scarecrow figure as he climbs aboard to greet the astonished Elliott, hatless, his clothes in tatters, blackened from head to foot by gunsmoke, spattered with blood.

"How goes the day?" asks Elliott, a fatuous question considering the state of the flagship.

"Bad enough," says Perry. "We have been cut all to pieces." Then to business: "Why are the gunboats so far behind?"

"I'll bring them up," says Elliott.

"Do so, sir," Perry responds shortly.

Elliott takes the rowboat and in a remarkable display of personal bravery rows off through heavy fire to call the smaller craft forward into battle by speaking-trumpet. He himself takes command of *Somers*, where he indulges in a curious display of temperament. A cannonball whizzes across the deck, causing Elliott to duck. A gun captain laughs. In a fury, Elliott strikes him across the face with his trumpet and then proceeds to arrest the sailing master, whom he believes to be drunk. But he gets the gunboats quickly into action and pours a heavy fire on the British ships.

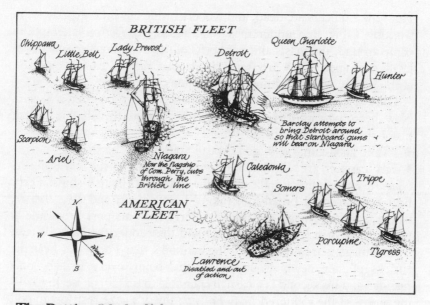

BRITISH FLEET

Chippawa · Little Belt · Lady Prevost · Detroit · Queen Charlotte · Hunter

Barclay attempts to bring Detroit around so that starboard guns will bear on Niagara

Scorpion · Ariel · Niagara Now the flagship of Com. Perry, cuts through the British line · Caledonia · Somers · Trippe

AMERICAN FLEET

N · W · E · S

Lawrence Disabled and out of action · Porcupine · Tigress

The Battle of Lake Erie: 2:40 p.m.

Perry is also in action. He has hoisted his personal flag on *Niagara* and is intent on cutting directly through the British line – an echo of Nelson's famous feat at Trafalgar.

Barclay, back on deck, his wound dressed, anticipates the tactic. A fresh breeze has sprung up; *Niagara* is bearing down at right angles to his ship. In a few minutes she can rake her from bowsprit to taffrail, the full length of the vessel, with her broadside of ten guns. It is a manoeuvre that every commander fears.

Barclay knows what he must do. He will have to wear his ship – bring her around before the wind – so that his own broadside of undamaged guns can be brought to bear upon *Niagara*. Before he can effect the manoeuvre he is struck down again by a charge of grape-shot that tears his shoulder blade to pieces, leaving a gaping wound and rendering his one good arm useless. At the same instant, his second-in-command, John Garland, falls mortally wounded. The ship is now in charge of Lieutenant George Inglis.

As Elliott's gunboats begin to rake the British vessels from the stern, Inglis tries to bring the badly mauled flagship around. But *Queen Charlotte*, which has been supporting Barclay in his battle with *Lawrence*, has moved in too close. She is lying directly astern and in the lee of *Detroit*, which has literally taken the wind out of her sails.

Her senior officers are dead, and Robert Irvine has little experience in working a big ship under these conditions. As *Detroit* attempts to come around, the masts and bowsprits of the two ships become hopelessly entangled. They are trapped. *Queen Charlotte* cannot even fire at the enemy without hitting fellow Britons.

Only seven minutes have passed since Perry boarded *Niagara*. Now he is passing directly through the ragged British line, a half pistol-shot from the flagship.

"Take good aim, boys, don't waste your shot!" he shouts.

His cannon are all double-shotted, increasing the carnage. As *Niagara* comes directly abeam of the entangled British ships, Perry fires his starboard broadside, raking both vessels and also *Hunter*, which is a little astern. On the left, Perry fires his port broadside at two smaller British craft, *Chippawa* and the rudderless *Lady Prevost*. The damage is frightful; above the cannon's roar Perry can hear the shrieks of men newly wounded. At this point, every British commander and his second is a casualty, unable to remain on deck. Looking across at the shattered *Lady Prevost*, Perry's gaze rests on an odd spectacle. Her commander, Buchan, shot in the face by a musket ball, is the only man on deck, leaning on the companionway, his gaze fixed blankly on *Niagara*. His wounds have driven him out of his mind; his crew, unable to face the fire, have fled below.

Detroit's masts crumble under Perry's repeated broadsides. *Queen Charlotte*'s mizzen is shot away. An officer appears on the taffrail of the flagship with a white handkerchief tied to a pike – Barclay has nailed his colours to the mast. *Queen Charlotte* surrenders at the same time, followed by *Hunter* and *Lady Prevost*. The two British gunboats, *Chippawa* and *Little Belt*, attempt to make a run for it but are quickly caught. To Perry's joy, his old ship, *Lawrence*, drifting far astern, has once again raised her colours, the British having been unable to board her.

It is three o'clock. Perry's victory is absolute and unprecedented. It is the first time in history that an entire British fleet has been defeated and captured intact by its adversary. The ships built on the banks of the wilderness lake have served their purpose. They will not fight again.

When Elliott boards *Detroit* there is so much blood on deck that he slips, drenching his clothing in gore. The ship's sides are studded with iron – round shot, canister, grape – so much metal that no man can place a hand on its starboard side without coming into contact with it.

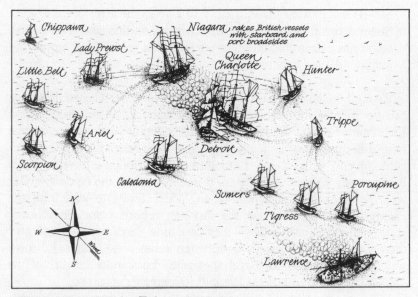

The Battle of Lake Erie: 3:00 p.m.

Elliott sends a man aloft to tear down Barclay's colours, saving the nails as a present for Henry Clay of Kentucky. Says Barclay, ruefully: "I would not have given sixpence for your squadron when I left the deck." He is in bad shape, weak, perhaps near death, from loss of blood and the shock of his mangled shoulder, ill-used once again in the final minutes of this astonishing contest.

Perry, meantime, sitting on a dismounted cannon aboard *Niagara*, takes off his round hat and, using it for a desk, scrawls out a brief message to Harrison on the back of an envelope. Its first sentence is destined to become the most famous of the war:

> We have met the enemy and they are ours. Two Ships, two Brigs, one Schooner and one Sloop.
>
> Yours, with greatest respect and esteem
>
> O.H. Perry

To William Jones, Secretary of the Navy, he pens a slightly longer missive to be borne personally to Washington by Dulaney Forrest, who still carries in his pocket the handful of grape-shot plucked from his waistcoat.

Sir – It has pleased the Almighty to give to the arms of the United States a signal victory over their enemies on this lake. The British squadron...have this moment surrendered to the force under my command after a sharp conflict....

Around the lake the sounds of the battle have been heard, but none can be sure of the outcome. At Amherstburg, fifteen miles away, Lieutenant-Colonel Warburton, Procter's deputy, watches the contest from a housetop and believes the British to be the victors. At Cleveland, seventy miles away, Levi Johnson, at work on the new court house, hears a sound like distant thunder, realizes the battle is under way. All the villagers assemble on Water Street to wait until the cannonade ceases. Because the last five reports come from heavy guns – American carronades – they conclude Perry has won and give three cheers. At Put-in Bay, only ten miles away, Samuel Brown watches the "grand and awful spectacle" but cannot be sure of the outcome because both fleets are half hidden by gunsmoke.

Perry returns to *Lawrence* to receive the official surrender. A handful of survivors greets him silently at the gangway. On deck lie twenty corpses, including close friends with whom he dined the night before. He looks around for his little brother, Alexander, finds him sound asleep in a hammock, exhausted by the battle. He dons his full-dress uniform and, on the after part of the deck, receives those of the enemy able to walk. They pick their way among the bodies and offer him their swords; he refuses to accept them, instead inquires after Barclay's condition. His concern for his vanquished enemy is real and sincere.

The September shadows are lengthening. Perry's day is over. The fever, which subsided briefly under the adrenalin of battle, still lurks. Oblivious of his surroundings, the Commodore lies down among the corpses, folds his hands over his breast, and, with his sword beside him, sleeps the sleep of the dead.

●

PUT-IN BAY, LAKE ERIE, September 11, 1813

The American fleet, its prizes and its prisoners, are back at anchorage by mid-morning. In the wardroom of the battered *Lawrence*, Dr. Usher Parsons has been toiling since dawn, amputating limbs. The seamen and marines are so eager to rid themselves of mutilated members that Parsons has had to establish a roster, accepting his patients for knife and saw in the order in which they were wounded. His task completed by eleven, he turns his attention to the remainder of the disabled; that occupies him until midnight. In all, he ministers to ninety-six men, saves ninety-three.

A special service is held for the officers of both fleets. Barclay, in spite of grievous wounds, insists on attending. Perry supports him, one arm around his shoulder. The effort is too much for the British commander, who is carried back to his berth on *Detroit*. Perry goes with him, sits by his side until the soft hours of the morning when Barclay finally drops off to sleep. The prisoners are struck by the American's courtesy. Now that the heat of battle has passed, he looks on his foes without rancour, makes sure his officers treat them well, urges Washington to grant Barclay an immediate and unconditional parole so that he may recover.

To Barclay, Perry is "a valiant and generous enemy." "Since the battle he has been like a brother to me," he writes to his brother in England. Later, the British commander, who will never again be able to raise his right arm above the shoulder, writes to his fiancée, offering to release her from their engagement. The spirited young woman replies that if there were enough of him left to contain his soul, she would marry him. The inevitable court martial follows, at which Barclay, not surprisingly, is cleared – his mutilated figure drawing tears from the spectators. But the navy, which has used him ill on Lake Erie with help that was too little and too late, puts him on the shelf. Almost eleven years will pass before he is promoted to post rank.

In the meantime, a more acrimonious drama is in the making. Most of Perry's officers are enraged at Elliott's behaviour during the action; but Perry, intoxicated by victory, is in an expansive mood. There is little doubt in his mind that Elliott has acted abominably, but in his elation, as he later tells Hambleton, there is not a man in his fleet whose feelings he would hurt. It is certainly in his power to ruin Elliott's career, but that is not his nature. Nor does he want the decisiveness of his victory marred by any blemish. "It is better to screen a coward than to let the enemy know there is one in the fleet," he remarks, quoting a long-dead British admiral.

In his official report, he cannot ignore his second-in-command; that would be tantamount to condemnation. So he laces his account of the battle with ambiguities:

At half past two, the wind springing up, Captain Elliott was enabled to bring his vessel, the Niagara, gallantly into close action.

And:

Of Captain Elliott, already so well known to the government, it would almost be superfluous to speak. In this action he evinced his characteristic bravery and judgement; and since the close of the action, has given me most able and generous assistance.

Perry shows the report to Elliott, who first says he is satisfied but later asks for changes. He does not like the reference to his ship coming into action so late. Perry, fearing he may have gone too far, refuses to revise the document.

- Elliott takes to his bed, calls for Dr. Parsons, who can find nothing wrong with him. He calls for Perry, who finds him in "abject condition" and listens sympathetically while Elliott laments that he has missed "the fairest opportunity of distinguishing [himself] that ever a man had." Elliott follows this up with a letter in which he reports that his brother has heard rumours that *Lawrence* "was sacrificed in consequence of a want of exertion on my part individually." He urges Perry to deny this allegation.

The good-natured Perry has already ordered his officers not to write home with their doubts about Elliott's conduct in action and to silence all rumours about any controversy. He can do no less himself. Thus he falls into Elliott's trap and writes a letter (which he will later describe as foolish):

...I am indignant that any report should be in circulation prejudicial to your character...I...assure you that the conduct of yourself...was such as to meet my warmest approbation. And I consider the circumstance of your volunteering and bringing the smaller vessels to close action as contributing largely to our victory....

This letter will be part of the ammunition that Elliott will use in his long and inexplicable battle for vindication. There is more: he is already twisting the arms of his own officers to prepare memoranda in his favour. And after Perry takes his leave of Lake Erie to go to another command, Elliott approaches Daniel Turner of *Caledonia* asking for a certificate praising his conduct in battle. Elliott tells

Turner he wants only to calm his wife's fears – she has heard the rumours – and promises on his honour to make no other use of the document. But after Turner complies, Elliott has the certificate published.

And to what end? In the hosannas being sounded across the nation, Elliott shares the laurels equally with his commander. Congress takes the unprecedented step of striking not one but two gold medals – the first time a second-in-command has received one. In this one divines the subtle hand of Elliott's friend and mentor, Mr. Speaker Henry Clay. Elliott's share of the prize money – a staggering $7,140 – also equals Perry's. (Chauncey, who begrudged the Erie fleet its seamen, gets one-twentieth of the total, almost thirteen thousand dollars.) As far as the public is concerned, Elliott is a hero. Why does he not keep quiet? But that would be contrary to Elliott's temperament; he is a man with a massive chip on his shoulder and an unbridled hunger for fame. He is also a man with a guilty conscience.

And so, as the news of the great victory spreads, as bonfires flare and triumphant salvos echo across the Union, as public dinners, toasts, orations, songs, and poems trumpet the country's triumph, the seeds of a bitter controversy begin to sprout.

Elliott cannot let the matter die. For the next thirty years the Battle of Lake Erie will be fought again and again, with affidavits, courts of inquiry, books, pamphlets, newspaper articles, even pistols. By 1818, Perry's own good nature evaporates; he calls Elliott "mean and despicable," retracts his letter when Elliott challenges him to a duel. Perry responds by demanding Elliott's court martial (a request that is pigeon-holed by the President). A hasty court of inquiry settles nothing, and even Perry's unfortunate death of yellow fever in 1819 does not still the verbal war. Elliott persists in his unflagging campaign for exoneration. In 1839, when James Fenimore Cooper enters the fray with a book that tends to support Elliott, Perry's friends rush again to his defence, and the literary battle goes on. Nor does it die until the last of the participants have gone to their final rest to join those others who, in the bloom of youth, bloodied the raw new decks of the two fleets that tore at each other on a cloudless September afternoon in 1813.

5

The Northwest Campaign: 3
RETREAT ON THE THAMES
September 14 – October 5, 1813

With Barclay's defeat, Erie becomes an American lake. Because Perry can cruise these waters with impunity, landing troops anywhere, the British cannot hope to hold the territory captured in 1812. Detroit must be evacuated; Amherstburg, on the Canadian side, is threatened. The British have two choices: to meet the coming invasion at the water's edge (always supposing they know where it will come), or retire at once to a defensive position up the valley of the Thames, keeping the army intact and stretching the American lines of supply. The British command favours retreat; the Indians want to stay and fight.

FORT AMHERSTBURG, UPPER CANADA, September 14, 1813

Tecumseh is in a violent passion. He has just come over from Bois Blanc Island in the Detroit River, where he and his followers are camped, to find that the fort is being dismantled. What is going on?

It looks very much as if Procter is planning to retreat; but Procter has been remarkably evasive with the Indians. On the day after the naval battle he actually pretended that Barclay had won.

"My fleet has whipped the Americans," he told the tribesmen, "but the vessels being much injured have gone into Put-in Bay to refit, and will be here in a few days."

Tecumseh, who is no fool, resents being treated as one. He does not care for Procter. The two have been at loggerheads since Brock's death, a year ago. Brock, in Tecumseh's view, was a *man*; Procter is fit only to wear petticoats. Now the British general fears to face his Shawnee ally with the truth.

Disillusion is gnawing at Tecumseh. Since 1808 he has been the supreme optimist, perfectly convinced that, aided by the compelling new religion of his mystic brother the Prophet, he can somehow weld all the warring and quarrelsome tribes into a mighty confederacy. He is in this war not to help the British but to help his people hold on to their hunting grounds and to their traditional life style. But the war has gone sour, and confederation is not as easy as it once seemed. He cannot convince the southern tribes to join him. And there is more than a suspicion that the young braves who still recognize his leadership are as interested in plunder and ransom money as they are in his grand design.

He is a curious mixture, this muscular Shawnee with the golden skin and hazel eyes who has renounced all pleasures of the flesh to funnel his energies toward a single goal. It is the future that concerns him; but now that future is clouded, and Tecumseh is close to despair. He has already considered withdrawing from the contest, has told his followers, the Shawnee, Wyandot, and Ottawa tribesmen, that the King has broken his promise to them. The British pledged that there would be plenty of white men to fight with the Indians. Where are they?

"The number," says Tecumseh, "is not now greater than at the commencement of the war; and we are treated by them like the dogs of snipe hunters; we are always sent ahead to *start the game*; it is better that we should return to our country and let the Americans come on and fight the British."

Tecumseh's own people agree. Oddly, it has been Robert Dickson's followers, the Sioux, and their one-time enemies the Chippewa, who have persuaded him to remain. But Dickson has gone off on one of his endless and often mysterious peregrinations through the wilderness to the west.

Now, with the fort being dismantled, Tecumseh has further evidence of Procter's distrust. Determined to abandon the British, he goes off in a fury to the home of Matthew Elliott, the Indian Department supervisor at Amherstburg. Ever since the Revolution, Elliott has been friend and crony to the Indians and especially to the Shawnee. At times, indeed, this ageing Irishman seems more Indian than Tecumseh. He fights alongside the Indians, daubed with ochre, has clubbed men to death with a tomahawk and watched others die at the stake – the ritual torture that Tecumseh abhors and prohibits. As events have proved, at both Frenchtown and Fort Meigs, he is less concerned about sparing the lives of prisoners than is Tecumseh. As a result he is, next to Procter, the man whom Harrison's Kentuckians hate most.

Elliott cringes under Tecumseh's fury. The Shawnee warns him that if Procter retreats, his followers will in a public ceremony bring out the great wampum belt, symbolic of British-Indian friendship, and cut it in two as an indication of eternal separation. The Prophet himself has decreed it. Worse, the Indians will fall on Procter's army, which they outnumber three to one, and cut it to pieces. Elliott himself will not escape the tomahawk.

For retreat is not in Tecumseh's make-up; he believes only in attack. The larger concerns of British strategy in this war are beyond him; his one goal is to kill as many of the enemy as possible. He has been fighting white Americans since the age of fifteen, when he battled the Kentucky volunteers. At sixteen, he was ambushing boats on the Ohio, at twenty-two serving as a raider and scout against the U.S. Army. He was one of the first warriors to break through the American lines at the Wabash during one of the most ignominious routs in American history when, in 1791, Major-General Arthur St. Clair lost half his army to a combined Indian attack. The following year Tecumseh answered the call of his elder brother to fight in the Cherokee war, and when his brother was killed became band leader in his stead, going north again to take part in the disastrous Battle of Fallen Timbers on the Maumee, where Major-General Anthony Wayne's three thousand men shattered Blue Jacket's band of fourteen hundred. On that black August day in 1794 Tecumseh, his musket jammed, did his best to rally his followers, waving a useless weapon as they scattered before the American bayonets.

Tecumseh believes in sudden attack: dalliance, even when justified, frustrates him; retreat is unthinkable. When Perry's fleet first appeared outside Amherstburg he could not understand why Barclay did not go out at once to face it.

"Why do you not go out and meet the Americans?" he taunted Procter. "See yonder, they are waiting for you and daring you to meet them; you must and shall send out your fleet and fight them."

Since those bloody days on the Wabash and Maumee, facing St. Clair and Wayne, Tecumseh has used another weapon – his golden voice – to frustrate William Henry Harrison's hunger for Indian lands. Now Harrison, the former governor of Indiana, who did his best to buy up the hunting grounds along the Wabash for a pittance, has Lake Erie to himself. He can land anywhere; and he has a score to settle with Tecumseh, who frustrated his land grab. Tecumseh, too, has a score to settle with Harrison, who destroyed the capital of his confederacy on the Tippecanoe. He cannot wait to get at the General; and he will use the weapon of his oratory to rally his people and blackmail the British into standing fast.

The following morning, he summons his followers from Bois Blanc Island. They squat in their hundreds on the fort's parade ground as

Tecumseh strides over to a large stone on the river bank. It is here that announcements of importance are made and here that Tecumseh, the greatest of the native orators – some say the greatest orator of his day – makes the last speech of his life.

It is to Procter, standing nearby with a group of his officers, that Tecumseh, speaking through an interpreter, addresses his words.

First, his suspicions, born of long experience, going back to the peace that followed the Revolution:

"In that war our father was thrown on his back by the Americans. He then took the Americans by the hand without our knowledge, and we are afraid that our father will do so again...."

Then, after a reference to British promises to feed the Indian families while the braves fought, a brief apology for the failure at Fort Meigs: "It is hard to fight people who live like ground hogs."

Then:

"Father, listen. Our fleet has gone out, we know they have fought. We have heard the great guns, but know nothing of what has happened to our father with one arm. Our ships have gone one way and we are much astonished to see our father tying up everything and preparing to run the other, without letting his red children know what his intentions are. You always told us to remain here and take care of our land.... You always told us you would never draw your foot off British ground. But now, Father, we see that you are drawing back, and we are sorry to see our father doing so without seeing the enemy. We must compare our father's conduct to a fat animal that carries its tail upon its back. But when affrighted, it drops it between its legs and runs off...."

Tecumseh urges Procter to stay and fight any attempt at invasion. If he is defeated, he himself will remain on the British side and retreat with the troops. If Procter will not fight, then the Indians will:

"Father, you have got the arms and ammunition.... If you have any idea of going away, give them to us.... Our lives are in the hands of the Great Spirit; we are determined to defend our land; and if it is his will, we wish to leave our bones upon it."

As always, Tecumseh's eloquence has its effect. Some of his people leap up, prepared to attack the British immediately if their leader gives the word. But Tecumseh is placated when Procter promises to hold a council with the tribesmen on September 18.

Procter faces serious problems. The fort is defenceless, having been stripped of its cannon to arm the new ship, *Detroit*. One-third of his troops have been lost to him as a result of Perry's victory. He is out of provisions and must call on Major-General Vincent's Centre Division to send him supplies overland, since the water route is now denied him by the victorious Americans. Harrison not only has a formidable attack force but he also has the means to convey it, unchallenged, to Canada. Procter's own men are battle weary, half famished, and despondent over the loss of the fleet.

He does not have the charisma to rally his followers – none of Brock's easy way with men, or Harrison's. He is in his fiftieth year, a competent enough soldier, unprepossessing in features, and not very imaginative. There is a heaviness about him; his face is fleshy, his body tends to the obese – "one of the meanest looking men I ever saw," in the not unbiased description of an American colonel, William Stanley Hatch. When Brock remarked that the 41st was "badly officered" he undoubtedly meant men like Procter; yet he also must have thought Procter the best of the lot, for he put him in command at Amherstburg and confirmed him as his deputy after the capture of Detroit.

Procter suffers from three deficiencies: he is indecisive, he is secretive, and he tends to panic. When Brock wanted to cross the Detroit River and capture William Hull's stronghold in a single bold, incisive thrust, Procter was against it. When Procter's own army crept up on the sleeping Kentuckians at the River Raisin, Procter hesitated again, preferred to follow the book, wasted precious minutes bringing up his six-pounders instead of charging the palisade at once and taking the enemy by surprise. When he was finally convinced of the fleet's loss on September 13, he held a secret meeting with his engineering officer, his storekeeper, and his chief gunner, ordered the dismantling of the fort and the dispatching of stores and artillery to the mouth of the Thames. But he did not tell his second-in-command, Lieutenant-Colonel Augustus Warburton, who is understandably piqued at being left in the dark. When Warburton protests, Procter curtly tells him he has a perfect right to give secret orders. A right, certainly; but it is an axiom of war that subordinates should be kept informed.

There are good reasons for Procter to withdraw from Fort Amherstburg. Harrison has total mobility. Perry's fleet can now land his troops anywhere along Erie's north shore to outflank the British and take them from the rear. But if Procter moves up the Thames Valley he can stretch Harrison's line of supply and buy time to prepare a strong defensive position. The bulk of the American force is made up of militia men who have signed up for six months. If past experience means anything, Harrison will have difficulty keeping them after their term is up, especially with the Canadian winter coming on.

He must move quickly if he is to move at all; otherwise Harrison will be at his heels, giving him no chance to prepare a defence on ground of his own choosing. And here Procter stumbles. Inexplicably, he has been told by his superiors *not* to retire speedily. "Retrograde movements...are never to be hurried or accelerated," Prevost's aide writes from Kingston. And De Rottenburg, at Four Mile Creek on Lake Ontario, believes that the enemy's ships are in no condition to move after the battle – therefore Procter should take time to conciliate the Indians.

Procter, by his secrecy, has already wasted time. Almost a week passes before the promised meeting with the tribesmen. Even if they agree to move with the British, the logistics will be staggering. With women and children, their numbers exceed ten thousand. All must be brought across from Bois Blanc Island and from Detroit (which the British will have to evacuate) and moved up the Thames Valley. The women and children will go ahead of the army along with those white settlers who do not wish to remain under foreign rule. The sick must be removed as well – an awkward business – together with all the military stores. It is a mammoth undertaking, requiring drive, organizational ability, decision, and a sense of urgency. Procter does not display any of these qualities. And when he hears from De Rottenburg, he is given plenty of excuse to drag his feet.

He meets the Indians on September 18. Tecumseh urges that Harrison be allowed to land and march on Amherstburg. He and his Indians will attack on the flank with the British facing the front. If the attack fails, Tecumseh says, he can make a stand at the River aux Canards, which he defended successfully the previous year. When Procter rejects this plan, Tecumseh, in a fury, calls him "a miserable old squaw." At these words, the chiefs leap up, brandishing tomahawks, their yells echoing down from the vaulted roof of the lofty council chamber.

The time for secrecy is past. Procter unrolls a map and explains his position to the Shawnee war chief. If the gunboats come up the Detroit River, he points out, they can cut off the Indians camped on the American side of the river, making it impossible for them to support the British. Harrison can then move on to Lake St. Clair and to the mouth of the Thames, placing his men in the British rear and cutting off

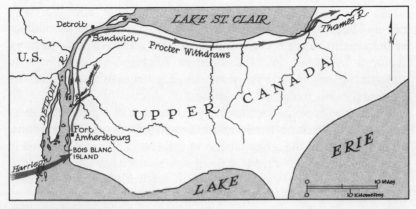

Procter Withdraws

all retreat. Tecumseh considers this carefully, asks many questions, makes some shrewd remarks. He has never seen a map like this before. The country is new to him, but he quickly grasps its significance.

Procter offers to make a stand at the community of Chatham, where the Thames forks. He promises he will fortify the position and will "mix our bones with [your] bones." Tecumseh asks for time to confer with his fellow chiefs. It is a mark of his flexibility that he is able to change his mind and of his persuasive powers that after two hours he manages to convince the others to reverse their own stand and follow him up a strange river into a foreign country.

Yet Tecumseh still has doubts. On September 23, after destroying Fort Amherstburg, burning the dockyard and all the public buildings, the army leaves for Sandwich. Tecumseh views the retreat morosely.

"We are going to follow the British," he tells one of his people, "and I feel that I shall never return."

The withdrawal is snail-like. It has taken ten days to remove all the stores and baggage by wagon and scow. The townspeople insist on bringing their personal belongings, and this unnecessary burden ties up the boats, causing a delay in transporting the women, children, and sick. Matthew Elliott, for example, takes nine wagons and thirty horses to carry the most valuable part of his belongings, including silver plate worth fifteen hundred pounds. The organization of the military stores is chaotic. Entrenching tools, which ought to be carried with the troops, are shifted to the bottoms of the boats after the craft are unloaded to take them across the bar at the mouth of the Thames. The rest of the cargo is piled on top, making them difficult to reach.

On the twenty-seventh, more than a fortnight after Barclay's defeat, Major Adam Muir destroys the barracks and public buildings at Detroit and moves his rearguard across the river. All of the territory captured by Brock in 1812 – most of Michigan – is now back in American hands. At five the same day, Lieutenant-Colonel Warburton marches his troops out of Sandwich.

That same evening, Jacques Bâby, a member of a prominent merchant and fur-trading family and a lieutenant-colonel in the militia, gives a dinner for the senior officers of the 41st in his stone mansion in Sandwich. Tecumseh attends wearing deerskin trousers, a calico shirt, and a red cloak. He is in a black mood, eats with his pistols on each side of his plate, his hunting knife in front of it.

Comes a knock on the door – a British sergeant announcing that the enemy fleet has entered the river and is sailing northward near Amherstburg. Tecumseh, whose English is imperfect, fails to catch the import of the message and asks the interpreter to explain. Then he rises, hands on pistols, and turns to General Procter.

"Father, we must go to meet the enemy.... We must not retreat.... If you take us from this post you will lead us far, far away...tell us Good-bye forever and leave us to the mercy of the Long Knives. I tell you I am sorry I have listened to you thus far, for if we remained at the town...we could have kept the enemy from landing and have held our hunting grounds for our children.

"Now they tell me you want to withdraw to the river Thames.... I am tired of it all. Every word you say evaporates like the smoke from our pipes. Father, you are like the crawfish that does not know how to walk straight ahead."

There is no reply. The dinner breaks up as the guests join the withdrawing army. Tecumseh has no choice but to follow the British with those warriors still loyal to his cause. By now these number no more than one thousand. The Ottawa and Chippewa bands have already sent three warriors to make peace terms with Harrison. The Wyandot, Miami, and some Delaware are about to follow suit.

In the days that follow, Henry Procter, obsessed by the problems of the Indians, abandons any semblance of decisive command. In 1812 the tribesmen were essential to victory; without them Upper Canada might well have become an American fief. Now they have become an encumbrance. Procter literally fails to burn his bridges behind him – an act that would certainly delay Harrison – because he believes that if he does so the Indians, who follow the troops, will think themselves

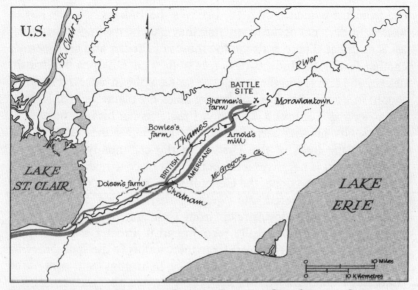

Retreat Up the Thames, September 27–October 5, 1813

cut off and abandon the British cause. To Lieutenant-Colonel Warburton's disgust, he purposely holds back the army in order to wait
for the Indians. He does not, however, give that reason to his second-
in-command but merely says that the troops should rest in their
cantonments because of wet weather.

Indeed, he tells Warburton very little. Nor does he stay with the
army. Mindful of his pledge to Tecumseh to make a stand at the forks
of the Thames, he dashes forward on a personal reconnaissance, leaving Warburton without instructions – an action his officers find extraordinary.

He cannot get the Indians out of his mind. Their presence haunts
him; the promises wrung from him at the council obsess him; Tecumseh's taunts clearly sting. And there is something more: his own superiors have harped again and again on the necessity of placating the
tribesmen. De Rottenburg has expressly told him that he must "prove
to them the sincerity of the British Government in its intent not to
abandon them so long as they are true to their own interests" (which,
translated, means as long as the Indians are prepared to fight for the
British). Prevost has ordered him to conciliate the Indians "by any
means in your power" – promising them mountains of presents if they
will only follow the army. It is clear that the high command, taking its

cue from the evidence of 1812, believes the Indians hold the key to victory; it does not occur to any that they may be the impediment that leads to defeat. There is also in the minds of Procter and his superiors another fear: if the Indians defect, may they not fall upon the British, destroy the army, and then swell the ranks of the invaders? Procter is caught in a trap: if he loses his native allies the blame will fall on him, but as long as Tecumseh is his ally, Procter is not his own man.

He sends his engineering officer, Captain Matthew Dixon, upstream to the forks of the Thames at the community of Chatham. Dixon's report is negative: it is not the best place to make a stand. But something must be done, the General says; he has promised Tecumseh. Dixon is badgered into agreeing that the tiny community of Dover, three miles downstream from Chatham, is a slightly better position, but he cannot really recommend it. Procter seizes on this, appoints an assistant engineer, Crowther, to fortify the spot, ordering him to dig entrenchments and to place light guns at two or three points.

His heart is not in it. He and Dixon take off immediately for Moraviantown, twenty-six miles upstream, a much better position already recommended by the eccentric militia colonel and land developer, Thomas Talbot. In his haste, Procter does not think to inform his second-in-command, Warburton, marching up the valley with the army.

The General's intentions are clear: the army will stand and fight at Moraviantown, not at the forks. But Henry Procter will always be able to say he kept his promise to Tecumseh.

•

FRENCHTOWN, RIVER RAISIN, Michigan Territory, September 27, 1813

As the British fire the public buildings in Detroit and move back into Canada, twelve hundred mounted Kentucky riflemen, led by the fiery congressman, Colonel Richard Johnson, gallop along the Detroit road to reinforce Harrison's invasion army. Here they pause at the site of their state's most humiliating defeat to find the bones of their countrymen still unburied and strewn for three miles over the golden wheatfields and among the apple orchards.

The grisly spectacle rekindles the volunteers' thirst for revenge. Here, on a bitterly cold day the previous January, Procter's Indians struck down the flower of Kentucky, massacring them without quarter, butchering the wounded, burning some alive after putting the torch to buildings, holding others for ransom. *Remember the Raisin!* is the only recruiting cry needed in the old frontier commonwealth. Kentucky now has more men under arms than any state in the Union.

The regiment halts to bury the dead. Captain Robert McAfee writes in his diary that "the bones...cry aloud for revenge.... The chimneys of the houses where the Indians burnt our wounded prisoners...yet lie open to the call of vindictive Justice...." The scene is rendered more macabre that night by a tremendous lightning storm "as if the Prince of the Power of the air...was invited at our approach to scenes of Bloodshed...."

Its task completed, the regiment rides on toward Detroit, where William Henry Harrison awaits them. Most have been in the saddle since mid-May, after Harrison had asked for reinforcements to relieve Fort Meigs. Richard Johnson was only too eager to answer the call. Without waiting for War Department approval, he issued a proclamation:

Fort Meigs is attacked – the North Western army is Surrounded... nobly defending the Sacred Cause of the Country.... The frontiers may be deluged with blood; the Mounted Regiment will present a Shield to the defenseless....
Every arrangement shall be made – there shall be no delay. The soldier's wealth is HONOR – connected with his Country's cause, is its Liberty, independence and glory, without exertions Rezin's [*sic*] bloody scene may be acted over again and to permit [this] would stain the national character....

Such purple sentiments spring easily from Richard Mentor Johnson's pen. At thirty-two a handsome, stocky figure with a shock of auburn hair, he has made a name for himself as an eloquent, if florid, politician. The first native-born Kentuckian to be elected to both the state legislature and the federal congress, he is a crony of Henry Clay and a leading member of the group of War Hawks who goaded the country into war. Like so many of his colleagues, he is a frontiersman by temperament, reared on tales of Indian depredations. His family were Indian fighters by inclination as well as of necessity. He has heard from his mother the story of one siege, when, as she was running from the blockhouse for water, a lighted arrow fell on her son's cradle. Fortunately for Richard Johnson it was snuffed out.

Unlike the aloof New Englanders or the hesitant Pennsylvanians, Kentuckians regard the invasion of Canada as a holy war, "a second revolution as important as the first," in Johnson's belief. It is also seen as a war of conquest: Johnson makes no bones about that. England must be driven from the New World: "I shall never die contented until I see...her territories incorporated with the United States."

The "men of talents, property and public spirit" who flock to Johnson's banner in unprecedented numbers – old Revolutionary soldiers, ex-Indian fighters, younger bloods raised on tales of derring-do – agree. All have made their wills, have resolved never to return to their state unless they come back as conquerors "over the butcherly murderers of their countrymen." Robert McAfee, first captain of the first battalion, is typical. On reaching the shores of Lake Erie he foresees in his imagination huge cities and an immense trade – the richest and most important section of the Union. "It is necessary that Canada should be ours," he writes in his journal.

Johnson and his brother, James, have fifteen hundred six-month volunteers under their command, each decked out in a blue hunting shirt with a red belt and blue pantaloons, also fringed with red. They are armed with pistols, swords, hunting knives, tomahawks, muskets, and Kentucky squirrel rifles. Their peregrinations since mid-May have been both exhausting and frustrating, for they have been herded this way and that through the wilderness for more than twelve hundred miles without once firing a shot at the enemy.

At last the action they crave seems imminent. Johnson can hardly wait to get at the "monster," Procter. His men are no less eager as they ride toward Detroit, swimming their horses across the tributary streams, on the lookout for hostile Indians, elated by news of the British withdrawal. On the afternoon of the thirtieth they reach their objective. The entire population turns out to greet them, headed by the Governor of Kentucky himself, old Isaac Shelby, who at Harrison's request has brought some two thousand eager militiamen to swell the ranks of the invading army.

The tide is turning for the Americans. Johnson learns that Harrison has already occupied Amherstburg, surprised that Procter abandoned it without offering resistance. Harrison now has a force of five thousand men, including two thousand regulars. He does not expect to catch Procter because the British have commandeered every horse in the country. It is all he can do to find a broken-down pony to carry the ageing Shelby.

Harrison has one hope: that Procter will make a stand somewhere on the Thames. His "greatest apprehensions," as he tells the Secretary of War, "arise from the belief that he will make no halt." In that case, perhaps he ought to move his army up the north shore of Lake Erie aboard the fleet, and attack the British rear.

At dawn on the morning of September 30 he and Shelby meet in a small private room in his headquarters at Amherstburg to discuss tactics. The Governor is here at Harrison's personal request, technically in command of all Kentucky militia.

"Why not, my dear sir, come in person?" Harrison asked him in a flattering letter. "You would not object to a command that would be nominal only. I have such confidence in your wisdom that you in fact should be 'the guiding head and I the hand.'"

Harrison – a scholarly contrast to the ragtag crew of near illiterates who officer the militia – cannot resist a classical allusion:

"The situation you would be placed in is not without its parallel. Scipio, the conqueror of Carthage, did not disdain to act as a lieutenant of his younger and less experienced brother, Lucius."

It is a shrewd move. Shelby, an old frontiersman and Revolutionary warrior, cannot resist Harrison's honeyed pleas. He is sixty-three, paunchy and double-chinned, with close-cropped white hair. But he commands the respect of Kentuckians, who call him "Old King's Mountain" after his memorable victory at that place in 1780 and flock to his command in double the numbers required.

Harrison wants the Governor's opinion: the army can pursue Procter by land up the Thames Valley or it can be carried by water to Long Point, along the lake, and march inland by the Long Point road to intercept the British.

Shelby replies that he believes Procter can be overtaken by land. With that the General calls a council of war to confirm the strategy. It opts for a land pursuit.

Harrison decides to take thirty-five hundred men with him, leaving seven hundred to garrison Detroit. Johnson's mounted volunteers, brought over early next morning, will lead the van. The remainder of the force, whose knapsacks and blankets have been left on an island in the river, will follow.

The General has the greatest difficulty persuading any Kentuckian to stay on the American side of the Detroit River. All consider it an insult to be left behind; in the end, Harrison has to resort to a draft to keep them in Detroit. The Pennsylvania militia, on the other hand, stand on their constitutional right not to fight outside the territorial limits of the United States.

"I believe the boys are not willing to go, General," one of their captains tells him.

"The boys, eh?" Harrison remarks sardonically. "I believe some of the officers, *too*, are not willing to go. Thank God I have Kentuckians enough to go without you."

Speed is of the essence. As Shelby keeps saying: "If we desire to overtake the enemy, we must do more than he does, by early and forced marches."

And so, at first light on October 2, as Procter dawdles, the Americans push forward, sometimes at a half run to keep up with the mounted men. Johnson asks Harrison's permission to ride ahead in search of the British rearguard. Harrison agrees but, remembering the disaster before Fort Meigs, adds a word of caution.

"Go, Colonel, but remember discipline. The rashness of your brave Kentuckians has heretofore destroyed themselves. Be cautious, sir, as well as brave and active, as I know you all are."

Johnson rides off with a group of volunteers. Not far from the Thames, they capture six British soldiers and learn that Procter's army is only fifteen miles above the mouth of the Thames. It is now nearly sunset, but when the regiment hears this, it determines to move on to Lake St. Clair. In one day Harrison's army has marched twenty-five miles.

The troops set off again at dawn. Since only the three gunboats with the shallowest draft can ascend the winding Thames, Oliver Hazard Perry, who is eager to see action, signs on as Harrison's aide. Harrison concludes that Procter is unaware of his swift approach, for he has not bothered to destroy any bridges to slow the American advance. Then, at the mouth of the Thames, an eagle is spotted hovering in the sky. Harrison sees it as a victory omen, especially after Perry tells him his seamen had noticed a similar omen the morning of the lake battle. The Indians, it seems, are not the only warriors who believe in signs and portents.

That afternoon, the army captures a British lieutenant and eleven dragoons. From these prisoners Harrison learns that the British have as yet no certain information of his advance.

By evening, the army is camped ten miles up the river, just four miles below Matthew Dolsen's farm at Dover, from which the British have only just departed. It has taken Procter's army five days to make the journey from Sandwich. Harrison has managed to cover the same ground in less than half the time.

●

DOLSEN'S FARM, DOVER, Upper Canada, October 3, 1813

Augustus Warburton is a confused and perplexed officer. Procter's second-in-command has no idea what he is to do because his commander has not told him. Word has reached him that the Americans are on the march a few miles downstream. His own men have reached the place where Procter decided to make a stand, but Procter has rushed up the river to Moraviantown, having apparently decided to meet the enemy there.

Now Captain William Crowther comes to Warburton with a problem. Procter has ordered him to fortify Dover; he wants to throw up a temporary battery, cut loopholes in the log buildings, dig trenches. But all the tools have been sent on to Bowles's farm seven miles upriver, and there are neither wagons nor boats to bring them back. Crowther is stymied.

It is too late, anyway, for Tecumseh, on the opposite bank, insists on moving three miles upstream to Chatham, at the forks. It was there that Procter originally promised to make a stand and, if necessary, lay his bones with those of the Indians. Tecumseh has not been told of any change of plans.

Nor has Warburton. His officers agree that the Indians must be conciliated. As a result, the army, which has lingered at Dolsen's for two days, moves three miles to Chatham and halts again. Tecumseh – not Procter, not Warburton – is calling the tune.

Tecumseh is in a fury. There are no fortifications at Chatham; Procter has betrayed him! Half his force leaves, headed by Walk-in-the-Water of the senior tribe of Wyandot. Matthew Elliott's life is threatened.

Elliott crosses the river and, in a panic, urges Warburton to stand and fight at Chatham.

"I will not, by God, sacrifice myself," he cries, in tears.

He is a ruined man, Elliott, in every sense, and knows it. Financially, he is approaching destitution. His handsome home at Amherstburg has been gutted by the Kentuckians – the furniture broken, fences, barns, storehouses destroyed. His personal possessions are in immediate danger of capture. And his power is gone: the Indians no longer trust him. Once he was the indispensable man, his influence over the American tribes so great that the British restored him to duty after a financial scandal that would have destroyed a lesser official. Now all that has ended. The frontier days are over. The Old Northwest, which Elliott and his cronies, Simon Girty and Alexander McKee, knew when they fought beside the braves against Harmar, St. Clair, and Wayne, is no more. Except for Tecumseh's dwindling band, the native warriors have been tamed. The old hunting grounds north of the Ohio are already threatened by the onrush of white civilization. Here on the high banks of the Thames, the faltering Indian confederacy will stand or fall.

Warburton asks Elliott to tell Tecumseh that he will try to comply with Procter's promises and make a stand on any ground of the Indian's choosing. He has already sent two messages to Procter, warning him that the enemy is closing in and explaining that he has moved forward to Chatham. But Procter goes on to Moraviantown regardless and, after sending his wife and family off to safety at Burlington Heights, remains there for the night.

The Indians are angered at Procter's inexplicable absence. Tecumseh's brother, the Prophet, says he would like personally to tear off the General's epaulettes; he is not fit to wear them. The army, too, is disturbed. Mutiny is in the air. There is talk of supplanting Procter with Warburton, but Warburton will have none of it, a decision that causes Major Adam Muir of the rearguard to remark that Procter ought to be hanged for being absent and Warburton hanged with him for refusing responsibility.

Early on the morning of October 4 (the Americans have been camped all night at Dolsen's), Warburton gets two messages. The first, from Procter, announces that he will leave Moraviantown that day to join the troops. The second, from Tecumseh, tells him that the Indians have decided to retire to the Moravian village.

Warburton waits until ten; no Procter. Across the river he can hear shots: the Indians are skirmishing with the enemy. Just as he sets his troops in motion another message arrives from Procter, ordering him to move a few miles upriver to Bowles's farm. The column moves slowly, impeded by the Indian women who force it to halt time after time to let them pass. At Bowles's – the head of navigation on the river – Warburton encounters his general giving orders to destroy all the stores collected there – guns, shells, cord, cable, naval equipment. In short, the long shuttle by boat from Amherstburg, which delayed the withdrawal, has been for nothing. Two gunboats are to be scuttled in the river to hinder the American progress.

At eight that evening the forward troops reach Lemuel Sherman's farm, some four miles from Moraviantown, and halt for the night. Here, ovens have been constructed and orders given for bread to be baked; but there is no bread, the bakers claiming that they must look first to their families and friends. Footsore, exhausted, and half-starved, their morale at the lowest ebb, the men subsist on whatever bread they have saved from the last issue at Dolsen's.

Tecumseh, meanwhile, has fought a rearguard action at the forks of the Thames – two frothing streams that remind him, nostalgically, of his last home, Prophetstown, where the Tippecanoe mingles its waters with those of the Wabash. In this strange northern land, hundreds of miles from his birthplace, he hungers for the familiar. His Indians tear the planks off the bridge at McGregor's Creek and when Harrison's forward scouts, under the veteran frontiersman William Whitley, try to cross on the sills, open fire from their hiding place in the woods beyond. Whitley, a sixty-three-year-old Indian fighter and Kentucky pioneer, has insisted on marching as a private under Harrison, accompanied by two black servants. Now he topples off the muddy timbers, falls twelve feet into the water, but manages to swim ashore, gripping his silver-mounted rifle. Major Eleazer Wood, the defender of Fort Meigs, sets up two six-pounders to drive the Indians off. The bridge is repaired in less than two hours, and the army pushes on.

That evening, Tecumseh reaches Christopher Arnold's mill, twelve miles upriver from the forks. Arnold, a militia captain and an acquaintance from the siege of Fort Meigs, offers him dinner and a bed. He is concerned about his mill; the Indians have already burned McGregor's. Tecumseh promises it will be spared. He sees no point in useless destruction; with the other mill gone, the white settlers must depend on this one.

In these last hours, fact mingles with myth as Tecumseh prepares for battle. Those whose paths cross his will always remember what was done, what was said, and hand it down to their sons and grandsons.

Young Johnny Toll, playing along the river bank near McGregor's Creek, will never forget the hazel-eyed Shawnee who warned him,

"Boy, run away home at once. The soldiers are coming. There is war and you might get hurt."

Sixteen-year-old Abraham Holmes will remember the sight of Tecumseh standing near the Arnold mill on the morning of October 5, his hand at the head of his white pony: a tall figure, dressed in buckskin from neck to knees, a sash at his waist, his headdress adorned with ostrich plumes – waiting until the last of his men have passed by and the mill is safe. Holmes is so impressed that he will name his first-born Tecumseh.

Years from now Chris Arnold will describe the same scene to his grandson, Thaddeus. Arnold remembers standing by the mill dam, waiting to spot the American vanguard. It is agreed he will signal its arrival by throwing up a shovelful of earth. But Tecumseh's eyes are sharper, and he is on his horse, dashing off at full speed, after the first glimpse of Harrison's scouts. At the farm of Arnold's brother-in-law, Hubble, he stops to perform a small act of charity – tossing a sack of Arnold's flour at the front door to sustain the family, which is out of bread.

Lemuel Sherman's sixteen-year-old son, David, and another friend, driving cows through a swamp, come upon Tecumseh, seated on a log, two pistols in his belt. The Shawnee asks young Sherman whose boy he is and, on hearing his father is a militiaman in Procter's army, tells him: "Don't let the Americans know your father is in the army or they'll burn your house. Go back and stay home, for there will be a fight here soon."

Years later when David Sherman is a wealthy landowner, he will lay out part of his property as a village and name it Tecumseh.

Billy Caldwell, the half-caste son of the Indian Department's Colonel William Caldwell, will remember Tecumseh's fatalistic remarks to some of his chiefs:

"Brother warriors, we are about to enter an engagement from which I shall not return. My body will remain on the field of battle."

Long ago, when he was fifteen, facing his first musket fire against the Kentuckians, and his life stretched before him like a river without end, he feared death and ran from the field. Now he seems to welcome it, perhaps because he has no further reason to live. Word has also reached him that the one real love of his life, Rebecca Galloway, has married. She it was who introduced him to English literature. There have been other women, other wives; he has treated them all with disdain; but this sixteen-year-old daughter of an Ohio frontiersman was different. She was his "Star of the Lake" and would have married him if he had only agreed to live as a white man. But he could not desert his people. Now she is part of a dead past, a dream that could not come true, like his own shattered dream of a united Indian nation.

In some ways, Tecumseh seems more Christian than the Christians, with his hatred of senseless violence and torture. He is considerate of others, chivalrous, moral, and, in his struggle for his people's existence, totally selfless. But he intends to go into battle as a pagan, daubed with paint, swinging his hatchet, screaming his war cry, remembering always the example of his elder brother Cheeseekau, the father figure who brought him up and, in the end, met death gloriously attacking a Kentucky fort, expressing the joy he felt at dying – not like an old woman at home but on the field of conflict where the fowls of the air should pick his bones.

●

LEMUEL SHERMAN'S FARM, Upper Thames, October 5, 1813

Procter's troops, who have had no rations since leaving Dolsen's, are about to enjoy their first meal in more than twenty-four hours when the order comes to pack up and march – the Americans are only a short distance behind. Some cattle have already been butchered, but there is no time to cook the beef and there are no pans in which to roast it. Nor is there bread. Ovens have been constructed but again the baker has run off. Some of the men stuff raw meat into their mouths or munch on whatever crusts they still have from the last issue; the rest go hungry.

There is worse news. The Americans have seized all the British boats, captured the excess ammunition, tools, stores. The only cartridges the troops have are in their pouches. The officers attempt to conceal that disturbing information from their men.

The army marches two and a half miles. Procter appears and brings it to a halt. Here, with the river on his left and a heavy marsh on his right, in a light wood of beech, maple, and oak, he will make his stand.

It is not a bad position. His left flank, resting as it does on the high bank of the river, cannot be turned. His right is protected by the marsh. The General expects the invading army to advance down the road that cuts through the left of his position. He plants his only gun – a six-pounder – at this point to rake the pathway. The regulars will hold the left flank. The militia will form a line on their right. Beyond the militia, separated by a small swamp, will be Tecumseh's Indians.

But why has Procter not chosen to make his stand farther upstream on the heights above Moraviantown, where his position could be protected by a deep ravine and the hundred log huts of the Christian Delaware Indians, who have lived here with their Moravian missionaries since fleeing Ohio in 1792? It is to this village that Procter brought his main ordnance and supplies. Why the sudden change of plan?

Once again the Indians have dictated the battle. They will not fight on an open plain; that is not their style. Procter feels he has no choice but to anticipate their wishes.

His tactics are simple. The British will hold the left while the Indians, moving like a door on a hinge, creep forward through the thicker forest on the right to turn Harrison's flank.

There are problems, however, and the worst of these is morale. The troops are slouching about, sitting on logs and stumps. They have already been faced about once, marched forward and then back again for some sixty paces, grumbling about "doing neither one thing or another." Almost an hour passes before they are brought to their feet and told to form a line. This standard infantry manoeuvre is accomplished with considerable confusion, compounded by the fact that Procter's six hundred men are too few to stand shoulder to shoulder in the accepted fashion. The line develops into a series of clusters as the troops seek to conceal themselves behind trees. Nobody, apparently, thinks to construct any sort of bulwark – entrenchments, earthworks, or a barricade of logs and branches – which might impede the enemy's cavalry. No one appears to notice that on the British side of the line there is scarcely any underbrush. But then, all the shovels, axes, and entrenching tools have been lost to the enemy.

The troops stand in position for two and a half hours, patiently waiting for the Americans to appear. They are weak from hunger, exhausted from the events of the past weeks. They have had no pay for six months, cannot even afford soap. Their clothes are in rags, and they have been perennially short of greatcoats and blankets. They are overworked, dispirited, out of sorts. Some have been on garrison duty, far away from home in England, for a decade. They cannot see through the curtain of trees but have heard rumours that Harrison has ten thousand men advancing to the attack. Many believe Procter is more interested in saving his wife and family than in saving them; many believe they are about to be cut to pieces and sacrificed for nothing. And so they wait – for what seems an eternity.

Tecumseh rides up. The men, he tells Elliott, seem to him to be too thickly posted; they will be thrown away to no advantage. Procter obediently robs his line to form a second, one hundred yards behind, with a corps of dragoons in reserve. Now the Shawnee war chief rides down the ragged line, clasping hands with the officers, murmuring encouragement in his own language. He has a special greeting for John Richardson, whom he has known since childhood. Richardson notes the fringed deerskin ornamented with stained porcupine quills, the ostrich feathers (a gift from the Richardson family), and most of all the dark, animated features, the flashing hazel eyes. Whenever in the future he thinks of Tecumseh – and he will think of him often – that is the picture that will remain: the tall sturdy chief on the white pony, who seems now to be in such high spirits and who genially tells Procter, through Elliott, to desire his men to be stout-hearted and to take care the Long Knives do not seize the big gun.

•

WILLIAM HENRY HARRISON, having destroyed Procter's gunboats and supplies, has crossed the Thames above Arnold's mill in order to reach the right bank along which the British have been retreating. The water at the ford is so deep that the men hesitate until Perry, in his role as Harrison's aide, rides through the crowd, shouts to a foot soldier to climb on behind, and dashes into the stream, calling on Colonel Johnson's mounted volunteers to follow his example. In this way, and with the aid of several abandoned canoes and keel boats, the three thousand foot soldiers are moved across the river in forty-five minutes.

William Whitley, the veteran scout, seeing an Indian on the opposite side, shoots him, swims his horse back across, and scalps the corpse. "This is the thirteenth scalp I have taken," he tells a friend, "and I'll have another by night or lose my own."

As the army forms up on the right bank, a message arrives for Harrison. A spy has reported that the British are not far ahead, aiming for Moraviantown. Harrison rides up to Johnson, tells him that foot soldiers will not be able to overtake Procter until late in the day, asks him to push his mounted regiment forward to stop the British retreat.

"If you cannot compel them to stop without an engagement, why FIGHT them, but do not venture too much," Harrison orders.

Johnson moves his men forward at a trot. Half a mile from the British line his forward scouts capture a French-Canadian soldier. The prisoner insists that Procter has eight hundred men supported by fourteen hundred Indians. When Johnson reveals he has only one thousand followers, his informant bursts into tears, begs him to retire. But Johnson has no intention of retreating. He sends back a message to Harrison that the British have halted and are only a few hundred yards distant. If they venture to attack, his men will charge them.

Procter does not attack, and the two armies remain within view of one another, motionless, waiting.

A quarter of an hour passes. Harrison rides up, sends Eleazer Wood forward to examine the situation through his spyglass. Behind him, the American column – eleven regiments supported by artillery – stretches back for three miles. Harrison holds a council of war on horseback. He sees at once that Procter has a good position and divines the British strategy: they will use the Indians on his left on the edge of the morass to outflank him. That he must frustrate. He will attempt to hold the Indians back with a strong force on his left and attack the British line with a bayonet charge through the woods. At the same time Johnson's mounted men will splash through the shallow swamp that separates the British from the Indians and fall on Tecumseh's tribesmen.

Harrison forms up his troops in an inverted L, its base facing the British regulars. Shelby is posted at the left end of the base (the angle of the L). Harrison takes a position on the right, facing Procter. The honour of leading the bayonet charge goes to Brigadier-General George Trotter, a thirty-four-year-old veteran. It is a signal choice, for a high proportion of Trotter's men come from the same Kentucky counties that bore the brunt of the Frenchtown massacre.

An hour and a half passes while Harrison forms his troops. The British, peering through the oaks, the beeches, and the brilliant sugar maples, can catch only glimpses of the enemy, three hundred yards distant. The Americans, waiting to attack, have a better view of the British in their scarlet jackets.

Meanwhile, Richard Johnson has sent Captain Jacob Stucker to examine the shallow swamp through which his troops must gallop in

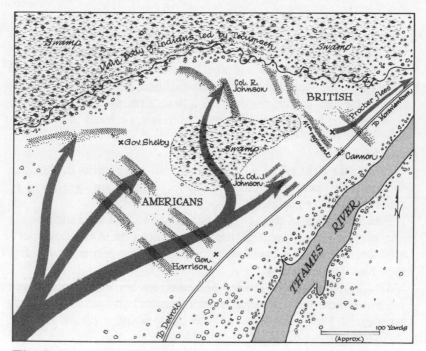

The Battle of the Thames

their attack on the Indians. Stucker returns with disappointing news: the swamp is impassable. Finally, the General speaks:

"You must retire, Colonel, and act as a corps of reserve."

But Johnson has a different idea:

"General Harrison, permit me to charge the enemy and the battle will be won in thirty minutes." He means the British – not the Indians.

Harrison considers. The redcoats are spread out in open formation with gaps between the clusters of men. The woods are thick with trees, but there is little underbrush. He knows that Johnson has trained his men to ride through the forests of Ohio, firing cartridges to accustom the horses to the sound of gunfire. Most have ridden horseback since childhood; all are expert marksmen.

"Damn them! Charge them!" says Harrison, and changes the order of battle on the spot.

It is a measure, Harrison will later declare, "not sanctioned by anything that I had seen or heard of." But he is convinced that this unorthodox charge will catch the British unprepared.

Now Stucker comes back with welcome news. He has found a way through the intervening swamp. It will not be easy, for the ground is bad. Johnson turns to his brother, James, his second-in-command.

"Brother, take my place at the head of the first battalion. I will cross the swamp and fight the Indians at the head of the second battalion." He explains his reason: "You have a family, I have none."

In the brief lull that follows, one of Harrison's colonels, John Calloway, rides out in front of his regiment and in a stentorian voice, shouts:

"Boys, we must either whip these British and Indians or they will kill and scalp every one of us. We cannot escape if we lose. Let us all die on the field or conquer."

Procter's repeated threat – that he cannot control the Indians – has been turned against him. He has so convinced the Americans that a massacre will follow a British victory that they are prepared, if necessary, for a suicidal attack.

The bugle sounds the charge. Seated on his horse halfway between the two British lines, Procter hears the sound and asks his brigade major, John Hall, what it means. The bugle sounds again, closer.

"It's the advance, Sir," Hall tells him.

An Indian scout, Campeaux, fires his musket. Without orders, the entire British front line discharges a ragged volley at the advancing horsemen.

In spite of their training, the horses recoil in confusion.

Procter looks toward the six-pounder on his left. "Damn that gun," he says. "Why doesn't it fire?"

But the British horses have also been startled by the volley. They rear back, become entangled in the trees, taking the six-pounder with them.

James Johnson rallies his men and charges forward as the second line of British defenders opens fire.

"Charge them, my brave Kentuckians!" Harrison cries in his florid fashion as the volunteers dash forward, yelling and shouting.

"Remember the Raisin!" someone shouts, and the cry ripples across the lines: *"Remember the Raisin! Remember the Raisin!"*

The volunteers hit the left of the British line. It crumbles. Captain Peter Chambers, one of the heroes of the siege of Fort Meigs, sees his men tumbling in all directions, tries vainly to rally them, finds himself swept back by the force of the onslaught.

"Stop, 41st, stop!" Procter shouts. "Why do you not form? What are you about? For shame. For shame on you!"

The force of the charge has taken Johnson's horsemen right through both British lines. Now they wheel to their left to roll up the British right, which is still holding.

"For God's sake, men, stand and fight!" cries a sergeant of the 41st. Private Shadrach Byfield, in the act of retreating, hears the cry, turns about, gets off a shot from his musket, then flees into the woods.

Not far away stands John Richardson, an old soldier at sixteen, survivor of three bloody skirmishes. A fellow officer points at one of the mounted riflemen taking aim at a British foot soldier. Richardson raises his musket, leans against a tree for support, and before the mounted man can perfect his aim drops him from his horse. Now he notes an astonishing spectacle on his right. He sees one of the Delaware chiefs throw a tomahawk at a wounded Kentuckian with such precision and force that it opens his skull, killing him instantly. The Delaware pulls out the hatchet, cuts an expert circle around the scalp; then, holding the bloody knife in his teeth, he puts his knee on the dead man's back, tears off the scalp, and thrusts it into his bosom, all in a matter of moments. This grisly scene is no sooner over than the firing through the woods on Richardson's left ends suddenly, and the order comes to retreat.

Procter, too, is preparing to make off. The gun crew has fled; the Americans have seized the six-pounder. Hall warns him that unless they move swiftly they will both be shot.

"Clear the road," Hall orders, but the road is clogged with fleeing redcoats. He suggests to the General that they should take to the woods; but Procter, stunned by the suddenness of defeat, does not appear to hear him. No more than five minutes have passed since Harrison's bugle sounded.

"This way, General, this way," says Hall patiently, like a parent leading a child. The General follows obediently. A little later he finds his voice:

"Do you not think we can join the Indians?" For Tecumseh's force on the right of the shattered British line is still fighting furiously.

"Look there, Sir," says Hall, pointing to the advancing Americans. "There are mounted men betwixt you and them." James Johnson's charge has cut Procter's army in two.

They are on the road, riding faster now, for the Americans are in hot pursuit. Procter is desperate to escape the wrath of the Kentucky volunteers, whose reputation is as savage as that of the Potawatomi who slaughtered their countrymen at the River Raisin. For all he knows they may flay him alive before Harrison can stop them.

As Captain Thomas Coleman of the Provincial Dragoons catches up, the General gasps out that he is afraid he will be captured. Coleman reassures him: some of his best men will be detailed to guard him. The General gallops on with the sound of Tecumseh's Indians, still holding, echoing in his ears.

As James Johnson's men drive the British before them, his brother's battalion plunges through the decaying trees and tangled willows of the small swamp that separates the Indians from their white allies. Richard Johnson's plan is brutal. He has called for volunteers for what is, in effect, a suicide squad – a "Forlorn Hope," in the parlance of both the British and the American armies. This screen of twenty bold men will ride ahead of the main body to attract the Indians' fire. Then, while the tribesmen are reloading, the main body will sweep down upon them.

There is no dearth of volunteers. The grizzled Whitley, a fresh scalp still dangling from his belt, will lead the Forlorn Hope. And Johnson will ride with them.

Off they plunge into the water and mud, into a hail of musket balls. Above the shattering dissonance of the battle another sound is heard – clear, authoritative, almost melodic – the golden voice of Tecumseh, urging his followers on to victory. Johnson's tactic is working: the Indians have concentrated all their fire on the Forlorn Hope, and with devastating results – fifteen of the twenty, including William Whitley, are dead or mortally wounded.

But Johnson faces a problem. The mud of the swamp has risen to the saddle girth of the horses. His men cannot charge. Bleeding from four wounds, he orders them to dismount and attack. An Indian behind a tree fires again, the ball striking a knuckle of Johnson's left hand, coming out just above the wrist. He grimaces in pain as his hand swells, becomes useless. The Indian advances, tomahawk raised. Johnson, who has loaded his pistol with one ball and three buckshot, draws his weapon and fires, killing his assailant instantly. Not far away lies the corpse of William Whitley, riddled with musket balls.

Beyond the protecting curtain of gunsmoke, the battle with the Indians rages on as Shelby moves his infantry forward to support the dismounted riflemen. Oliver Hazard Perry, carrying one of Harrison's dispatches to the left wing, performs a remarkable feat of horsemanship as his black steed plunges to its breast in the swamp. The Commodore presses his hands to the saddle, springs over the horse's head to dry land; the horse, freed of its burden, heaves itself out of the swamp with a mighty snort; as it bounds forward, Perry clutches its mane and vaults back into the saddle without checking its speed or touching bridle or stirrup.

Word spreads that Richard Johnson is dead. An old friend, Major W.T. Barry, riding up from the rear echelon to examine the corpse, meets a group of soldiers bearing the Colonel back in a blanket.

"I will not die, Barry," Johnson assures him. "I am mightily cut to pieces, but I think my vitals have escaped." One day he will be vice-president.

Behind him, the cacophony of battle continues to din into his ears as Shelby's force presses forward through the trees. The volume rises in intensity: the advancing Kentuckians shouting their vengeful battle cry; the Indians shrieking and whooping; wounded men groaning and screaming; horses neighing and whinnying; muskets and rifles shattering ear drums; bugles sounding; cannon firing.

The smoke of battle lies thickly over forest and swamp, making ghosts of the dim, painted figures who appear for an instant from the cover of a tree to fire a weapon or hurl a tomahawk, then vanish into the gloom. They are not real, these Indians, for their faces can be seen only in death. Which are the leaders, which the followers? One man, the Kentuckians know, is in charge: they can hear Tecumseh's terrible battle cry piercing the ragged wall of sound. For five years they have heard its echo, ever since the Shawnee first made his presence felt in the Northwest. Yet that presence has always been spectral; no Kentuckian on the field this day – no white American, in fact, save Harrison – has ever seen the Shawnee chief or heard his voice until this moment. He is a figure of legend, his origins clouded in myth, his persona a reflection of other men's perception. Johnson's riders, firing blindly into the curtain of trees, hating their adversary and at the same time admiring him, are tantalized by his invisibility.

Suddenly comes a subtle change in the sound. Private Charles Wickliffe, who has been timing the battle, notices it: something is missing. Wickliffe, groping for an answer, comes to realize that he can no longer discern that one clear cry, which seemed to surmount the dissonance. The voice of Tecumseh, urging on his followers, has been stilled. The Shawnee has fallen.

The absence of that clarion sound is as clear as a bugle call. Suddenly the battle is over as the Indians withdraw through the underbrush, leaving the field to the Kentuckians. As the firing trails off, Wickliffe takes out his watch. Exactly fifty-five minutes have elapsed since Harrison ordered the first charge.

As the late afternoon shadows gather, a pall rises over the bodies of the slain. There are redcoats here, their tunics crimsoned by a darker stain, and Kentuckians in grotesque attitudes that can only be described as inhuman, and Indians, staring blankly at the sky, including several minor chieftains, one dispatched by Johnson, another by Whitley.

But one corpse is missing. Elusive in life, Tecumseh remains invisible in death. No white man has ever been allowed to draw his likeness. No white man will ever display or mutilate his body. No headstone, marker, or monument will identify his resting place. His followers have spirited him away to a spot where no stranger, be he British or American, will ever find him – his earthly clay, like his own forlorn hope, buried forever in a secret grave.

•

JOHN RICHARDSON, fleeing from James Johnson's riders, charges through the woods with his comrades, loses his way, finds himself unexpectedly on the road now clogged with wagons, discarded stores and clothing, women and children. Five hundred yards to his right he sees the main body of his regiment, disarmed and surrounded by the enemy. Instinctively, he and the others turn left, only to run into a body of American cavalry, the men dismounted, walking their horses.

Their leader, a stout elderly officer dressed like his men in a Kentucky hunting jacket, sees them, gallops forward brandishing his sword and shouting in a commanding voice:

"Surrender, surrender! It's no use resisting. All your people are taken and you'd better surrender."

This is Shelby. Richardson, whose attitude towards all Americans is snobbishly British Canadian, thinks him a vulgar man who looks more like one of the army's drovers than the governor of a state – certainly not a bit like the chief magistrate of one of His Majesty's provinces.

He swiftly buries his musket in the deep mud to deny it to the enemy and surrenders. As the troops pass by, one tall Kentuckian glances over at the diminutive teen-ager and says: "Well, I guess now, you tarnation little Britisher, who'd calculate to see such a bit of a chap as you here?" Richardson never forgets that remark, which illustrates the language gulf between the two English-speaking peoples who share the continent.

Shadrach Byfield at this moment, having fled into the woods at the same time as Richardson, has encountered a party of British Indians who tell him Tecumseh is dead. They want to know whether the enemy has also taken Moraviantown and ask Byfield whether he can hear American or British accents up ahead. At the forest's edge, Byfield hears a distinctive American voice cry, "Come on, boys!" The party retreats at once. Terrified that the Indians will kill him, he gives away what tobacco he has in his haversack and prepares to spend the night in the woods.

Major Eleazer Wood is in full pursuit of Procter, but the General eludes him, stopping only briefly at Moraviantown and pressing on to Ancaster, so fatigued he cannot that evening write a coherent account of the action. Wood has to be content with capturing his carriage containing his sword, hat, trunk, and all his personal papers, including a packet of letters from his wife, written in an exquisite hand.

Moraviantown's single street is clogged with wagons, horses, and half-famished Kentuckians. The missionary's wife, Mrs. Schnall, works all night baking bread for the troops, some of whom pounce on the dough and eat it before it goes into the oven. Others upset all the beehives, scrambling for honey, and ravage the garden for vegetables, which they devour raw.

Richardson and the other prisoners fare better. Squatting around a campfire in the forest, they are fed pieces of meat toasted on skewers by Harrison's aides, who tell the British that they deplore the death of the much-admired Tecumseh.

Now begins the long controversy over the circumstances of the Shawnee's end. Who killed Tecumseh? Some give credit to Whitley, whose body was found near that of an Indian chief; others, including Governor Shelby, believe that a private from Lincoln County, David King, shot him. Another group insists that the Indian killed by Richard Johnson was the Shawnee; that will form the most colourful feature of Johnson's subsequent campaign for the vice-presidency.

But nobody knows or will ever know how Tecumseh fell. Only two men on the American side know what he looks like – Harrison, his old adversary, and the mixed-blood Anthony Shane, the interpreter, who knew him as a boy. Neither is able to say with certainty that any of the bodies on the field resembles the Indian leader.

The morning after the battle, David Sherman, the boy who encountered Tecumseh in the swamp, finds one of his rifled flintlock pistols on the field. That same day, Chris Arnold comes upon a group of Kentuckians flaying the body of an Indian to make souvenir razor strops from the skin.

"That's not Tecumseh," Arnold tells them.

"I guess when we get back to Kentucky they will not know his skin from Tecumseh's," comes the reply.

In death, as in life, the Shawnee inspires myth. There are those who believe he was not killed at all, merely wounded, that he will return to lead his people to victory. It is a wistful hope. "Skeletons" of Tecumseh will turn up in the future. "Authentic" graves will be identified, then rejected. But the facts of his death and his burial are as elusive as those of his birth, almost half a century before.

As the Americans bury their dead and those of their enemy in two parallel trenches, Shadrach Byfield moves through the wilderness with the Indians, still fearful that he will be killed by his new companions. Toward sunset on his second night in the wild, to Byfield's relief and delight the party stumbles upon one of his comrades, also drifting about in the woods. That night they sleep out in the driving rain, existing on a little flour and a few potatoes. The following night they find an Indian village where they are treated kindly and fed pork and corn. At last, after a further twenty-four hours of wandering, their shoes now in shreds, they run into a group of fifty escapees whom Lieutenant Richard Bullock has gathered together. With Bullock in charge, the remnants of the 41st make their way to safety.

John Richardson, meanwhile, is marched back to the Detroit River with six hundred prisoners. Fortunately for him, his grandfather, John Askin of Amherstburg, has a son-in-law, Elijah Brush, who is an American militia colonel at Detroit. Askin writes to his daughter's husband to look after his grandson. As a result, Richardson, instead of being sent up the Maumee with the others, is taken to Put-in Bay by gunboat, where he runs into his own father, Dr. Robert Richardson, an army surgeon captured by Perry and assigned to attend the wounded Captain Barclay.

The double victories on Lake Erie and the Thames tip the scales of war. For all practical purposes the conflict on the Detroit frontier is ended. At Twenty Mile Creek on the Niagara peninsula, Major-General Vincent, expecting Harrison to follow up his victory, falls into a panic, destroys stocks of arms and supplies, trundles his invalid army back to the protection of Burlington Heights. Of eleven hundred men, eight hundred are on sick call, too ill to haul the wagons up the hills or through the rivers of mud that pass for roads.

De Rottenburg is prepared to let all of Upper Canada west of Kingston fall to the Americans, but the Americans cannot maintain their momentum. Harrison's own supply lines are stretched taut; the Thames Valley has been scorched of fodder, grain, and meat; his six-month volunteers are clamouring to go home. Harrison is a captive of America's hand-to-mouth recruiting methods. He cannot pursue the remnants of Procter's army, as military common sense dictates. Instead, he moves back down the Thames, garrisons Fort Amherstburg, and leaves Brigadier-General Duncan McArthur in charge of Detroit.

The British still hold a key outpost in the Far West – the captured island of Michilimackinac, guarding the route to the fur country. It is essential that the Americans seize it; with Perry's superior fleet that should not be difficult. But the Canadian winter frustrates this plan. For that adventure the Americans must wait until spring. Instead, Harrison takes his regulars and moves east to Fort George, from which springboard he hopes to attack Burlington Heights.

Once again victory bonfires light up the sky; songs written for the occasion are chorused in the theatres; Harrison is toasted at every table; Congress strikes the mandatory gold medal. One day, William Henry Harrison will be president. An extraordinary number of those who fought with him will also rise to high office. One will achieve the vice-presidency, three will rise to become governors of Kentucky, three more to lieutenant-governor. Four will go to the Senate, at least a score to the House.

For Henry Procter there will be no accolades. A court martial the following year finds him guilty of negligence, of bungling the retreat, of errors in tactics and judgement. He is publicly reprimanded and suspended from rank and pay for six months.

Had Procter retreated promptly and without encumbrance, he might have joined Vincent's Centre Division and saved his army. But it is the army he blames for all his misfortunes, not himself. In his report of the battle and his subsequent testimony before the court, he throws all responsibility for defeat on the shoulders of the men and officers serving under him. The division's laurels, he says, are tarnished "and its conduct calls loudly for reproach and censure." But in the end it is Procter's reputation that is tarnished and not that of his men. To the Americans he remains a monster, to the Canadians a coward. He is neither – merely a victim of circumstances, a brave officer but weak, capable enough except in moments of stress, a man of modest pretensions, unable to make the quantum leap that distinguishes the outstanding leader from the run-of-the-mill: the quality of being able in moments of adversity to exceed one's own capabilities. The prisoner of events beyond his control, Procter dallied and equivocated until he was crushed. His career is ended.

He leaves the valley of the Thames in a shambles. Moraviantown is a smoking ruin, destroyed on Harrison's orders to prevent its being used as a British base. Bridges are broken, grist mills burned, grain destroyed, sawmills shattered. Indians and soldiers of both armies have plundered homes, slaughtered cattle, stolen private property.

Tecumseh's confederacy is no more. In Detroit, thirty-seven chiefs representing six tribes sign an armistice with Harrison, leaving their wives and children as hostages for their good intentions. The Americans have not the resources to feed them, and so women and children are seen grubbing in the streets for bones and rinds of pork thrown away by the soldiers. Putrefied meat, discarded in the river, is retrieved and devoured. Feet, heads, and entrails of cattle – the offal of the slaughterhouses – are used to fill out the meagre rations. On the Canadian side, two thousand Indian women and children swarm into Burlington Heights pleading for food.

Kentucky has been battling the Indians since the days of Daniel Boone. Now the long struggle for possession of the Northwest is over; that is the real significance of Harrison's victory. The proud tribes have been humbled; the Hero of Tippecanoe has wiped away the stain of Hull's defeat; and (though nobody says it) the Indian lands are ripe for the taking.

The personal struggle between Harrison and Tecumseh, which began at Vincennes, Indiana Territory, in 1810, has all the elements of classical tragedy. And, as in classical tragedy, it is the fallen hero and not the victor to whom history will give its accolade. It is Harrison's fate to be remembered as a one-month president, forever to be confused with a longer-lived President Harrison – his grandson, Benjamin. But in death as in life, there is only one Tecumseh. His last resting place, like so much of his career, is a mystery; but his memory will be for ever green.

6

THE ASSAULT
ON MONTREAL
October 4 – November 12, 1813

With Michigan Territory and Detroit back in American hands and the campaign on the Niagara peninsula at a standstill, the United States reverts to its original strategy – to thrust directly at the Canadian heartland, attacking either Montreal or Kingston and cutting the lifeline between the Canadas. Two armies – one at Fort George, a second at Sackets Harbor – will combine for the main attack. A third, at Plattsburgh on Lake Champlain, will act in support, either joining in the massive thrust down the St. Lawrence or creating a diversion if the attack should focus on Kingston.

SACKETS HARBOR, NEW YORK STATE, October 4, 1813

Major-General James Wilkinson, Dearborn's replacement as the senior commander of the American forces, returns to his headquarters after a month at Fort George, shivering from fever, so ill that he must be helped ashore. He has been ailing for weeks; as a result, the projected attack on Montreal – or will it be Kingston? – has moved by fits and starts. The combined forces from Sackets Harbor and Fort George should have been at the rendezvous point – Grenadier Island, near the mouth of the St. Lawrence – long before this. Winter is approaching, but they have only just begun to move.

At fifty-six, Wilkinson is an odd choice for commander-in-chief. He is almost universally despised, for his entire career has been a catalogue of blunders, intrigues, investigations, plots, schemes, and deceptions. Outwardly he is blandly accommodating, with a polished, easy manner. Behind those surface pretensions lurks a host of less admirable qualities: sensuality, unreliability, greed for money, boastfulness, dishonesty. No other general officer has pursued such an erratic career. Long before, as brigadier-general, he was forced to resign because of his involvement in a cabal against George Washington. As clothier-general he resigned again because of irregularities in his accounts. As a key figure in the "Spanish Conspiracy," a plan to split off the southwest into a Spanish sphere of influence, he resigned once more. His colleagues are unaware that he has taken an oath of

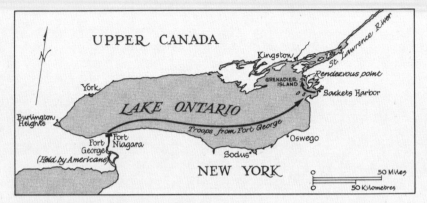

Lake Ontario, October, 1813

allegiance to the Spanish crown and draws a pension from that government of four thousand dollars a year.

Yet he is nothing if not resilient. After the Spanish scandal he rejoined the army, rose again to brigadier-general, plotted to discredit his commander, Anthony Wayne, then narrowly escaped indictment for his association with Aaron Burr. He faced a court martial for conspiracy, treason, disobedience, neglect of duty, and misuse of public money but, to President Madison's dismay, the court cleared him. Now here he is, the President's deputy, in charge of the most important military post in the United States – a living example of the poverty of military leadership in his country's army.

He has been too long away from his headquarters; indeed, it is questionable whether he should have left, for the Secretary of War, John Armstrong, has quit Washington to be at the centre of the war and has all but taken over in his absence. Sick or not, the shivering general must look in on Armstrong, who shares quarters with Wilkinson's second-in-command, the ineffectual Morgan Lewis, who is Armstrong's brother-in-law.

Armstrong would like to have Wilkinson's job. He fancies himself a shrewd military strategist and is not without experience, having served on the staff in the Revolution and later as a brigade commander in the militia. He likes to be called General and peppers his letters to his army commanders with military axioms and advice. Madison has no confidence in him, and James Monroe, the Secretary of State, is an avowed enemy; but Armstrong, through a politically opportune marriage, has powerful friends in New York who helped him secure his present post.

The Secretary's instincts are often sound but his execution indecisive. It has always been obvious to him that the key to victory in Canada lies in the capture of Kingston, but in his orders to Wilkinson he has covered himself carefully to escape blame for future defeat. Kingston, he declares, "represents the *first* and *great* object of the campaign." Then he equivocates, explaining that it can be attacked in two ways: directly by assault, or indirectly by sweeping down the St. Lawrence to Montreal, thus cutting its supply line. The Secretary is an expert at making the obvious appear significant. Whether Wilkinson chooses to attack Kingston or Montreal, Armstrong can always point out that he suggested an alternative course.

Now here he is at Sackets Harbor, a handsome figure, about to turn fifty-six, with a proud, unlined face, regular features, and hooded eyes, aristocratic by nature, pugnacious by temperament – "eminently pugnacious," in Martin Van Buren's phrase – ambitious, caustic, but like Wilkinson outwardly convivial.

They make a strange pair, the general and the politician who hold the fate of Canada in their hands. Friends once, then enemies, they are friends again, or seem to be. While serving together in 1792 they had such a falling out that Armstrong, charged by Wilkinson with fraud, left the army in disgust. That has been patched up; Wilkinson is the Secretary's choice as commander. But it is an uneasy alliance. To the ailing general, Armstrong's presence is unsettling. He feels his command undermined, his prestige lessened, for the Secretary has been bustling about, making free with advice that, not surprisingly, is accepted as command.

Wilkinson is so sick that he has almost ceased to care. Weakened by a series of paroxysms, he tells Armstrong he is incapable of command and wants to retire. The Secretary insists he is indispensable, assures him that he will soon recover, and remarks to one of his staff, "I would feed the old man with pap sooner than leave him behind." It is indicative of their relationship that the "old man" is scarcely a year older than Armstrong.

Indecision marks their deliberations. Neither can make up his mind whether the main attack should be on Kingston or on Montreal. Whichever objective one favours, the other opposes. Almost at their first encounter, Wilkinson vigorously espouses Montreal. Armstrong differs but covers himself with a cloud of ambiguities. A fortnight later both men trade positions, Armstrong arguing that circumstances have changed. But when Wilkinson asks for a direct order in writing, the

Secretary declines, referring him to his earlier letter about "direct" and "indirect" attacks.

It is becoming obvious that neither man expects an attack on Kingston or Montreal to succeed; in this documentary confrontation they are carefully protecting themselves from future charges of failure.

Armstrong, the would-be commander, is the author of a pompous little book entitled *Hints to Young Generals*. "The art of war," he has written, "rests on two [principles] – concentration of force and celerity of movement." It cannot be said that the army is moving with celerity at Sackets Harbor. Nineteen days are spent loading the boats with provisions, a task the contractor's agent believes could be done in five. The boats are encumbered with hospital stores instead of guns and powder, and these stores are scattered throughout the flotilla without any plan.

This is especially significant because the squadron, when it does move, will resemble a floating hospital – a term specifically used by William Ross, the camp surgeon. In September, some seven hundred men and officers lie ill; that number will double within two months.

The chief causes are bad food – which, in Dr. Ross's words, has "destroyed more soldiers than have fallen by the sword of the enemy" – and wretched sanitation. The meat is rotten, the whiskey adulterated, the flour so bad that "it would kill the best horse in Sacket's Harbor." The greatest offender is the bread, which when examined is found to contain bits of soap, lime, and, worst of all, human excrement. The bakers take their water from a stagnant corner of the lake, no more than three feet from the shore. Into the lake pours all the effluent from a cluster of latrines a few yards away. Naked men knead the dough. Nearby is a cemetery housing two hundred corpses, together with the contents of a box of amputated limbs marked "British arms and legs," buried in no more than a foot of sandy soil. But although the troops are weak from dysentery and the leading officers have been warned of the problem, nothing is done. His subordinates are convinced that Wilkinson is too ill to be told and too weak (from the same condition) to act upon the information if he were.

The word from Major-General Wade Hampton, meanwhile, is not such as to inspire confidence. Hampton's army of four thousand regulars and fifteen hundred militia at Lake Champlain has been ordered to support Wilkinson's attack. The difficulty is that Hampton hates Wilkinson so much that he will not take orders from him. Indeed, he has secured the ambiguous agreement of the Secretary of War that his will be a separate command. Unfortunately, Armstrong has also assured Wilkinson that Hampton really will act under his orders. The result is that although Wilkinson has sent directions to Hampton, two hundred miles away, Hampton has not deigned to answer. In the end all communication between the two generals has to be passed through Armstrong.

Hampton's army has reached Châteauguay Four Corners, just south of the border, after a dismal attempt to follow Armstrong's instructions to create a diversion near the Canadian village of Odell-town. The attack failed on September 21 because of unseasonably hot weather. Horses and men were so desperate with thirst that the entire force had to withdraw and march seventy miles to its present situation.

Now Hampton too seems to be covering himself against failure. He reports that his troops are raw and that illness is increasing daily. "All I can say is it shall have all the capacity I can give it," he writes, lamely.

Armstrong tells him to hold fast at Four Corners "to keep up the enemy's doubts, with regard to the real point of your attack" – a necessary order, since Armstrong himself does not know where the real point of attack will be. Finally, on October 16 he instructs Hampton to move down the Châteauguay River and cross the border, either as a feint to support the thrust against Kingston or to await the main body of Wilkinson's army on its movement down the St. Lawrence to Montreal.

At this point, more than half of Wilkinson's combined forces have yet to reach the rendezvous point at Grenadier Island. A winter storm has been raging for a week, lashing the waters of the lake with rain, snow, and hail. Those few boats that do set off are destroyed or forced back to harbour. Do Wilkinson and Armstrong really believe they can seize Canada before winter?

By October 19, when the weather abates and the main body sets off, the ground is thick with snow. And still no one can be sure whether Kingston or Montreal will be the main point of the attack.

●

CHÂTEAUGUAY FOUR CORNERS, New York State, October 21, 1813

For the past eighteen days, two Canadian farmers, Jacob Manning and his brother, David, have been held captive by the Americans in a log stable on Benjamin Roberts's farm, where Wade Hampton's army

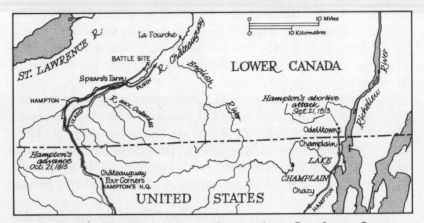

Wade Hampton's Movements, September–October, 1813

is camped. Suddenly word comes that the Major-General himself wishes to speak to them.

The Mannings are spies – part of a small group recruited by the British from the settlers of Hemmingford and Hinchinbrook townships just north of a border that was, until war broke out, little more than an imaginary line. This is smugglers' country. The settlers know one another intimately and, no matter what their allegiance, still continue an illicit trade – the Americans sneaking barrels of potash into Canada for sale in Montreal, the Canadians slipping over the line, pulling hand sleds loaded with ten-gallon kegs of hard-to-get whiskey. So much beef is shipped into Canada for the British Army that herds of cattle have left discernible tracks in the woods along the Hinchinbrook frontier.

For some time the Mannings have been supplying the British with reports of American troop movements. But on the night of October 2, an American patrol descended on their farmhouse near Franklin and surprised the two brothers asleep. Since that night they have been held under suspicion.

They are brought under guard to Hampton's headquarters at Smith's Tavern, where the Major-General himself receives them. A large and imposing Southerner in his sixtieth year, Hampton is known for his impatience, his hauteur, and his hasty temper. Subordinates and superiors find him difficult to get along with, perhaps because he is a self-made man with all the stubbornness, pride, and ego that this connotes. An uneducated farm boy – orphaned early in life by a

Cherokee raid that wiped out most of his family, including his parents – he is well on his way to becoming the wealthiest planter in the United States. He has a hunger for land – greed might be a better word – and has made a fortune in speculation, much of it bordering on the shady. In South Carolina he is the proprietor of vast plantations that support thousands of slaves, some of whom wait upon him here at Four Corners, to the raised eyebrows of the northern settlers. He is both a politician and a soldier, with a good Revolutionary record and a background that includes a stint in Congress and several other public offices. Now, entering his seventh decade, he seems to have lost his drive – the panache that made him one of General Thomas Sumter's most daring officers. He is not popular. Morgan Lewis has flatly refused to serve under him; several other officers at Fort Niagara have sworn they would resign their commissions if Hampton were placed in charge of that frontier.

His orders are to cross the border and march down the Châteauguay to the St. Lawrence. If Wilkinson attacks Kingston, this move will confuse the British. Otherwise, his army will join Wilkinson's on its sweep to Montreal.

Hampton is as much in the dark regarding British and Canadian strength and intentions as the British are of American strength and strategy. That is why he has called for the Manning brothers. He wants David Manning to take his best black charger, gallop to Montreal, and bring him back an estimate of the British defence force there. There will be no danger, the General assures Manning; no one will suspect him, and if he does his job well there will be a handsome reward.

Manning refuses.

"Are you not an American?" Hampton demands.

"Yes," says Manning. "I was born on the American side and I have many relations, but I am true to the British flag."

He is a Loyalist – a Tory who refused to fight against the British during the Revolution and was forced to move north of the border.

Hampton's famous temper flares. He roughly tells the Manning brothers that they are in his power and will be sent to the military prison at Greenbush if they do not toe the line.

The two backwoodsmen are not cowed. They reply, cheekily, that anything will be better than confinement in a filthy stable; perhaps they will be treated like human beings at Greenbush.

Hampton tries a different tack, asks if there is a fort at Montreal.

When they tell him that none exists, he refuses to believe it. He takes the two men to the tavern window overlooking the Roberts farm and proudly points out the size of his army.

Spread out before them, the brothers see an imposing spectacle: thousands of men striking their tents, cavalry cantering about, the infantry drilling in platoons. Clearly, Hampton is about to move across the Canadian border.

The General proudly asks how far the Mannings think a force of that size can go. Again, Jacob Manning cannot resist a cheeky answer.

"If it has good luck it may get to Halifax," he says – for Halifax is the depot to which prisoners of war are sent.

Angered, Hampton orders his officer of the guard, a local militia-man named Hollenbeck, to take the brothers back to the stable and keep them there for three days to prevent word of his advance reaching the British.

But Hollenbeck is an old friend and neighbour.

"Do you want anything to eat?" he asks.

"No," says Jacob.

"Well, then, put for home," says Hollenbeck. Off go the brothers with news of Hampton's advance.

Theirs is not the only intelligence to reach the British. Hampton's forward troops under Brigadier-General George Izard are already across the border. At four o'clock they reach Spears's farm at the junction of the Châteauguay and Outarde rivers and rout a small Canadian picket, which sounds the alarm. For weeks the border country has been in a state of tension, not knowing exactly where the American attack on Lower Canada will come. Now it is clear that Hampton's main force will advance along the cart track that borders the Châteauguay. His object is the St. Lawrence River and, surely, Montreal.

In the coming battle the defence of Canada will fall almost entirely to the French-Canadian militia. More than three hundred are already moving up the river road to a rendezvous point in the hardwood forest not far from the future settlement of Allan's Corners – the Sedentary Militia from Beauharnois in homespun blouses and blue toques, and two flank companies of the 5th Battalion of Select Embodied Militia in green coats with red facings. This is the notorious Devil's Own battalion recruited from the slums of Montreal and Quebec, and so called because of its reputation for thievery and disorder.

The following morning a more reliable force of Canadian Fencibles and Voltigeurs arrives. The latter unit consists not of habitants but of voyageurs, lumbermen, and city-bred youths. They have been drilled all winter like regulars by their leader, a thirty-five-year-old career soldier, Lieutenant-Colonel Charles-Michel d'Irumberry de Salaberry. They wear smart grey uniforms and fur hats and are used to fighting in their bare feet.

De Salaberry, who has been given charge of the Châteauguay frontier by his superior, the Swiss-born Major-General de Watteville, is that unique product of Lower Canada, the French-Canadian aristocrat. But he is no fop. De Rottenburg refers to him as "my dear Marquis of cannon powder." Short in stature, big-chested and muscular, he is a strict disciplinarian – brusque, impetuous, often harsh with his men. Dominique Ducharme, the victor at Beaver Dams, now back in Lower Canada, cannot forgive him for dispatching him to track down six deserters, whom he ordered shot. (Ducharme, had he known what would be their fate, would have let them escape.) De Salaberry's Voltigeurs, however, admire their leader because he is fair minded.

> This is our major, [they sing]
> The embodiment of the devil
> Who gives us death.
> There is no wolf or tiger
> Who could be so rough;
> Under the openness of the sky
> There is not his equal.

In the de Salaberry vocabulary, one word takes precedence over all others: honour. He cannot forget his father's remark to Prevost's predecessor, Sir James Craig. The elder de Salaberry openly opposed Craig, who wanted to destroy the rights of French Canadians. When Craig threatened to remove his means of livelihood, Ignace de Salaberry retorted: "You can, Sir James, take away my bread and that of my family, but my honour – never!"

The Voltigeurs no doubt know the story of the scar their colonel carries on his brow. It goes back to his days in a mixed regiment in the West Indies, when a German duellist killed his best friend.

The duellist: "I come just now from dispatching a French Canadian into another world."

De Salaberry: "We are going to finish lunch and then you will have the pleasure of dispatching another."

But it is the German who is dispatched, de Salaberry merely scarred.

He has been a soldier since the age of fourteen; three younger brothers have already died in the service. His father's patron and his own was the Duke of Kent, father of a future queen. The Duke prevented him from making an unfortunate marriage; the bride he later chose is a seigneur's daughter.

For weeks, de Salaberry has been spying on Hampton's pickets at Châteauguay Four Corners. Now he is prepared to meet the full force not far from the confluence of the Châteauguay and the English River.

He has chosen his position with care. Half a dozen ravines cut their way through the sandy soil at right angles to the Châteauguay River. These will be his lines of defence. The first three are only two hundred yards apart, the fourth half a mile to the rear. At least two more lie some distance downriver near La Fourche, where Major-General de Watteville's reserves and headquarters will be stationed.

By mid-day on October 22, de Salaberry has his axemen constructing breastworks of felled trees and tangled branches on the forward tip of each ravine. A mile or more in front of the leading ravine – a coulee forty feet deep on Robert Bryson's farm – they build a vast abatis extending in an arc from the river's gorge on the left to a swamp in the forest on their right.

The axemen are still hacking down trees and piling up slash when de Salaberry is reinforced in a dramatic fashion. In Kingston, on October 21, Sir George Prevost had decided to send a battalion of Select Embodied Militia – a mixed bag of French-Canadian and Scottish farmers – to Châteauguay. He called on their commander, Lieutenant-Colonel George Macdonell, to ask how soon the battalion could be under way.

"As soon as my men have done dinner," replied the Colonel, who is known through the county as Red George to distinguish him from a score of other Glengarry Macdonells.

Now Prevost has come post-haste to Châteauguay where, to his astonishment, he encounters Red George. The battalion has made the trip in just sixty hours without a man absent.

That same day, October 24, as Hampton's main body moves up along the road his engineers have hacked through the bush, a spy watches them go by and carefully counts the guns, the wagons, and the troops, immediately sending detailed reports to the British.

More than fourteen hundred of Hampton's militiamen, he writes, have refused to cross the border. The Americans are badly clothed, having so little winter gear that they have had to cast lots for great-coats. The Virginians are not used to the Canadian weather. One regiment of a thousand Southerners has lost half its force to "a kind of distemper." He has also heard a report that Major-General Wilkinson is bringing his army down the St. Lawrence by boat and plans to join Hampton in an assault on Montreal.

Now the British are aware of the full American strategy. Hampton has upwards of four thousand men assembled at Spears's farm. All that stands between him and the St. Lawrence are the sixteen hundred militiamen seven miles downriver. The brunt of the attack will be borne by de Salaberry's three hundred Canadian Voltigeurs and Fencibles manning the forward ravines. They wait behind the tangle of roots and branches, knowing that they are heavily outnumbered and outgunned. The spy has counted nine pieces of field artillery, a howitzer, and a mortar and suspects there is more moving toward the Canadian lines by an alternative route.

Who is this secret agent who seems to know everything that is going on at Spears's farm and Four Corners? He is, of course, David Manning, the Loyalist farmer, whom Wade Hampton believes to be safely behind bars at Greenbush. But Hampton has not reckoned on the uncertain loyalties of the border people. He does not know, will never know, that Hollenbeck, his sergeant of the guard, is not only David Manning's friend and neighbour but also an informant who is perfectly prepared to salute the Stars and Stripes in public while secretly supplying the British with all the information and gossip they require.

●

SPEARS'S FARM, Châteauguay River, Lower Canada, October 25, 1813

Major-General Wade Hampton considers the problem of de Salaberry's defence in depth and realizes he cannot storm those fortified ravines without serious loss. He decides instead on a surprise flanking movement that will take the French Canadians in the rear.

He summons Robert Purdy, Colonel of the veteran U.S. 4th Infantry, and gives him his orders. Purdy will take fifteen hundred elite troops, cross the Châteauguay River at a nearby ford, proceed down the right bank under cover of darkness, bypass de Salaberry's defences on the opposite shore, recross the river at dawn by way of a second ford, and attack the enemy from behind their lines. Once Hampton hears the rattle of Purdy's muskets, he will launch a frontal attack on the abatis, thus catching de Salaberry's slender force between the claws of a pincer.

It is an ingenious plan on paper, impossible to carry out in practice. Hampton is proposing that Purdy and his men, accompanied by guides, plunge through sixteen miles of thick wood and hemlock swamp in pitch-darkness. That would be difficult in familiar territory; here it becomes a nightmare. The guides prove worthless, have, in fact, warned Hampton that they are not acquainted with the country. But Hampton is bewitched by a fixed idea; nothing will swerve him.

The result is disaster. Hampton accompanies the expedition to the first ford, then returns to camp. The night is cold; rain begins to fall; there is no moon. On the far side of the river Purdy's men flounder into a creek, stumble through a swamp, trip over fallen trees, stagger through thick piles of underbrush. Any semblance of order vanishes.

After two miles the guides themselves are lost. Purdy realizes he cannot continue in the dark. The men spend the night in the rain, shivering in their summer clothing, unable to light a fire for fear of betraying the plan.

At the camp, Hampton receives a rude shock. A letter arrives from the Quartermaster General relaying Armstrong's instructions to build huts for the army's winter quarters at Four Corners – south of the border. *Winter quarters at Four Corners!* Hampton has been expecting to winter at Montreal. The order can have one meaning only: Armstrong doubts that the expedition will reach its objective. The fight goes out of Hampton. Heartsick, he considers recalling Purdy's force but realizes that in the black night it cannot be found.

Dawn arrives, wan and damp, the dead leaves of autumn drooping wetly from the trees. In a tangle of brush and swamp, Purdy shakes his men awake. On the opposite bank, the American camp is all abustle, the forward elements already in motion along the wagon road that leads to the French-Canadian position.

In spite of his intelligence system, de Salaberry is not expecting an attack this morning. A party of his axemen, guarded by forty soldiers, is strengthening the abatis a mile in front of the forward ravine when, at about 10 A.M., the first Americans come bounding across the clearing, firing their muskets. De Salaberry, well to the

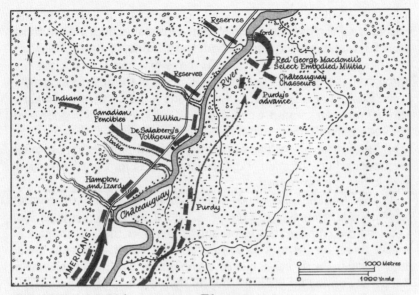

The Battle of Châteauguay: Phase 1

rear, hears the staccato sounds of gunfire, moves up quickly with reinforcements. The workmen have scattered, and the Americans, cheering lustily, push forward, only to be halted by musket fire.

De Salaberry – a commanding figure in his grey fur-trimmed coat – moves forward on the abatis, climbs up on a large hemlock that has been uprooted by the wind, and, screened from enemy view by two large trees, watches the blue line of Americans moving down the river road toward him. The firing has sputtered out; the expected attack does not come.

Hampton is waiting to hear from Purdy across the river. The Americans settle down to cook lunch. On the Canadian side of the abatis a company of Beauharnois militia kneel in prayer and are told by their captain that having done their duty to their God, he now expects they will do their duty to their King.

Meanwhile, de Salaberry's scouts have discovered Purdy's presence on the east bank of the river – a few stragglers emerging briefly from the dense woods along the far bank. Purdy is badly behind schedule; his force of fifteen hundred has got no farther than a point directly across from de Salaberry's forward position. Back goes word to Red George Macdonell, who has been given the task of guarding the ford in the rear. Macdonell sends two companies of his Select

Embodied Militia across the river to reinforce a small picket of Châteauguay Chasseurs who, despite their formidable title, are untrained local farmers, co-opted into the Sedentary Militia of Lower Canada.

The Canadians move through the dense pine forest, peering through the labyrinth of naked trunks, seeking the advancing Americans. Purdy's advance guard of about one hundred men is splashing through a cedar swamp when the two forces meet. Both sides open fire. Macdonell's men stand fast, but the Chasseurs turn and flee. The American advance party also turns tail and plunges back through the woods where the main body, mistaking them for Canadians, opens fire, killing their own men.

Purdy, thinking the woods full of enemies, attempts to regroup and sends a messenger to Hampton, asking for reinforcements. The courier heads for Spears's farm, only to discover that Hampton is no longer there, having moved downriver. As a result, Hampton has no idea whether Purdy has achieved his objective. Nor can he tell what is happening on the far bank because of the thickness of the forest.

Finally, at two o'clock Hampton decides to act. He orders Brigadier-General George Izard to attack in line. Izard, another South Carolina aristocrat, is a professional soldier of considerable competence. His well-drilled brigade moves down the road toward the vast tangle of the abatis.

Behind their breastwork, de Salaberry's Voltigeurs watch as a tall American officer rides forward. After the battle is done, some will claim to remember his cry in French, which will become a legend along the Châteauguay:

"Brave Canadians, surrender yourselves; we wish you no harm!"

At which de Salaberry himself fires, the American drops from his horse, and the battle – such as it is – is joined.

De Salaberry shouts to his bugler to sound the call to open fire. The noise of sporadic musketry mingles with the cries of a small body of Caughnawaga Indians stationed in the woods to the right of the Canadian line. The Americans, firing by platoons, as on a parade ground, pour volley after volley into the woods, believing that the main Canadian force is concentrated there. The lead balls whistle harmlessly through the treetops.

Now Red George Macdonell sounds his own bugles as a signal that he is advancing. Other bugles take up the refrain; de Salaberry sends buglers into the woods to trumpet in all directions until the Americans believe they are heavily outnumbered. Izard hesitates – a fatal error,

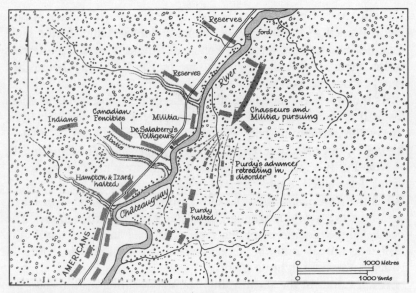

The Battle of Châteauguay: Phase 2

for he loses momentum. Two other ruses reinforce his misconception about the Canadian strength. Some of Macdonell's men appear at the edge of the woods wearing red coats, then disappear, reverse their jackets, which are lined with white flannel, and pop out again, appearing to be another corps. In addition, twenty Indians are sent to dash through the forest to the right of the Canadian line, appearing from time to time brandishing tomahawks. The ruse is similar to the one used by Brock against Hull the previous year: the Americans are led to believe that hundreds of savages are lurking in the depths of the woods.

"Defy, my damned ones!" cries de Salaberry. "Defy! If you do not dare, you are not men!"

The battle continues for the best part of an hour, the Americans firing rolling volleys, platoon by platoon, the half-trained Canadians returning the fire raggedly. There are few casualties on either side. Izard does not attempt to storm the abatis.

Now de Salaberry turns his attention to the action on the far side of the river. The two Canadian companies that drove off Purdy's forward troops have been advancing cautiously toward his position and are now tangling with his main force.

De Salaberry hurries to the river bank, climbs a tree, and begins to

225

shout orders to Captain Charles Daly of the Embodied Militia, speaking in French so the Americans cannot understand him. At the same time he lines up his force of Voltigeurs, Indians, and Beauharnois militia along his side of the river to fire on Purdy's men, should they emerge from the woods.

As the two forces face each other in the swampy forest, Daly orders his men to kneel before they fire, a manoeuvre that saves their lives. Purdy's overwhelming body of crack troops responds with a shattering volley, but most of it passes harmlessly over the Canadians' heads.

Now Purdy's force swoops forward on the river flank of the Canadians, determined to take them from the rear. The situation is critical, but as the Americans burst out of the woods and onto the river bank, de Salaberry, watching through his glass, gives the order to fire. The bushes on the far side erupt in a sheet of flame. The Americans, badly mangled, retreat into the forest; exhausted by fourteen hours of struggle, they can fight no more.

A lull comes in the skirmishing. Hampton, sitting his horse on the right of his troops, is in a quandary. A courier has just swum the river with news of Purdy's predicament. The Major-General is rattled, angry at Purdy for not reporting his position sooner, unaware that the original message has gone astray.

He considers his options. Izard has not attempted to storm the abatis; to do so, Hampton is convinced, would cause heavy casualties. He believes there are five to six thousand men opposing him. In fact, there is only a fraction of that number. De Salaberry has perhaps three hundred men in his advanced position. Macdonell has about two hundred in reserve. The remainder (apart from the two companies across the river) are several miles back at La Fourche, where the English River joins the Châteauguay. These do not number more than six hundred, and none have been committed to battle. De Salaberry, either by accident or by design, has failed to inform Major-General de Watteville of the American advance—a delinquency that nettles his senior and might easily provoke a court martial in the event of failure.

De Salaberry is a bold officer. His defensive position is strong. But it is Hampton's failure of nerve more than de Salaberry's brilliance of execution that decides the outcome of the so-called Battle of Châteauguay. In reality, it is no more than a skirmish, with troops on both sides peppering away at each other at extreme range and to little effect. De Salaberry, on his side of the river, has lost three men killed, eight wounded.

Hampton's heart is not in it. Purdy is bogged down, the afternoon is dragging on, rain is in the offing, twilight but a few hours away. A host of emotions boils up inside the hesitant commander: jealousy of Wilkinson, who will gain all the glory if Hampton, by a victory, helps him to seize Montreal; anger at Armstrong, who he rightly believes is resigned to defeat; and, most telling, a lack of confidence in himself. He does not have the will to win. Much of his force has yet to be engaged in battle. His artillery has not been used. Izard's brigade has fallen silent. Suddenly, the Major-General sends an order to Purdy to break off the engagement on the right bank and tells his bugler to sound the withdrawal.

De Salaberry's men watch in astonishment as the brigade retires in perfect order. Oddly, they make no attempt to harass it, waiting instead for a rally that never comes. Their colonel, expecting a renewed attack at any moment, has sent back word to all the houses along the river to prepare for a retreat and to burn all buildings. It is not necessary.

Of this Colonel Purdy, hidden in the forest, is unaware. As the sun sets he starts to move his wounded across the river on rafts and sends a message to his commander asking that a regiment be detached to cover his own landing. He is shocked and angered to discover that Hampton has already retreated three miles, deserting him without support.

The following morning the once elite detachment straggles into Hampton's camp, many without hats, knapsacks, or weapons, their clothing torn, half starved, sick with fatigue, their morale shattered. Purdy is thoroughly disgusted. Several of his officers have behaved badly in the skirmish, but when Purdy tries to arrest them for desertion or cowardice, Hampton countermands the order. Purdy reports to the General that someone in the commissary is selling the troops' rations, but Hampton brushes away the complaint. The sick, in Purdy's view, are being so badly neglected that many have died from want of medical care. In common with several other officers, Purdy is convinced that Hampton is drinking so heavily that he is no longer able to command.

De Salaberry, meanwhile, feels snubbed by the British high command. Sir George Prevost, who arrived on the field with de Watteville shortly after the victory, is his usual cautious self. The brunt of the struggle has been borne by a handful of French-Canadian militia. One thousand fresh troops, held in reserve, are available to harass the enemy. De Salaberry is eager to do just that, but neither senior commander will allow it. Both are remarkably restrained in their congratulations, perhaps because of de Salaberry's delinquency in not informing them of the American attack. And de Salaberry himself is embittered because, he believes, he has not been given sole credit for repulsing the invaders. "It grieves me to the heart," he declares to the Adjutant-General, "to see that I must share the merit of the action." For Prevost and de Watteville insist on a portion of the glory.

Hampton meanwhile orders his entire force back across the border to Four Corners "for the preservation of the army" – a statement that would astonish the British, who are convinced that the Americans are planning a second attack. On October 28, Indian scouts confirm Hampton's decision.

It has been, as de Salaberry asserts in a letter to his father, "a most extraordinary affair." In this battle in which some 460 troops forced the retirement of four thousand, the victors have lost only five killed and sixteen wounded with four men missing. (The American casualties number about fifty.) It has been a small battle but for Canada profoundly significant. A handful of civilian soldiers, almost all French Canadian, has, with scarcely any help, managed to turn back the gravest invasion threat of the war. Had Hampton managed to reach the St. Lawrence to join with Wilkinson's advancing army, who would give odds on the survival of Montreal? And with Montreal gone and Upper Canada cut off, the British presence in North America would be reduced to a narrow defensive strip in the lower province. On a military sand table, the battle of Châteauguay seems no more than a silly skirmish. Yet without this victory, what price a Canadian nation, stretching from sea to sea?

●

GRENADIER ISLAND, Thousand Islands, New York State, October 28, 1813

"All our hopes," James Wilkinson writes to the Secretary of War, "have been very nearly blasted." Two days have passed since Hampton's defeat at Châteauguay (a calamity unknown to Wilkinson) and the great flotilla designed to conquer Montreal – or will it be Kingston first? – is still stuck at its rendezvous point. The troops are drenched from the incessant rains, boats are smashed, stores scattered, hundreds sick, scores drunk.

Wilkinson puts the best possible face on these disasters, relying on the Deity to solve his problems:

"Thanks to the same Providence which placed us in jeopardy, we are surmounting our difficulties and, God willing, I shall pass Prescott on the night of the 1st or 2nd proximo, if some unforeseen obstacle does not present to forbid me."

Unforeseen obstacles have already presented themselves in quantity. On the journey from Sackets Harbor to Grenadier Island – a mere eighteen miles – the flotilla was scattered by gales so furious that great trees were uprooted on the shores. Some boats have not yet arrived.

A third of all the rations have been lost. It is virtually impossible to disentangle the rest from the other equipment. Shivering in the driving rain, the men have torn the oilcloths off the ration boxes for protection, so that the bread becomes soggy and inedible. Hospital stores have been pilfered – the hogsheads of brandy and port wine, which the doctors believe essential for good health, tapped and consumed. The guard is drunk; the officer in charge finds he cannot keep his men sober. The boats are so badly overloaded that they have become difficult to row or steer. Sickness increases daily. One hundred and ninety-six men are so ill that Wilkinson – himself prostrate with dysentery – orders them returned to Sackets Harbor. In spite of the army's shortage of rations, the American islanders prefer to sell their produce to the British on the north shore. When Jarvis Hanks, a fourteen-year-old drummer boy with the 11th U.S. Infantry, tries to buy some potatoes from a local farmer for fifty cents a bushel, the man refuses, saying he can get a dollar a bushel in Kingston. That night, Hanks and his friends steal the entire crop.

Some of the officers are still half convinced that Wilkinson intends to attack Kingston. Chauncey, in fact, does not learn until October 30 that the Major-General has made up his mind to take the flotilla down the river, joining with Hampton to attack Montreal. The Commodore is, in his own words, "disappointed and mortified." He clearly does not believe that such a plan has much chance of success, for the season is far advanced.

Three brigades finally set out for the next rendezvous point, at French Creek on the American side of the river directly opposite

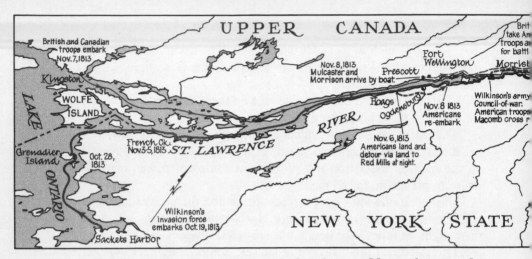

Wilkinson Moves on Montreal, October 31–November 11, 1813

Gananoque. Brigadier-General Jacob Brown manages to get down the river; bad weather forces the other two back. The bulk of the army arrives on November 3, followed by Wilkinson, now so ill that he has to be carried ashore.

The disillusioned Chauncey, who feels that his navy has been relegated to the position of a mere transport service for the army, is supposed to be guarding the entrance to the St. Lawrence to protect Wilkinson's flotilla from pursuit by British gunboats. But while Chauncey's squadron lurks in the south channel, Sir James Yeo's daring second-in-command, Captain William Howe Mulcaster (the same officer who refused the Lake Erie command) nips down the north channel, evades the Americans, moves down to French Creek, skirmishes with Brown's brigade, then whips back to Kingston to report at last that Montreal is the enemy's objective.

The tangle with Mulcaster again delays Wilkinson. The full flotilla does not leave French Creek until November 5.

Providence has at last smiled on the ailing general; the valley of the St. Lawrence is bathed in an Indian summer glow as six thousand men in 350 boats, forming a procession five miles long, slide down the great river, flags flying, brass buttons gleaming, fifes and drums playing, boatmen chorusing. There is one drawback: Mulcaster is not far behind.

On November 6, the flotilla reaches Morristown. Wilkinson is four days later than his most pessimistic promise to Armstrong. Now he must halt, for he fears the British guns at Prescott, a dozen miles

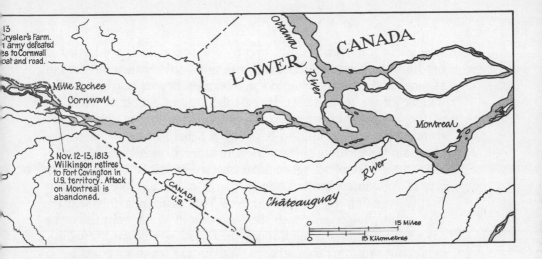

downstream. He decides to strip his boats of all armament, march his men along the river bank, hauling the supplies in wagons, and pass Prescott with the lightly manned boats under cover of darkness. That will cost him another day.

While the boats are being unloaded and the troops formed, he issues a proclamation to the British settlers along the river, urging the farmers to remain at home, promising that the persons and property of non-combatants will be protected.

These sentiments might as well be directed to the wind. This is Loyalist country, and the settlers are already priming their muskets to harass the American flotilla. The river shortly becomes a shooting gallery, with gunfire exploding from the bushes at every twist in the channel.

At noon, Colonel William King, Hampton's adjutant-general, arrives with the official news of the débâcle at Châteauguay. Morgan Lewis takes King downriver to find Wilkinson, who is reconnoitring Prescott. The three men sit on a log as King describes Hampton's defeat, adding that "our best troops behaved in the most rascally manner."

"Damn such an army!" Wilkinson cries. "A man might as well be in hell as command it."

Still, Hampton's force remains intact – that is some consolation. The two armies number close to eleven thousand men – more than enough, surely, to seize Montreal.

At eight that night the river is shrouded in a heavy fog. Brown, the officer of the day, gives the order to move. Out into the water they go with muffled oars. The fog lifts, and Brown's leading gig is subjected to a fearful cannonade. Fifty twenty-four-pound balls are hurled at her from the Canadian shore but with no effect, for the guns are out of range and set too high to do any damage. Brown halts the flotilla, waiting for the moon to set. Its pale light, gleaming on the bayonets of the troops trudging along the shore, has helped identify the manoeuvre to the British, as have signal lights flashing in the homes of certain Ogdensburg citizens friendly to the British cause.

In the midst of all this uproar the irrepressible Winfield Scott arrives. Wilkinson had left him in charge of a skeleton command at Fort George until relieved by the New York State militia. Now, having left his own brigade with the Secretary of War's permission, he has ridden for thirty hours through the forests of northern New York in a sleet storm. Taken aboard Wilkinson's passage boat, he is stimulated by the bursting of shells and rockets and the hissing of cannonballs. Scott finds it sublime, though he distrusts and despises his general – an "unprincipled imbecile," in Scott's acid view. Years before he was court-martialed for referring publicly to Wilkinson as a liar, a scoundrel, and a traitor. But the ambitious Scott has learned that the road to promotion and power must not be strewn with invective and keeps his feelings to himself. The two men, who have no use for one another, conceal their mutual antipathy behind masks of cordiality.

Wilkinson leaves the passage boat and returns to his gig. Scott, knowing his reputation, is convinced he is drunk, but it is more likely that he is simply intoxicated from repeated draughts of opium, prescribed to ease his dysentery, an ailment that has now spread to most of the older officers, including his second-in-command, Morgan Lewis.

Wilkinson's condition is so serious that he is finally forced to go ashore and relieve himself at Daniel Thorpe's farmhouse on the river bank a mile below Ogdensburg. Benjamin Forsyth of the rifle company meets him and helps him up the bank with the aid of another officer. Wilkinson is muttering to himself, hurling imprecations at the British, threatening to blow the enemy's garrison to dust and lay waste the entire countryside. The two officers sit him down by the hearth, post a guard at the door to keep the spectacle from prying eyes, and try to decide what to do. By this time Wilkinson is singing bawdy songs and telling obscene stories, to the horror of Thorpe, who also believes him to be drunk. Finally, the General begins to nod and, to the relief of all, allows himself to be put to bed.

November 7 dawns clear and bright, a perfect day for sailing. But the British have reinforced every bend with cannon and sharp-shooters. Wilkinson detaches an elite corps of twelve hundred soldiers to clear the bank, with Forsyth's riflemen detailed as a rearguard. By nightfall the flotilla has moved only eight miles.

Wilkinson is losing his nerve. In his weakened condition he imagines himself in the grip of forces he cannot control. Providence has been fickle, wrecking all his plans for a speedy descent down the river. He has little faith in his own army, especially the contingent from Sackets Harbor. He knows that he has been held up too long, giving Mulcaster every chance to catch him from the rear: the word is that two armed schooners and seven gunboats have already reached Prescott carrying a thousand – perhaps fifteen hundred – men. In his fevered imagination, the General magnifies the forces opposed to him. The farmers on the Canadian shore have been purposely stuffing their interrogators' heads with wild stories about the dangers ahead – the terrifying rapids, batteries of guns at every narrows, savage Indians prowling the forest, no fodder for the horses. It is said that the army will face five thousand British regulars and twenty thousand Canadian militia – a fantastic overstatement.

On November 8, Wilkinson, who can hardly rise from his bunk, calls a council of war. It agrees, hesitantly, to continue on to Montreal. Still concerned about the forces gathering on the Canadian side, the Major-General orders Jacob Brown to disembark his brigade and take command of the combined forces clearing the north shore.

Ahead lies the dreaded Long Sault, eight miles of white water in which no boats can manoeuvre under enemy fire. Brown's job is to clear the banks so that the flotilla can navigate these rapids without fear of attack. Harassed now from the rear, Wilkinson cannot get under way until Brown reaches the head of the rapids. Wilkinson moves eleven miles and, with Mulcaster nipping at his heels, stops again.

The following day, November 10, Mulcaster's gunboats move in to the attack. At the same time, Brown's force on the shore runs into heavy resistance. By the time Brown has cleared the bank, the pilots refuse to take the boats through the white water. The flotilla moves two miles past John Crysler's farm to Cook's Point, a mile or two above the Long Sault. The troops on shore build fires from the farmers' rail fences and shiver out the night in the rain and sleet. Jarvis Hanks, the drummer boy in the 11th, pulls a leather cap over his head and curls up so close to the fire that by morning both his cap and his shoes are charred. Brown, meanwhile, has gone aboard Wilkinson's passage boat to find out exactly who is in charge. But Wilkinson is too sick to see him. It has taken eight days for the fleet to move eighty miles. A log drifting down the river could make the same distance in two.

•

JOHN CRYSLER'S FARM, St. Lawrence River, Upper Canada, November 11, 1813

Dawn breaks, bleak and soggy. John Loucks, one of three troopers in the Provincial Dragoons posted with three companies of Canadian Voltigeurs and a few Indians a mile ahead of the main British force, spots a movement through the trees ahead. A party of Americans is advancing from Cook's Point, where Wilkinson's flotilla is anchored. A musket explodes from the woods on his left, where a party of Indians is stationed. The Americans reply with a volley that kicks the sand in front of the troopers' horses. Off goes young Loucks at a gallop, heading for the headquarters of the British commander, Lieutenant-Colonel Joseph Wanton Morrison.

As the three dragoons dash through the ranks of the 49th Regiment, Lieutenant John Sewell is in the act of toasting a piece of breakfast pork on the point of his sword. He needs hot nourishment, for he has slept on the cold ground all night, his firelock between his legs to protect it from the icy rain, laced with sleet. Now it seems, there will be no time for breakfast, as his company commander shouts to him:

"Jack, drop cooking, the enemy is advancing."

The British troops are scrambling into position behind a stout rail fence, but the warning is several hours premature. All that Loucks has encountered is an American reconnaissance party. A regular officer chides him gently for his precipitate gallop: it is perfectly all right to fall back, he explains, but it is bad form to ride so fast in the face of the enemy.

At his headquarters in the Crysler farmhouse, hard by the King's Highway that runs along the river bank, Colonel Morrison assesses his position. He has been chasing Wilkinson in Mulcaster's gunboats for five days, ever since word reached Kingston that the main American attack would be on Montreal. Now he has caught up with him. Will the Americans stand and fight or will the chase continue? With a force of only eight hundred men to challenge Wilkinson's seven

234

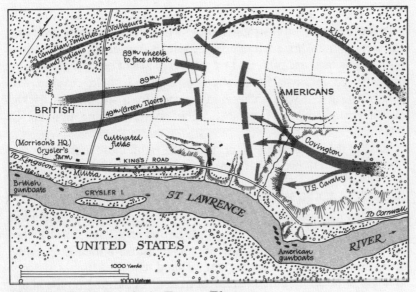

The map contains the following labels: Canadian Fencibles and Indians, Voltigeurs, Ripley, 89th wheels to face attack, 89th, AMERICANS, BRITISH, 49th (Green Tigers), (Morrison's HQ) Crysler's Farm, Cultivated fields, Covington, To Kingston, Militia, KING'S ROAD, British gunboats, CRYSLER I., ST LAWRENCE, U.S. Cavalry, To Cornwall, UNITED STATES, American gunboats, RIVER, 1000 Yards, 1000 Metres

The Battle of Crysler's Farm: Phase I

thousand, Morrison is not eager for a pitched battle. But if he must have one, it will be on ground of his choosing – a European-style battle here on an open plain where his regulars can manoeuvre, as on a parade ground, standing shoulder to shoulder in two parallel lines, each man occupying twenty-two inches of space, advancing with the bayonet, wheeling effortlessly when ordered, or moving into eche-lon – a staggered series of platoons, each supporting its neighbour.

This is the kind of warfare for which his two regiments have been trained: Brock's old regiment, the 49th, known as the Green Tigers both from the facings on their lapels and for the fierceness of their attack; and his own regiment, the 89th. The Green Tigers have had their fill of fighting, from Queenston to Stoney Creek, but the 89th are new to North America. Morrison, their commanding officer and senior commander on the field, has just turned fifty. Like his father before him, he has served half his life in the British Army, shifted from continent to continent wherever his country needs him, from Holland, where he was wounded, to the Caribbean, to Canada. He has never handled a battalion in battle; but he has been singled out as an attentive and zealous officer, and he has solid support in John Harvey, his second-in-command, and Charles Plenderleath of the 49th, both veterans of Stoney Creek.

He has chosen his position carefully, anchoring his thin line between the river on his right (where Mulcaster's gunboats will give support) and an impenetrable black ash swamp about half a mile to his left. His men are protected by a heavy fence of cedar logs, five feet high. Ahead for a half-mile stretches a muddy field covered with winter wheat, cut with gullies and bisected by a stream that trickles out of the swamp to become a deep ravine running into the St. Lawrence.

Behind the fence, the 49th occupies the right, close to the river and to the King's Highway that runs along the bank. The 89th is on the left, nearer the swamp; its soldiers wear scarlet coats, but the battle-seasoned 49th hide their distinctive tunics with grey overcoats.

Half a mile forward of this main body are lighter troops, including Canadian Fencibles. Another half-mile farther on are the skirmishers – Indians and Voltigeurs, the latter almost invisible in their grey home-spun, concealed behind rocks, stumps, and fences.

Though heavily outnumbered, Morrison is counting on the ability of the British regulars to hold fast against the more individualistic Americans. Here the contrast between the two countries, so recently separated and estranged, becomes apparent. Wilkinson's men are experienced bush fighters, brought up with firearms, blooded in frontier Indian wars, used to taking individual action in skirmishes where every man must act on his own if he is to escape with a whole skin. But the British soldier is drilled to stand unflinching with his comrades in the face of exploding cannon, to hold his fire until ordered so that the maximum effect of the spraying muskets can be felt, to move in machine-like unison with hundreds of others, each man an automaton. The British regular follows orders implicitly; the American volunteer is less subservient, sometimes to the point of anarchy. This British emphasis on "order" extends, in Canada, to government. If the Canadians accept a form of benevolent dictatorship, or at least autocracy, it is because they have opted for a lifestyle different from that of their neighbours, a lifestyle based on British attitudes and institutions. Under the impetus of war, that attitude is hardening.

Morrison has one advantage of which he is unaware. The American high command is prostrate. In separate boats anchored at Cook's Point, the chief of the invading army and his second-in-command both lie deathly ill, unable to direct any battle. Lewis, confined to a closet-like cabin and dosing himself on blackberry jelly, is even less capable than his enfeebled superior. Wilkinson, unable to rise from his bunk, awaits word from Jacob Brown on shore that the rapids ahead have been cleared of British troops. At 10:30 a dragoon arrives with the expected reassurance. The Commander-in-Chief is in a quandary. Mulcaster is directly astern. What if the British gunboats should slip past him? He gives a tentative order to the flotilla to get under way and orders Brigadier-General Boyd, on land, to begin marching his men toward Cornwall. Even as he does so he is alerted to the presence of British redcoats on Crysler's field. At the same time Mulcaster begins to lob shot in his direction. Wilkinson decides to destroy the small British force before moving on.

This confusion and delay does not sit well with John Boyd on shore. Since early morning, he has been subjected to a variety of conflicting orders. At noon, a violent storm further reduces the morale of the troops who have now been under arms for nearly forty-eight hours. Boyd rides impatiently to the river bank where he finally receives a pencilled order to put his troops in motion in twenty minutes as soon as the guns can be put ashore. It is the last order he receives from Wilkinson.

Boyd will command the American forces in the battle to follow. A one-time soldier of fortune who for twenty years sold his services to a variety of Indian princes, including the Nizam of Hyderabad and the Peshwa of Poona, he exchanged his turban and lance in 1808 for a colonel's eagle in the U.S. 4th Infantry. Commissioned brigadier-general at the opening of the war, he does not enjoy the esteem of his peers. Brown cannot stand him. Scott considers him imbecilic. Lewis, in a vicious indictment, describes him as "a combination of ignorance, vanity, and petulance, with nothing to recommend him but that species of bravery in the field which is vaporing, boisterous, stifling reflection, blinding observation." Not the best man to put up against British regulars.

Boyd's first move is to send Lieutenant-Colonel Eleazar Ripley's regiment across the muddy fields and over a boggy creek bed to probe Morrison's forward skirmishers in the woods on the British left. Ripley advances half a mile when a line of Voltigeurs suddenly rises from concealment and delivers two volleys at his men who, disregarding the cries of their officers, leap behind stumps and open individual fire until, their ammunition exhausted, they run back out of range. Ripley retires with them but soon returns to the attack with reinforcements and drives the Voltigeurs back.

John Sewell, the British lieutenant whose breakfast was so rudely

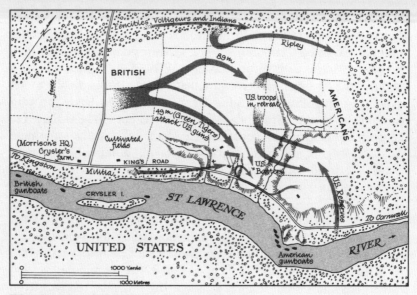

The Battle of Crysler's Farm: Phase 2

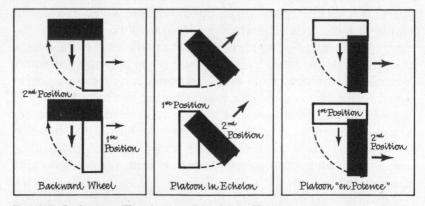

British Infantry Tactics at Crysler's Farm

interrupted, is standing with his fellow Green Tigers in the thin line formed by the two British regiments when he sees the grey-clad Voltigeurs burst from the woods on his left, pursued by the Americans. The situation is critical. If Ripley's men can get around the 89th, which holds the left flank, and attack the British from the rear, the battle is as good as lost.

Morrison now executes the first of a series of parade-ground manoeuvres, wheeling the entire 89th Regiment from its position in line, facing east, to face north – *en potence*, to use the military term. Emerging from the woods, the Americans encounter a solid line of scarlet-coated men firing muskets in unison. They break and run. The contrast between the fire of the opposing forces is so distinct that the women and children hiding in Captain John Crysler's cellar can easily tell the American guns from the British: the former make an irregular pop-pop-pop; the latter, at regular intervals, resound "like a tremendous roll of thunder."

Thwarted in his attempt to turn the British left, Boyd now advances his three main brigades across the open wheatfields in an attempt to seize the British right. Leonard Covington, the forty-five-year-old Marylander who commands the 3rd Brigade – a veteran of Anthony Wayne's frontier army – is fooled by the grey coats of the 49th directly in front of him.

"Come, lads, let me see how you will deal with these militia men," he shouts.

But the disguised Tigers are already executing another familiar drill – moving into echelon, a line of staggered platoons, which, supported by six-pounders, fire rolling volleys against the advancing Americans.

The action has now become general, a confused mêlée of struggling men, half obscured by dirty grey smoke, weaving forward and backward, floundering in the ankle-deep mud, splashing and dying in the stream beds, tumbling into gullies, clawing their way out of ravines until no one, when it is over, is able to produce a coherent account of exactly what went on.

Certain key moments emerge from the fog of battle. In one of several assaults on the British line, Brigadier-General Covington falls mortally wounded while attempting to seize the British cannon. His second-in-command is also killed. This critical loss, followed by the loss of two more senior officers, causes confusion in the American 3rd Brigade.

At about the same time, the American artillery, hauled from the boats and late getting into position, begins to harass the advancing British. Morrison orders Plenderleath to attack the guns with the heavy troops of the 49th, for unless they can be silenced the grapeshot will cut the outnumbered British to pieces.

Plenderleath's Green Tigers are about 120 yards from the enemy. Off they go through the deeply ploughed field, trampling the grain, kicking up the mud, tearing down two snake fences that bar their path, unable to fire back as they struggle with the heavy logs under a galling hail of shot from the American six-pounders.

John Sewell, advancing with his company into the hail of grape, sees his captain killed, takes over, and suddenly spies a squadron of American dragoons galloping down the King's road on his right. He realizes the danger: if the horsemen get around the flank, they can wheel about and charge the British from the rear. Fortunately, another drill book manoeuvre exists to meet this threat. Captain Ellis on the right wing executes it under Plenderleath's command, wheeling his men backward to the left to face the line of cavalry. Sewell notes that the entire movement, which the Americans believe to be a retreat, is carried out with all the coolness of a review as the commands ring out over the crash of grape and canister: *Halt...Front... Pivot...Cover...Left wheel into line...Fire by platoons from the centre to the flank.* The effect is shattering as the wounded American horses, snorting and neighing, flounder about, their saddles empty.

At the same time, a light company of the 89th stationed well ahead of the main ravine charges the American artillery, captures a six-pounder, and kills its crew. By now the whole American line is giving way, and the retreat is saved from becoming a rout only by the presence of American reserves.

Wilkinson, who has spent the day in his bunk lamenting his ill fortune at not being with his men, tries to prevent a pell-mell rush to the boats, exclaiming that the British will say that the Americans were running away and claim a victory. He sends a message to Boyd, asking if he can maintain himself on the bank that night to preserve some vestige of American honour. Boyd's answer is a curt *No*: the men are exhausted and famished; they need a complete night of rest.

Boyd now busies himself with the mandatory report of the day's action, which is, as always in defeat, a masterpiece of dissembling. He cannot actually claim victory but comes as close to it as he can, larding his account with a litany of alibis:

> ...though the result of this action were not so brilliant and decisive as I could have wished, and the first stages of it seemed to promise, yet when it is recollected that the troops had been long exposed to hard privations and fatigues, the inclement storms from which they could have no shelter; that the enemy were superior to us in numbers [sic], and greatly superior in position, and supported

by 7 or 8 heavy gunboats; that the action being unexpected, was necessarily commenced without much concert; that we were, by unavoidable circumstances long deprived of our artillery; and that the action was warmly and obstinately contested for more than three hours, during which there were but a few short cessations of musketry and cannon; when all these circumstances are recollected, perhaps this day may be thought to have added some reputation to the American arms. And if, on this occasion, you shall believe me to have done my duty, and accomplished any of your purposes, I shall be satisfied....

Wilkinson, in his report to the Secretary of War, does not shilly-shally. He inflates the British strength from 800 to 2,170, bumps up the British casualties from 170 to 500, and declares that "although the imperious obligations of duty did not allow me sufficient time to rout the enemy, they were beaten...."

But it is Wilkinson who is beaten. "Emaciated almost to a skeleton, unable to sit my horse, or to move ten paces without assistance," he seeks an excuse to give up the grand campaign and receives it the morning after the battle in the form of a letter from General Hampton.

The two armies were supposed to meet just below the Long Sault, at St. Regis opposite Cornwall. Wilkinson's flotilla makes the passage, but Hampton is not there and never will be. It is impossible, he reports, to transport enough supplies to the St. Lawrence to feed the army; his arrival would only weaken the existing force; the roads are impracticable for wheeled transport; his troops are raw, sick, exhausted, dispirited. He intends to go back to Plattsburgh on Lake Champlain and strain every effort to throw himself on the enemy's flank along the old Champlain-Richelieu invasion route. This is mere posturing. He intends to do nothing.

Now Wilkinson has his scapegoat. Montreal, just three days downriver, is virtually defenceless. Hampton's apparent feint at Châteauguay and his sudden withdrawal has convinced Prevost to withdraw the bulk of the British troops to Kingston. Wilkinson still has some seven thousand soldiers. But neither he nor his generals have the will to continue. A hastily summoned council of war agrees to abandon the enterprise.

Wilkinson goes to some effort to make it clear that the defeat of the grand plan is entirely Hampton's fault. In his General Order on November 13 he announces that he is "compelled to retire by the extraordinary unexampled, and apparently unwarrantable conduct of Major General Hampton."

To Armstrong he writes that, with Hampton's help, he would have taken Montreal in eight or ten days. Now all his hopes are blasted: "I disclaim the shadow of blame because I have done my duty.... To General Hampton's outrage of every principle of subordination and discipline may be ascribed the failure of the expedition...."

The army drifts eighteen miles down the St. Lawrence to Salmon Creek and moves up that tributary to the American hamlet of French Mills, soon to be known as Fort Covington in honour of the dead general. Here, in a dreary wilderness of pine and hemlock, with little shelter and hard rations, it passes a dreadful winter. Sickness, desertions, and venality do more damage than any British force. Clothing is hard to come by. Little Jarvis Hanks, the drummer boy, has no pantaloons and is forced to tailor himself a pair out of one of his two precious blankets. Driven to subsist on contaminated bread, the men sicken by the hundreds and die by the score. So many men are mortally stricken that funeral dirges are banned from the camp for reasons of morale. By the end of the year almost eighteen hundred are ill. Food is so scarce the sick must subsist on oatmeal, originally ordered for poultices. All of the efficient officers have gone on furlough or are themselves ill with pneumonia, diarrhea, dysentery, typhoid, or atrophy of the limbs, a kind of dry rot. The remainder, ex-ward politicians mostly, fatten their pocketbooks by selling army rations to British and Americans alike, and drawing dead men's pay.

The defeat on the St. Lawrence wrecks the careers of the men who bungled the grand attack. Wilkinson, convalescing in a comfortable home at Malone, New York, and bitterly blaming everybody but himself for the débâcle, must know that his days are numbered. Hampton will shortly resign, to the relief of all. Lewis and Boyd have each taken a leave of absence and will not be heard of again.

Jacob Brown, promoted to major-general, and George Izard, Hampton's efficient second-in-command, represent the new army. When the force at French Mills breaks up the following February, Brown takes two thousand men to Sackets Harbor to continue the struggle for the Niagara frontier while Izard marches the rest to Plattsburgh.

Along the St. Lawrence, the settlers begin to rearrange the fragments of their lives. The north shore has been heavily plundered of cattle, grain, and winter forage. Fences have been ripped apart to build fires – the sky so illuminated it sometimes seemed as if the entire countryside was ablaze. Cellars, barns, and stables have been looted. Stragglers, pretending to search for arms, rummaged through houses, broke open trunks, stole everything from ladies' petticoats to men's pantaloons. Fancy china, silver plate, jewellery, books – all went to the plunderers in spite of Wilkinson's proclamation that private property would be respected.

The American advance has left a legacy of bitterness. Dr. William "Tiger" Dunlop, an assistant surgeon with the 89th, working with the wounded of both armies in the various farmhouses that do duty as makeshift hospitals, discovers that he cannot trust some of the Loyalist farmers near the stricken Americans, so great is their hatred of the enemy.

Fortunately, this brief explosion in their midst marks the last military excursion down the great river. For John Crysler and his neighbours, the war is over. In spite of James Wilkinson's hollow boast that the attack on Montreal is merely suspended and not abandoned, the St. Lawrence Valley will never again shiver to the crash of alien musketry.

7

THE NIAGARA IN FLAMES
November – December, 1813

With the news of Procter's defeat on the Thames, General Vincent hastily moves his Centre Division back to Burlington Heights, leaving the Niagara peninsula a no-man's land. The Americans, hived in Fort George, cannot break out except for brief forays against the surrounding countryside. The regulars have departed to join Wilkinson. William Henry Harrison and his men have come and gone. The new American commander, Brigadier-General George McClure, a New York militia officer, is planning to move up the peninsula with his citizen soldiers in an attempt to dislodge Vincent's army.

SHIPMAN'S CORNERS (St. Catharines), Upper Canada, November 28, 1813

Captain William Hamilton Merritt and two of his Provincial Dragoons, their uniforms concealed by long greatcoats, lurk by a bridge over Twelve Mile Creek, spying out the countryside. Disloyalty is rife; traitors abound. Joseph Willcocks, the Canadian turncoat, is an hour away, riding at the head of an armed troop of former Canadians on one of his nightly attacks against his one-time neighbours. To young Captain Merritt's bitter disappointment, he has just missed tangling with him.

Two dissident Canadians mistake the three dragoons for members of the invading army. From them, Merritt learns that the Americans are marching out of Fort George, heading for Burlington Heights, and that their advance post is already at Shipman's.

Merritt is forty miles from the nearest British post. If the Americans discover his presence he will certainly be captured – and there are enough enemy sympathizers about to spread the news. These are confusing times. Villages change hands, often overnight. Pickets, advance parties, mounted marauders from both sides gallop about seeking each other and often confusing themselves, for it is not always possible to tell friend from foe: men from both sides speak the same language; not everyone wears a uniform, and some who do so, like Merritt and his men, are disguised.

The three dragoons retire slowly through the night until they reach

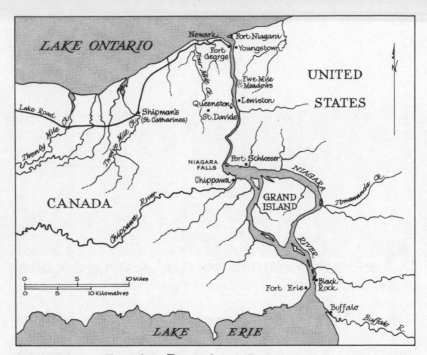

The Niagara Frontier, December, 1813

the Runchey farmhouse at Twenty Mile Creek. Here they run directly into two enemy horsemen, and an odd little charade takes place. Merritt, posing as an American, affects a Yankee accent. The Americans, seeing through the deception, pretend to be British. A scuffle follows and shots are fired, just as two more horsemen ride up.

These are also Merritt's men – his sergeant-major and his cornet, Amos McKenney, both hot on the trail of another traitor – but Merritt does not recognize them in the dark, and an incredible mixup ensues. Merritt shoots off McKenney's cap, believing him to be an American. McKenney's horse, startled by the shot, lurches and throws him to the ground. Merritt's own horse is exhausted from the night ride, and so the young captain leaps into the empty saddle and dashes away. Only when he reaches headquarters at Dundas and recognizes the bridle does he realize, with a sinking heart, that he may have shot his best friend and comrade.

McKenney is not dead, only unhorsed and stunned. He lights out for the woods, spends the rest of the night stumbling through the undergrowth, trying to keep away from the enemy whom he can hear crashing through the bushes, hot on his trail. When dawn arrives, the "enemy" turns out to be his own sergeant-major, who has also spent the night fleeing from an unseen adversary—who turns out to be McKenney. The embarrassed pair make their way back to Dundas, to the relief of their crestfallen commander.

At twenty, William Hamilton Merritt is that inevitable product of war—a young-old man. He has already had more than a year of almost uninterrupted warfare—a mounted guerrilla veteran of a dozen skirmishes, hair-breadth escapes, shoot-outs, midnight rides, sleepless nights, sudden forays, hurried retreats. He is well educated, having studied the classics under John Burns, the Presbyterian minister at Newark, and mathematics and surveying under Richard Cockrel, the noted Ancaster schoolmaster—learning that will stand him in good stead in the future when he builds the first Welland Canal. At sixteen, Merritt operated a two-hundred acre farm and a general store. At nineteen, his commercial ambitions were interrupted by the war. He served in his father's Niagara Light Dragoons until the unit was disbanded in the spring of 1813. From that point on, as far as Merritt was concerned, it was somebody else's war. But General Vincent had other ideas. Here was a man who knew every back road, lane, and creek bed in the Niagara peninsula and—equally important—was conversant with the loyalties of every settler. Who better to raise and lead a troop of fifty Provincial Dragoons? Since that time, Merritt has been in the thick of it.

Since October, all his energies have been funnelled into a single purpose: he desperately wants to capture the traitor Willcocks, who briefly kidnapped his father. The elder Merritt is now safely returned to Shipman's, the rest of the family scattered about the peninsula. Young Merritt cannot understand why the British do not drive the Americans back across the Niagara River. What is the army about, he keeps asking himself. Why doesn't Vincent go on the attack? Have our great men given up the idea of regaining the country?

He is still puzzling over this lack of initiative at a party on November 29 when a midnight order calls on him to move at once with his dragoons to Forty Mile Creek. He is to join Colonel John Murray, the army's inspecting field officer, who is close on the trail of the treasonous Willcocks. "King Joe," as Merritt sardonically calls him, is reported to be in the vicinity with 250 men, but when Merritt's troop arrives after an all-night ride, they have already slipped away.

By this time Brigadier-General George McClure's main army of sixteen hundred New York militia has reached Shipman's. Willcocks, acting as his advance scout, somehow manages to inflate Murray's light force into an army. He warns McClure that two or three thousand British troops are on their way to meet the American threat.

Does McClure believe this nonsense, or is he merely seeking a way out? His bravado is well known, his bravery held in lower esteem. "Your general will lead you to victory and share the dangers with you," he told his brigade in September. Now, on the strength of a rumour, he is prepared to fold up and retire.

He calls the usual council of war. His officers tell him what he wants to hear: it would be madness to go on. And so it would, for the British, having beaten Wilkinson, are now able to rush regular troops back to Upper Canada and, with a new commanding general, Gordon Drummond, in charge, to go immediately on the offensive.

The morning after the council, McClure counts his men to discover that six hundred – one-third of his army – have not waited for their December 9 discharge but have simply deserted. In a panic, he realizes that he has left Fort George almost defenceless. Seizing some cattle and flour from the settlers, he makes a hasty withdrawal.

Now the eager Murray asks Vincent's permission to move forward but is told he cannot take his main body past Forty Mile Creek or his outposts past Twelve Mile Creek. Vincent, it appears, is no more anxious to tangle with McClure than the American is with him. His health has failed him and he is about to be replaced.

Merritt worries about his father. On December 8 he persuades the commander of Murray's advance picket to let him go on to Shipman's to round up any suspicious characters who may be helping the Americans. His real purpose is to bring his father to safety. That done he returns to Forty Mile Creek where he receives a stiff dressing-down from Colonel Murray for disobeying orders. But a moment later Murray himself disobeys instructions. When Merritt reports a rumour that McClure has threatened to lay waste the countryside if the British dare advance, Murray agrees to move his entire force forward to Twenty Mile Creek, in direct contravention of Vincent's orders. To Merritt, this is not far enough; he fears for the safety of the community at Shipman's.

He returns to Twelve Mile Creek and publicly assembles all the available militia, a ruse that convinces McClure's scouts that the greater part of Vincent's Centre Division has already reached that spot.

Merritt has had little sleep for three nights. At two on the morning of December 10, having just bedded down in a nearby farmhouse, he is dispatched on another errand – to ride immediately to Beaver Dams to prevent a cache of flour from falling into American hands. When he returns to Shipman's, the exhausted dragoon is surprised to discover that Colonel Murray has moved forward. Orders or no orders, the aggressive Murray is determined to march on Fort George this very night. The town of Newark is in flames, burned by the Americans: every house, every barn, every shop, every public building. It is a bad business; but Merritt cannot help a moment of inward elation, for it means that the Americans are leaving Canada.

•

NEWARK, UPPER CANADA, December 10, 1813

Snow. Snow falling in a curtain of heavy flakes. Snow blowing in the teeth of a bitter east wind off the lake. Snow lying calf deep in the streets, whirling in eddies around log buildings, creeping under doors, piling in drifts at the base of snake fences. Snow clogging the brims of top hats, crusting mufflers, whitening horses' manes, smothering the neat gardens of summer. No day, this, to be out in the storm; better to crouch by hearth or kitchen stove, making peep-holes in the frosted windows from which to view the white world from behind the security of solid walls. But not on this day, for there is no security in Newark. Before darkness falls there will be few walls standing in this doomed village.

On Queen Street, in Joseph McCarthy's store, a violent quarrel is in progress. The American commander, George McClure, is hotly defending his decision to burn the town against the vehement protests of Dr. Cyrenius Chapin, the partisan leader from Buffalo.

McClure is in a near panic. Armstrong has ignored his repeated request for reinforcements. Harrison and his veterans are gone. With the threat to Montreal at an end, the British can again turn their attention and their troops to the Niagara country. Fort George is virtually defenceless, for all of McClure's militia, having reached the end of their period of enlistment, have recrossed the river in a body and are dispersing to their homes. Threats, bribes, entreaties have not persuaded them to stay. Indeed, they have been in a state of near mutiny on learning that they will not receive their pay before demobilization. McClure has gone to the extreme of offering an extra two dollars a month to any man who will remain. To his chagrin and disgust, dozens take the money, then desert.

To hold the captured British fort – the only American foothold on the peninsula – McClure has some seventy regulars plus Joseph Willcocks's small corps of about one hundred Canadian Volunteers. Merritt's hoax has convinced the General that the entire British army is on its way from Twelve Mile Creek. Willcocks has just lost five men, one of whom has been handed over to the Indians – an act that strikes terror into the hearts of others. A council of war has speedily concluded that the fort must be abandoned and destroyed before the British arrive.

McClure attempts to justify the decision to burn the town by brandishing a letter from Armstrong, written the previous October:

Understanding that the defense of the post committed to your charge may render it proper to destroy the town of Newark, you are hereby directed to apprise its inhabitants of this circumstance, and invite them to remove themselves and their effects to some place of greater safety.

This is hardly a *carte blanche* to destroy the village, since McClure has no intention of defending the fort. He argues, however, that the British mean to attack Fort Niagara, the American stronghold across the river. By burning Newark he will deny them comfortable billets.

McClure is not much of a soldier. A Londonderry Irishman, he has been carpenter, miller, contractor, merchant, land speculator, and, above all, a New York State politician. The spoils have included a judgeship and command of the 8th Brigade of state militia, the latter an inconsequential post because there are no militia left to command. Like so many other political appointees to military rank, he is a better boaster than tactician. Chapin, himself a citizen soldier, has little use for him. He censures McClure for countenancing the plundering of buildings and the burning of private homes by the undisciplined militia during an abortive October venture to Twenty Mile Creek; indeed, Chapin suspects that McClure shared in the spoils. On his part, the General hates Chapin, calls him a "damned rascal," and has been heard to wish that the enemy would capture him.

Does McClure really intend to burn Newark for the reasons he advances to Chapin? If he means to deny the British shelter, why does he not destroy the new barrack buildings at Fort George? Why does he not burn the fifteen hundred new tents that lie within its walls? Is there, perhaps, a second, more emotional reason to visit such misery on the women, children, and non-combatants of Newark?

Behind the bumbling militia general there can be discerned a more intriguing figure, another enemy of Chapin's and one of McClure's chief advisers, the turncoat Joseph Willcocks. Now a commissioned lieutenant-colonel in the American army, Willcocks is a former resident of the doomed community. It was from here that he edited his virulent newspaper, the *Upper Canadian Guardian or Freeman's Journal.* That publication was not designed to placate the true-blue Loyalists who make up the town's elite and whom the Americans, with memories of the Revolution, still disparage as "Tories."

Now, as McClure rides through the streets of the Loyalist village at the head of his burning party, torches and lanterns lit, directing his men to various corners of the town to fire houses and public buildings, Willcocks rides beside him, settling old scores and cursing anyone who protests as a Tory.

He is a curious, even baffling specimen, this Willcocks. His motivations are more complex than those of his two chief associates, Benajah Mallory, now his second-in-command, and Abraham Markle. Like so many of their fellow citizens, these two came to Canada from the United States, lured by cheap land and low taxes; in spite of service in the Upper Canadian legislature, their loyalties have never been firm. But Willcocks is not an American. He is the scion of an upper-class British family living in Ireland. He fought for the British at Queenston Heights. Why is he presiding at the destruction of his adopted village?

The answer lies partly in Willcocks's mercurial personality and partly in his continuing search for a patron – a father figure, perhaps – who can advance his interests. He is a handsome man at forty, reasonably well educated and with an aptitude for making friends, though it is noticed that the friends he makes are generally those who can give him a push up the ladder of his ambition.

His first patron in Upper Canada was a distant cousin, Peter Russell, who, as Administrator of the province, was the most powerful man next to the governor. Russell gave him a job and a home but threw him out when Willcocks made advances to the Administrator's half-sister.

His next backer was Chief Justice Allcock, with whom he also lived and whose influence secured him a better post as Sheriff of York. When Allcock was moved to Lower Canada, Willcocks sought a new benefactor and found him in the person of the new Puisne Judge of the Court of King's Bench, Robert Thorpe. That encounter marked a watershed in Joseph Willcocks's life. Under Thorpe's dark influence, the model civil servant became a thorn in the side of the government that employed him. Thorpe was aggrieved at not being appointed Chief Justice and shortly became the backer of those opposition elements in the legislature who gathered about the Irish lawyer and malcontent, William Weekes. If Weekes was Thorpe's tool, so was Willcocks. Having lost his government job and launched his scrappy little newspaper, Willcocks became a member of the lower house. And after Weekes was killed in a duel in 1806, Willcocks became the centre of the opposition forces.

In Willcocks's resistance to the closed circle of elitists at York can be seen the faint stirrings of a movement, interrupted by war, that a quarter of a century later will burst into open revolt. His Irish upbringing, his re-education under Thorpe and Weekes, his breach with Russell – all these have contributed to a vaguely formed political philosophy that makes him a foe of arbitrary power. In his newspaper, Willcocks hinted so broadly at bribery in the legislature that he was thrown in jail. It did not disconcert him. He fought hard, if vainly, for common school education – an American idea shunned by those who believe that schooling should be reserved for the sons of the privileged. He also opposed the strengthening of the militia. At the war's outset he successfully blocked Isaac Brock's call to suspend the laws of *habeas corpus* and to invoke martial law. "I am flattered at being ranked among the enemies of the King's Servants in this colony," he declared. "I glory in the distinction."

Then, suddenly, he reversed himself to become Isaac Brock's humble and obedient servant. It is these sudden right-angle turns in Joseph Willcocks's chequered career that baffle his friends and disconcert his enemies. Brock, who had every reason to hate and despise him, went out of his way to meet him and beg his aid. Among the proud and stiff-necked arbiters of the province's destiny, Brock must have stood out as a man of exquisite charm and affability. Once again Willcocks found himself in the shadow of an older patron, this time the most powerful man in the province, one who made a point of flattering him. Would he undertake a mission of some delicacy in the interests of his country? Willcocks succumbed and was dispatched to secure the loyalty of the Grand River Indians. Later, still under Brock's influence, he fought bravely at Queenston where his patron was killed.

Brock's crusty successor, Roger Sheaffe, no diplomat, had little time for such as Joe Willcocks. But the Americans had. During the second occupation of York, when the Americans seemed to be winning, some of Willcocks's friends went over to the enemy. Willcocks joined them, and here he is in Newark again, the civil servant-turned-radical-turned-soldier-turned-traitor, riding beside his commander, a green band and a white cockade in his hat identifying him proudly as a Canadian Volunteer, shouting threats and imprecations at his former neighbours.

Many have not heeded McClure's warning, given early this morning, believing that the threat to burn the town is an empty gesture. Now, roughly turned out into the blowing snow, they see their homes and all their belongings consumed by fire. The able-bodied citizens are with the militia or in prison at Fort Niagara. Only women, children, and sick old men remain. Two babies are born this night in the light of the leaping flames.

Mrs. Alex McKee, whose husband is a prisoner at Niagara, struggles to save what she can. Her family owns seven buildings, including two houses, a well-stocked store, and a soap and candle factory. They pack fifteen trunks with their most valuable effects and ship them off to Eight Mile Creek to be buried and covered with brushwood. She saves one article – a large teatray – as a sleigh to protect her little daughter's bare feet from the snow. It is a vain effort; the child's toes are soon frozen.

Eliza Campbell, widow of the fort major, cannot leave her home because she has three small children to care for. She lives in a handsomely furnished storey-and-a-half building, surrounded by two acres of land with fruit trees and a barn. Now, forced from her house without time to gather anything but money, she watches as the soldiers plunder her furniture and fire the two buildings. A moment later, one of Willcocks's men takes all her money.

John Rogers, a boy of nine, watches his mother carry a beautiful mantelpiece out into the street before her house is reduced to ashes. His parents have friends and relatives among the American officers but have been told that if their home were to be spared, they would be tagged as disloyal by their neighbours.

Mrs. William Dickson lies ill in bed in her handsome mansion, the first brick house in Newark. Her husband, a brother of the Robert Dickson whom the Sioux call the Red-Haired Man, is a prisoner in Fort Niagara. Like others who are unable to walk, Mrs. Dickson is carried out of her house, bed and all, and plumped down in the snow while Willcocks's men put the torch to the building, destroying everything – damask curtains, cherry and walnut furniture, a full set of India table china, stores, stoves, clothing, pictures, and, above all, one of the finest libraries in Upper Canada – a thousand books purchased in England at a cost of three thousand dollars. It is surely no coincidence that Dickson has long been an enemy of Joseph Willcocks – ever since the day, seven years before, when he killed Willcocks's political patron, William Weekes, in a duel.

McClure's intelligence, much of it based on Willcocks's exaggerated reports, is faulty. The British as yet have no intention of attacking either Fort George or Fort Niagara. But Colonel Murray, seeing the flames from a distance, decides to ignore his orders, march on the town, and seize the fort. He calls out the militia, instructs Captain Merritt to commandeer axes and scaling ladders, and puts his column in motion. Refugees are already streaming out of the town seeking shelter. The nearest farmhouse, four miles away, cannot handle them all. Some women and children walk up to ten miles that night through the swirling snow. The spectacle enrages Murray's men, fuelling a desire for revenge that Murray is in no mood to dampen.

At nine in the evening, Murray's advance enters the smouldering village. McClure's troops make a hasty retreat across the ice-choked Niagara River. They have blown up Fort George's main magazine and spiked the guns but left the new barracks intact, together with a quantity of ammunition and all fifteen hundred tents.

By the time William Merritt enters the town, Newark is a heap of coals, the streets clogged with furniture and only one house still standing – that of his brother-in-law. Ninety-eight houses, barns, and stables have been destroyed. Four hundred people are homeless. All public buildings – jail, court house, library – are in ashes. Two churches have been fired. In McEwen's smokehouse, the refugees seek what shelter they can. Others crouch against chimneys or in root houses or cellars, hastily roofed with boards.

In the hearts of the homeless and the soldiers there is one common emotion: a desire for retaliation. The senseless burning of Newark will send an echo down the corridors of history, for it is this act, much more than the accidental firing of the legislature at York, that provokes a succession of incendiary raids that will not end until the city of Washington itself is in flames.

●

ST. DAVIDS, UPPER CANADA, December 18, 1813

It is close to midnight as Colonel John Murray looks over the force that is about to march to the river and embark on the attack against Fort Niagara, the American stronghold on the far side. He turns to Captain Thomas Dawson of the grenadiers of the 100th, who will lead the Forlorn Hope:

"What description of men have you got, Dawson, for the advance? Can you rely on them?"

"I can, Colonel. I know every one of them. They can all be depended on."

"Yes, Dawson, I dare say, but what I mean, are they a desperate set? I want men who have no conscience, for not a soul must live between the landing place and the fort. There must be no alarm."

"They are just that description of men, Colonel."

They are, in fact, the flower of Upper Canada. Young Allan MacNab is here, not yet turned sixteen; one day he will be premier. Lieutenant Richard Bullock, one of the few officers who escaped capture at the Thames, is here, and half a dozen officers from the Lincoln Militia – Loyalists with names like Kerby, Ball, Hamilton, and Servos, local gentry burning for revenge after the destruction of Newark.

The secret attack on the American fort has been a week in the planning, ever since McClure's hasty departure from Fort George. For the past several days, Merritt and his dragoons have been gathering boats for the midnight voyage across the river. Exhausted from lack of sleep and a bout of grippe brought on by fatigue and cold, Merritt finds to his bitter disappointment that he can no longer stand upright and must miss the night's excitement.

Lieutenant-General Gordon Drummond – De Rottenburg's replacement as commander in Upper Canada and as Prevost's second-in-command – has come down from Little York to St. Davids to mastermind Murray's attack. A bolder and more innovative leader than his predecessor, he has left nothing to chance. The force of 562 men is taken from the 100th Regiment, the Royal Scots, and the veteran 41st. The Forlorn Hope will dispose of the American advance guard. One body will storm the main gate of the fort; another will attack the southern salient; a third will scale the eastern bastion. One officer, Daniel Servos, carries a stick of cordwood to jam into the gate if necessary. A party of axemen has been detailed to chop down the pickets and open the way to the fort's rear. Silence is essential. Oars are to be muffled, muskets carried at the shoulder, unloaded, bayonets fixed, to prevent the clash of arms. The troops have all been warned that any sound will bring instant death. The killing is to be silent. "The bayonet is the weapon on which the success of the attack must depend," Drummond declares.

The boats slip across the narrow river in just fifteen minutes, landing two and a half miles above the fort. It is intensely cold, the night moonless, a soft blanket of snow muffling the sound of marching feet.

At Youngstown, Captain Dawson and his enormous sergeant, Andrew Spearman, spot an American soldier posted outside a tavern door. This must be the advance guard. Spearman creeps up on the shivering sentry, chokes him into silence, demands the official countersign, then dispatches him with a single bayonet thrust.

Some of the Forlorn Hope peer through the window. The twenty members of the American picket are inside, protecting themselves from the cold. The officers are playing whist. When it is all over someone will claim that one of the Americans asked, "What's trump?" and one of the Canadians replied, "Bayonets are trump!" Perhaps; it is a night for legend.

The door crashes open; the Forlorn Hope dashes in – young Allan MacNab in the forefront. The advance guard dies under the bayonets of the British and the force moves on. A mile or so later a second picket is also dispatched, silently, ruthlessly, and the company marches on along the frozen river road.

What Murray does not know is that two days before, a deserter has alerted McClure to the possibility of just such an attack. McClure has warned the fort's commander, Captain Nathaniel Leonard, to keep his men on guard and to place grenades at strategic points to resist the enemy.

Fort Niagara is no easy target. Its bastions bristle with twenty-seven pieces of artillery. Three strong towers overlook the palisades. Four hundred and thirty men, of whom some fifty are sick, guard the ramparts. But where are these men? Sound asleep in their tents, in spite of the warning. Where is McClure? In Buffalo, attempting to justify his attack on Newark. And where is Captain Leonard? At home with his family, three miles beyond. The evidence suggests that the captain is more than a little drunk and that his officers, after a night of gaming and tippling, are sleeping it off in the belief that the threatened attack, which has failed to materialize on two previous nights, is merely a figment of the deserter's imagination.

The ice crackles under the tread of the soldiers' boots, but the sound is borne away on the gusts of a northeast wind. Only one man is on horseback: Lieutenant-Colonel Hamilton of the British 100th, who, having lost a leg in Holland, cannot march but refuses to remain behind. Suddenly Hamilton's horse neighs loudly. From a stable near the fort comes an answering neigh. The force halts at once. Surely these sounds must alert the garrison! *Silence.* Relieved, the men shuffle forward.

At three o'clock they reach the main gate to find the drawbridge down. They have arrived at the very moment when the sentries on the river side are being changed. Spearman, the big sergeant, advances alone across the bridge, reaches the sentry box, is challenged, gives the countersign, and in an approximation of a Yankee accent says he has come from Youngstown. As the sentry turns, Spearman strangles him to death.

Shouting and cheering, the storming party dashes across the bridge, awakening the garrison. A cannon booms from the roof of one of the towers. Lieutenant Maurice Nolan of the 100th rushes through the lower door and vanishes into the gloom. His comrades hear the clash of steel on steel, the hoarse roar of musketry. Nolan is dead, his chest pierced by a bayonet, a musket ball, and three buckshot. Three American corpses lie beside him, one killed by a pistol shot, the others with their skulls cleft by sword blows. In a fury, Nolan's men proceed to massacre the survivors until other officers stop them.

Meanwhile, Major Davis Byron Davies of the 100th is attacking a second blockhouse. Random fire has already killed one of his men, wounded two others. Davies seizes an American prisoner, threatening him with instant death unless he guides him to the inner stairs, waits until he hears the Americans reloading their muskets, seizes the interval to force the door, and in the light of flaming torches carried by his men finds his way up the twisting staircase, shouting to his followers to bayonet everybody. The Americans have no stomach for the fight; one man is killed; sixty-four surrender.

Panic-stricken, a group of Americans tries to escape from the sally port, only to be driven back by the grenadiers of the Royal Scots. Colonel Murray saves most of their lives by making them lie down, receiving a painful bayonet wound in the hand for this act of mercy.

It is soon over. The Americans have lost sixty-five dead and sixteen wounded, all by the bayonet, the British six dead, five wounded. Fourteen officers, including the tardy Captain Leonard, who returns at dawn, are captured with 350 others. The considerable booty includes twenty-nine cannon, seven thousand muskets and rifles, seven thousand pairs of shoes, and a vast cache of clothing, much of it originally captured from the British, the whole being valued at one million dollars. To William Hamilton Merritt's delight, Murray allows him and his troops a share of the prize money as a reward for their services. Every private soldier will receive two pounds sterling, the officers much more.

At five that morning a cannon shot from the newly captured fort signals victory to Major-General Phineas Riall, the peppery little Irishman who has replaced the ailing Vincent as officer commanding the Centre Division. Riall has been waiting on the far shore for this signal to invade Lewiston with a thousand men and five hundred Indians.

Drummond has agreed to use the natives only if they can be kept under control – a specious argument, surely. Does Drummond, of all people – the first Canadian-born general officer – actually believe the Indians can be controlled? Or that Matthew Elliott and William Caldwell, the Indian Department officers who will lead them in battle, will be able to control them? They have shown no disposition to do so on previous occasions.

Riall's force lands without opposition at Five Mile Meadows, half way between Lewiston and the lake. There is little to stand in his way as he sets out to make a clean sweep up the river. The handful of militia at Lewiston has deserted. Their commander was told to expect a three-cannon warning from Fort Niagara if invasion came; he ignored the single cannon shot at three o'clock – the only gun fired by the defenders – believing it a false alarm. Snug in bed, the citizens now find the British and Indians on their doorsteps. They flee from their homes, half-dressed, many without shoes or stockings, the men on horseback, the roads leading to Buffalo a tangle of wagons, farmers' carts, and sleighs, many toppling over, passengers cursing their drivers, in the pell-mell escape.

Mrs. Solomon Gillette, waiting for her husband to return home, hears the sound of the signal cannon, wakes her ten-year-old son, Orville, and sets about milking. The task is nearly complete when blood-curdling yells split the air. Three Indians in war paint and feathers appear, loot the barn, drink the milk, head for the house.

Orville dashes off, dodging between the haystacks; but his mother cannot flee, for she has left three younger children in the house. More Indians arrive, seize a demijohn of whiskey, threaten to kill the children. She holds the two youngest in her arms while Jervis, aged seven, clings to her skirts. Through the open door she spies a British officer, resplendent in scarlet, and springs into the street, pleading for rescue. The Indians fire a volley. Little Jervis falls dead at her feet. As the officer dashes up to save the surviving trio, one of the Indians tears the scalp from the dead child's head.

At the same time, on Centre Street, her husband, Solomon, is taken prisoner. As he is led away he sees his eldest boy, Miles, aged nineteen, being brought along the opposite side by a party of tribesmen. Miles, a veteran of the Battle of Queenston Heights, struggles with his native captors, shoots one, tries to break away, and is shot and scalped in front of his father. Mrs. Gillette and her two babies make their way through the snow for 270 miles, finally reaching her father's farm in Columbia County. It is June before she learns that ten-year-old Orville is safe and Christmas before she knows that her husband is alive and a prisoner in Canada. The shattered family is not reunited until the spring of 1815.

Joseph Willcocks's second-in-command, Benajah Mallory, arrives post-haste with sixty turncoat Canadian Volunteers to fight a delaying action that will allow the settlers time to escape. But soon every building in the vicinity is reduced to ashes. Within a day, the Niagara frontier from the fort to Tonawanda Creek, including the Tuscarora village, Lewiston, Youngstown, and Manchester (the future Niagara Falls), have been depopulated and reduced to smoking ruins.

For this devastation Brigadier-General McClure is blamed. In Buffalo he is the subject of universal excoriation for what one American (in the *Pittsburgh Gazette*) calls the "wanton and abominable act" of firing Newark. As he marches at the head of his men down the main street, his ears ring with cries and taunts: "Shoot him down! Shoot him!" Cyrenius Chapin's followers lead the pack, some even firing their muskets at the embattled general. Chapin is briefly jailed for mutiny but almost immediately released by the citizens themselves.

McClure cannot stay in Buffalo. He is a pariah. Brigadier-General Timothy Hopkins finds that the militia will not serve under him. His own soldiers have lost confidence in him. His officers are convinced that he is unfit to command. Universally detested, he slinks off to Batavia and turns his militia command over to Major-General Amos Hall.

The British, meanwhile, are advancing on Fort Schlosser. Marching with the advance is the indestructible Private Shadrach Byfield of the 41st light company, back in service again after his escape on the Thames and fresh from the attack on Fort Niagara. A mile and a half from its objective, the group seizes a forward guardhouse, manages to take eight prisoners before the rest escape. Byfield and a handful of men are ordered to guard the prisoners while the main force moves on to Schlosser.

The night is dark, the countryside unknown, the trails through the woods labyrinthine. Byfield's party takes the wrong fork and almost immediately runs into trouble. Footsteps can be heard behind them. Friend or enemy? No one wants to find out, but at last Byfield volunteers to go back alone, runs into a shadowy figure – an American – threatens to blow his brains out, and makes him a prisoner. It is the officer of the guard who made his escape during the confusion of the attack.

An affecting little scene follows. The American complains that someone has stolen his boots. Byfield rummages in his pack and generously offers him a pair of his own as well as a tot of rum to warm him, whereupon the prisoner breaks into sobs, exclaiming he had not expected to be treated so well.

There are more tears to come. As Byfield brings his prisoner to Fort Schlosser, now in British hands, he spots the body of an American officer sprawled on the floor. His captive spots it too and begins to weep bitterly, for this battered and bleeding corpse was once his dearest friend.

Byfield and the others burn the fort, destroy all the buildings, throw the provisions into the river. Then, on December 22, all of the army save for a small garrison force at Fort Niagara returns to the Canadian side, and the people of Buffalo and Black Rock, who have been expecting an imminent attack, breathe more easily. Their relief is premature. A week later, the attack is launched.

•

BUFFALO, NEW YORK, December 30, 1813

Margaret St. John – the widow St. John, as she is now known – has no sense of danger, even though she can hear the booming of cannon downriver at Black Rock. She has seen General Amos Hall's troops move out, two thousand strong, with men like Chapin and Mallory in the van, and is convinced the militia can thwart any British attempt at landing.

She is not easily rattled, for she is a child of the frontier: her father was a long-time missionary to the Indians. She has lived all her life in log communities, in the shadow of dark forests, always on the rim of civilization. She has raised eleven children under the most primitive conditions, often without a doctor's help. Now, at forty-five, she is self-reliant, domineering, a little irritable at times, but always in total control.

She has no way of knowing that the American defence of Black Rock is a total disaster, that almost half of General Hall's volunteers have fled at the first alarm, that the British, having launched a successful two-pronged attack, are even now marching on Buffalo, fourteen hundred strong, with the Indians in the vanguard, their passage only slightly impeded by a few bold defenders.

Like a clap of thunder the alarm gun booms, and panic grips the village. The first of the retreating militia come dashing through town, followed by a column of refugees. The terrible word *Indians!* passes, in a scream, from house to house.

The flight from Buffalo begins at once as horses, oxen, and sleighs are commandeered; as babies are thrown into open carts along with furs, jewellery, bread, silverware, provisions. Those who cannot find transport set out on a dead run through the light snow over half-frozen ruts.

Into the St. John cottage at the corner of Main and Mohawk comes an old friend, Dr. Josiah Trowbridge. He begs the widow to leave at once, warns that the Indians will kill her if she stays, offers her his horse, promises to take care of the children.

"I can't do it," says Margaret St. John. "Here is all I have in the world, and I will stay and defend it."

All she has in the world are two buildings: the big family house which, since the accidental drowning of her husband and one son the previous summer, has been leased as a hotel, and the little unfinished storey-and-a-half cottage into which she and eight of her children have been forced to squeeze.

Across Main Street, her son-in-law, Asaph Bemis, is hastily packing a wagon. He offers to take the six youngest St. John children, three boys and three girls, along with his own wife and baby to safety. He packs them in with the bedding and household goods, whips his horses and is off.

The Indians are advancing down Guideboard Road, the militia fleeing ahead. One of Mrs. St. John's neighbours, Job Hoysington, stops; he wants one more shot at the redskins, he says. The others dash on, leaving him behind. His scalped corpse and rifle will not be found until the snow melts in the spring.

Next door to the St. Johns lives Sally Lovejoy, a tall, spirited woman of thirty-five. She, too, has no intention of leaving unless she can take her big trunk, containing her most precious belongings, with her. When no wagon can be found to handle the trunk, she determines to stay. Her husband, Henry, is fighting with the militia. Young Henry, her thirteen-year-old son, wants to fight, too; during Bisshopp's raid on Black Rock he carried a musket bigger than himself. Now his mother tells him to run away:

"Henry, you've fought against the British: you must run. They'll take you prisoner. I am a woman; they'll not harm me."

The town is in a state of anarchy. People are fleeing in every direction, some heading up Seneca Street toward the Indian reservation, others galloping up Main toward Williamsville or Batavia, more moving up the beach toward Pratt's Ferry at the river and on to Hamburg.

An ox team lurches by, pulling a sled crammed with wounded soldiers; another, loaded with household goods, carries a settler's family and three exhausted women who have begged a ride; a ragged party of militia straggles through town, still carrying the muskets they have never fired. Friendly Seneca Indians clip-clop past on ponies, their women up behind, babes in arms. Children are lost and found again. One woman, holding her baby, tumbles off her horse into a bed of quicksand and is hauled out at the last moment. A farmer from Hamburg arrives with a load of cheese, grasps what is happening, dumps his wagon and loads it with refugees.

Families are separated. Job Hoysington's wife, unable to wait any longer for her husband (already dead), sets out on foot with her six children, turns two of them over to a passing rider, and does not locate them for weeks; they are found in two separate counties, miles apart. Few save anything of value, and those who try are often thwarted. One silversmith throws his stock into a pillowcase; he hands it to a stranger who offers to save it but is never seen again.

Some stay to fight. One group, led by one of Oliver Hazard Perry's naval gunners, rushes to the river where the *Chippawa*, late of Perry's fleet, is wintering. They seize an old twelve-pound cannon and trundle it up Main Street to the corner of Niagara. There they see the British advancing – a long line of brilliantly uniformed men, bayonets gleaming in the morning sunlight.

The cannon speaks, without much effect. It is so badly overloaded by the eager civilians that on the third shot it bounds off the carriage.

Dr. Cyrenius Chapin is convinced that further resistance is useless. He determines to surrender the town to the British.

"Don't fire that gun," says Chapin.

Robert Kane, a mason by trade, doesn't want to give up.

"I *will* fire it," says Kane. "I will cleave any man who touches it."

Seth Grosvenor runs up to the St. John cottage looking for help to hoist the heavy gun back on its carriage. But every able man has gone.

Grosvenor is in tears.

"If I had help," he says, "I could drive the British back."

At this moment, Mrs. St. John sees a group of men on horseback coming from Court Street. She runs out into the road as the leading rider draws rein.

"For mercy sake's do turn back and help Mr. Grosvenor manage that cannon and defend the town," she cries, "and let General Hall go; he must be an awful coward."

The rider raises his hat but trots on with the others. Somebody tells Mrs. St. John that she has been talking to the General himself. Well, she retorts, if she had known that she would have had more to say.

Suddenly the Bemis wagon, with the St. John children hanging on for dear life, flies past. At North Street they found the way blocked by oncoming Indians – friendly Senecas pursued by British tribesmen. With bullets whizzing around his head, Asaph Bemis managed to turn the cart around and now, as he rattles down Main Street, calls to his mother-in-law that he must take the lakeshore road but will be back for the rest of the family as quickly as possible.

As the wagon passes the head of Niagara Street, young Martha St. John looks out and catches a confused glimpse of the British army drawn up on Niagara Square and a man on horseback facing them holding a white flag over one shoulder. It is 10 A.M. The man is Cyrenius Chapin, who has tied the flag to his cane. The British accept his surrender but later repudiate it because Chapin has no official standing in the community. He is made prisoner once more, being placed under heavy guard because of his previous escape. He has already sent his two daughters, aged eleven and nine, out of town on foot to try to reach his farm at Hamburg, ten miles away. He has no idea where they are now.

Down the street at Pomeroy's Bakery some famished militiamen are gobbling up Pomeroy's bread when the cry comes, "Run, boys, run!" Looking north, they see a long line of Indians trotting down Washington Street in single file. Gripping the bread in one hand and their muskets in the other, they flee the village.

Several Indians and their women are in the St. John house, looking for plunder. Next door, Mrs. St. John sees an Indian pulling down the curtains from Mrs. Lovejoy's windows. Her spirited neighbour grapples with the invader.

"Don't risk your life for property," cries Mrs. St. John.

But Mrs. Lovejoy replies, "When my property goes, my life shall go with it."

Each witness to the grisly scene that follows will remember it from a slightly different focus. Mrs. Lovejoy struggles with the Indian over – what? A silk shawl? The blankets? The curtains? One thing is clear to Mrs. St. John, watching in dismay through her window: she sees her neighbour strike at the Indian with a carving knife; she sees him raise his hatchet; she sees the hatchet fall. But she does not dare enter the house to determine Sally Lovejoy's fate.

A British colonel rides up.

"Why are you not away?" he asks, crossly.

She replies that she has nowhere to go but the snow, asks protection for her house. He sends her to Major-General Riall, who gives her his own interpreter as a guard.

Now, from the corner of Main and Seneca comes a crackle of flames, a whiff of wood smoke. An officer and a squad of men are moving from house to house, torches in hand. Soon the Lovejoy home is fired. Mrs. St. John and her two remaining daughters, Maria and Sarah, with the help of Pettigrew, the hired man, go into the house, take out the body of Mrs. Lovejoy, and lay it on a pile of boards beside a fence. Then they manage to extinguish the fire. At night, with the help of old Judge Walden, the women carry the corpse back into the house and place it on the cords of the bedstead. Later, some of the villagers return to visit the home and are moved to tears by the spectacle of Sally Lovejoy, clad in her black silk dress, her long, ebony hair reaching through the cords to the floor.

Meanwhile, the Bemis family and the six younger St. John children have reached Pratt's Ferry to find a long queue waiting to cross the river. Men, women, children, soldiers, oxen, horses, wagons of every description from great timber haulers to tiny go-carts scarcely big enough for a baby mill about at the water's edge.

Suddenly, Martha St. John hears a loud groan from the multitude and, turning, sees tall pillars of brown smoke billowing above the treetops. As the refugees realize that their homes are being destroyed, a sound of wailing and sobbing, mingled with women's shrieks, ripples across the crowd.

The Bemises are among the last to get across the river; after nineteen trips, James Johnson, the ferryman, gives up and follows the others in their flight. The family's destination is a tavern at the little community of Willink. Three miles before they can reach it, the wagon breaks down. The three St. John sisters, Margaret, Parnell, and Martha, decide to trudge on through the deep snow, leaving the Bemis couple and the four younger children to spend the night in the cart. As they pick their way along the strange road their nerves are shaken by a weird spectacle: wads of burning matter from Buffalo, born on the wind, hurtle over their heads like meteors.

It is past dawn when, numb with cold, they finally reach the tavern. In a large room in front of a log fire they recognize their neighbours. Here are the two Chapin girls, who have walked ten miles from Buffalo through the snow. And here is the family of Samuel Pratt, whose wife, Sophia, seeing Martha blue with cold, takes the girl in her arms by the fire and rubs her frostbitten fingers. There is breakfast for all, for the resourceful Mrs. Pratt was in the act of baking bread when the alarm sounded; she stuffed the dough into a pillowcase and brought it with her.

Shortly afterwards the rest of the St. John family arrives, carried by the two horses, having spent a ghastly night in the cold.

In the days that follow, the widow St. John struggles to save her cottage. The British are determined to burn every house in Buffalo as well as all public buildings, army stores, and – this is the official reason for the attack – four schooners from Perry's fleet, which are stranded for the winter at the river's mouth.

The morning after the attack, the St. John barn goes up in flames. "They say I must burn your barn," cries old Pettigrew, the hired man, wiping his eyes.

"Oh well," says Mrs. St. John, "it cannot be helped." He takes a burning brand from the hearth and sets it on fire.

They cannot save the big house, which is her livelihood. When the

British first fire it, she and her daughters struggle to extinguish the flames with pails of water from the well. But the respite is brief.

In vain Mrs. St. John exclaims that the British, by burning the hotel, are destroying her income.

"We have left you one roof, and that is more than the Americans left for our widows when they came over," she is reminded. The St. John hotel goes up in flames, as does the Lovejoy home next door, corpse and all; thus are the Canadians avenged for the burning of Newark.

The flames of Buffalo die down, but this is not the end. Fire breeds fire, revenge seeds more revenge. Before this war is ended, more homes will be put to the torch on both sides of the border, from the humblest cottage to the executive mansion of the President himself.

The British depart, keeping a garrison in Fort Niagara. The people of Buffalo trickle home to the blackened ruins of their village. The St. John children are shocked at the spectacle before them: all that is left of their big house are the cellar walls, two chimneys, and the front step. The frontier from Buffalo through Black Rock to Eighteen Mile Creek is a blackened smear. The British have destroyed 333 buildings. In Buffalo only three are still standing – the jail and the blacksmith shop, which would not burn, and the little cottage on Main Street, just twenty-two feet square, that the widow St. John, through the force of her will, managed, against all odds, to preserve.

8

MARKING TIME
January to June, 1814

With the burning of Buffalo, the campaign of 1813 ends. It is again too cold to fight. Since the war began, only a few square miles of territory have changed hands: the British hold Michilimackinac Island; the Americans occupy Amherstburg. Both sides change their high commands and prepare for another invasion, neither knowing where it will come. On Lake Ontario and Lake Champlain the rival navies engage in a new shipbuilding contest, constructing the world's largest lake vessels. And in St. Petersburg, Russia, three American diplomats try vainly to negotiate for peace with the British, with the Tsar as mediator.

ST. PETERSBURG, RUSSIA, January 6, 1814

The Russian Christmas. It is bitterly cold; the Fahrenheit thermometer shows twenty-five below. A skin of ice glitters on the colossal bronze statue of Peter the Great; a crust of snow sheaths the cornice of the church of St. Catherine; a frieze of icicles droops from the carved façades of the Hermitage and the Winter Palace. On the gravelled promenades, the snow squeaks beneath the runners of the one-horse sleighs that dart along the frigid banks of the Neva.

It is eleven o'clock. Above the great colonnade of the new church of Our Lady of Kazan – perhaps the most magnificent building in the city – the bells are ringing for a *Te Deum* to mark the recent successes of the Allies over Napoleon. Just one year ago, all Europe was opposed to Russia; now all Europe is with her in the holy crusade against the French. Wellington is through the Pyrenees and into France – and the Iberian peninsula is lost to Bonaparte. Blücher and Bernadotte have stopped him at Leipzig. The Continental system is smashed, the Empire crumbling.

Within the great church, dwarfed by the lofty domes, the gigantic columns, the gargantuan icons, a thin congregation listens to a proclamation from the Tsar, read by a chamberlain. The Russian Emperor is absent at army headquarters in Frankfurt, but the Empress is here, of course, and several grand dukes and at least one grand duchess. The diplomatic corps, however, is poorly represented. Thus the three Americans present, in their blue and gold uniforms (newly designed for such occasions), are more than usually conspicuous and more than usually uncomfortable. The church doors are continually opening and shutting, and after two hours of hymns, prayers, and chanting, they are thoroughly chilled.

The trio's discomfort is more than physical. Two are fed up with Russia, and each is fed up with the others' company. They are supposed to be treating for peace through the good offices of the Emperor Alexander, but now, with Napoleon approaching final defeat, peace with England seems nearly as distant as the Emperor himself. For almost six months they have waited for some official word: will the British agree to accept Alexander as a mediator in the dispute with their former colony? They are fairly certain that the answer is No, but it has not come officially; so they remain, diplomatic prisoners, shackled to a chill environment by the constraints of protocol.

All three are distinguished public servants, but none more distinguished than the leader of the delegation, John Quincy Adams, an old Russia hand who has been Minister Plenipotentiary here in St. Petersburg since 1809. Son of the second president of his country, a former senator, he has only recently turned down a confirmed appointment to the Supreme Court.

See him now, standing rigidly beneath the vaulted dome (for, as one of his colleagues has ruefully observed, no one sits down in a Russian church) — a short, stout figure of forty-six, the humourless face as chilly as the Russian winter, the high, bald pate gleaming like polished marble. If he is impatient with the interminable ceremony he gives no sign; yet for Adams this is time pirated from intellectual inquiry. He begrudges every wasted moment, does his best to stay out of society's grasp, rises before six, beds down early, feels a sense of overpowering guilt if he cannot spend at least five hours daily in reading and study. He gobbles up everything: science, philosophy, the classics, the Bible. No night passes in which he does not set out the minutiae of the day in a voluminous journal. In this exhaustive work every official gesture is recorded along with his own reading and observations — everything save his deepest, most intimate emotions. Gazing at the sky one frosty November night in 1813, he observes a constellation that he cannot identify, marks down the position on a slip of paper, leafs through Lalande's *Astronomy*, discovers to his discomfiture that it is the constellation Orion — one familiar to every schoolboy. *Mortification!* To be ignorant of something he should have known thirty years before! He must, of course, record his own humiliation in his journal: "I am ashamed at my age," he writes, "to be thus to seek for the very first elements of practical astronomy."

To James Ashton Bayard, standing next to him, Adams is the coldest of fish: "He has little talent for society and does [not] appear to enjoy it. His address is singularly cold and repulsive. His manners are harsh and you seldom perceive the least effort to please anyone." These first impressions, expressed a few days after his initial encounter with Adams, have hardened during the ensuing months, exacerbated no doubt by Bayard's own ill health (a concomitant of the wretched Russian weather) and his increasing homesickness.

As senators, Bayard and Adams were political opponents and, in a sense, still are. Bayard, a Federalist, was originally opposed to the war but, unlike some of his colleagues, supported the government once the declaration was made. He knows that the war – "a hopeless project" – has been tearing his country apart and feels it his solemn duty "not to refuse to the government any means in my power which could aid in extricating the Country from its embarrassments." Of the three envoys he is the least sophisticated – a tall, greying senator from Delaware, ill at ease in court circles, unable to make small talk in diplomatic French, unaccustomed to the finger-bowl etiquette of multi-course banquets.

The third member of the trio, Albert Gallatin, is Bayard's direct opposite, an alert and cultured Genevan who has served his adopted country as Secretary of the Treasury for almost thirteen years. He is fluent in French, witty, and has no trouble fitting into the Russian social routine, which, beginning as it does at two in the afternoon and ending at two or three the following morning, encourages the kind of late rising that is anathema to Bayard and Adams. Yet Gallatin is no lie-abed. Of the three, his mind is the sharpest, his diplomatic talents the most polished. He is about to turn fifty-three, a swarthy, compact figure with a flat, forthright face and a prominent nose. Nor has his career reached its peak: more than three decades of public service lie before him.

Gallatin and Bayard share apartments in the same building – the best rooms in the city – but each man keeps to himself, the two scarcely speaking except on official business, each going his own way in a separate carriage. On this Christmas night, with the *Te Deum* finally at an end, Bayard makes his way to Adams's quarters to pour out his resentment at his fellow lodger, who he imagines has adopted a superior air toward him. Gallatin, at the moment, is in a curious position. He has only recently learned that the Senate has refused to ratify his appointment as envoy. Though the Russians continue to treat him as a diplomat, he is, in fact, only a private citizen. Bayard does not trust him. He is convinced that Gallatin, on his return to Washington, will blame the failure of the peace negotiations on the Senate's rejection.

Adams does not yet know it, but Bayard has been making equally unkind remarks about him, Adams, in private. After six months in the Russian capital, Bayard is at the end of his tether. At first it was all very novel, very entrancing. The orphan boy from Philadelphia, sought out with his colleagues for special treatment by his Russian hosts ("a rare act of civility not heretofore experienced by any Foreigner"), was subjected to a glittering circuit of architectural wonders – palace after palace, church after church, museum after museum. There were country weekends in dazzling châteaux, theatre parties, operas, recitals, and, above all, banquets where under glistening chandeliers he rubbed shoulders with dukes and duchesses, counts and countesses, princes and princesses, never at ease with the gold and silver plate, never certain of which arm to offer to what lady. He quickly tired of all this magnificence: "There is nothing so homely in my own Country, the sight of which would not please me better...."

As Bayard's exile lengthened, the social circus palled the more. The waters of the Neva brought on attacks of diarrhea. The Russian women began to look unattractive. Their dress he found tasteless, their dinners laborious; the weather was "gloomy and detestable" and the people "as cold as their climate in its most frosty season."

For Gallatin, who moves easily among the nobility – staying for supper at the homes of his hosts, playing endless games of Boston, strolling through the gardens with the ladies, joking in his exquisite French – the long wait is just as frustrating. He has not come here to socialize but to try to end a war that neither side wants to continue.

Yet it does continue, for there is the matter of national honour. The Americans have no intention of asking the British to discuss peace terms; they must never be seen to come on bended knee! On the contrary, they hope to get a good deal more out of the peace agreement than they originally expected. James Monroe, the American Secretary of State, believes that the United States can annex all or most of Canada as it has recently acquired Louisiana. It would be, he argues, in Great Britain's best interests because she would no longer

274

have to bear the expense of supporting her North American colonies. The Americans, in fact, are prepared to offer advantages in trade as part of the bargain.

But all this depends on the British accepting the mediation that Alexander I, Emperor of Russia, has happily extended. There is the rub. It has long been obvious to the three envoys that the British have no intention of accepting the offer – have, indeed, officially rejected it. From the British point of view, the war in North America is a family quarrel to be settled directly between the belligerents without the interference of a foreign potentate. The Americans have already been made aware of this, but until they hear *officially* – from the Tsar himself – it would be a breach of protocol to leave the country, a rebuff to a friendly nation. And so the war goes on; men die in the mud of Crysler's Farm and the swamps of Châteauguay; women and children shiver, homeless, in the snows of Newark and Buffalo; farm boys cough out their lives in the tattered tents of French Mills.

The situation is complicated by the war in Europe, the difficulty and slowness of communication, the byzantine manoeuvrings of the Russian court, and the Emperor's own vain, wistful fancy that, in the end, the British may come round. The envoys have never met Alexander; he is hundreds of miles away, his days fully occupied with the problem of Napoleon. Their only contact with the Russian Emperor is through his foreign minister, the courtly Count Romanzoff, who is, unfortunately, so out of favour with his royal master that he is not always aware of what is going on.

The envoys have been trapped in the sunless Russian capital since July. Now it is January and still no word from the Tsar of all the Russias – a sign of poor Romanzoff's fall from grace. The delay is maddening. A letter takes two months to reach Washington; that means a four-month hiatus before any report can be acknowledged. News of the war is obtained tardily from the English newspapers. In the American view, these are dreadfully biased, although it has not been possible to disguise the magnitude of Barclay's defeat on Lake Erie. But the Americans have yet to learn of Wilkinson's disastrous attempt on Montreal or of the attacks along the Niagara frontier.

Gallatin, who now considers himself a private citizen no longer bound by official etiquette, is determined to leave as soon as possible. Bayard wants to leave with him – an intention that offends Adams's sense of protocol. Adams is also irked to learn that the pair are planning to visit the Emperor Alexander at Frankfurt and then proceed to

London, apparently to sound out the British on the subject of direct peace talks. The fact that the two have concocted the plan behind his back annoys him almost as much as the plan itself. For Adams is convinced that neither man can do any good by going to England "unless our Government has totally changed its principles."

The rock on which any peace negotiations must founder, in Adams's view, is the matter of impressment. The forcible seizure of British deserters from American ships on the high seas is the only remaining reason for this savage border war. Madison has explicitly told his envoys that the question of impressment cannot be set aside. But the British have flatly announced that they will refuse to discuss it. After their weary internment in the Russian capital, both Gallatin and Bayard have softened on the matter. Their inclination now is to yield; it seems the only way peace can be obtained.

Meanwhile, Adams helps Bayard prepare a note to Count Romanzoff that will allow him to leave the country without creating an international incident. He is determined to depart on the twenty-first – six months to the day after his arrival. Delicate negotiations follow; more "notes" – the mortar of diplomacy – are exchanged. On the eighteenth a note arrives from the Count indicating that if Bayard sends another note asking for an audience of leave, he can immediately quit Russia. "No words can express my joy," he scribbles in his diary. Off goes the note on the twentieth. Back comes another on the twenty-first: the Empress Mother will receive him on the twenty-third.

On that day, a Sunday, the dowager receives him. They discuss the war, agree on the hope that it will not last long. *We know you are against the war*, the Empress murmurs...*and that you should be glad of.* He presses his lips to her wrinkled paw, bows his way out, moves on to the apartments of the Grand Dukes Nicholas and Michael and the Grand Duchess Ann, nibbles at their outstretched knuckles. Finally, he is free.

The following day, a little procession takes off for the west – Bayard in a four-horse calèche, Gallatin in a four-horse carriage, six servants bringing up the rear in a six-horse landau. Somehow Gallatin's carriage becomes separated on leaving the city, runs into a snowbank, and is stalled for several hours. Bayard trots on. It will be May, and the start of a new campaign along the embattled border, before the two reach London.

John Quincy Adams is relieved to see the last of them. In his view, three heads are not better than one. The endless, niggling arguments over the precise phrasing of diplomatic notes is such that one took an entire week to compose; Adams is convinced that he could have done it alone in two hours. "In the multitude of counsellors there is safety," he has noted, "but there is not despatch." It is a portent of things to come.

In the frustrating months of waiting, Adams, the clear thinker, the scientific dabbler, the cool logician, has come perilously close to paranoia, half-convinced that his two colleagues, who make a habit of going directly to Count Romanzoff, are conspiring behind his back, trying to manoeuvre him out of the peace negotiations – a suspicion reinforced by their joint trip to London. Now a few days after their departure, the consul, Levitt Harris, comes to him to report what Bayard has been saying behind his back. The alleged remarks are scarcely damaging, but they fuel Adams's own suspicions that Bayard has also been turning Gallatin against him. He tells Harris that he hopes "never again to be placed in relations which would make it necessary to associate with Mr. Bayard." It is a vain fancy. When peace negotiations finally begin the two men will find themselves colleagues once more. But many months will pass and much blood be spilled before that becomes a reality.

●

YORK, UPPER CANADA, February 15, 1814

In the charred capital, His Honour, the President of the Legislative Council and Administrator of the Province, is pleased to open the session of both houses with what the official proceedings will describe (as always) as "a most gracious speech." The setting is new – Jordan's Hotel and Tavern must do duty as a public edifice now that the Parliament Buildings lie in ashes – and so is the President himself, who has come down from Kingston for the occasion.

He is Lieutenant-General Gordon Drummond, an unknown quantity to the handful of legislators assembled to hear him (their number depleted by capture and disaffection). They know, of course, that he is a Canadian, the first native-born general officer to take command of both the army and the civil government. He is forty-two, a New Brunswicker who has been a soldier since the age of seventeen. He must have military talent: he rose from lieutenant to colonel in just three years. His regiment, the famous 8th or King's, saw bloody action in Holland and continued to distinguish itself under its Canadian leader in the West Indies, the Mediterranean, and Egypt.

Since 1811, Drummond has been Sir George Prevost's second-in-command in Canada. Clearly he is made of sterner stuff than the despised Sheaffe or the easy-going De Rottenburg. But is he another Brock? He is certainly as handsome as Brock – with his angular, chiselled face, his thin aristocratic nose, and his dark, tight curls. (Does he use a curling iron in the fashion of the time?) John Strachan, the armchair general, who is not a member of the legislature but whose long shadow hangs over it, has reservations. Drummond, Strachan finds, is an excellent man "and a very superior private character," but somehow he lacks Brock's panache. "He seems to be destitute of that military fire and vigour of decision which the principal commander of this country must possess in order to preserve it...."

Nonetheless, in his speech to the legislature Drummond is forthright. He knows what he wants. He wants one-third of each militia regiment embodied for up to twelve months' military service. He wants the wretched provincial roads improved. He wants to continue the practice of banning all distillation of grain, for the province is teetering on the edge of starvation and every kernel of wheat, oats, and rye is needed for food. Most of all he is concerned about disaffection. The jail at York is bursting with prisoners accused of treason and sedition. The population is heavily American – at best apathetic, at worst disloyal.

So Drummond demands stern measures: a denial of the right of *habeas corpus* in certain cases; the right to confiscate the property of convicted traitors; the right to enforce martial law when necessary. The legislature allows him the first two. When it denies him the third Drummond makes it very clear who is in charge. His executive council, which he dominates (it has been reduced to three members), hastily gives him the power he seeks. He expects the lower house to censure him for it, as it censured De Rottenburg, but without it he cannot impress provisions for his troops from the reluctant settlers. Democracy, such as it is in Upper Canada, goes out the window as Drummond shows his iron fist.

He feels shackled by lack of money. At Long Point and Port Dover, debts incurred by Brock eighteen months before have yet to be paid. In consequence, the settlers will not sell their produce to the army. Small debts cannot be discharged because neither coinage nor army bills are available in denominations under twenty-five pounds. If a merchant is owed twenty pounds, he collects nothing; if he is owed forty pounds, he loses fifteen. What money does come in is scarcely enough to pay off old debts. As a result, Drummond is forced to accept loans from York merchants to cover the spending.

There are further complications: Canadians, prejudiced against paper money, want gold because the Americans are flooding the country with forged bills. There is also the problem of compensation. Everybody from John Crysler on the St. Lawrence to Isaac Dolsen on the Thames is demanding relief for war damages. Early in March, with the legislature still in session, Drummond pays a flying visit to the Thames Valley and returns to report that the entire region has been drained of its resources. There is no house that does not have a claim for reparations. The mills have been burned, the houses looted, the livestock killed or dispersed. Drummond estimates that at least thirty thousand pounds will be needed just to pay existing obligations.

The troops are in a state of discontent over the lack of pay. Some have received nothing for six months. At Fort Niagara, the captured stronghold on the American side of the river, Colonel Robert Young reports an increasing number of desertions among soldiers who are usually steady and well behaved. Pay is not the only problem. The men of Drummond's old regiment, the King's, are suffering so badly from ague and dysentery that the regiment's medical officer recommends its immediate removal. By mid-March, Major-General Riall, Vincent's replacement, reports that desertions have been increasing to an alarming degree from "that cursed Fort," as he calls it.

Riall wants to reduce the garrison and decrease the area of the fort. But Drummond has no intention of abandoning his toehold on the American bank of the Niagara. When the invasion comes, the five or six hundred men hived in the fort can stand off at least ten times their number. The best Drummond can do is to replace the King's with another regiment. Meanwhile, Riall must hold his thin line along the river, as Brock did before him, and be prepared to deploy at the moment the enemy's invasion point is known.

As soon as the river and the lakes are open the British 103rd will reinforce Riall's Centre Division (now called the Right). Drummond does not relay to Riall Prevost's assessment of that regiment: "...men who [have] long lost sight of everything that is honest and honourable. Convicts taken from the hulks to be made soldiers – but who answer to no other purpose than that of bringing the profession into discredit and disrepute...." Of all the corps last sent to Canada, Prevost believes the 103rd to be the worst. On a recent foray to destroy American stores and river craft, fifty-one of its members deserted to the enemy.

Drummond has no idea where the Americans will strike. Their movements, are, to say the least, confusing. The best part of an American division has moved from French Mills (Wilkinson's winter quarters) to Sackets Harbor and then on toward the Niagara frontier, only to turn about and march back again. Drummond cannot know it, but this is the result of an ambiguous order sent by the Secretary of War and misinterpreted by Jacob Brown. Drummond determines to sit tight, maintain his main force at Burlington Heights, and when the American intentions are known, march at the head of his army to reinforce Major-General Riall's slender defence along the Niagara.

At the moment, the weather is his enemy. An unexpected mild spell in February has frustrated a daring and unconventional attack that Drummond planned against the American fleet, wintering at Put-in Bay. The plan called for seventeen hundred men to hack a road through the forest, seize Amherstburg, cross the Detroit River, and push on to attack the ships with bill hooks, hatchets, and muskets. But the ice is too soft and the expedition must be aborted. At the same time the weather along the Niagara is so bad, the snow so deep, that no progress can be made to strengthen "that cursed Fort."

In mid-March, Drummond prorogues the legislature and returns to his headquarters at Kingston. One further problem continues to occupy him: he is convinced that some exemplary trials are needed "to overawe the spirit of disaffection in the province." John Beverley Robinson, the youthful acting attorney general, is preparing abstracts against some thirty persons for high treason. Most have left the country, but there are eight or nine who he believes can be convicted. An additional twenty remain to be indicted. These will be civil trials. As Robinson points out, "Executions of traitors by military power would have comparatively little influence. The majority of people would consider them arbitrary acts of punishment."

The accused traitors are Canadian civilians who joined groups of armed American raiders under Joseph Willcocks's second-in-command, Mallory, during the guerrilla activity the previous November. Captured by the Oxford and Norfolk militia during two encounters at Port Dover and Chatham, they have been languishing in the York jail, waiting to be tried by a special commission.

Robinson is convinced that the trial must take place as close to the homes of the accused as possible – in the London district. He well knows that the settlers in that region are generally indifferent to the interests of the autocratic government at York (in which they have little real say) and, if not indifferent, are often actively pro-American. But now the war has come to their doorstep. Willcocks, Mallory, Markle have all conducted raids on their settlements, robbing them of cattle and household goods, burning barns and homes, making prisoners of those neighbours who have joined the militia. The accused are known to them as men who actively supported the raiding parties. Some of the prospective jurors, in Robinson's words, "voluntarily resorted to arms to subdue them." Therefore it is fair to suppose that "men who risqued their lives in the apprehension of these traitors will be well satisfied to have them punished as they deserve."

To all this Drummond assents. He is anxious to have the trials take place as swiftly and as publicly as possible. For the future security of the province, a number of unfortunate farmers are shortly to be brought before a jury of their peers at the Union Hotel in Ancaster (for the London district is held to be too close to the border) and, in accordance with the ancient law still on the statute books, to be hanged, drawn, and quartered if found guilty. Nothing else, the authorities are convinced, will serve to stiffen the spines of a wavering population.

●

GOTHENBURG, SWEDEN, April 14, 1814

Henry Clay, Speaker of the House of Representatives, and his colleague, Jonathan Russell, the two newest members of what is now a five-man American peace commission, step off the gangplank of the U.S. corvette *John Adams*, which has brought them here from New York. Since the bay is choked with ice and the river frozen, they must travel twelve miles by sleigh to reach their lodgings in the heart of the town, where they confidently expect to meet the three other plenipotentiaries, now charged with dealing directly with the British – but on neutral ground.

But where *are* the others? Where are Adams, Bayard, and Gallatin, the original threesome who are to form part of the expanded commission? And where are the British negotiators? Nobody knows. Clay and Russell dispatch notes to Amsterdam and St. Petersburg informing the missing trio of their new appointment. A week passes before they learn that Bayard and Gallatin are in London. As for Adams, he has not yet left the Russian capital, but long before the letter can reach him he will be off to Reval on the Gulf of Finland, waiting for the ice to shift in the Baltic. Men of goodwill on both sides have been murmuring about peace in North America for the best part of a year, but the possibility of any face-to-face negotiation seems as remote as ever.

The five wanderers have been chosen partly for their public stature, partly for their negotiating ability, partly for what they represent. Adams and Bayard are both known to be, in James Monroe's words, "friendly to peace" – especially Bayard, a confirmed Federalist, whose party has always opposed the war. Russell and Clay are in the other camp, notably the silver-tongued Clay who, as leader of the War Hawks, helped goad the country into war in 1812. Monroe, the Secretary of State, has regional considerations also in mind. Thus Adams represents the Eastern states, Bayard the Middle, Clay the South and West, and Russell the commercial interests. As for Gallatin, as a former member of the Cabinet he stands as a buffer, the great conciliator between hawks and doves, eastern and western interests. For the negotiators must negotiate with each other as well as with the enemy.

Clay comes to Gothenburg reluctantly. He would much rather remain in Washington as Speaker, but he cannot in conscience resist this call to public service. America needs tough-minded men who will stand up to the nefarious British, and Clay is nothing if not tough-minded. It is possible to believe that without his persistence in the winter of 1811-12, the United States might not have gone to war.

His instructions and those of his colleagues are clear. The most important item on the future agenda is that of impressment. "This degrading practice must cease; our flag must protect the crew; or the United States cannot consider themselves an independent Nation." The words are Monroe's, but they might easily have sprung from Clay's own lips in the months before war was declared. Impressment is what this brutal, frustrating, inconclusive war is all about – that and the British Orders in Council establishing a blockade on the high seas. Those Orders were repealed, not at the eleventh hour, alas, but at the thirteenth, a tardiness on Britain's part that frustrated any hope of peace. Now, however, Monroe and his president, James Madison, are insisting that the whole matter of blockades – their legality and illegality – be settled by formal treaty.

Third, but not least, is the question of Canada. Here the American government's view has hardened. Canada – or at least part of it – must be ceded to the Union. Joint use of the Great Lakes will surely mean another war; it was in those common waters that the British gained control of the Indians with the resultant massacres: "The cupidity of the British Traders will admit of no control. The inevitable consequences of another war, and even of the present, if persevered in by the British Government, must be to sever those provinces by force from Great Britain. Their inhabitants themselves, will soon feel their strength, and assert their independence."

Nothing can be settled, however, until the British appoint negotiators, and this has not been done. Clay is eager to get started, but events seem to be moving at the speed of treacle. He wants Gallatin and Bayard to get to Gothenburg as quickly as possible. What are they doing in the enemy capital, anyway? Yet neither man shows any sign of moving, while Russell, the former American chargé d'affaires in London, must go off to Stockholm to present his credentials as American ambassador to Sweden. Like Adams, he will hold two jobs at the same time.

So Clay frets, all alone, in Gothenburg. He is not used to sitting still, has none of John Quincy Adams's cool patience. (That earnest diplomat is bettering himself in Reval waiting for the ice to break by working his way through the Duc de Sully's interminable memoirs of life under Henry IV of France.) Clay, the hot-tempered Kentuckian, is used to getting his way, whether in a duel, a poker game, or on the floor of the House. Now, as he paces impatiently about his new lodgings – a lank, nervous figure, his long, bony face reflecting his frustration – he must know that events have overtaken him, "wonderful events...astonishing events," to be sure, but events, nevertheless, that may have an adverse effect on the peace talks.

He is scarcely in Gothenburg a week before the news filters through that the Allies have seized Paris (on March 31), that Napoleon has abdicated, and that a new Bourbon king, Louis XVIII, is about to ascend the throne. Clay is bowled over by this dramatic and unexpected news. Napoleon, the master of Europe for more than a decade, humbled and shipped off to an obscure Mediterranean isle! Clay has anticipated peace, but *this* – this is like a revolution! No human sagacity could have foreseen it, he tells the American ambassador in Paris.

Bayard and Gallatin, who arrived in London in the midst of its delirium over Bonaparte's downfall, report to Clay some of the new facts of life. As the bells peal and the rockets explode and the people cheer the end of twenty years of war, Gallatin explains that "the complete success obtained by this country in their European contest has excited the greatest popular exultation, and this has been attended with a strong expression of resentment against the United States."

The popular feeling is entirely in favour of continuing the war. People talk of taking over the Great Lakes, pushing back the American border, dividing the Union by seducing New England back into the Imperial fold. The British now have a seasoned army sitting idle, which they cannot demobilize too quickly, as well as a superabundant naval force. The people are demanding "the chastisement of America," and even though their political leaders are less eager to continue the war, "they will not, certainly, be disposed to make concessions, nor probably displeased at a failure of negotiations." Impressment will never be repealed.

In spite of Clay's earnest hope that he will shortly leave London for Gothenburg, Gallatin is determined to stay, hoping to open direct negotiations with the British leaders, especially Lord Castlereagh, the foreign secretary.

Indeed, it has become clear that the Swedish city is the wrong place for negotiations. The British much prefer a neutral town – in Holland, say – as close as possible to London, for it is obvious that the real negotiations will be in the hands of Lord Liverpool, the Prime Minister, Lord Bathurst, the colonial secretary, and Castlereagh. Whoever are chosen as plenipotentiaries will be little more than messenger boys for the trio of peers at Whitehall. Both Gallatin and Bayard are agreed on the need for a change of location.

Meanwhile Clay receives disturbing news from Crawford, the American ambassador in Paris, who tells him that unless America either excludes the whole question of impressment from the agenda, or at least agrees to postpone it, there is no chance for any peace negotiation. The matter, he points out delicately, has become largely academic: the European war is over; Britain has too many sailors, does not need to impress anyone.

There is more. The news of Wilkinson's disgrace the previous November on the St. Lawrence has placed "all the continental powers under the direct influence of our enemy." The posturing general has turned America's potential friends against her.

The British are taking their own time naming envoys to the peace talks, which, it is finally decided, will be held at Ghent in Belgium. At last, on May 15, Christopher Hughes, secretary to the American mission, who has begged to go to London, learns unofficially who they are to be: Admiral Gambier, "a Mr. Golsby (or Goldburn)," and a Mr. Adams. They are, in short, nonentities, unknown to the Americans, equally unknown to the British public.

Admiral James Gambier, aged fifty-eight, is a blundering and sedentary flag officer with remarkably little sea experience (less than six years), known as much for his failures as for his successes, as well as for his piety and his narrow morality, which some call hypocrisy.

Henry Goulburn is so little known that Hughes, among others, gets his name wrong. He is an under-secretary for war and the colonies, a run-of-the-mill diplomat at thirty but more forceful than his two colleagues.

William Adams is an obscure Admiralty lawyer, placed on the commission because of his expertise in maritime law, on which much of the future negotiation is expected to hinge.

The choice of this threesome suggests two British attitudes. First, they hold the Americans in contempt. The United States has sent a first-class team of plenipotentiaries to Europe; the British have responded with second-class negotiators. Second, as suspected, the real decisions will be made by Great Britain in Whitehall, not at Ghent. But the British, in their hauteur, have placed themselves at a disadvantage. Their choices are no match for five tough, high-powered Americans.

In Gothenburg, winter gives way to spring, but Henry Clay is in no mood to bask in the zephyrs of late May. With Russell still in Stockholm he is all alone, his sense of isolation aggravated by a lack of knowledge of the outside world. Two weeks have passed without news from England, and the last letter could scarcely have improved his temper – a burbling report from Hughes, the commission secretary, exclaiming over the beauty of the English lawns and gardens, the extraordinary size of the capital, and "the perfect state of cultivation" of the countryside. Clay does not need this kind of report from enemy territory; it is bad enough to be cooped up here in a foreign town whose very Englishness has given it the sobriquet of "Little London."

Clay is eager now for peace, as he once was for war, but events are moving at a crawl. The boredom is driving him to distraction. He has no one to talk to, having dispatched his secretary to Amsterdam to intercept the latest news from Washington. Adams is somewhere in mid-Baltic among the ice floes, a fortnight overdue. Hughes remains in London, against Clay's wishes, goggling over the estates of the aristocrats. Gallatin is there too, still trying to see the Tsar of Russia, who has thus far eluded him – still hoping to get the negotiations moving. Bayard has set out for Ghent but has got no farther than Paris. "Perhaps never was a joint mission so disjointed & scattered," Russell remarks in a moody letter from Stockholm.

Clay will not soon find an outlet for his frustration. Two more months will slip by before the British and Americans finally meet face to face at the Hôtel d'Alcantara in Ghent. Meanwhile, the same spring that brings a bloom to the pasque flower in Sweden heralds a renewal of the war in Canada. Men are dying from musket fire and round shot, and the bloodiest battles still lie ahead.

•

WITH THE BRITISH FLEET, blockading Sackets Harbor, New York, May 24, 1814

Lieutenant-General Gordon Drummond has come down from Kingston to board Commodore James Yeo's spanking new flagship, *Prince Regent*. His purpose: to reconnoitre the Americans' chief naval base and centre of operations. Yeo and his opposite number, the sleepy-eyed Chauncey – those two "heroes of defeat," in Winfield Scott's sardonic phrase – have both declined to fight a decisive battle. Theirs has been a war, instead, of carpenters and shipwrights. All winter long at Kingston and Sackets Harbor, hundreds of men have been hammering at vessels that will never fight, each one bigger and better armed than the last. Now Drummond intends to discover how far the American shipbuilding program has progressed and, if possible, to frustrate it.

He would dearly love to mount an all-out attack on Sackets Harbor, wreck the garrison, and destroy Chauncey's partly built fleet. That would give the British undisputed control of Lake Ontario, where the fortunes of war have see-sawed over the past eighteen months. But the base is well fortified. Drummond needs at least eight hundred reinforcements to make the attempt. These the cautious governor general Sir George Prevost has denied him, fearing that it would denude Lower Canada of regular troops, leaving Montreal open to American capture.

Drummond arrives aboard *Prince Regent* to find Yeo lying in his cabin, prostrated by illness (as who is not in this war of invalids?). The following morning, May 25, the General sets off in a canoe to look over the harbour. He approaches within a mile and a half, peers through his glass, observes that Chauncey's new vessels have their topgallants across and are ready to take to the lake except for the largest ship, *Superior*, which is not yet rigged.

Once this sixty-four-gun double-decker is launched, the two fleets will again be almost equal in firepower. All winter long the rival commanders have struggled to outbuild each other. When Chauncey learns that Yeo is constructing the largest ship ever to ply an inland lake – almost as large as Nelson's *Victory* – he orders that his own flagship be increased in size. When Yeo, in reply, undertakes to build the largest ship in the world – *St. Lawrence*, a gigantic three-decker, mounting 120 guns – Chauncey makes plans to go him one better.

The road from Albany to Sackets is jammed with wagon trains hauling supplies for the new fleet. On Canada's Atlantic coast, four sloops of war are laid up in order to supply seamen for the vessels being built at Kingston. Every skilled carpenter in Montreal has been rounded up to work on the British fleet. At Sackets Harbor, four hundred shipwrights are toiling in shifts. The cost on both sides is horrendous. The British have secretly hired two hundred ox teams from Vermont and New Hampshire to haul guns and cable to Kingston. It costs two thousand pounds to bring six thirty-two-pounders into the naval yard, a thousand pounds to haul in a single large cable from Sorel. Small wonder that the government's bills in Upper Canada go unpaid.

Shortly after Drummond returns to *Prince Regent*, one of his spies confirms his assessment. *Superior* is still short of heavy guns, rigging, and cable, all held up at Oswego Falls because of the British blockade. As long as the fleet lurks outside the harbour, these essentials, which can be moved only by water, are denied to Chauncey: his biggest ship lies helpless and unarmed.

The American commander, however, has a plan to run the blockade using nineteen bateaux, which move at night, hide in small inlets by day. Drummond discovers the scheme, sends off a detachment of gunboats to capture the blockade runners. The Americans flee up a winding creek, the Big Sandy, and ambush their pursuers, killing, wounding, or capturing the entire British force. From this point the Americans haul their cannon, cable, and supplies sixteen miles overland to the shipyard. With the naval balance about to change again on the lake, Drummond and Yeo call off the blockade.

Will the enemy now attack Yeo before his great ship, still building at Kingston, is ready? Drummond does not believe they will – not until *their* great ship is ready. Even then, he suggests, they are unlikely to seek an encounter. He advises Yeo to stay on the defensive until the mighty *St. Lawrence* is ready to sail. Then, perhaps, the British can venture out of Kingston harbour and destroy the American fleet. Drummond does not consider a more likely possibility – that Chauncey, discovering Yeo's superiority, will commence construction of another ship to equal the odds, that Yeo will then follow suit, and that long after the war is over four more great vessels, all unfinished, never to be launched, will be on the ways at Kingston and Sackets Harbor, preparing to fight a battle that can never take place.

•

BUFFALO, NEW YORK, June 4, 1814

Winfield Scott, newly promoted to brigadier-general, has been drilling his raw recruits unmercifully since March 24, preparing for an expected invasion of Canada. Now he draws up his brigade in a hollow square on the training ground to witness the execution of five men sentenced to be shot for desertion. The prisoners stand before them, dressed grotesquely in white robes – their winding sheets – with white caps on their heads and red targets over their hearts.

Five graves stand open before them. Beside each grave lies a coffin. Each of the condemned men is made to kneel between coffin and grave as the firing party approaches. For every prisoner there are twelve riflemen.

Officers load the weapons, return them to the firing party. The chaplain murmurs a short prayer. The white caps are pulled down over the eyes of the victims. As soon as the order is given, the guns explode and five men drop as one, some toppling into the open graves, others sprawling across their coffins. One struggles feebly. A sergeant approaches, aims the muzzle of his piece a yard from the victim's head, blows him into eternity.

Suddenly a murmur ripples across the ranks as one of the corpses slowly rises to his knees and is helped to his feet.

"By God," he says, "I thought I was dead!"

He has been judged too young to die. This is Brigadier-General Scott's blunt method of telling him he has been reprieved by having his men fire blank cartridges.

The gesture is typical of Scott, a harsh disciplinarian and self-taught tactician who has, at last, been given the command he has sought for so long. Brevetted a brigadier-general in March, he is now, at twenty-eight, the youngest general officer in the American army and the symbol of a new attitude. The tired veterans of another war – Hampton, Wilkinson, Dearborn, and others – are out of the army. John Armstrong has all but scrapped the stale tradition of seniority. George Izard, aged thirty-eight, has been promoted; so has Eleazar Ripley, aged thirty-two. And Jacob Brown, at thirty-nine, is now major-general in command of the Northern Army. Amos Hall no longer leads the New York militia. His replacement is Henry Clay's congressional crony and War Hawk, the ebullient Peter B. Porter.

In this new pantheon one name is unaccountably missing, that of William Henry Harrison, surely an able commander and, some believe, the best-qualified man to lead the new invasion. But Harrison has resigned. He cannot – *will* not – work under Armstrong, cannot abide the Secretary's repeated interference in his command. Armstrong, on his part, has accepted Harrison's resignation without demur. For the Secretary of War, William Henry Harrison is too independent.

The new head of the Northern Army, Jacob Brown, is an aggressive and imaginative commander but with little regular experience, and certainly no tactician. He remains at his headquarters at Sackets Harbor and leaves the training of the army to Winfield Scott at Buffalo. Scott is in his element. No more ambitious officer exists in the United States. For two years he has actively sought promotion, frustrated to the point of fury by the imbecilities – a typical Scott word – of the past two years. Compromised at Queenston Heights by a well-meaning but green commander, deserted by a craven militia, captured, and imprisoned by the British in the winter of 1812-13, held back during the attack on Fort George by the incompetence of Boyd, maddened by Wilkinson's posturing on the St. Lawrence, he is finally on his own, able at last to put into practice those military theories that he has soaked up from his voluminous reading.

He may not know everything about war, but he acts as if he does. His fellow officers shrink from arguments on tactics or strategy, for Scott is able at a moment's notice to clinch the debate by quoting an incontrovertible authority. His baggage wagon carries Scott's considerable library – a variety of military works, biographies of the great soldiers of history, and the latest texts on drill and strategy imported from Europe. In future years, when Scott is the nation's leading soldier, this will come to be known as "the Scott tradition."

In Scott, the army has found a remarkable commander. He is a little pompous and more than a little vain but has reason to be both. He has studied Greek, Latin, and French, rhetoric, metaphysics, mathematics, political economy, philosophy, and law. He is an omnivorous reader: Plutarch, Shakespeare, Milton, Adam Smith, John Locke. He rides well, holds his liquor, plays chess, knows how to keep a conversation going. He is also a gourmet who believes that a knowledge of good food and its preparation is one of the accomplishments of a gentleman and a soldier – a view not lost on the army cooks.

He is also pugnacious. As a boy of thirteen he defended his Quaker schoolteacher from a drunken brawler, knocking the man down with a single blow. A furrowed skull is evidence of a successful duel. In his full-dress uniform, the long-legged Scott – a towering six-foot-five – cuts a handsome figure and knows it. When he received his first uniform – a sartorial symphony of blue and gold, scarlet and white – he strutted for two hours before two full-length mirrors, admiring himself.

He is a man of colossal ego, superbly confident of his own abilities, which, happily for him, are considerable. Here at Buffalo his military library comes into its own. Since the government has not provided him with a text on infantry tactics, Scott has dug into his baggage to discover a dog-eared copy of the French regulations issued by Napoleon and has made it his military Bible. Since March he has been acting as a drill sergeant, beginning with the officers, teaching them to march in column and line, to wheel and deploy, to load and fire their muskets with some degree of efficiency, to charge with fixed bayonets.

For three months, ten hours a day, Scott drills his men, allowing nothing to interrupt him except darkness or rain. Once the officers are schooled, the lower ranks are put to work. In the morning, the corporals drill their squads. At eleven, the captains take over. At one the entire brigade, complete with officers and musicians, turns out for four more hours. To Jarvis Hanks the drummer boy, who has come overland from French Mills with his comrades, Winfield Scott is "the most thorough disciplinarian I ever saw."

There has been some grumbling and a flurry of desertions. But now with four corpses lying on the drill ground and a fifth prisoner fainting dead away from the shock of his resurrection, there will be no more. Indeed, officers and men alike are gaining a new respect for themselves, as well as for their commander, who now finds them "healthy, sober, cheerful and docile." Scott has left nothing to chance. A stickler for cleanliness, he has borne down so hard on sanitary conditions that the army has lost only two men from illness.

The camp is secure. Scott has organized night patrols, guards, sentinels, outposts. He insists on civility, etiquette, and courtesy and lays down rules to enforce "these indispensable outworks of subordination." Woe to the soldier who forgets to salute a junior lieutenant! Woe to the officer who fails to return the salute.

He also has at his command an intelligence arm – a small force of spies, which he personally directs. They are mainly Americans with friends living north of the border, or disaffected Canadians who can come and go fairly freely. Scott's practice is to throw them out to the rear of the British right flank as far as Burlington Heights and even to York. The spies hide in the homes of sympathizers who visit the British posts to find out for them what Scott wants to know.

Scott has at least one captive traitor in the British midst, an anonymous captain in one of the regular regiments who has volunteered to pass along military secrets. "I hold him," Scott tells Armstrong in his florid fashion, "by one of the strongest cords that bind the human heart – a sentiment of steady and determined revenge. I know his private history."

Thus, the new brigadier is able to inform the War Department in Washington of the exact British strength at York, Lake Simcoe, Burlington Heights, Fort George, Fort Niagara, Queenston, Chippawa, and Fort Erie. He has details of new fortifications, emplacements, blockhouses, supply depots. He knows the topography of the Niagara peninsula, the distance between communities, the state of the roads, the best places to effect a landing. In short, he is preparing for the next invasion of Canada, carefully and methodically. His men, in his own words, "sigh for orders to beat up the enemy's quarters."

Some, however, have carried the beating up too far in the smash-and-grab raids launched by the Americans along the shoreline of Lake Erie. Abraham Markle, the man who directs Scott's spies to the homes of dissident Canadians, is not above settling old scores – and therein lies danger. Markle is a crony of Joseph Willcocks, an officer in the Canadian Volunteers, a former member of the Upper Canadian legislature who defected about the same time as his fellow turncoat.

He is responsible for urging that the homes of old Revolutionary Tories in the Long Point area be destroyed. On May 16, he guided a raiding party across the lake, ostensibly to destroy public property. Instead, it burned every house, barn, and private building between Port Dover and Turkey Point – an act of revenge, for their owners were among those who burned Buffalo the previous December.

That is too much for Scott. The last thing he wants is a continuation of the tit-for-tat incendiary war that flared up the previous winter. He calls a court of inquiry which disavows the act, but it is too late. Sir George Prevost is outraged; he has already indicated that as far as the British are concerned, vengeance for the destruction of Newark ended with the burning of Buffalo. Now he asks the navy, patrolling the eastern seaboard, to act to deter further American raids. Vice-Admiral Alexander Cochrane is happy to co-operate. He issues an order to "destroy and lay waste such towns and districts as you may find assailable...." The firing of private property becomes official British policy. It will not be tempered until Washington itself is in flames.

•

FRANKFORT, KENTUCKY, June 6, 1814

It is late evening. From the open window of the dining room in Weisinger's Tavern on the outskirts of town comes the sound of revelry and hoarse voices raised in song. What is this? "Rule Britannia"? "God Save the King"? It is too much for the crowd of Southerners gathered below the open windows. They surge forward, maddened by the foreign voices, and try to rush the stairs, only to be halted by Dan Weisinger himself, a man of substance and authority who has been selling claret to the revellers at thirty dollars a case and has no intention of losing their custom.

The celebrants are prisoners of war. The captured officers from Barclay's fleet are here as are those of the 41st taken at the Battle of the Thames. The group includes the young gentleman volunteer from Amherstburg, John Richardson, now a tall seventeen-year-old.

After eight months in captivity, things have eased. No longer fettered in stifling prisons, Richardson and his comrades are on parole, dressed in the grey cotton blouses affected by Kentucky riflemen. A Frankfort banker has guaranteed their bills so that they are able this night to celebrate the birthday of the mad old king, George III, in a style to which, as officers of His Majesty, they have become accustomed.

For John Richardson it has been a remarkable experience, thanks largely to the American connections of his maternal grandfather, the Canadian fur trader John Askin, Sr., who is the father-in-law of Elijah Brush, the American commander of the militia at Detroit. For many a family living along the international border this is a civil war in more than one sense, for the Brush family has been remarkably civil to their enemy kinsman.

In Chillicothe, another member of the family, Henry Brush, took Richardson under his wing, supplied him with a private apartment, regular meals, and a horse. As Richardson put it, "no individual in the character of a prisoner of war had less reason to inveigh against his destiny."

Now he is in Frankfort with the others. The news of Napoleon's defeat has put a new complexion on the war. Lodged in the town's principal hotel, they are paid the regulation three shillings a day — more than sufficient for their board, which includes three hearty meals and all the whiskey they can drink.

In the garden, taking their daily constitutional, the British have been objects of an intense if hostile interest by the long-limbed Kentuckians who come to stare and gibe, surprised to discover that their enemies are white and not like the Indians, as they have been taught to believe. When the prisoners reply to the Kentuckians' jeers in kind, young Richardson records the odd comments, delivered "in their usual nasal drawling tone."

Tarnation if these Britishers don't treat us as if we were their prisoners than they ours.

Roar me up a sapling if they aren't mighty saucy.

By Christ, I've the swiftest horse, the truest rifle, and the prettiest sister in the whole state of Kentucky, but I'd give 'em all to have one long shot.

This zoo-like atmosphere is soon dissipated as the government puts the prisoners on parole and tells them they can leave for Canada if they can pay their way. The field officers depart; the others remain, enjoying the run of the town.

Most Kentuckians cannot forget that some of these men were present at the River Raisin and again at Fort Meigs, when the Indians had their way with wounded prisoners. Yet there are others, perhaps with stronger reasons to be bitter, who have long since forgiven and forgotten. One of these is George Madison, the American major who surrendered to Procter at the Raisin. Another is Madison's friend Betsey Hickman, daughter of the disgraced General Hull and widow of Captain Paschal Hickman who, after his capture at Frenchtown, was tomahawked by the Potawatomi and allowed to choke to death in his own blood.

Major Madison cannot forget that the British in Lower Canada treated him well. He determines to return the compliment and helps arrange parole for the officers. As for Betsey Hickman, she has known Richardson since he was a small boy, for the Hulls of Detroit and the Askins of Amherstburg were old friends and neighbours before the war. As far as she is concerned, such friendships cannot be shattered by politics, and so John Richardson becomes a regular guest in her home.

He is more than a little in love with the buxom Betsey, even though she has three teen-aged daughters not much younger than himself. In spite of the tragedies of the previous eighteen months – her father sentenced to be shot, her husband cruelly slaughtered – she retains her beauty and her good humour. She is both rich and desirable. When a tall, husky Kentuckian named James starts to pay her court, Richardson seethes. In the younger man's mind, James is "a man of vulgar bearing and appearance...evidently little used to the decorum necessary to be preserved in the society of females." When James goes so far as to smoke a cigar in the presence of ladies, Richardson cannot resist a comment on his bad manners. James glares at him, leaves the room, and from then on appears to avoid the youth.

Meanwhile, word has arrived of a prisoner exchange. Richardson hurries to the Hickman home to murmur his goodbyes, then, late at night, heads back to his quarters only to find the malevolent James barring his path.

"You have escaped me once," says James (or so the future novelist and playwright will recall it), "but I'll take good care you don't again."

A stiletto flashes. A hand grips Richardson by the collar. He wriggles free, dashes off, hears a shrill whistle from behind as a group of James's friends leap from their hiding place in pursuit. Fear spurs him on – up a slope, over a garden wall, down a pathway, through a stubborn gate, home to the tavern.

Next day Richardson loses no time in recounting the story to the Hickman family, whereupon, to his immense satisfaction, the spirited

Betsey announces that James will never again darken her door. It is as well Richardson is leaving, for James is armed, but a paroled prisoner is allowed neither weapons nor a lock on his door.

Off goes Richardson next morning with his fellow officers, each attired in a light Kentucky frock fastened by a red Morocco belt with a silver buckle. They mount their horses and follow their escort through the streets, heading north toward Canada with the blessings of George Madison and a knot of friends ringing in their ears and the scowls of the rest of the populace engraved on their memories. Richardson half expects another ambush or perhaps a single shot from a long Kentucky rifle; as the company trots along he examines every tree lest it hide an enemy. There is nothing.

John Richardson's war is over, but his life is just beginning. The events of these crowded teen-age years will become grist for the literary mill he is constructing; and the people he has encountered — Tecumseh, Betsey, George Madison's daughter Agatha, even the ill-humoured James — will, in thin fictional disguises, achieve an immortality of sorts in the literary works that flow from his pen.

●

ANCASTER, UPPER CANADA, June 18, 1814

John Beverley Robinson, acting attorney general for the province, veteran of Queenston Heights, leading member of the ruling aristocracy, ward and disciple of the Reverend Dr. John Strachan, is penning a careful letter in his slanting copperplate to General Drummond, via his aide, Captain Robert Loring.

He weighs his words carefully, for, as a result of what he writes, some men will die gruesomely while others will live. At the Union Hotel on the main street of this little village, the trials for high treason, soon to be known (a little unfairly) as the Bloody Assizes, are coming to an end. It is Robinson's task to sum up the evidence for Drummond and to indicate which of the guilty men should be executed and which, if any, should be reprieved.

A handsome, personable young man with delicate, almost feminine features, at the age of twenty-three he carries the burden of justice in Upper Canada on his shoulders. (The solicitor general, D'Arcy Boulton, captured en route to England, now languishes in a French jail.) He is not without experience of the world. He has seen men die, including his predecessor, John Macdonell, Brock's stricken aide, who was also the senior partner in the law firm to which Robinson was articled. He owes his present position to John Strachan and to Mr. Justice William Dummer Powell, one of the three senior jurists who have been taking the treason cases here in rotation.

Strachan, who has an ability to spot talent, took Robinson under his wing as a small boy, paid his tuition at his famous Cornwall school, invited him into his household, counselled him, and ever since has bombarded his protégé with letters of advice, reproof, praise, caution. For most of his life, young Robinson has struggled to achieve the standards his foster father set for him. It has not been easy.

Like many others this sickly spring, he has been so ill that it has required an enormous effort to come from York to Ancaster to preside at the prosecution of the twenty-one men charged with high treason. Yet come he must, "for I shall enjoy very little rest or comfort until these prosecutions are ended."

Strachan cannot resist telling him how to run the trial:

"Do not indulge yourself in asperity of expression against the Prisoners – a dignified statement of the magnitude of their crime will have more weight.... In addressing the jury appeal to their reason rather than their passion.... Much depends upon the success of the first trial, bring forward the greatest offender.

"In regard to your opposing Barristers. Be cool – neither harsh nor supercilious. Boldly demand authorities for random objections. This will frequently confound the objector....

"Be not surprised at unexpected objections.... On such occasions you may assume a bolder tone – remind the court that the public have rights as well as their Prisoners, that if frivolous objections are allowed to defeat substantial justice Society cannot exist...."

Whether or not Robinson has taken Strachan's advice, he has been remarkably successful. Of seventeen persons tried, thirteen have been convicted. Four trials remain, but two will have to be held over until the fall, for the evidence arrived too late. The others proceed on the morrow.

Robinson has handled the cases without any Crown officers to assist him, with no one to share the responsibility of public prosecutor, with the enemy in possession of part of the district in which the court sits. He has been meticulously correct, resisting all pressure for summary justice, some of which comes from the Administrator himself, for Drummond keeps importuning him to speed things up and to offer the wavering public some spine-stiffening examples of treason unmasked before the summer campaign gets under way.

Now Robinson, mulling over the records of the accused, decides that eight have no claim to mercy. The remainder, he suggests, might escape with something less than the maximum penalty, but "an unconditional free pardon should in no case be granted." There are some extenuating circumstances, however.

There is, for instance, the confused case of Samuel and Stephen Hartwell, former Americans who returned to their native country immediately war was declared and were captured at Detroit as bona fide prisoners of war. Upper Canada is full of people not unlike the Hartwells – recent arrivals from the United States who do not yet think of themselves as British or Canadian, who have little interest (and even less say) in the government of the province, whose loyalties are tenuous if not non-existent, who have no desire to fight their former countrymen, and who may, indeed, feel that they are traitors if they do. Unlike the Hartwells, who made their personal loyalties clear at the outset and crossed back over the border, most of these rootless farmers sit tight, suppress their feelings, try to stay out of trouble. Technically the Hartwells are traitors, but Robinson is well aware of the problem and realizes that "from the former relations between the two countries many cases of such nice discrimination may arise." That being the case, "perhaps from political motives even, it is best not to strain the law to its utmost rigor...."

There is also the murky case of Jacob Overholzer, "an ignorant man from Fort Erie of considerable property and a good farmer...not a man of influence or enterprise [who] it is thought acted as he did from motives of personal enmity to the persons thus taken away who are not of themselves men of good character." Ninety-six of Overholzer's neighbours have signed a petition asking a pardon for this "unfortunate but honest old man," whom they describe as "peaceable, sober and industrious...and a good neighbour." No other prisoner has received such an accolade.

Overholzer is a victim of circumstance, a model farmer and also a newly arrived American, a target for private grudges and public revenge by reason of the depredations of the enemy along the Niagara. After the burning of Newark some of his neighbours threatened to seize his land and burn his buildings. Three of his enemies stole his horses, harnesses, and household goods. When Overholzer complained to the authorities, the thieves turned on Overholzer, branding him as a traitor for his part in a recent American raid. This confused series of charges and countercharges might well have blown over had it not been for the temper of the times. The magistrate who heard the case originally dismissed the charges as nothing more than an example of unneighbourly spite. Now they have been dredged up again, and Overholzer's defence is rejected.

Robinson leaves the matter of clemency to Drummond, but urges that one or two sentences be carried out as swiftly as possible, to awe the populace. The following Monday – June 20 – the last two accused are found guilty. On Tuesday, the convicted men are brought from the temporary jail in the Union Mill, a building owned, ironically, by Abraham Markle, another traitor tried *in absentia*. Standing in the dock, with the public looking on, the fifteen farmers listen to the sentence in the form presented for centuries by the Common Law:

"That each of you are to be taken to the place from whence you came and from thence you are to be drawn on hurdles to the place of execution, whence you are to be hanged by the neck, but not until you are dead, for you must be cut down while alive and your entrails taken out and burned before your faces, your head then to be cut off and your bodies divided into four quarters and your heads and quarters to be at the King's disposal. And may God have mercy on your souls."

Thomas Scott, the Chief Justice, hastens to assure Drummond that "in point of fact this sentence is never exactly executed; the executioner invariably taking care not to cut the body down until the criminal is dead, but the sentence of the law is always pronounced." He adds that "the impressions which those convictions have made on the public mind will be, so far as I can judge, striking and lasting...."

It is Scott's view, and Robinson's, that only the worst of the traitors need be executed, perhaps one for each of the London and Niagara districts, "since example is the chief end of punishment and...the punishment of a few would have an equal, and I even think a more salutary effect in this province, than the punishment of many."

Scott adds that "the very novelty and horror of the punishment of that crime will have a most powerful effect...."

Upper Canada has always been a docile and law-abiding province. Scott, speaking for the ruling clique, wants to keep it that way. For beneath the placid surface can be discerned the ferment of American-style democracy and republicanism, the political philosophies of the enemy, fuelled by American victories on Lake Erie and the Thames. That must be stamped out ruthlessly.

Drummond mulls over Robinson's and Scott's advice, decides that the eight listed in Robinson's letter shall die. At Burlington Heights, on July 20, the sentences are carried out after a fashion. A rude gallows with eight nooses awaits the victims, who are driven in two wagons to the scene. Once the nooses are adjusted, the wagons are driven off, leaving the prisoners to strangle. Their contortions are such that a heavy brace comes loose and falls, striking one of the dying men on the head and mercifully putting an end to his struggles. Later all eight heads are chopped off and publicly exhibited.

Of the remainder of the accused, one manages to escape. Three are eventually banished from Canada for life. But Garrett Neill, "an ignorant and inconsiderable man," Isaac Pettit, who joined the rebels because he could not stand to be called a coward, and Jacob Overholzer, the victim of his neighbours' rancour in this incendiary conflict, surrender to a different fate. Confined in the crowded and stinking military prison at Kingston, they contract a virulent form of typhus and succumb, one by one, to the disease three months after the war is over.

9

THE STRUGGLE
FOR THE FUR COUNTRY
May — September, 1814

The watershed of the Upper Mississippi, though technically American, is an economic no-man's land, where British traders operate easily. Guarding the entrance to this domain is Michilimackinac Island, ceded to the United States after the Revolution and captured by the British in July, 1812. For economic reasons as well as military, the Americans must recapture it. The lateness of the season prevented such an expedition following Harrison's victory on the Thames in October, 1813. But there is no doubt that, when spring comes, the Americans will try again.

MICHILIMACKINAC ISLAND, Lake Huron, May 18, 1814

To the infinite relief of the half-starved British garrison, a long line of bateaux, laden with stores, provisions, weapons, and soldiers, arrives at this captured American fort after more than three weeks of battling the shrieking gales and grinding ice floes of the great inland sea. The new commander, Lieutenant-Colonel Robert McDouall of the Glengarry Fencibles, a Scot with eighteen years' regular service, steps ashore and takes command from Captain Richard Bullock of the 41st.[*]

The British are determined to hold this great lump of Precambrian schist, for if they lose it they lose control of the western fur trade. Every craft moving southwest toward Green Bay, or to the Wisconsin-Fox portage, or to the headwaters of the Mississippi-Missouri system must come within reach of its guns. Sir George Prevost, the Governor General, is well aware of its significance. As he explains in a letter to Lord Bathurst: "Its geographical position is admirable. Its influence extends and is felt amongst the Indian tribes at New Orleans and the Pacific Ocean; vast tracts of country look to it for protection and supplies, and it gives security to the great establishments of the Northwest and Hudson's Bay Companies by supporting the Indians on the Mississippi."

---

[*] Not to be confused with Lieutenant Richard Bullock, also of the 41st, a coincidence of nomenclature that has misled many historians.

Prevost is convinced that Mackinac is the only barrier preventing American expansion westward to the Red River. If it falls, the enemy will monopolize the fur trade of the Northwest.

Washington's first blunder of the war – some say the greatest – was the failure to alert the American commander at Michilimackinac that war had been declared. The subsequent British occupation inspired the northwestern tribes to join the British and led directly to the loss of Detroit. Now, with Detroit again in American hands and control of Lake Erie wrested from the British, this mini-Gibraltar is in peril.

All winter long, Captain Bullock has been doing his best to strengthen the fort. The garrison has survived only through careful rationing. The troops have been without meat since March, existing on local corn and fish. Now, on this bright May day, soldiers and civilians crowd to the shoreline to help unload the barrels and sacks of provisions.

Until this moment, the beleaguered Bullock had no idea whether the first boats to arrive after the spring breakup would fly the Stars and Stripes or the Union Jack. But while the Americans dallied, McDouall dared. By crossing the lake at the moment of the breakup, he has beaten the enemy to the island and shortened the odds against its capture.

He is a courageous and resourceful officer, a former aide to Procter and a veteran of the midnight battle at Stoney Creek. He brings with him ninety members of the Royal Newfoundland Regiment, together with a party of shipwrights, twenty-one seamen, eleven gunners in charge of four field pieces, and twenty-nine large bateaux. The journey has been made from York through the snows along the old overland route to Nottawasaga Bay and then across the lake, the boats dodging between the grinding floes, the men half frozen on the oars. Yet McDouall has lost only one boat and managed to save its cargo and its crew.

A few days later a second reinforcement arrives – two hundred picked Indian warriors, mainly Sioux and Winnebago, led by the Red-Haired Man, the legendary Robert Dickson. McDouall has certainly heard of Dickson – who has not? – the most celebrated Indian leader in the Northwest, the most admired and the most mysterious. Like McDouall, he is a Scot, gigantic of frame and full of face, with a shock of flaming hair that has given him the Sioux cognomen of *Mascotopah*. No other white man commands the respect of the tribes as Dickson does; the contrast between him and some other leading members of the Indian Department is startling. Unlike Matthew Elliott (dead now of exhaustion and old age), he is highly literate. Unlike Thomas McKee, a hopeless drunkard, he is temperate. Unlike John Norton, who is jealous of his superiors and suspected by some of his followers, he commands the absolute loyalty, even love, of his people. Most of the others forsook their Indian women for white brides; not Dickson. He remains faithful to his Sioux wife. One cannot imagine Dickson standing by, as Elliott and the others did at Fort Miami, while the tribesmen attacked defenceless prisoners; he will not allow his people to kill or torture captives. No one in the department matches his reputation for humanity, courage, integrity, zeal.

That is Sir George Prevost's assessment. Dickson and his Indian followers were the key to the capture of Michilimackinac by the British in 1812. The following January, the Governor General persuaded the Red-Haired Man to give up the fur trade and become a government employee — agent to the Indians of the Northwest. When Elliott and his colleagues at Amherstburg tried to put obstacles in Dickson's way, Prevost promoted him to a separate command, naming him Assistant Superintendent of Indian Affairs in Michigan Territory and all captured lands, reporting directly to Procter.

Thus Dickson is both diplomat and military leader. His task is to unite all the diverse and squabbling tribesmen against the Long Knives. In this cause, his peregrinations are extraordinary. He vanishes into the wilderness for months at a time, turns up unexpectedly, vanishes again. Though no one can ever be sure where Dickson is, one thing is certain: he covers astonishing distances in remarkably short periods of time. Leaving Montreal in mid-January, 1813, he set off on a fifteen-hundred-mile journey that few, if any, have equalled, travelling to Fort George, Amherstburg, Detroit, the Wabash, Chicago, Green Bay, and eventually arriving at Prairie du Chien on the upper Mississippi in mid-April. He went on to Mackinac, took part with his Indians in the siege of Fort Meigs and the attack on Fort Stephenson, pushed on to Kingston to pick up presents for the Indians, moved overland from York by way of Lake Simcoe and the Nottawasaga River, crossed Lake Huron to Mackinac again, then set off for Garlic Island on Lake Winnebago, where he spent the winter.

He has lived a life of hardship without complaint while his brothers, Thomas and William, occupy fine homes at Queenston and Newark. On Lake Winnebago, while the Americans were burning William's brick mansion in Newark, the Red-Haired Man was close to starvation. By February, he and his Indians had only eight handfuls of wild rice, ten pounds of black flour, two shanks of deer, three frozen cabbages, and a few potatoes left on which to exist.

By March, his situation was desperate. "I am heartily sick of this place," he wrote. "There is no situation more miserable than to see objects around you dying of hunger and [to be] unable to give them but little assistance. I have done what I could for them and in consequence will starve myself."

He loves his people. He could easily leave them, but that is not his way. He hangs on until the snow melts in April, then goes off to Prairie du Chien to recruit more followers to the British cause. That accomplished, he sets off with his tribal army to defend Michilimackinac.

With Dickson's arrival, McDouall seizes the opportunity to deliver to the assembled chiefs the kind of flowery speech required of army commanders. He chooses the King's birthday – the same day on which John Richardson and his fellow prisoners decide to toast their sovereign in the hostile Kentucky capital.

The Americans, McDouall asserts in his Scots burr, are intent on destroying the Indians and seizing their lands:

"My children, you possess the Warlike spirit of your fathers. You can only avoid this horrible fate by joining hand in hand with my warriors in first driving the Big Knives from this Island and again opening the great road to your country...."

The speech is popular and so is the speaker. The Indians like the way McDouall treats them. Dickson finds "the greatest satisfaction in conducting the Indian business in conjunction with him."

The British are ready, and indeed eager, to defend the island; but the Americans do not come. The Indians grow restless. Some want to head down the lake and fight the enemy on the water – a dangerous proposal in the light of the Americans' known naval strength.

Then, on June 21, two voyageurs beach a small bark canoe under the brow of the frowning cliffs and inform McDouall that an American raiding party, three hundred strong, has seized Prairie du Chien on the Upper Mississippi. Its leader is General William Clark, Governor of Missouri Territory. The following day, the Tête du Chien, one of the leading chiefs of the Winnebago, arrives with a grisly tale. Clark, on capturing the settlement, seized eight Winnebago, cajoled them at first with kindness, set food before them, and then as they were eating had them murdered in cold blood. Only one escaped. Worse was to follow. Clark shut up four others in a log building and then shot them. One was the Tête du Chien's brother, and another the wife of Wabasha, first chief of the Sioux.

The Indians are screaming for revenge, and McDouall is faced with a difficult decision. His task is to hold the fort: dare he chance an expedition down the Mississippi to recapture the outpost and to exact revenge for Clark's depredations? To do so is to weaken his own position and to leave Michilimackinac wide open to enemy attack from across the lake.

He has little choice. If he does not accede to the Indians' wishes he loses the support of the tribes. If that happens the Americans will win the Upper Mississippi – the gateway to the Canadian Northwest: "The total subjugation of the Indians on the Mississippi would either lead to their extermination...or they would be spared on the express condition of assisting them to expel us from Upper Canada."

The chiefs of the Winnebago and the Sioux ask two favours of McDouall. They want a white man from the Indian Department to command the expedition, and they want an artillery piece. McDouall cannot spare more than eighteen of his regulars, but he assigns Sergeant James Keating of the Royal Artillery to accompany a force of civilian volunteers with a brass three-pounder. William McKay, an officer of the North West Company, is appointed temporary lieutenant-colonel in charge of the force. Two members of the Indian Department, Thomas G. Anderson and Joseph Rolette, decked out in red coats and epaulettes, with red feathers in their hats, are detailed to raise two companies of local volunteers while Dickson detaches part of his Indian force – two hundred Sioux, three hundred Winnebago.

On June 28, this hastily assembled strike force sets off down Lake Michigan to be joined by seventy-five Menominee, twenty-five Chippewa, and a company of Green Bay Fencibles, while McDouall, in his fort above the cliffs of Mackinac, awaits the inevitable attack upon his island.

•

MICHILIMACKINAC ISLAND, Lake Huron, July 26, 1814

Daybreak. From the island's highest promontory, McDouall's sentinels see the blurred outlines of half a dozen sailing ships emerging from the fog – part of Perry's former fleet on Lake Erie. The long-expected invasion of the island is about to begin.

McDouall cannot understand why the Americans have waited so long. The breathing space of several weeks has given him time to strengthen his defences. If the Americans had come even a week or so earlier, he would not have had at his disposal those Indians who have just returned from the expedition down the Mississippi. He would like to have the remainder of the Mississippi force, but at least he has the consolation of knowing that the Union Jack flies over Prairie du Chien. The upper river is a British waterway and will remain so if McDouall can hold Michilimackinac.

Why the delay? The answer is to be found in American procrastination, hesitancy, bad planning, wrong decisions. The expedition was projected as long ago as April, then cancelled (in the mistaken belief that the British were not eager to command the upper lakes), and revived again. The fleet did not sail until July, when it set out for a British supply base reported at Macadesh Bay on the southeastern extremity of Lake Huron. Nobody, as it turned out, knew how to get there. Nobody had thought to bring a pilot who could lead the fleet through the maze of fog-shrouded islands and sunken rocks behind which the bay was concealed.

At that point, the fleet's commander, Captain Arthur Sinclair, in an incredible decision overruled the army commander, Lieutenant-Colonel George Croghan, defender of Fort Stephenson. Croghan wanted to make sail for Mackinac without delay; Sinclair insisted on first attacking and burning the deserted British fort on St. Joseph's Island, forty miles to the north.

Now, at last, the Americans are standing off Mackinac – the big brigs *Lawrence* and *Niagara*, the smaller schooners *Scorpion* and *Tigress*, and two gunboats. With one thousand soldiers, Croghan outnumbers the defenders two to one. On the island, the older settlers gaze upon the fleet with mixed feelings, some anxious for an American victory so that they may renew acquaintances and cement old loyalties, others fearful that should the invasion succeed, they may be hanged as traitors. Allegiances on this rock-bound island are fragile. In two decades it has changed hands three times.

From his vantage point in the fort, 120 feet above the village, McDouall is uneasy. His defences are in good shape, but he has only 140 soldiers. The Indians are an unknown quantity, "as fickle as the wind." Worse, he is desperately short of supplies. Dickson's followers have so badly depleted his stores that he has had to refuse rations to their wives and children and to reduce those of his white garrison. The enemy can beat him merely by sitting still, blockading the island, starving him into submission.

But the Americans plan an assault. The big guns are already booming, but the range is too far; and when the fort's cannon return the fire, the fleet moves into the lee of Bois Blanc Island. Here McDouall's sentries spot an American work party on shore, clearing an area for artillery. Three hundred Indians in bark canoes swiftly put a stop to that, seizing one luckless American who has tarried too long to pick raspberries. The British save him from death and from him learn something of the enemy strength and plans.

It is Croghan's idea to land on a beach on the southwest side of the island where an open field and a sparse woods, almost devoid of undergrowth, will allow him to fight a set-piece battle, which the Indians abhor. He intends to "annoy the enemy by gradual and slow approaches." Incredibly, nobody on the American side has paid any attention to the island's natural defences. When Sinclair attempts to batter the fort with his guns, he discovers he cannot elevate them enough to do any damage. The shells fall harmlessly in the gardens of the villagers, who have sought safety within the bastion. Sinclair now realizes that the island is "a perfect Gibraltar." One hundred and twenty feet above the fort the British have a second gun, which Sinclair's naval cannon cannot reach. Faced with the loss of artillery support, Croghan decides to launch his assault from the only other beach on the island, at its far northwest corner – a fatal mistake.

This is ideal Indian country. A labyrinth of trees and tangled undergrowth extends almost to the water's edge, cut by narrow footpaths and thin cart tracks, unsuitable for the massing of troops or guns. Equally serious is the distance of this landing place from the army's objective. The fort lies at the other end of the island, three miles away, at the crest of a steep slope. McDouall's men are already blocking all the paths but one (which they will use) to slow the assault.

Fog shrouds the lake. A week passes before the ships can move. Then, on August 4, in clear weather, the fleet moves up to within three hundred yards of the beach and one thousand men push off in rowboats, supported by a sheet of fire from the American carronades.

In one of these craft stands Croghan's young deputy, Major Andrew Hunter Holmes, resplendent in blue and gold. Croghan's guide, Ambrose Davenport, a Mackinac resident exiled to the United States after the British victory in 1812, has urged Holmes to wear nothing more distinct than a common hunting suit, lest the Indians make him a target. But the stubborn major declares that the uniform was meant to be worn, and he intends to wear it. If it should be his day to fall, he says, then he is willing to die.

The troops land in a hail of musket balls. The thickets are alive with Indians, gorgeously plumed, hideously painted. Croghan halts his men at the edge of a small clearing. In the woods, at the far end he can see the British line, two artillery pieces at its centre, the riflemen forming an arc on either side.

McDouall has stripped his fort of defenders, leaving only twenty-five untrained militia behind, taking the field with 140 soldiers and some 350 tribesmen. The regulars lurk behind a ridge, protected by a hastily built abatis of roots and tangled branches. The Indians hold the flanks.

McDouall's two guns, a six-pounder and a three-pounder, open fire but without effect. The Americans return it. Now McDouall's defensive strategy is thrown into disarray by a false rumour. Sinclair's two brigs, it is said, are landing men farther down the island. To prevent entrapment, he pulls back. Most of the Indians follow.

A small group of Menominee – Dickson's followers – hold fast on the left flank under their celebrated chief, Tomah, concealed behind rocks, boulders, and trees that they have hacked down to form a breastwork. One of the younger braves, Yellow Dog, wants to follow McDouall and turns to his uncle, L'Espagnol, a huge, rawboned Menominee, said to be part Spanish.

"Let us go with the others," says Yellow Dog.

"No," says L'Espagnol. "I shall remain; if you wish to go you can, but you ought to show proper respect for your uncle by standing by him."

At this juncture, Croghan determines to outflank the retiring British by circling around their left on the lake side. He orders Major Holmes to lead his men in a charge through the woods.

Yellow Dog spots the gaudily dressed officer, his silver braid glinting in the sunlight. As a reward for his fidelity, L'Espagnol gives the young man the honour of shooting the American leader. On come the enemy, the officers casually swinging their swords. The Indians, uttering their war cry, open fire. Yellow Dog's gun misses fire, but Holmes falls dead with five bullets in his body, one of them from L'Espagnol's gun. The warrior runs forward, seizes Holmes's cap and sword, and vanishes into the forest.

The charge peters out as quickly as it began – and at fearful cost. Holmes's second-in-command falls, seriously wounded. Two of the senior officers are mortally stricken. McDouall, hearing the Indian cries, returns only to be forced back by Croghan's regulars advancing in ragged line. But the Indians on the flanks – the same Indians McDouall despised as "fickle as the wind" – are too much for the Americans. At last Croghan realizes what he should have known at the outset – that he cannot possibly move his men three miles through this snarled jungle, especially with the guns on the heights above him.

He has lost twenty dead, forty-four wounded. The Indians scalp the corpses, loot their belongings, and are prevented from killing the wounded only by McDouall's stern discipline.

Holmes's body, stripped, is found by his black servant who hides it under a covering of bark until a truce party recovers it the following day. It is taken aboard *Lawrence* which, with the gunboats, is returning to Detroit loaded with one hundred sick and wounded and a portion of the soldiers. But Sinclair and Croghan remain on Lake Huron with *Niagara*, *Tigress*, and *Scorpion*, determined to blockade the lake. If the Americans cannot take the British stronghold by force, they intend to starve it into surrender.

●

NOTTAWASAGA BAY, Georgian Bay, Lake Huron, August 13, 1814

Sinclair's reduced fleet anchors in the small harbour, debouching men and guns to attack the British supply base a mile or so up the Nottawasaga. In this way he hopes to strangle the supply line to Mackinac Island. A prisoner from a British gunboat, captured during the excursion to St. Joseph's Island, has described this secret route, which runs from Little York to Lake Simcoe, across a short portage into the Nottawasaga River, and thence down to Georgian Bay. Sinclair has also learned that the British sloop *Nancy* is expected to take on supplies for Mackinac deposited earlier at the river's mouth. What he does not know is that Lieutenant Miller Worsley of the Royal Navy has been alerted to their presence.

When McDouall saw the American fleet hovering off his shore, he realized that he must get word to Nottawasaga to hold back *Nancy* for fear of capture. To carry this message by fast canoe across three hundred miles of treacherous water to the British post up the river he chose a remarkable man, Robert Livingston. An Indian Department courier, Livingston knows every foot of the fur country. He has logged nine thousand miles by canoe in the service of his department. In this war he has been taken prisoner twice, escaped twice, suffered five wounds, two of which have not yet healed. A tomahawk cost him the sight of his right eye, a musket ball is lodged in his thigh, spear wounds have scarred his shoulder and forehead. No matter; he has managed to beat the American navy to the river's mouth to find the sloop loaded with six months' provisions, ready to sail. Warned by Livingston of the American presence on the lake, Worsley and his twenty-one seamen haul the little craft three miles up the narrow, winding river, impeded by overhanging boughs and rocks jutting from the shallow water. They conceal the vessel behind a bald ridge, protected by a hastily built blockhouse and a twenty-four-pound cannon, then await developments.

Their attempt at concealment fails. Sinclair and Croghan can see the vessel's masts above the ridge. Worsley and Livingston with twenty-one sailors, nine voyageurs, and twenty-three Indians are badly outnumbered by Croghan's three hundred assault troops. The next day, the Americans hammer at the blockhouse with a four-pounder, to no effect. At noon they unload two howitzers, move them forward under cover, and lob shells into the British position. There is a shattering explosion: a shell has hit the magazine. Worsley leads his men into the forest as a train of powder, previously laid, sputters its way to *Nancy*, blowing up the ship and everything aboard – shoes, leather, candles, flour, pork – all destined for the starving fort.

Sinclair spots a packet flung from the exploding blockhouse – correspondence between McDouall and Montreal. Now for the first time he has an inkling of the island's desperate condition. He can safely return to Lake Erie with Croghan leaving *Tigress* and *Scorpion* behind, one to hover at the mouth of the Nottawasaga, the other to guard the entrance to the French River, the terminal point on the Ottawa River portage route. If the two schooners do their job, nothing will get through to Michilimackinac. If necessary, he tells *Tigress*'s commander, he may also cruise around St. Joseph's Island to intercept the great fur canoes of the North West Company. Thus, with total command of the huge lake, the Americans can squeeze the British dry and seize the fur country.

But Sinclair has reckoned without young Miller Worsley who, with his men, has retreated fifteen miles up the Nottawasaga. Here,

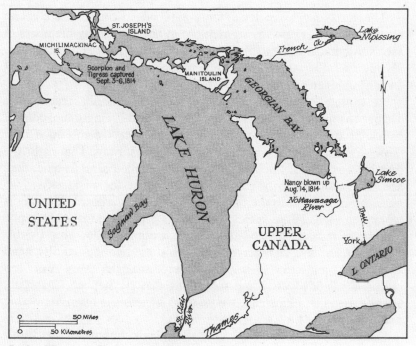

Lake Huron, Summer, 1814

unknown to the Americans, is another cache of supplies: one hundred barrels of flour, two big bateaux, and the canoe that Livingston brought from Mackinac. On August 18, Worsley and Livingston load men and provisions into the three craft and set off to row and paddle for 360 miles along the north shore to the British garrison.

Six days later, within eight miles of St. Joseph's Island, they are greeted by an unexpected sight: the two American schooners, *Tigress* and *Scorpion*, cruising in tandem down the Detour channel, seeking the North West Company's fur canoes. At once Worsley hauls up his boats, conceals the supplies, crams all the men into Livingston's big canoe, and as dusk falls slips past the enemy at a distance of no more than one hundred yards.

When he reaches Michilimackinac on August 31, he finds the garrison on half rations, eating their horses and paying ballooning prices to the settlers — a dollar and a half for a loaf of bread. McDouall is more than willing to fall in with Worsley's bold offer to lead an attack on both American vessels to clear the lake of the enemy.

The next day, Worsley's force sets off in four bateaux. The naval commander and his seamen are in one boat. Fifty members of the Newfoundland Fencibles, experienced boatmen and fishermen, occupy the other three. Robert Dickson follows with two hundred Indians in nineteen canoes.

At sunset on September 2, this formidable flotilla reaches the Detour channel. The following day Worsley and Livingston paddle off by canoe to seek the American schooners. They come upon one, *Tigress*, anchored in the channel only six miles away. That night the four bateaux set out, the men rowing with muffled oars. At nine, they see the dark outline of the schooner against the night sky. Two bateaux slip around to the port side, two to the starboard. Worsley is within ten yards of the vessel before he is hailed. He makes no reply. A burst of musket fire and the roar of a cannon follow, but by this time his men have clambered aboard and are fighting hand to hand with officers and crew. It is a short, fierce struggle; every American officer is wounded including the sailing master, Stephen Champlin, Perry's friend and kinsman, whose thigh bone is shattered, rendering him a cripple for life.

Somebody tries to burn *Tigress*'s signal book, but one of the British seizes it. Now Worsley has the flag code. He sends Livingston off in a canoe to find *Scorpion*. Livingston returns in two hours to report the schooner fifteen miles down channel but beating up toward *Tigress*.

Worsley plans a bold deception. He will keep the American pennant flying, hide his soldiers, dress the officers in American uniforms. The charade is in readiness when *Scorpion*, unsuspecting, comes up and anchors two miles away on the night of September 5.

At dawn, Worsley slips his cable and bears down on the other ship, using his jib and foresail only. His men lie on deck, hidden under their greatcoats. The signal flags deceive the Americans; no officer walks *Scorpion*'s deck. A gun crew, busy scrubbing the planking, pays no attention to *Tigress* until it is within ten yards.

By then it is too late. The grappling-irons are out, the muskets are exploding, men are pouring over the side, seizing the bewildered Americans. It is over in five minutes, to Sinclair's subsequent mortification.

Thus ends the war on the northern lakes. Mackinac Island is relieved. Lake Huron is again an English sea. The fur country, almost as far south as St. Louis, is under British control and will remain so until the horse trading at Ghent restores the *status quo*.

IO

THE LAST INVASION
July — November, 1814

Unable to seize either Kingston or Montreal, the Americans decide to make another drive at the Niagara peninsula. Jacob Brown, newly promoted to major-general, plans to seize Fort Erie, march down the Niagara and, with the help of the navy, capture Fort George, then move on to Burlington Heights. With the European war ended, Britain is planning to ship massive reinforcements to Canada, but these have not yet arrived. When Lieutenant-General Gordon Drummond asks Sir George Prevost for more men, he is told there are none to spare. His five thousand troops, scattered from York to Fort Erie, are not enough to contain the enemy attack.

BEFORE FORT ERIE, Upper Canada, July 3, 1814

It is two o'clock on a black, rainy morning when Winfield Scott in the lead boat of the American invasion force, thirty-five hundred strong, leans over the bulwark to check the depth of the water with his sword. It is less than knee deep. As musket balls whiz above his head, Scott leaps over the side and is about to shout "Follow me!" when the boat swerves in the current and he steps into a hole.

"Too deep!" gurgles Scott, as he disappears below the surface.

The warning cry prevents 150 men from drowning. The boat backs water as her crew struggles to haul the big brigadier-general, heavily encumbered by cloak, high boots, sword, and pistols, aboard. No one laughs; Scott is sensitive about his dignity. A moment later, in the shallows of a small cove near Fort Erie, he goes over the side again. His men follow. The British pickets gallop away.

Thus begins the third major invasion of the Niagara frontier, proposed less than a month before – and in the most casual fashion – by John Armstrong, the American Secretary of War.

"To give...immediate occupation to your troops, and to prevent their blood from stagnating, why not take Fort Erie?" the Secretary suggested to Major-General Jacob Brown, almost as though he were planning a weekend outing. Scott, with his sense of history, would have liked to wait a day and seize his objective on the anniversary of his country's independence, but the impatient Brown is not to be delayed. After capturing Fort Erie, he plans to seize the strategically important bridge over the Chippawa and march downriver to Fort George, where he fully expects Commodore Chauncey to be waiting, ready to give him heavy support from his reinforced fleet.

One officer opposes Brown's plan. Scott's fellow brigadier-general, Eleazar Wheelock Ripley, believes the force is too small to make an impression upon the peninsula and that if the British dominate Lake Ontario the Americans are likely to be cut off and captured. When Brown attempts to reason with him, Ripley sullenly offers his resignation. Brown curtly tells him to follow orders, and Ripley does so – but tardily. Ripley goes down in Brown's mental notebook as a hesitant, untrustworthy officer.

The British garrison at Fort Erie is heavily outnumbered by Ripley's and Scott's regulars and by more than one thousand militia volunteers and Indians under Amos Hall's replacement, Congressman Peter B. Porter. At five it surrenders. For the Americans it has been a long, weary day; after more than twenty-four hours of constant movement, young Jarvis Hanks, the drummer boy, cannot stay awake and finds himself dropping off to sleep while on the march.

But the following day – July 4 – is as glorious as its name: the rain dispersed, the sky cloudless, a haze of heat already shimmering over the grain fields and fruit orchards that border the Niagara. Through this smiling countryside, for twelve hours Winfield Scott and his brigade drive back the forward elements of Major-General Phineas Riall's thinly extended Niagara army, the soldiers on both sides choking in the dust and sweating in the blazing sunlight.

At dusk, the British withdraw across the Chippawa bridge to the safety of their entrenched camp. Scott prudently moves back a mile behind Street's Creek.

Riall has been on the gallop since eight in the morning, gathering his troops and dispatching appeals to York for reinforcements. At the British camp on the north side of the Chippawa, all is fever and bustle as troops and refugees pour in. Riall's defensive position is well chosen, for the sluggish creek is unfordable, and there is no other bridge for miles upstream. The Chippawa cuts the peninsula in two: no invading force can roll up the frontier without seizing and holding this bridge.

To frustrate such an attempt, Riall has his army dug in on the north side of the creek and an artillery battery on the south side amid a cluster of houses and warehouses that forms the community of Chippawa. The settlement marks the southern terminus of the portage route around Niagara Falls, where schooners and wagon trains switch cargoes to circumvent the great cataract. Tomorrow it will be a battlefield. The residents have already fled to the protection of the British camp, and a long line of refugees snakes along behind.

For more than twelve months these victims of a baffling and mysterious war – old men, women, small children – have been harassed and plundered by raiding parties from across the river. Their horses are spavined, for the best animals have all been stolen or eaten. The remaining wagons are broken down. Everything of value has long since been taken – livestock, flour, bacon, household goods, silverware, cutlery. Half starved through the winter, their able-bodied men seconded to the militia, their fields sometimes unsown, oftener ravaged, they cross the bridge and seek a camping place in the open fields beyond the British lines.

As dusk falls, Winfield Scott's advance brigade is reinforced by Ripley. A force of Pennsylvania militia under Peter B. Porter is also on the way. By noon the following day, Jacob Brown will have five thousand fighting men and Seneca Indians to contest the bridge at the Chippawa. Riall will have two thousand. As midnight approaches and more reinforcements straggle into camp and bed down, the two armies, more than a mile apart, slumber and await the approach of a bloody tomorrow.

●

CHIPPAWA, UPPER CANADA, July 5, 1814

It is seven o'clock of a bright midsummer morning. Captain Joseph Treat of the U.S. 21st Infantry has been up all night on picket duty. He is lame, worn down by fatigue and burdened by extra responsibility, for the second-in-command of his company is not only ill but also under arrest. As well, a fall from a horse a few days earlier has rendered him unfit for duty. But he has refused to report sick and has marched with his regiment to Street's Creek.

As the lemon sun begins to warm the meadows along the Niagara, an order reaches him to march his forty men back to camp. Comes a rattle of musketry from the British picket lines. Treat's men throw themselves to the ground, hidden in the waist-high grass. He orders them to their feet, but when the enemy fires again his new recruits break and run toward the rear, directly into the muzzles of their own cannon.

Treat, running after his men, calls on them to halt, form up, return and face the enemy. At this moment, Major-General Jacob Brown arrives on the scene.

The new commander of the Army of the North is a big, handsome figure, with a smooth oval face and clear searching eyes. He comes from a long line of Pennsylvania Quaker farmers but has also been schoolmaster, surveyor, land speculator, and – more significantly – a smuggler. Smuggling is an honourable calling in Sackets Harbor, Brown's home; most of the male populace engages in it. Brown, however, is no minor smuggler. A road is named for him, Brown's Smuggler's Road, and his nickname, "Potash Brown," comes directly from the illicit potash trade across the border. His smuggler's resourcefulness – aggressive action, swift decisions – has already stood him in good stead as an army commander; he is several cuts above the posturing and indecisive leaders he has replaced. Quick to act, he is also quick to anger – too quick, sometimes. His worst fault is a refusal ever to admit he is wrong. Now he is enraged at what he sees: an officer running away with his men in the face of enemy fire. As Treat tries vainly to explain, his sergeant runs up to report that one of the men hiding in the grass has not risen. Brown is aghast: a wounded man deserted by his cowardly officer! Captain Treat again tries to explain, but Brown brusquely sends him off to bring back the wounded man, then strips him of command, charges him with cowardice, and rides away. Treat is outraged; it will take ten months and all his persistence to clear his name.

All that morning, to Brown's annoyance, the skirmishing continues. The Americans are camped on the south side of Street's Creek, the British on the north side of the Chippawa. Between these two streams lies an empty plain, three-quarters of a mile wide, bordered on the east by the river, on the west by a forest. At noon, Brown determines to clear the forest of British pickets – Indians and militia – who are exposing his whole camp to a troublesome fire.

He decides to employ Peter B. Porter's mixed brigade of Indians and Pennsylvania militia who, having crossed the river at midnight, are marching toward the camp. He rides out to meet them and explains his plan.

Porter is touchy where the militia are concerned and jealous of the regulars who, he believes, get better treatment than his civilian army. Brown flatters him, explaining that it is necessary to drive the British out of the forest and that the militia and Indians are better equipped for bush fighting than the regulars.

Porter suspects he is about to become a sacrificial goat. He can see no prospect of glory in this kind of skirmish, which can end only in retreat. And Porter desperately needs a moment of glory after the humiliations visited on him at Black Rock. (Can he ever forget being forced from his home in his nightshirt?) He is a pugnacious man with a pugnacious face – bulldog nose, snapping black eyes – pugnacious in politics (Henry Clay's leading War Hawk) and pugnacious in war. He does not lack zeal: he has scoured the countryside for volunteers, not always with success. Almost half of his Pennsylvanians have refused to cross into Canada – another setback to add to his litany of mortifications. But he has, by dint of oratory and persuasion, managed to attract four hundred Senecas to the American cause.

Brown hastens to assure the belligerent militia general that there is not a single British regular on the south side of the Chippawa – only militia. At the moment this is true. Further, he promises that Winfield Scott's brigade will cover Porter's right in case the British should attack.

Porter agrees. The Pennsylvanians are less than enthusiastic. Their rations have been left behind. At two o'clock the troops are given two biscuits per man, the first food they have eaten that day. Captain Samuel White, who expects to enjoy a good supper later on, gives one of his biscuits away, only to learn, belatedly, of the projected attack. When Porter calls for volunteers, White and two other officers, with some 150 others, volunteer as privates.

White watches in fascination as the Indians tie up their heads with yards of white muslin, then paint their faces, making red streaks above the eyes and forehead, rubbing their hands on burnt stumps to streak charcoal down their cheeks. That accomplished, Porter leads his force of several hundred in single file through the woods on the left.

He does not know, of course, that Phineas Riall, the British commander, has decided to mount an all-out attack on the American position. Riall has sent a screen of militia and Mohawks under John Norton to cover his right flank in the same woods through which Porter's men are advancing. At the same time he is forming up his regulars to cross the Chippawa bridge and advance against Jacob Brown's army.

Riall is a Tipperary Irishman, short, stout, near-sighted, gutsy, but without much fighting experience. He is impetuous to the point of rashness. He has badly underestimated the size of the enemy force and believes, wrongly, that the enemy plans a two-pronged attack, with Chauncey's fleet bombarding the lakeshore above Newark. Consequently, he has weakened his force by sending a regiment back to Queenston. Yet he does not order out the militia from the neighbouring countryside or call on the 103rd Regiment, eight hundred strong, at Burlington Heights, which could be rushed to the scene within two days. When the three hundred members of the exhausted and badly mauled King's Regiment arrives from York early in the morning, Riall decides he has an army strong enough to attack.

Besides the King's, he has two regular regiments: the Royal Scots under Lieutenant-Colonel John Gordon and the 100th under the remarkable Marquis of Tweeddale, a physical giant, famous as a swordsman, horseman, gambler, and fox hunter, thrice wounded under Wellington, limping from a game leg. A recent arrival, Lord Tweeddale comes to Canada with a towering reputation for chivalry, dash, and eccentricity. Stories about him are rife in the camp: how, on one memorable long march with Irish recruits, he appointed a rear-guard with shillelaghs to hurry on the laggards; how he knocks his men down when they get drunk, bails them out when they are in trouble, thinks nothing of leaping from his horse and shouldering a private soldier's knapsack to march as an example to his troops; how he once risked his life under fire to swim a river and rescue the wife of a German hussar, forgotten during a retreat. His baggage on the Peninsula included cases of champagne and claret, which he often served in his own mess to captured officers. At his waist he carries two pistols presented by Wellington himself following a cavalry action.

Lord Tweeddale is in bed, suffering from a violent case of ague – a vague term that could mean anything from influenza to malaria – when he receives Riall's order. He replies that he is "in the cold fit of the disease" but expects the hot fit shortly. Riall agrees to postpone the attack for an hour when, presumably, the Marquis will be hot enough for action. By four o'clock the troops are drawn up on a plain between the two creeks, hidden from the Americans by a screen of bushes along the Chippawa.

At this moment, Peter B. Porter is moving his men in file through the woods, blissfully unaware of his predicament. Just ahead, masked by trees and underbrush, a strong enemy column is advancing toward

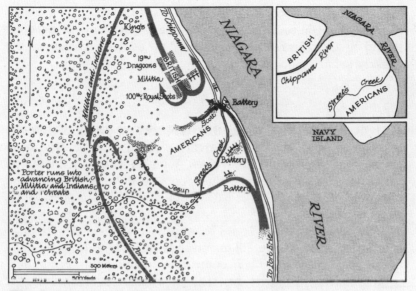

The Battle of Chippawa

him. A few yards to his right, on the plain beyond the forest's rim, Riall's scarlet-coated regulars are drawn up in battle order, bayonets gleaming. When he realizes that he is caught between the two forces, Porter shouts the traditional cry: "*Sauve qui peut.*" In an instant his column is in full retreat, the Indians bounding ahead, many carrying their small sons, whom they have brought into battle, on their shoulders. Porter himself is scarcely able to keep ahead of the pursuing British until he reaches the safety of Street's Creek. Once again, the bellicose congressman has been frustrated in his search for glory.

Not all of his men outrun the enemy. Captain Samuel White, who volunteered to fight as a private under Porter, is surrounded by enemy Indians with two fellow officers from the Pennsylvania militia, Lieutenant-Colonel John Bull and a Major Galloway. An Indian seizes his coat, another his vest, a third his neck-cloth. Soon he is stripped to his shirt and pantaloons. Everything including his watch is taken.

Galloway has lost his boots and must walk barefoot. A more ghastly fate awaits the Colonel. The party has proceeded less than half a mile to the rear when one of the guard whoops, raises his rifle, and shoots him through the body. Bull falls, reaches out to Galloway for help, and is dealt a tomahawk blow through the skull. His captors scalp him and leave the corpse where it fell. As they hurry their two remaining prisoners through the woods, White expects a similar fate at any moment. A vagrant thought courses through his mind: why hadn't he eaten the second biscuit in his rations while he had the chance? If he lives, he is unlikely to have supper.

●

MAJOR-GENERAL JACOB BROWN sees the clouds of dust and hears the firing in the forest. He rightly concludes that the British are moving to the attack. It is five o'clock. Winfield Scott, in full uniform, has decided, in the cool of the afternoon, to drill his brigade in grand evolutions on Dan Street's meadow. But now his commander dashes up on horseback.

"You will have a battle!" cries Brown, and quickly outlines the situation. Scott is sceptical. He will march and drill his brigade, he says, but he does not believe he will encounter five hundred of the enemy.

Nonetheless, he moves his men at a smart double across the Street's Creek bridge. To his discomfiture, he discovers that the British have placed nine field guns on the far side. Fortunately, the grape and cannonballs pass harmlessly over the heads of the jogging soldiers. The drummer, Jarvis Hanks, watches them skip across the surface of the creek. Nathan Towson, perhaps the best artillery officer in the American army, has already brought his own guns down and is replying to the British volleys.

From his position in front of Chippawa Creek, Riall, the British commander, sees Scott's brigade advancing and is deceived by their uniforms. Unable to obtain regulation U.S. Army blue cloth, Scott has had to outfit his men in grey.

"Why," exclaims Riall, "it is nothing but a body of Buffalo militia!" (warm memories of the rout at Black Rock the previous December).

Scott forms his troops into line and, because he believes a commander should appear a little arrogant before a battle, roars out a rallying cry to his troops. Independence Day is over but:

"Let us make a new anniversary for ourselves!"

As the Americans, dressing smartly by the right, begin a steady advance under British artillery fire, Riall revises his opinion.

"Why, those are regulars!" the little Irishman exclaims, with an oath.

The months of parade-ground toil are paying off. Scott's men move inexorably forward, halting, loading, firing in unison. Young Hanks stands by the side of Sergeant Elias Bond, drum slung over one shoulder, holding the sergeant's ramrod in his other hand, saving so much time that the sergeant manages to get off sixteen rounds before advancing.

Scott's line comes on in perfect order, Towson's battery of twelve-pounders covering his right. On his left flank, Major Thomas Jesup with the 25th Regiment, pushing through the woods only just vacated by Porter's fleeing militia, manages to outflank the British. Noting this, Scott decides upon a difficult manoeuvre, holding back his centre and advancing his wings so that they extend beyond the British flanks, half surrounding the columns. Cannonballs tear into the advancing line, but the Americans close up the ranks with the steadiness of veterans.

Brown now orders Eleazar Ripley's brigade forward to support Scott. In the 21st Battalion a brand-new private marches in the ranks, musket on shoulder. He is Captain Joseph Treat, victim of the morning's encounter with Brown, still smarting from the unfairness of his dismissal.

Scott has no idea where Ripley's brigade is – or Porter's. He continues to move back and forth around his U-shaped formation, encouraging his men. Towson's accurate fire has all but silenced the British cannon. A shot strikes the British magazine, reducing the British stock of ammunition, throwing the gunners into confusion. Towson now begins to belabour the British columns with canister.

The British, only two hundred yards from the American line, attempt a charge through the deep furrows and three-foot grass of the meadow. They are beaten back. Gordon, the colonel of the Royals, falls, shot in the mouth, unable to speak. The Eighth Marquis of Tweeddale, riding at the head of his regiment, is forced to dismount. The fire from Towson's canister is now so heavy – the big iron balls spraying in every direction – that both British regiments come to a standstill. Lord Tweeddale calls to the captain of his grenadier company to resume the advance, but even as the order is given, the officer is killed. He calls to a lieutenant, who at that moment is grievously wounded. He calls to his next in line, a young subaltern; he, too, is killed. A ball ploughs into Tweeddale's game leg, cutting his Achilles tendon; he cannot move. His men hoist him onto his horse and begin to take down a fence to let him through to the rear. Up rides a squadron of American cavalry, their commander demanding Tweeddale's surrender. The imperturbable peer retorts that he will order his men to shoot the officer and fire on his squadron if he does not retire on the instant. As the Americans turn back, Tweeddale turns over his command to the only officer remaining on his feet, and rides away.

The British line is breaking. Winfield Scott, preparing for a bayonet charge, rides out in front of the 11th Infantry and cries:

"The enemy says the Americans are good at long shot but cannot stand the cold iron. I call upon you instantly to give the lie to the slander. *Charge!*"

It is all but over. Riall, who has exposed himself fearlessly, riding out in front of his troops during the entire encounter almost as if he were courting death, realizes he must withdraw. He calls upon the King's Regiment, held in reserve, to cover the retreating troops as they move across the Chippawa bridge, ripping up the planking as they go. Miraculously he is unscratched, though his cloak is riddled with bullet holes. He leaves behind mounds of dead, among them some of his bravest officers. In little more than two hours he has lost almost one-third of his effective force.

The Americans do not pursue. Riall is too well entrenched, his guns too well positioned. A light rain sweeps across the battlefield as Scott's men trudge back through the mud. As dusk falls the two armies occupy the identical positions they did the previous evening, with one difference: more than eight hundred men are dead, wounded, or missing.

•

CAPTAIN SAMUEL WHITE, herded as a prisoner through the woods and fields, continues to ask himself why he and his fellow Pennsylvanian, Major Galloway, are still alive. His captor slips in a furrow, falls, but never relaxes his grip. For an instant the American contemplates escape, but realizes that that would mean instant death. Ahead, he can see the last of the British retreating across the Chippawa bridge. The Indians push White forward with such violence that he almost falls. They gain the bridge with the last of the rearguard, the American cannonballs rolling after them, one shot falling within yards of White himself. A moment later, the bridge is destroyed.

Now, thinks White, I'm safe. The British will protect me.

To his indignation, they do nothing of the sort but urge the Indians to run the prisoners still farther:

Who have we got there – a damn Yankee? Well, damn him, run him well, he's not half run yet.

White is almost at the end of his tether. It's impossible, he thinks; I cannot run twenty rods farther. But run he must; mouth agape, breath coming in hoarse gasps – and not for twenty rods but for more than a mile to the Indian encampment, poked in the back whenever he slackens pace.

At last, at the rear of the camp, he is halted and allowed to collapse. It is some time before he can find his voice to ask for water.

Eventually, a group of Canadian officers arrive. The Indians disperse, and White is taken to the British camp, where he is reunited with Major Galloway. The two are taken to Riall's headquarters, where the testy general peppers them with questions, few of which seem relevant.

Riall asks the size of Brown's army, but when White replies that it numbers five thousand, Riall refuses to believe him.

"That is not true, sir, you know it is not, you have more than double that number."

Commanders do not like to be beaten except by an overwhelming force, and Riall, the wishful thinker, is no exception.

The prisoners sleep that night on bare ground. Soaked with sweat after his exertions, Captain White shivers with cold until the sergeant in charge lends him his coat and a kerchief to cover his head. Equally welcome is a tot of rum. The sergeant himself has been a prisoner, knows what it is like, remembers that he was well treated by his American captors. But he is not allowed to draw rations for his charges and so must feed them from his own supply.

On the afternoon of the third day White sees a British horseman racing down the banks of the Chippawa at full speed to report that the Americans are bridging the creek upstream and are about to outflank the British position.

The camp comes alive. Horses are hitched to gun tumbrels; baggage wagons are heaped with supplies; cannons roar on both sides as the British artillery covers Riall's retirement. Soon the army is in full retreat along the road toward Queenston as Winfield Scott, swimming the Chippawa at the head of his brigade, occupies the abandoned camp.

White and three fellow prisoners march at the rear of the retiring army, watching with amusement as camp kettles tumble out of the escaping wagons, rattling at high speed along the river road. Riall, who realizes at last that he is outnumbered, decides to retreat to Fort George. There he will try to hold on until his superior, Gordon Drummond, can arrive with reinforcements. Drummond, at Kingston, makes plans to leave immediately for the head of the lake, pushing on the 89th Regiment (victors at Crysler's Farm) and the Glengarry Light Infantry. But it will be some time before these can reach the Niagara frontier. Meanwhile, Riall's situation is critical. The Americans occupy Queenston Heights. Fort George cannot hold out long against enemy bombardment. If Chauncey's fleet arrives from Sackets Harbor it can blast these crumbling defences into rubble with its naval guns. Once again, the peninsula is in peril.

All this is of no consequence to Captain Samuel White and his fellow prisoners. Before reaching Fort George they are marched to a large brick house surrounded by British troops. From the windows, White can see wounded officers being carried toward Newark, each in a blanket held by four men. The prisoners have no rations – the entire garrison is close to starvation from lack of supplies. When at last they are given beef, they eat it raw, being too ravenous to wait to cook it.

A few days later they are herded aboard a schooner bound for York, so crowded with wounded men that they are forced to remain on deck for the entire journey. Luckily, one of the officers gives them a bottle of rum. It is the last liquor White will see until the following March when, with the war over and after many hardships, he finds himself safely home in Adams County, Pennsylvania.

●

QUEENSTON, UPPER CANADA, July 10, 1814

Second-Lieutenant David Bates Douglass has just arrived on the Niagara frontier, fresh from West Point, with a company of young engineers. Here, on the heights above the town, almost at the very spot where Brock fell, he looks down on the American camp and feels a surge of emotion.

On the horizon, five miles distant, he can see the silvery surface of Lake Ontario. Three hundred feet below, cutting through a jungle of foliage, the Niagara plunges out of the turmoil of the rapids and wriggles toward open water. He gazes down with pounding heart on the village of Queenston, surrounded by an open plain, white with American tents. He can see long lines of troops under arms, columns in motion, cavalry galloping about, gunners drilling – no fancy plumage, no glitter, only hundreds of men in close-buttoned grey tunics and plain white belts, wielding Brown Bess muskets. (These distinctive uniforms, Winfield Scott's makeshifts, will soon be adopted permanently for the cadets at West Point in recognition of the victory at Chippawa.) In the distance, near the river's mouth, Douglass spots a flash of colour – the Union Jack waving over the two forts, Niagara and George – and, here and there, as the sun's rays catch it, the glitter of an enemy bayonet.

His company descends the heights and enters the vast semicircle of tents. The troops are in good spirits, some splashing about in the river. Jarvis Hanks disports himself by leaping from the third storey of a dockside warehouse, thirty feet above the swirling Niagara, thinking of the mill pond back home in the green mountains of Vermont.

Jacob Brown has no time for such frivolity. A dozen problems occupy the American commander's mind. He has lost confidence in one of his brigade commanders, Eleazar Ripley, who has disapproved of the campaign from the start. Can this force of fewer than five thousand actually hope to conquer the Niagara peninsula and hold Upper Canada? Ripley thinks not; such an action can only lead to a senseless effusion of blood. To the impetuous Brown, Ripley is far too cautious. Brown prefers Scott's panache. The big brigadier's tactics may occasionally be questionable – he took a long chance at Chippawa, advancing so swiftly that his flanks were unprotected – but his very audacity makes up for it.

Brown has reason for his impatience. He has rushed his army to Queenston because he believes he has a rendezvous this day with Commodore Chauncey and the fleet. With Chauncey's ships transporting men and guns from Sackets Harbor, Brown is confident he can take Fort George and then move up the peninsula, seizing Burlington Heights, York, and finally Kingston, effectively ending the war.

But there is no sign of Chauncey. For three days, Brown waits and frets. On July 13, he dispatches a letter by express:

I have looked for your fleet with the greatest anxiety since the 10th.... For God's sake let me see you...at all events have the politeness to let me know what aid I am to expect from the fleet of Lake Ontario.

But there is no unified command among the U.S. forces, no chief of combined operations. The navy is a law unto itself, jealous of its prerogatives. What Brown does not know is that Chauncey lies so ill with fever that he can scarcely make a decision. One thing, however, is clear: the ailing commodore has no intention of turning his spanking new vessels over to a second-in-command; nor does he intend to use them as mere transports for the army. These are *fighting* ships, not barges! In his myopia, Chauncey conceives that his only duty is to do battle with the British fleet – in his own time. And there is nothing anybody can do about that – not Brown, not Armstrong, not even the President.

Brown is aware that as each day passes the British forces grow stronger. The frontier is in a ferment. Guerrilla warfare rages on both sides. The militia in the London district is called out. Civilians harry the troops. Farmers leave their fields and flock into Burlington Heights and to Twenty Mile Creek, where Major-General Riall has his headquarters.

The Canadian population is so hostile to the invaders that, in an act of revenge, the troops of Colonel Isaac Stone descend upon the Loyalist village of St. Davids and burn it to the ground. Brown, in one of his furies – and with bitter memories of the retaliation that followed McClure's ravaging of Newark – dismisses Stone. The Colonel pleads that he, personally, was three miles away at the time, but Brown is not in a mood to accept excuses. The accountability for the outrage, he says, must rest with the senior officer. It is a harsh principle, indicative of Brown's frustration.

He cannot even blockade Fort George from his position at Queenston. Parties continue to slip in and out of that thinly held garrison. On July 20, Brown – still expecting the fleet – moves his army up before the fort, a move urged by the aggressive Winfield Scott against the advice of most senior officers.

But Scott can do no wrong in Brown's eyes. Hanks, the drummer boy, watches wide-eyed as the tall brigadier rides forward within range of the British cannon, telescope in hand, to reconnoitre the fort. A shell buzzes toward him. Scott raises his sword, sights it at the bomb, sees that it will fall directly upon him, spurs his horse, wheels about and escapes. A moment later, the missile drops on the exact spot he has vacated.

Without siege guns, Brown realizes he can do nothing against the fort. Those guns are at Sackets Harbor and can be transported to the scene only by Chauncey's fleet – and there is no sign of Chauncey. Chagrined, Brown moves his army back to Queenston, having lost two days in a pointless exercise. At last, on July 23, he learns the hard truth: a letter from Sackets Harbor makes it clear he will get no help from the navy.

The odds have changed dramatically. Brown's army has been reduced to twenty-six hundred effective soldiers. But the British have somewhere between three and four thousand. Lieutenant-General Drummond is on his way from York to take personal command. Morrison's 89th has arrived to reinforce Riall. The British have sent troops across the Niagara to the American side, apparently planning to march up the river and threaten Brown's flank and rear. All of Brown's reserve supplies are at Fort Schlosser, in the direct path of this movement. Brown loses no time. On July 24, he moves back to Chippawa. There he will attempt to refit and reinforce his army and, leaving both forts in British hands, bypass them and move up the peninsula to seize Burlington Heights.

The zealous Winfield Scott does not want to wait. So eager is he for the contest that he wants to move on Burlington that very night. Brown restrains him. Sometimes Scott is *too* eager, a failing that will be brought home to both men in less than twenty-four hours at the junction of Portage Road and Lundy's Lane.

•

CHIPPAWA, UPPER CANADA, July 25, 1814

It is five o'clock of a sultry day, the Americans at rest or drill, bathing, washing clothes, checking arms. David Douglass watches curiously as Winfield Scott's brigade heads out in column across the creek in the direction of the Falls.

His friend and superior, Colonel Eleazer Wood, explains what is happening. The British are believed to be crossing the Niagara at Queenston to seize Lewiston, dash upriver, overwhelm the American depot at Fort Schlosser opposite the American camp, and threaten Brown's army. More troops are thought to be moving toward the American camp on the Canadian side. Scott has been ordered to march on Queenston – an action designed to force the enemy back to the Canadian side of the river – and report on the British dispositions.

Douglass, eager to be part of the action, gets permission to ride with Wood in the vanguard of Scott's brigade.

Actually, the Americans are misinformed. Brown has been operating on rumour. He is convinced that the main British attack will come on his supply depot at Schlosser, directly across the river, but Gordon Drummond, now on the scene, has cancelled that movement. In fact, his deputy, Riall, is massing British troops three miles away at Lundy's Lane, the main route between the Falls and the head of Lake Ontario. Riall has established a strong defensive force on this road to keep watch on the American camp at Chippawa. Drummond, meanwhile, having landed at the mouth of the Niagara, is marching to Riall's aid with eight hundred men.

Brown's weakness is his stubbornness and inflexibility. He finds it difficult to change his mind once it becomes fixed – a trait that has been impressed on the unfortunate Captain Treat and also on the cautious brigadier, Ripley. Earlier in the day, Colonel Henry Leavenworth, officer of the day, reported seeing two companies of British infantry and a troop of dragoons at Wilson's Tavern near the Falls. Leavenworth tries to warn Brown that these must be the advance guard of the British army; he cannot believe that Drummond would trust such a force so close to the enemy without sizeable support. But Brown cannot be budged. Off goes Scott toward Queenston with Nathan Towson's artillery, dragoons and volunteers – upwards of twelve hundred men. But Riall has three times that number, with more on the way.

The widow Wilson's tavern, one of the few buildings not burned by American partisans, overlooks the famous Table Rock, just above the Falls. As Scott's column comes into view, David Douglass sees eight or ten British officers hastily mount their horses. Some ride off briskly, but three or four face about and coolly examine the advancing Americans through glasses. They wait until the column is within musket shot, whereupon their leader, an officer "of dignified and commanding mien," waves a military salute, wheels and rides away. In the distance, through the woods beyond, Douglass can hear a series of bugle signals.

Wood and Douglass are the first men to enter the tavern.

"Oh, sirs!" cries Mrs. Wilson, "if you had only come a little sooner you would have caught them all."

"Where are they and how many?"

"It is General Riall," says the widow, "with eight hundred regulars, three hundred militia and Indians, and two pieces of artillery."

At this moment Winfield Scott enters, questions the tavernkeeper closely, then sends Douglass back to camp with word that Scott is about to engage the British army at Lundy's Lane.

It does not occur to the eager brigadier-general to wait for reinforcements from Brown or even to sound out the enemy's strength. It is an axiom of warfare that one does not engage an entrenched enemy piecemeal. But the aggressive Scott moves forward blindly until, suddenly, he realizes that he is heavily outnumbered by the forces directly ahead of him. The widow Wilson's information, perhaps by design, was deceptive.

Scott is now within cannon shot of the red frame Presbyterian church, which occupies a high knoll one hundred yards to the left of the river road. To the right of the church is a small graveyard, and below it an orchard. The British hold the knoll and the ground around it, their line in the shape of a crescent with seven big field guns at the centre. Scott is caught in the curve of this crescent. Behind the ridge, Lieutenant-General Gordon Drummond's advancing reinforcements, including the veteran 89th, are already forming up.

What is Scott to do? Fall back? He does not know that Riall is preparing to do just that, believing, in his own blindness, that Brown's entire army is before him. Only Drummond's timely arrival countermands Riall's order to withdraw.

Scott ponders. He is in a tight spot. If he advances he may be torn to shreds. If he turns back, he may panic the main army. There is another consideration, undoubtedly the paramount one for a man like Scott. He and his brigade have a reputation to uphold. His name is magic; his men can do no wrong. Can he suffer the ignominy of a retreat? A more cautious, less egotistical officer – Ripley, for one – might accept that. Scott cannot. He decides to push ahead against overwhelming odds, not waiting for Brown's army, to glory, honour, and acclaim, even if it means the sacrifice of his brigade.

On his right, between road and river, is a thick wood. Scott orders Major Thomas Jesup to creep through this covering with his battalion, work around the British flank, and seize the Queenston road in the rear. With the support of Towson's artillery, he himself will lead a frontal assault on the hill.

Jesup finds a narrow trail through the woods, moves slowly forward, and, as darkness begins to fall, hits the British in the flank, driving back a detachment of militia and two troops of dragoons. He is about to cross the Queenston road to attack the batteries at the rear of the knoll when he realizes that more British reinforcements are on their way from Queenston. If he crosses the road, he will be caught between two bodies of the enemy. He switches plans, determines instead to harass the new arrivals.

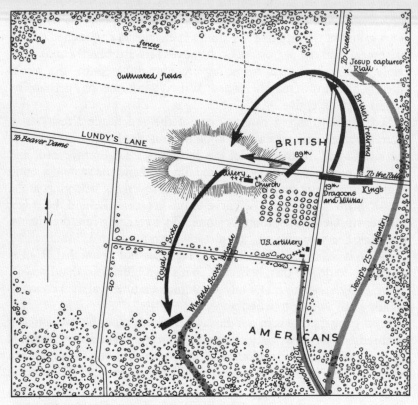

The Battle of Lundy's Lane: Phase 1

It is now so dark that it is impossible to distinguish friend from foe. On Jesup's flank, one of his captains is surprised by a party of men emerging from the gloom.

"Make way there, men, for the General," a British voice barks out.

"Aye, aye, Sir!" comes the quick-thinking reply.

As his aide rides past, the Americans surround the British general and his staff.

"What does all this mean?" asks the astonished Riall.

"You are prisoners, Sir," comes the answer.

"But I am General Riall!"

"There is no doubt on that point; and I, Sir, am Captain Ketcham of the United States Army."

Riall, bleeding from a wound that will cause him to lose his arm, mutters, half to himself:

"Captain Ketcham! *Ketcham!* Well, you *have* caught us, sure enough."

Jesup's prisoners, who include Drummond's aide, Captain Robert Loring, are sent back to Scott, eliciting a cheer from his hard-pressed brigade. For Scott is in trouble, his three battalions torn to pieces by the cannon fire of the British. The 22nd, its colonel badly wounded, breaks and runs into the 11th in the act of wheeling. That battalion breaks too, its platoons scattering, all its captains killed or wounded, its ammunition expended. The brigade has been reduced to a single battalion, the badly mauled 9th, reinforced by a few remnants of the beaten regiments. The attack is a failure.

British reinforcements are pouring in – Drummond's detachment from Queenston, another twelve hundred from Twelve Mile Creek. Winfield Scott can only hope that his message has got through to Brown and aid is on its way.

•

DAVID BATES DOUGLASS, his horse lathered, crosses the Chippawa bridge, the distant sound of cannon fire assaulting his ears, and reports directly to Major-General Brown, who immediately orders out Ripley's brigade to reinforce the embattled Scott. He does not, however, immediately send off Porter's Pennsylvania militia; clearly the stubborn commander is not yet convinced that the entire British force on the Niagara frontier is engaged at Lundy's Lane. And so the American army goes into battle piecemeal.

Douglass's commander, Colonel William McRee, sends him back to the scene of the action. It is dark when he arrives at Wilson's Tavern, brilliantly lit and ready to receive the wounded. He rides on, soon sees the dim outlines of a hill surmounted by flashing cannon. Wounded soldiers limp past as he gallops on, the balls whizzing over his head, knocking the limbs off trees.

As Douglass reaches Scott's lines, Colonel McRee overtakes him.

"Come," says McRee, "let's see what these fellows are doing."

The two ride down to the left of the action, guided in the pitch dark by the flash of musketry. McRee spurs his horse directly toward the British lines, draws up at the foot of the knoll, examines the action, turns to his junior.

"That hill is the key to the position and must be taken," he says.

Brown gallops up. Ripley's force is not far behind, the men advancing on the run to keep up with their mounted leader. It is Brown's intention to withdraw Scott's shattered brigade and to move Ripley's fresh troops into line. A wan moon, half obscured by the smoke of battle, occasionally reveals the carnage on the hill above – heaps of corpses, grey uniforms intermingled with scarlet.

McRee advises Brown that victory lies in the seizure of the British cannon on the brow of the hill, just below the church. As Ripley's troops move into line, Brown turns to Colonel James Miller, a veteran of Tippecanoe and the siege of Detroit:

"Colonel Miller, will you please to form up your regiment and storm that height."

"I'll try, sir," replies Miller, and this modest reply becomes in the years that follow an American rallying cry on the order of *Don't give up the ship* and, as well, the motto of Miller's regiment, the 21st.

Miller does more than try. Brown has dispatched Robert Nicholas's raw 1st Regiment, newly arrived from garrison duty on the Mississippi frontier, to act as a diversion to "amuse the infantry," as he quaintly puts it. Nicholas's troops give way in disorder, but Miller, on their left, leads his three hundred men forward under cover of the shrubbery to the shelter of a rail fence, directly below the guns. He can see the slow matches of the British gunners glowing in the dark, only a few yards away. He whispers to his men to lean on the fence, gain their breath, aim carefully, and fire. A single volley routs the gunners and Miller's regiment has possession of seven brass cannon. But the British line rallies, surges forward with fixed bayonets, and a hand-to-hand battle follows, the blaze of the opposing muskets crossing one another – the Americans, as is their custom, loading their muskets with one-ounce iron balls and three buckshot to add to the carnage. The guns remain in their hands.

It is ten o'clock. The moon is down. In the blackness of a hot night the armies struggle for two hours for possession of the guns with what one of Miller's officers calls "a desperation bordering on madness." Seldom more than twenty yards apart, the opposing lines occasionally glimpse the faces of their enemies and the buttons on their coats in the flash of the exploding muskets. Drummond, cold as ice, refuses to give an inch. Ripley's men, moving to support Miller, can hear the British commander's rallying cry: "Stick to them, my fine fellows!" Ripley orders his men to hold their fire until their bayonets touch those of their opponents, so that they can use the musket flashes to take aim.

Later, the surviving participants will try to bring order out of chaos in the reports they submit, writing learnedly of disciplined flank attacks, battalions wheeling in line, withdrawals, charges, the British left, the American right, making the Battle of Lundy's Lane sound like a parade-ground exercise. But in truth the actual contest, swirling around the shattered church on the little knoll, is pure anarchy – a confused mêlée in which friend and foe are inextricably intermingled, struggling in the darkness, clubbing one another to death with the butts of muskets, mistaking comrades for foes, stabbing at each other with bayonets, officers tumbling from horses, whole regiments shattered, troops wandering aimlessly, seeking orders.

In the blackness, a British non-commissioned officer approaches David Douglass and salutes, mistaking him for one of his own officers:

"Lieutenant-Colonel Gordon begs to have the three hundred men, who are stationed in the lane below, sent to him, as quick as possible, for he is very much pressed."

Douglass draws him closer, pretending not to hear distinctly, and when he approaches, seizes his musket and draws it over the neck of his horse. The man is mystified:

"And what have I done, Sir? I'm no deserter. God save the King and dom the Yankees!"

In the darkness, the light company of the British 41st is almost shattered by an American ruse. Shadrach Byfield, his stomach warmed by a noggin of rum after a seven-mile dogtrot from Queenston, hears someone in a loud voice call upon his captain to form up on the left. Who is calling? From what regiment? It is too dark to tell, but the regiment's guide insists the voice belongs to an enemy. The bugle sounds for the company to drop. A moment later it is hit by a musket volley; two corporals and a sergeant are wounded. Byfield and his fellows leap up, fire back, and charge forward, driving the Americans away.

Jacob Brown, having sent Miller up the hill to seize the British guns, moves along the Queenston road with his aides to the rear of Lundy's Lane and is almost captured in the dark. Only the cry of a British officer – "*There are the Yankees!*" – saves him. Now he comes upon Major Jesup, fighting his way back to rejoin Scott's shattered brigade. Wounded and in pain, Jesup asks for orders and is told to form on the right of the American 2nd Brigade.

Confusion! The British reinforcements, hurried into the line in the dark, mistake friends for enemies. The Royal Scots pour a destructive

337

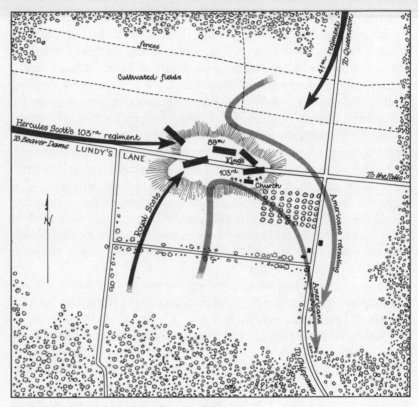

The Battle of Lundy's Lane: Phase 2

fire into the Glengarry Fencibles stationed in the woods to the west of the church. The British 103rd blunders by error into the American centre and is extricated only with difficulty and heavy casualties.

Jacob Brown vaguely discerns a long line of soldiers in the dark, tries to discover who they are, rides out in front. The line appears to be advancing. An aide spurs his horse, rides forward, and in a firm voice cries out: "What regiment is that?"

"The Royal Scots, Sir," comes the unexpected reply.

Brown and his suite throw themselves behind their own troops to await the attack.

Porter's Pennsylvanians have arrived at last and are placed on the left flank of the American regulars in time to face a British charge.

"Show yourselves, men, and assist your brethren!" cries Porter.

Alexander McMullen, one of the Pennsylvania volunteers, hears a shower of musket balls pass over his head like a sweeping hail storm. Fortunately for him, the British on the knoll above are having difficulty depressing their weapons.

The battle seesaws. A pause follows each rally while each side distributes cartridges and flints or searches the bodies of the dead for ammunition. Now, as Porter's corps ascends the hill, a stillness falls over the battlefield. The two armies face each other, neither moving. Finally, McMullen hears a British officer's voice inquiring hoarsely if the Americans have surrendered.

No reply. Nobody moves.

A young lieutenant named Dick at last breaks the silence: *We will NEVER surrender!*

On the American right some of Joseph Willcocks's turncoat Volunteers falter and fall back, firing their muskets sporadically without orders. The British respond with a shower of lead, and the militia turns and bolts. As the Pennsylvania officers try to rally their men, Colonel Nicholas's regulars interpose themselves between the fleeing militia and the British. Again silence, save for the murmurs of the volunteers and the groans of the dying.

Ripley, hard pressed with the British again advancing, asks Brown to order up Scott's brigade – or what is left of it – for support. Brown hesitates. Scott's badly mauled force is the only reserve he has. If he commits it now he will have nothing left with which to deal the enemy a finishing blow should the tide of battle turn. Nonetheless, he grants Ripley's request.

Winfield Scott forms up his skeleton brigade in a second line behind the American right wing. He has decided upon another bold stroke – a dash past the captured guns, piercing the British line and rolling around to take it from the rear.

"Are these troops prepared for the charge?" he asks Henry Leavenworth.

The loyal Leavenworth, the only surviving battalion commander, is given no chance to reply.

"Yes, I know, they are prepared for anything!" Scott cries and orders them into close column, shouting out an order that has almost become a cliché: "Forward and charge, my brave fellows!"

The tired troops follow their commander into the jaws of disaster. Gordon Drummond has anticipated the move and protected his flanks with the battle-seasoned 89th Regiment, whose commander, Morrison, has already left the field, grievously wounded. Kneeling in the cover of a grain field, the British regulars hold their fire, await Drummond's order, and, at twenty paces, let loose a volley that routs Scott's troops. The British pursue the fleeing Americans at bayonet point.

In the darkness and smoke, all is confusion. Forced down the hill and to the left of the line, Scott – who has had two horses shot from under him – again tries to lead a charge. The 89th, in hot pursuit, mistakes his force for their fellow battalion, the Royal Scots, and lets him escape.

Now Scott finds himself with the remainder of his assault party directly in front of two British regiments, the 103rd and the 104th. Fortunately for him, *they* mistake him for the British 89th.

"The 89th!" warns a British officer, just as his men are about to decimate Scott's ranks.

"The 89th!" call out the Americans, realizing the British mistake.

Scott leads his detachment back toward his own lines, only to blunder into two more British regiments, the real Royal Scots and the 41st, who are too far forward of their own line. A bitter hand-to-hand struggle ensues, the opposing troops standing toe to toe, slashing and hacking at each other. Up come the Glengarries to support the British regulars, but they too are confused in the darkness, mistaking the Royals and 41st for American regiments. As the two British forces grapple with one another, Scott's men are able at long last to retire.

Scott moves to Jesup's detached battalion on the extreme right of the American line and asks after his wound. A moment later he is prostrated by a one-ounce ball that shatters his left shoulder joint. Scott is in a bad way, for he is a mass of bruises from two falls from horseback and from the rebound of a spent cannonball that ploughed into his right side. Two men move him to the rear and place him against a tree where, on reviving, he finds he cannot raise his head from pain and loss of blood.

Brown, meanwhile, is on the far side of the field with Porter's volunteers. A musket ball passes through his right thigh, but he remains on his horse. His aide falls mortally wounded. Now the American commander suffers a violent blow from a spent cannonball. Badly winded and bleeding, he determines to turn his command over to Scott. On learning that Scott is wounded, he passes it to Ripley.

It is past eleven o'clock and the battlefield is silent. As if by agreement, both sides cease fighting. Henry Leavenworth, in command of Scott's brigade, counts his men, finds he has fewer than two hundred, confers with Jesup, agrees that the troops ought to return to camp.

The British have quit the hill and may at any moment cut off the American withdrawal. Almost every battalion commander has been disabled; the men are exhausted and suffering from a raging thirst, for there is no water. Some have left the field. There are no reserves; Brown has committed every man.

For Alexander McMullen of the Pennsylvania militia, these will be, in retrospect, the most trying moments of his life. Sweating heavily during the attack up the hill, he had opened his vest and shirt. Now he shivers in the night air, and not only from the midnight chill; the prospect of imminent death disturbs him more. He hopes against hope that he will not have to struggle one more time up that terrible slope, now strewn with corpses.

It is clear to all, including Brown, that the army must retire. Major Hindman of the artillery encounters the wounded general, who orders him to collect the guns and march to camp.

But how are the captured guns to be removed? Most of the horses are dead, the caissons blown up, the guns unlimbered, the men exhausted, the drag ropes non-existent. Hindman decides to try to bring away one of the brass twenty-four-pounders, assigns a junior officer, Lieutenant Fontaine, to get it ready, then goes in search of horses. But Drummond, bleeding from a wound in the neck, is already forming his battle-weary British for a final assault. Once more his battered battalions press up the slope and retrieve the guns just as Hindman returns with horses and wagons. Fontaine dashes through the ranks on horseback; the rest of his party is captured.

The British are too exhausted to harass the retreating Americans. Most of the men have marched eighteen miles on this hot July day, some twenty-one. They throw themselves down among the corpses and in their sleep are scarcely distinguishable from the dead. Ripley's troops straggle back to the camp at Chippawa, plunge into the river to slake their thirst, then fall into their tents.

It has been the bloodiest battle of the war, the casualties almost equal on both sides. The British count some 880 officers and men killed, wounded, or captured, the Americans almost as many (although some will charge that Brown has purposely underestimated his returns). William Hamilton Merritt, leader of the Provincial Dragoons and now an American captive, is one who will not fight again.

Both sides claim victory. Drummond reports that the day has "been crowned with complete success by the defeat of the enemy and his retreat to the position of Chippawa...."

Brown declares that "the enemy...were driven from every position they attempted to hold...notwithstanding his immense superiority both in numbers and position, he was completely defeated...."

Nothing will ever shake Winfield Scott's conviction that the Americans won a brilliant victory, for which he was largely responsible. Certainly his men bore the brunt of the fighting. Of a total of 860 American casualties, Scott's brigade suffered 516. Scott is contemptuous of Brown; he considers him a flawed commander and is stung by Brown's report of the action, which, he feels, does not give him sufficient praise. It is "lame and imperfect, unjust and incomplete."

A few doubts are raised about Scott's wisdom in immediately attacking Riall's position. Was such rashness necessary? Would it not have been better to wait for the rest of the army? Did not Scott, in his search for glory, needlessly sacrifice hundreds of men? After all, what advantage did the Battle of Lundy's Lane give to Brown's army, apart from raising American morale?

These hard questions are drowned in the chorus of jubilation that follows the battle. Scott, in dreadful pain, his life at times despaired of, achieves during his convalescence a triumph that might have brought a blush to the cheek of a Roman conqueror. Medals, swords, banquets, addresses, honours of every kind – including a promotion to major-general – are heaped upon him. A national hero, he can do no wrong. He will continue to serve his country for another half century, every ambition achieved – General-in-Chief, Old Fuss and Feathers, the Nestor of the Republic – all because of a bloody and indecisive battle fought on a Stygian night at the margin of Lundy's Lane.

•

CHIPPAWA, UPPER CANADA, July 26, 1814

In his tent at 1 A.M., the wounded Jacob Brown sends for Brigadier-General Ripley, orders him to reorganize the troops, feed them, and then with every available man march back to the battlefield at dawn to meet the British.

It is a foolish order. Ripley's effective force does not exceed fifteen hundred. It is scarcely conceivable that they can retake the hill after only a few hour's sleep. Nonetheless, Ripley sets off the following morning at daybreak.

Samuel Tappan, a company commander in the 21st Regiment, marches with him. Tappan's situation suggests Ripley's problem. The previous day he took forty-five men into battle of whom seventeen were casualties. But such is the state of confusion and morale in Brown's battered army that Tappan has been able to muster only nine men on this march back down the Queenston road.

Ripley sends Tappan and another officer forward through the woods on the left to reconnoitre. As the two emerge from the thickets a mile from the battlefield, they see Drummond's army posted on the heights above, the guns on a knoll near the road, the flanks protected by the river on one side and a thick forest on the other. Tappan realizes that the Americans are outnumbered.

Neither side has any stomach for a fight. Ripley withdraws to Chippawa and prepares to move the entire army farther back. Brown is furious. He has lost all confidence in Ripley, who he is convinced "dreaded responsibility more than danger." On his shoulders he places all the blame for the loss of the British guns and, by implication (though he can never say it), for the defeat at Lundy's Lane – forgetting his own harsh retort to the disgraced Colonel Stone, after the burning of St. Davids, that accountability must rest with the senior officer.

Ripley demands a court of inquiry – he has many supporters, including Miller and Jesup – but the President intervenes before the first witness is finished. Congress has already decided that Ripley and everybody else involved in the battle is a hero. Nobody in Washington wants to sully the legend of victory at Lundy's Lane with adverse testimony.

Brown is borne across the Niagara with the other wounded, but the recriminations do not end. His report of the battle, dictated to an aide, does not satisfy some of the chief participants. Three of Scott's commanders – Leavenworth, Jesup, and Colonel Hugh Brady of the 22nd – are bitter, feeling that they have been denied the kind of glowing praise that will bring them glory and promotion. Porter, too, is bitter: his militiamen have not received proper credit for their part in the Battle of Chippawa; they have been treated as "the tools and drudges of the regular troops." He himself has not been given the command he expects. He frets, in a letter to the Governor of New York, that because his casualties are so low "it will seem that we were cowardly and did not do our duty."

It is well that his men are not privy to that callous statement. As Ripley prepares to withdraw to Fort Erie, one of Porter's men, the Pennsylvanian Alexander McMullen, passes down his own line and views "a scene of distress...which I hope I may never witness again." Porter may bemoan his few casualties, but it seems to McMullen that every tent contains at least one wounded man, each still wearing his blood-soaked uniform. John McClay, the company quartermaster, struck in the forehead by a musket ball, his skull cracked open, lies groaning on his back, his face covered with gore, a wild look in his eyes. In a nearby house, his cousin, Thomas Poe, lies mortally wounded. McMullen helps carry him across to the waiting boats. Poe shakes his hand weakly.

"Alexander," he says, "you will never see me again in this world." A few minutes later he expires.

McMullen notes that of one hundred men who came with him from Franklin County, only twenty-five are whole. He counts forty wagons moving toward the river, loaded with wounded men. Knocked about in the lumbering carts, they suffer horribly.

McMullen begins to feel giddy. Attacked by a high fever and a violent headache, he scrambles into one of the wagons, where the jolting all but deranges him. He climbs out, attempts to walk, falls, is finally helped along by one of the regulars.

In a meadow near Fort Erie, the army halts. The men drop where they stand. David Douglass, the engineer who brought Scott's message to Brown the previous day, is so tired he stretches out on the first available wagon and slumbers without complaint on a heap of crowbars, pickaxes, and spades. Alexander McMullen flops down in the meadow under a single blanket as the rain pours down in torrents.

The British do not have the strength to follow. In a crumbling log shack near Lundy's Lane, the assistant surgeon of the 89th, Dr. Dunlop, struggles to save the wounded. The chief surgeon is so ill he has been shipped home. The chief assistant, also ill, has exhausted his strength helping bring down the wounded. Tiger Dunlop works alone.

The casualties lie in tiered berths from which they must be moved in order to have their wounds dressed – an excruciating operation. As more men are herded into the makeshift hospital, they are laid on straw on the floor. By noon, Dunlop has 220 men to attend.

There is no time for niceties. Limbs that might be saved are amputated to forestall gangrene. The heat is stifling, the flies thick. Maggots breed in open wounds, causing dreadful irritation. For two days and nights, Dunlop seldom sits down, pausing only to eat and change his clothes. On the third day he collapses, and for five hours nothing can wake him. Refreshed, he plunges in again.

An American militiaman is brought in – a big, powerful farmer from New York State, about sixty years old. He is suffering grievously. A ball has shattered his thigh bone, another has passed through his body, wounding him mortally. His ageing wife arrives from across the river under a flag of truce to find her husband writhing in agony on a bed of straw. Stunned at what she sees about her, she takes her husband's head in her lap, the tears running down her face, and sits in a stupor until awakened by a groan from the dying man. She clasps her hands together, looks about her wildly, and cries out:

"O that the King and the President were both here this moment to see the injury their quarrels lead to – they surely would never go to war without a cause that they could give as a reason to God at the last day, for thus destroying the creatures that He hath made in his own image."

Half an hour later, her man is dead.

●

BLACK ROCK, NEW YORK STATE, August 13, 1814

Well before dawn, eleven hundred British soldiers under the command of Lieutenant-Colonel J.G.P. Tucker slip across the Niagara River to the American side in nine boats on a mission, which, if successful, could force the enemy out of Canada.

The Americans have retreated to the protection of Fort Erie and are constructing a vast fortified camp, with the original fort forming a bastion at one corner. They are supplied and reinforced by rowboats from Buffalo and protected by batteries set up along the American side of the river. Tucker's task is to destroy the supply depots, disperse the troops at Black Rock, and wreck the batteries, leaving the American flank exposed. If he succeeds, the Americans will not be able to hold Fort Erie, and Gordon Drummond will not have to mount a long and costly siege.

These are seasoned troops. Half come from the veteran 41st Regiment, which has fought in Upper Canada since the start of the war. Only a hard core of originals remain, however. Private Shadrach Byfield of Wiltshire is one. Of the 110 men in his company who marched into Detroit with Isaac Brock in the summer of 1812, fewer than fifteen are left. Most, including Byfield himself, have been wounded at least once.

At twenty-five, Shadrach Byfield is a survivor. He missed death by inches at the River Raisin, survived the bloody siege of Fort Meigs, escaped from the ditch after the failed attack on Fort Stephenson, was one of the few who slipped through Harrison's fingers after the débâcle on the Thames, took part in the capture of Fort Niagara, emerged unscratched after storming up the hill at Lundy's Lane. Now, as dawn breaks, he prepares once more to face hostile guns.

Tucker is counting on surprise. He expects to land before dawn, seize the bridge over Sacjaquady Creek, and move to his objective. But the Americans are waiting for him behind a breastwork of logs. The far side of the bridge, obscured from the attackers, has also been rendered impassable.

As Tucker's force lands and moves up the narrow path in the dark, three hundred sharpshooters, protected by the logs, begin to pick them off.

A strange thing happens: the veterans are seized by an unaccountable panic. They crouch, duck, flatten themselves in the face of the deadly fire. It is more than possible that they have seen enough fighting for a time, that they are used up by the bloody events of the previous week. Nevertheless, their officers rally them, and the column moves on, dashing across the bridge at the double quick only to discover that the planking at the far end has been torn up. The column recoils, but its momentum is such that many of the men are thrown into the water. An attempt is made to rebuild the floor of the bridge, but the American riflemen keep up such a steady fire that the task must be abandoned.

Shadrach Byfield, staring across the creek, sees one of the Americans climb above the breastwork only to fall back, struck by a British ball. At almost the same moment a bullet strikes Byfield's right arm, just below the elbow. One of his comrades cuts his uniform away, and Byfield staggers to the rear, finds a doctor, and asks him to amputate the arm. The surgeon refuses, believes the limb can be saved, orders Byfield into one of the boats.

To General Drummond's disgust, the remains of Tucker's entire force returns to Canada, its mission a failure.

"The indignation excited in the mind of the Lieut.-General...will not permit him to expiate on a subject so unmilitary and disgraceful," his General Order declares. "...it is...the duty of all officers to punish with death on the spot any man under their command who may be found guilty of misbehaviour in front of the enemy.... Crouching, ducking, or laying down when advancing under fire are bad habits and must be corrected."

With the Americans daily reinforcing their camp at Fort Erie, Drummond has been cheated of an easy victory. It will now require a vigorous and undoubtedly a bloody effort to dislodge them.

To Shadrach Byfield, all this is of minor importance. The doctors have done their best to save his arm, but mortification has set in. It must come off. That is a heavy blow, for he is a weaver by trade.

He seeks out a fellow soldier whose own arm has recently been amputated.

"Bill, how is it to have the arm taken off?"

"Thee woo't know, when it's done," Bill reassures him.

Several orderlies are detailed to blindfold and hold him down before the surgeon goes to work with knife and saw, but Byfield waves them away. There'll be no need of that, he says, stolidly. The operation seems to take forever and is very painful, but he bears it well. Then, his stump dressed, he goes off to bed, mercifully groggy from a draught of mulled wine.

Later, he asks for his severed arm. An orderly replies casually that it has been thrown onto a dung heap. Enraged, Byfield leaps out of bed, tries to strike the man with his one good hand. Then, nothing will do but that he search through the heap, find the missing appendage, look about for lumber, somehow manage to nail a coffin together, and give his arm a decent burial.

Byfield's fighting days are over. He returns to England where he and his family must make do on a pension of nine pence a day, later raised to fifteen through his own importuning. One night he dreams that he is working at his old trade, wakes his wife, tells her he is certain that, arm or no arm, he can weave cloth.

"Go to sleep," says she. "There was never such a thing known as a person having but one arm to weave."

But in his sleep Byfield works out his destiny. The following day he visits a blacksmith, draws the design of an instrument similar to one in his dream and, thus equipped, finds work at his former trade with a clothier at Staverton Woods, not far from his home in Wiltshire. There, from time to time, he looks back on his youthful adventures. Those memories begin to blur until he cannot quite remember which battle came first or what the places were called or what his companions looked like. Certain incidents stand out sharply – the spectacle of an Indian throwing a wounded man into the fire after Lundy's Lane, for instance – but it is all a little unreal, rather like one of his dreams. Only his missing forearm testifies to the reality of his experience on the embattled border of a strange, cold colony, an ocean and more away.

•

THE BRITISH CAMP before Fort Erie, Upper Canada, August 14, 1814

After a week of bombarding the American fortifications, Lieutenant-General Gordon Drummond is convinced that the time has come to attack. A shell has just landed on the American magazine chest. Drummond is certain that it has caused heavy casualties. With the Americans off balance he will this very night assault the fort from three sides.

Drummond and his opposite number, Brigadier-General Edmund Pendleton Gaines (Ripley's replacement) are like blind men, groping to test each other's strength. Both have miscalculated. Because the British entrenchments are hidden behind a screen of trees, Gaines can only guess at Drummond's force, which he estimates at five thousand. Actually, Drummond has fewer than three thousand men. Drummond is misled by his spies and informers into believing the Americans have fifteen hundred troops. In fact, Gaines has almost twice that number. Drummond has made another error: the explosion of the magazine has produced few casualties. And Gaines, shrewdly reading his opponent's mind, is now expecting an immediate attack.

Drummond plans a simultaneous assault on each of the three major gun batteries that protect the corners of the fifteen-acre encampment. The camp is surrounded on three sides by embankments, ditches, and palisades. Directly ahead, at the near corner, not more than five hundred yards from the forward British lines, the Lieutenant-General can see the outlines of the old fort, now bristling with cannon. One hundred and fifty yards to the left, on the edge of the lake, is a second artillery battery commanded by David Douglass. The two are connected by a vast wall of earth, seven feet high, eighteen feet thick. Half a mile up the lake, and also connected to the fort by an enclosed rampart, is Nathan Towson's battery of five guns, perched on a conical mound of sand, thirty feet high, known as Snake Hill and joined to the lake by a double ditch and abatis. If Drummond's plan succeeds,

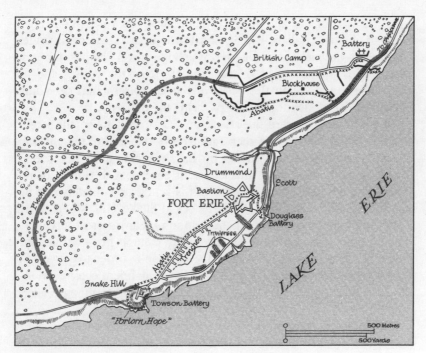

The Siege of Fort Erie

his assault forces will strike all three batteries at the same time and seize the encampment.

At 4 P.M. his main force sets off. Its task is to attack Towson's battery on Snake Hill. Drummond orders it to march down the Garrison Road, screened from view by the forest, to rendezvous on the far side of the American encampment, and to attack at two the following morning. The General orders the troops to remove the flints from their firelocks and to depend entirely upon the bayonet, identifying the enemy in the dark by their white pantaloons. Loud talking is prohibited and the roll is to be called every hour to frustrate desertions.

This last is a curious instruction. Does Gordon Drummond actually expect a body of his men to steal away in the dark of the night? Clearly he does. The bulk of the thousand-man force attacking the Towson battery is made up of soldiers from the de Watteville regiment, a foreign corps recruited twenty years before in Switzerland but shattered during the Peninsular campaign and now heavily interlaced with prisoners of war and deserters from Napoleon's armies – French, German, Dutch, Italian, Polish, and Portuguese. Their commander, Lieutenant-Colonel Victor Fischer, is an able officer; he has under his command a smattering of British regulars from the King's and the 89th. They may stiffen the backs of the less-disciplined de Watte-villes, but the motley foreign corps forms the majority.

Drummond considers the attack on Snake Hill to be the key to success. If Fischer and his men can capture that end of the encampment, victory is certain. But why has he committed his poorest troops to this critical night attack? In his eagerness to rid the peninsula of the invading army, Drummond is acting precipitately. He has not bothered to reconnoitre the defences at Snake Hill, where a vast abatis of tangled roots and branches can inhibit any assault force. Nor does he plan to soften those defences with cannon fire – he has purposely refrained from bombarding the position in order to conceal his real purpose from Gaines. Secure in his overconfident conviction that the Americans are outnumbered and demoralized, he plunges ahead in the belief that he can conquer by surprise alone.

He has divided his force. While Fischer assaults the far end of the camp, two smaller detachments will attack the near end. The General's nephew, Lieutenant-Colonel William Drummond of Keltie, will lead 360 men against the ramparts of the original fort. Lieutenant-Colonel Hercules Scott will lead another seven hundred against the Douglass battery on the lakeshore and against the embankment that connects it to the old fort. Scott's regiment is the notorious 103rd, originally the New South Wales Fencibles, known in that colony as "the rum regiment," brought up to strength before sailing for Canada by the recruitment of released convicts. Two of its companies are composed of boys below fighting age.

Two more antithetic characters than Hercules Scott and William Drummond could scarcely be found in a single army corps. Scott is a bitter man who despises his commanding officer. He does not believe that the assault on the American encampment has any hope of success. But he is a courageous officer and can be expected to do his duty. He sleeps that night in the drenching rain under a piece of canvas suspended from a tree and jauntily tells his surgeon, "We shall breakfast in the fort in the morning." Privately he is less optimistic; he has already written out a brief will and mailed it to his brother, for he is half convinced that he will not return from the attack.

Only in this respect does he resemble the General's nephew. Every army knows at least one field officer like William Drummond – colourful, dashing, eccentric, ruthless – the sort of leader that men will follow into the mouths of cannon. Such men rarely rise above field rank, for they are either killed in action or barred from promotion by their own quirkiness. There does not seem to be a nerve in Drummond's body. Perhaps he lacks the imagination to be afraid. He is a fatalist who spends the day in high spirits, spinning yarns with a wide circle of cronies, then as the bugles sound turns solemnly to his friends, and remarks:

"Now, boys! We never will all meet together here again; at least I will never again meet you, I feel it and am certain of it."

A thick rain is falling; soon it becomes a torrent. The General's nephew leaves the leaky hut in which the others are smoking and talking, finds a rocket case, stows himself away in it, and is soon fast asleep as if this were not his last day on earth.

Beyond the American camp, the same downpour soaks Fischer's mixed bag of British regulars and foreign mercenaries as they move through the forest.

It is two in the morning. In a clump of dripping oaks, three hundred yards in front of Snake Hill, a picket of one hundred Americans hears the steady *swish-swish* of the approaching column and sounds the alarm. Surprise, the essence of Drummond's plan, has not been achieved.

Towson's artillery is already in action. The British attackers are illuminated in a sheet of flame, a pyrotechnical display so bright that Snake Hill will shortly be dubbed Towson's Lighthouse.

Now Fischer comes up against the formidable abatis that the Americans have constructed between Snake Hill and the lake – thousands of tree trunks, four to six inches in diameter, their branches cut off three feet above the base, pointing in all directions and forming an impassable tangle. Unable to breach this labyrinth and the embankment behind it, Fischer's Forlorn Hope dashes around the end on the American left and into the lake in the hope of taking the defenders from the rear. The current is swift, the channel a maze of slippery rocks. The men struggle in waist-deep water. Part of the Forlorn Hope does reach the rear of the battery to fight hand to hand with the defenders, but two companies of Eleazer Wood's 21st, especially detailed for such an emergency, pour a galling fire on those who follow.

Panic seizes the men of the de Watteville regiment struggling in the water. Some, dead or badly wounded, are being borne into the Niagara River by the stiff current. Shouting wildly, they break in confusion, turn tail, and plunge directly into the King's, carrying those veterans with them like a torrent. Only the seasoned 89th holds fast. The hundred men of the Forlorn Hope who have managed to penetrate the American defences are killed or captured.

Fischer, meanwhile, is attempting to storm the Towson battery with the rest of his force, only to find that his scaling ladders are too short to reach the parapet. Worse, he cannot reply to the heavy fire being poured down on him because, to ensure secrecy, his men have been ordered to remove the flints from their muskets. He charges the parapet five times before giving up. His losses are heavy. Many of the de Watteville regiment have deserted and are hiding in the woods. The King's, too, have been badly mauled during the panic. Only the 89th, which maintained its order, is intact.

Drummond's principal attack has failed. Success now depends entirely on the forces of his flamboyant nephew and those of the embittered Hercules Scott.

●

AT THE OTHER END of the American camp, David Bates Douglass has kept his men on the *qui vive*, warned by his commander, Brigadier-General Gaines, that a British attack is certain. Midnight passes without incident; then two o'clock. Nothing. Stretched out on his camp bed, Douglass begins to doubt that the assault will come. Slowly, the tension that has been keeping sleep away subsides and he slips into slumber.

Still asleep, he hears – what? A musket shot? Or is it part of his dream? Another volley follows. His body responds before his brain; he is on his feet before he is awake. In the distance, on the far left, comes another volley. This is no dream!

The cry "To arms! To arms!" ripples along his line of tents. The reserve is aroused and formed in the space of sixty seconds. On Douglass's left, the American 9th battalion, bayonets fixed, has already formed a double line. His own corps is wide awake and standing to their guns, the primers holding their hands over the priming to protect it from dampness, the firemen opening their dark lanterns, lighting their slow matches.

Up the river, at Snake Hill, the sky is brilliantly lit with rocket flares, bomb bursts, and musket fire. The sound of small arms and artillery, blended together, becomes a continuous roar like a stupendous drum roll.

Douglass has seen the signal rockets rise from the woods in front of him in answer to those from Fischer's column, but there is yet no hint of an attack on his battery. As the minutes tick by, tension starts to build.

"Why don't the lazy rascals make haste?" someone whispers.

It is another axiom of war that the more complex the plan the more unlikely it is of success. Drummond's three attacks were supposed to take place simultaneously – difficult enough in broad daylight, let alone pitch darkness. Hercules Scott's men should have assaulted Douglass's position the instant Fischer's rockets went up, but his battalion is still moving along the lakeshore, just below the embankment, as yet unseen but certainly heard. The tramp of seven hundred pairs of feet on the soft sand and the low whispers of the officers keeping their men together carries clearly through the night air:

"*Close up...Steady!...Steady men, steady...Steel...Captain Steel's company.*"

The sound of plodding feet grows louder. Then, as if on a signal, a sheet of fire blazes, and the batteries along the entrenchment from the water to the fort open up in reply.

It is three o'clock. Douglass is firing his cannon at point-blank range, cramming each to the muzzle with round shot, canister, and bags of musket balls – stuffing each barrel so full that he can touch the last piece of wadding with his hand.

From the direction of the old fort comes a sudden cry:

"Cease firing! You are firing on your own men!"

As Douglass considers, the fire slackens momentarily. But the voice was stiffly British; this, he guesses is a *ruse de guerre*. A second voice calls out in an American twang:

"Go to hell. Fire away, there, why don't you?" and the cannonade continues.

Hercules Scott's column surges forward with scaling ladders, seeking to surmount the breastwork. Again and again the British are repulsed. Of twenty officers, only four escape without wounds. More than half the regiment are casualties. By dawn it is clear that the attempt has failed.

On Scott's right, Drummond of Keltie is more successful. He forms up his men in a deep ravine, unbuckles his sword, and asks his friend Dunlop, the surgeon, to keep it for him; he prefers a boarding pike and pistol. Then he leads his 350 men in a dash across the open plain to the fort.

Twice his men attempt to scale the walls with ladders and are beaten back. Finally, hidden under the smoke of the big guns, they creep along the outer ditch, scale the north bastion of the old fort, and leap into the upper storey.

"Give the damn Yankees no quarter!" shouts William Drummond.

The gunners desert their cannon as British and Americans struggle hand to hand with pikes, bayonets, spears. One of the American defenders, Lieutenant John McDonough, badly wounded by a bayonet, asks for quarter, but Drummond, in a rage, shoots him with his pistol. It is his final act. A moment later, the General's brash nephew falls dead, shot through the heart and bayoneted.

The British manage to take possession of one side of the fort but are subject to heavy fire from the blockhouse above. The battle seesaws, neither side giving way, until suddenly beneath their feet comes a trembling followed by a roar and an appalling explosion. The magazine in the north bastion has blown up, either by accident or by design.

Douglass, over a hundred yards away, feels the ground shake under him, then sees a jet of flame shoot up from the fort for more than a hundred feet into the night sky, followed by a shower of stone, earth, chunks of timber, bits of human bodies. One of his own men falls dead, struck by the debris.

The carnage is ghastly. The Americans, protected by the walls of the barracks, are spared, but the British attackers are torn, crushed, mangled. Some, flung from the parapet, die on the bayonets of their comrades in the ditch below. Nothing can stem the panic that follows. Believing the entire fort to be mined, the men break and flee across the plain to the safety of the British trenches.

Only a few escape the blast. Captain John Le Couteur, who made the snowshoe trip from New Brunswick in 1813, is blown off the parapet, falling twenty feet into the ditch, winded but unharmed. As he dashes toward the British camp, he sees an officer on a stretcher and asks who it is.

"Colonel Scott, sir, shot through the head."

Le Couteur can see the bullet wound in Hercules Scott's forehead. The commander of the British 103rd can no longer speak, and only the slight pressure of his hand reveals that he is conscious. He has only moments to live.

At this spectacle, Captain Le Couteur flings down his sabre and cries out: "This is a disgraceful day for Old England!"

"For shame, Mr. Le Couteur," someone calls. "The men are sufficiently discouraged by defeat."

"Don't blame him," says another. "It's the high feeling of a young soldier."

Another officer turns about – General Drummond.

"Where is Colonel Scott?" the General asks.

"Oh, Sir! He is killed, just being brought in by his men."

"Where is Colonel Drummond?"

"Alas, Sir! He is killed, too. Bayoneted."

At the memory of his commander's death and that of three-quarters of his own men, Le Couteur bursts into tears.

The General is heartsick, and not just over the death of his nephew. Clearly he has underestimated the size of the American force and the strength of its defences and overestimated the effect of his artillery barrage. He has no time for recriminations. If the American commander knows what he is about, he will counter-attack at once while the British are off balance and in disarray and before Fischer's broken column can return. Drummond has fewer than one thousand effective troops to put into the line. They wait in their trenches for the counter-blow. It does not come. Brigadier-General Gaines has not grasped his opponent's weakness.

The British losses are appalling. More than nine hundred men – one-third of the army – are dead, wounded, or missing. Six battalions are so badly shattered they are no longer fit for field duty. The drummer Jarvis Hanks, visiting the ditch outside the fort in the morning, counts 190 bodies, the faces burned black, many horribly mutilated, one or two still alive but dying, a confusion of torn arms and legs heaped about, one human trunk bereft of head or limbs, "too sickening to look upon." Men move about in the ditch picking the pockets of the dead and dying. William Drummond's body lies under a cart, naked except for his shirt. American soldiers have looted it of epaulettes, money, and a gold watch.

Gordon Drummond blames both the "misconduct of this foreign corps," the de Watteville regiment, and the happenstance of the explosion for his misfortune. It is the failure of the mission more than the deaths of good men that appalls him. "The agony of mind I suffer from the present disgraceful, and unfortunate conduct, of Troops committed to my superintendence wounds me to the Soul," he writes to Sir George Prevost. He does not consider that his own hasty planning and faulty intelligence may have contributed to the débâcle. But then, no commander on either side during this maladroit war has yet written – will ever write – "I blame myself."

Prevost knows better. He chides Drummond gently in two letters, which the Americans intercept and Drummond never receives. It has been, the Governor General remarks, "a costly experiment," but no doubt the Lieutenant-General will profit from the experience. He can say no more; Drummond is the best he has. He can scarcely replace him.

Gaines is jubilant, but his elation is short lived. Gordon Drummond has no intention of abandoning the investment of Fort Erie. The cannonade increases in fury. One aiming point is the chimney above Gaines's headquarters. On August 29, a shell strikes it, drops through the roof, smashes the General's writing desk, and wounds him so badly that he is evacuated to Buffalo, his part in the war at an end.

Within the encampment, as the rain pelts down and the bombardment goes on and autumn approaches, elation gives way to dismay. Was Ripley right, after all? Is it possible for the invasion force to seize the peninsula and march on to conquer York and Kingston? The Americans have won a significant victory on paper, but nothing has changed. They hold exactly fifteen acres – no more, and Drummond's army blocks any further advance.

•

THE BRITISH CAMP before Fort Erie, September 17, 1814

Tiger Dunlop, the British army surgeon, is at dinner, well behind the lines, when the sound of gunfire interrupts his meal. Two American columns have left the safety of the fort and are attacking the British batteries two miles in front of the main camp. Jacob Brown, back on the Canadian side, is making one last attempt to break Gordon Drummond's siege of the American encampment.

Dunlop rushes out without waiting for orders. By the time he reaches the forward trenches with the other officers, the skirmish is all but over. He sees the Indians bounding forward, yelling and flinging their tomahawks. He comes upon American corpses, their skulls cleft to the eyes by the throwing hatchets. He searches the battlefield for wounded men and comes upon one of his bandsmen carrying in a blanket a mortally wounded American officer, gulping water from a canteen. Dunlop proposes to dress his wounds, but the officer refuses.

"Doctor," he gasps, "it's all in vain, my wound is mortal and no human skill can help me – leave me here with a canteen of water and save yourself. . . ."

Dunlop takes him back to a hut; when he returns from his medical duties, the American is dead. Dunlop asks his identity and is told he is Jacob Brown's confidant and David Bates Douglass's friend, Colonel Eleazer Wood, the engineer.

Dusk is falling as the Americans regain the shelter of their fort and the British return to their camp. Two British batteries have been damaged, at appalling loss. Brown counts 511 casualties, Drummond 565. Both sides claim victory, each exaggerating the other's strengths and losses. Neither will admit it, but the war on the Niagara frontier has again reached a stalemate. Drummond is low on ammunition and food, his troops miserable and diseased, desertions on the increase, his camp a heaving swamp. He is reinforced the next day but still has no more than two thousand effectives. On September 21, in a driving torrent of rain, he abandons the siege and moves quietly back to the original British position on Chippawa Creek. Brown, his own strength diminished by British cannon fire and the disastrous sortie, is too weak to follow. The two forces resemble equally matched prize-fighters, staggering about the ring in the last round, scarcely able to raise their arms in combat.

Both commanders are hungry for fresh troops. On September 28, George Izard arrives at Batavia, New York, having marched all the way from Lake Champlain with four thousand seasoned American troops. He is determined to drive the British out of Fort Niagara, but Brown wants instead to repeat the Battle of Chippawa. On October 10, Izard moves his army across the river and three days later is skirmishing with the British outposts at Street's Creek. In all this there is a weary sense of *déjà vu*.

Drummond suffers an agony of frustration. His force is not strong enough to go on the attack, but he is convinced that with two more regiments he could drive the Americans back across the river and finish the war in Upper Canada. He pleads with Prevost for supplies and men. Commodore Yeo is sitting at Kingston with the fleet. The new ship, *St. Lawrence*, is almost ready. Why can't the navy supply him?

Drummond's frustrations are nothing compared to Izard's. In his projected sweep across the Chippawa and up the peninsula to seize Burlington Heights and York, the Major-General has counted on Chauncey. Now he discovers to his chagrin that the American commodore, having learned of Yeo's superiority on the lake, has fled to the shelter of Sackets Harbor and will not come out. Izard cannot conceal his bitterness; Chauncey's timidity has destroyed all hope of any forward movement.

Drummond, meanwhile, is feverishly awaiting the arrival of the 9th Regiment from Kingston. Yeo reluctantly agrees to carry some troops and provisions across the lake but is so fearful of overloading his great new ship, *St. Lawrence*, that he carries only a small number of men; the rest are forced to struggle on by land over roads little better than rivers of mud. Drummond is as bitter at Yeo's caution as Izard is at Chauncey's. To both naval commanders their ships are too precious to be risked in battle and too grand to be used as transports.

Both opposing generals are dispirited and both are ill. Drummond is so sick that he asks to be sent home. Izard is so sick he cannot write to the Secretary of War. The troops on both sides are weak from dysentery. The weather grows worse each day.

The fight has gone out of the men on the Niagara frontier. The American militia, without pay for three months, are mutinous. Izard can see no practical reason to remain on the Canadian side of the river and so, after several days' wait for clement weather, embarks his troops. By November 1 all are back on their own soil. Nobody has the temerity to recall the gloomy prophecies of the perverse and discredited brigadier-general Eleazar Ripley.

And what of Fort Erie, over which so much blood has been spilled? In Izard's view, it is worthless: "It commands nothing, not even the entrance of the strait." It is "a weak, ill planned...hastily repaired redoubt."

On November 5, Gordon Drummond, guided by a sixth sense, dispatches James FitzGibbon, one-time leader of the Bloody Boys and now a captain with the Glengarry Light Infantry, to travel upriver to see what is happening at the fort. FitzGibbon finds it deserted. The Americans have blown up the works, dismantled everything of value, and vanished across the Niagara.

FitzGibbon rides through the rubble of the deserted encampment. Except for a dozen cases of damaged cartridges, the enemy has left nothing. Five months have passed since Winfield Scott first leaped ashore in its shadow. Yet no territory has been captured; none given up. The invasion has ended just as the last one did the previous December. Thousands are dead, more are crippled, hundreds are in prison. In the glowing reports of the opposing commanders, scores of officers have achieved immortality of a sort, their deeds of heroism, zeal, steadfastness, loyalty, leadership, and resolve recorded for all time. But where in this crumbling, rain-swept redoubt – its walls spattered with old blood, its ramparts scarred by cannon fire – is the glory? Where the victory? Here, as at Chippawa and Lundy's Lane, the dead lie mouldering in common graves. To what purpose have they fought? For whose honour have they bled? For what noble principle have they fallen? Even the suave diplomats, charged with treading the delicate pathway toward peace in the ancient Flemish city of Ghent, can no longer be certain.

II

THE BURNING OF WASHINGTON

August, 1814

Heeding Sir George Prevost's request to create diversions along the eastern seaboard of the United States in support of the struggle in Canada and also as a reprisal against American raids on Canadian private property – especially the vengeful burning of Port Dover in the spring – British ships have for months been harassing settlements on Chesapeake Bay. Now, with the war in Europe ended and reinforcements available, the British plan to attack the gunboats guarding Washington and, at the same time, mount a land raid on the capital.

BENEDICT, CHESAPEAKE BAY, MARYLAND, August 19, 1814

Lieutenant George Gleig, an eighteen-year-old subaltern in the British 85th, clambers off a landing launch, loaded down with equipment, sweltering in his thick wool uniform, feeling the effects of ten weeks on shipboard. Since leaving France at the end of May he has been almost constantly cooped up in a tiny stateroom with forty fellow officers, without exercise, subject to seasickness, threatened with typhoid – not the best preparation for a long march in the August heat with the prospect of a battle at the end.

The villagers have deserted Benedict, but now the empty streets come alive as forty-five hundred British soldiers – Wellington's Invincibles – pile out of the boats and sort themselves into three brigades. Some begin to forage for extra food. Gleig finds three ducks, and the following morning he and his friend Lieutenant Codd manage to buy a pig, a goose, and a couple of chickens from a solitary farm wife. But before they can enjoy their feast, the bugle sounds assembly.

As the three brigades march off toward Washington, their commander, Major-General Robert Ross, a blue-eyed Irishman of forty-seven, one of Wellington's best officers, rides past to the cheers of his men. Ross has some doubts about this venture. His troops, languishing aboard ship, are badly out of shape. He has no cavalry and only three small field guns. The terrain ahead, cut by streams and bordered by forests, can be easily defended. He has been persuaded, however, by his naval colleague, Rear-Admiral George Cockburn, that a two-pronged attack up Chesapeake Bay is practical – with the fleet seizing the American flotilla of gunboats and the army marching on the capital by a parallel route.

Ross is new to North America, but Cockburn has been skirmishing off the coast for more than a year and knows every inlet in the long, narrow bay. At forty-two he is a seasoned commander, famous for his lightning thrusts at American seaboard settlements. In an earlier decade he might have been a buccaneer. The plan to seize and burn Washington is his.

Ross's column manages only six miles. The march is a horror, the men groaning under their heavy baggage, choking with dust, half dead from heat and fatigue. Scores fall exhausted by the wayside. George Gleig has never felt so tired, though he remembers that during the Peninsular campaign he often marched thrice this distance without difficulty.

Surprisingly, the British advance is unimpeded. No one has blocked the road or burned any bridges. Except for a few shots fired from the woods there is no harassment on the flanks, no attempt at ambush. The real enemy is the weather. In August, Maryland is a furnace.

Still, General Ross has misgivings. Admiral Cockburn, having chased the Americans into a cul-de-sac and forced them to blow up their gunboats, arrives on horseback to stiffen his colleague's resolve. The high command is also nervous. At two in the morning of August 24, both commanders are awakened by a courier from their commander-in-chief, Vice-Admiral Sir Alexander Cochrane, who orders them to return at once.

A whispered argument follows between Ross and Cockburn as Ross's aides strain to listen. Clearly Cockburn wants to go on, in spite of orders. They hear the phrase "stain upon our arms." They hear him pledge success. They see Ross waver and finally, as dawn breaks, see him strike his head and say: "Well, be it so, we will proceed."

George Gleig has spent a sleepless night on picket duty, two miles ahead of the main British force, with only sixteen men, fearing imminent capture. He has no time to rest, for when he returns to camp at five, the army is ready to march. He can hardly drag one foot ahead of the other, but he knows that Washington is only a few miles ahead, across the Potomac. Just past the community of Long Old Fields the road forks, one route leading directly to the capital, the other circling around to the right, a longer distance through the village of Bladens-

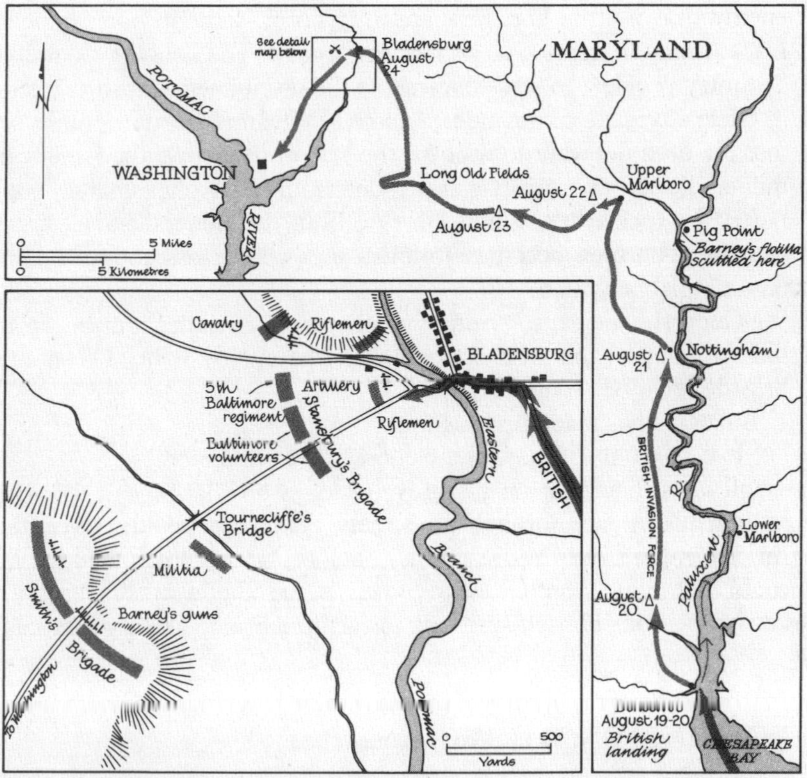
See detail map below
Bladensburg
August 24
MARYLAND
POTOMAC
WASHINGTON
RIVER
Long Old Fields
Upper Marlboro
August 22
August 23
5 Miles
5 Kilometres
Pig Point
Barney's flotilla scuttled here
Cavalry
Riflemen
BLADENSBURG
5th Baltimore regiment
Artillery
Stansbury's Brigade
Riflemen
Baltimore volunteers
Eastern
BRITISH
Tournecliffe's Bridge
Militia
Branch
Barney's guns
Smith's Brigade
To Washington
Potomac
500
Yards
August 21
Nottingham
BRITISH INVASION FORCE
R.
Patuxent
Lower Marlboro
August 20
August 19-20
British landing
CHESAPEAKE BAY

The British March on Washington, August 19–24, 1814

burg. Ross leads his weary men onto the direct fork, then suddenly reverses his column and opts for the Bladensburg road. His plan is to throw the Americans off guard; they will not have been expecting this. Nor have his men. By the time they reach the village in the scorching sun, they have marched fourteen miles and some are lying dead from exhaustion by the wayside.

It is noon as the troops trudge into the village. They have already seen huge clouds of dust in the distance and realize that the Americans are marching to meet them. But Bladensburg is empty of the enemy; the Americans have not fortified it, an error that causes relief. Few have the stomach for street fighting.

On the heights above the village, directly ahead and beyond the single bridge that crosses the Potomac's shallow eastern branch – surprisingly still intact – George Gleig in the light brigade can see the enemy drawn up in line. Few are in uniform, some in blue, some in black, many in hunting jackets or frock coats. To Gleig they look like "country people," in stark contrast to the disciplined British regulars.

Gleig's brigade commander, Colonel William Thornton, thinks so, too. He does not want to wait for the rest of the army: the American militia, he insists, cannot stand a determined bayonet charge, supported by rocket fire. When Harry Smith, the General's aide, urges caution, Thornton becomes furious, and when Ross supports him, Smith is flabbergasted.

"General," he says, "neither of the other brigades will be up in time to support this mad attack and if the enemy fight, Thornton's brigade must be repulsed."

But Ross has made up his mind.

"If it rain militia," says the General, "we will go on."

Off goes Thornton on his grey horse, sword flashing in the sun, leading his brigade through the streets. As he reaches the river, the American guns open up. A moment before, George Gleig had felt he could not move another step; now, as the Battle of Bladensburg begins, he finds himself sprinting toward the bridge like a young colt.

•

WASHINGTON, D.C., August 24, 1814

Brigadier-General William Winder, the Baltimore lawyer placed in charge of the defence of Washington, worries and frets. For five days, without much sleep, he has been trying frantically to raise a force of militia to oppose the British, whose intentions he does not know and cannot guess. For most of the night he has been stumbling about on foot, his horse played out, his right arm and ankle in pain from a fall in a ditch. His own subordinates cannot find him and, for a time, believe him a captive of the British.

Now, having inspected the forces guarding the bridge over the east branch of the Potomac – the entrance to the city – he snatches an hour's sleep on a camp cot. If the British do intend to attack Washington, he reasons, they will probably come this way by the direct route from Long Old Fields. On the other hand, they may have another objective – Annapolis, perhaps, or Fort Warburton. He cannot tell. It is also possible they may take a more roundabout route to the capital, through Bladensburg. What to do? If he goes to Bladensburg, he leaves the other route wide open.

366

Few believe the British intend to attack Washington. The Secretary of War is one doubter. "They certainly will not come here," John Armstrong has declared. "What the devil will they do here? No! No! Baltimore is the place...that is of so much more consequence." This incredulity helps explain why so few have answered the call to arms.

Winder's military career has not been glorious. Captured by the British as he blundered about in the dark at Stoney Creek and exchanged a year later, he holds his present post partly because he is available and partly because he is a nephew of Maryland's governor, whose state has not been the most enthusiastic supporter of the war. That blood relationship, however, has not paid off. Of six thousand Marylanders called out by federal draft on July 4, only 250 were under Winder's command the day the British landed. The Pennsylvania record is even worse. That state was supposed to supply five thousand men but has sent none because its militia law has expired, and no one has yet got around to renewing it.

Winder should have fifteen thousand men – the number called for by the government. Two days before he could count only three thousand. Now, with the redcoats only eight miles away, more troops are trickling in. None are trained because the government would not call on them until the danger was "imminent." And some will not see action because of a maddening bureaucracy. As Winder fidgets and waits for word of the British line of march, seven hundred frustrated arrivals from Virginia are vainly attempting to get arms from the War Department. The clerk in charge arrives at last and begins doling out flints, one at a time, counting each carefully. When an officer tries to speed things up, he starts the count over again. These men will not see action today.

Because he cannot be sure of the British intentions, Winder has had to divide his forces. Two thousand Marylanders under Brigadier-General Tobias Stansbury occupy Bladensburg. Some arrived only the previous night and have hardly had time to settle in. Another six hundred are on their way from Annapolis; Winder does not know where they are. At the Potomac bridge on the eastern outskirts of Washington, ready to march in either of two directions, he has fifteen hundred District of Columbia militia under Brigadier-General Walter Smith. In addition, there are a handful of regulars, a couple of hundred dragoons, and four hundred naval men, anxious to get into action now that the flotilla has been destroyed.

The sun is scarcely up before Winder receives mortifying news from General Stansbury at Bladensburg. Fearing the British may take another route and cut him off, he has moved his exhausted Marylanders out of the village and back toward Washington. Winder orders him forward again. Stansbury's troops, who have been up most of the night, return as far as the heights above Bladensburg, commanding the bridge across the river, but do not occupy the village.

At ten, Winder's scouts gallop in and the General finally learns the British intentions: they have taken the longer route through Bladensburg. That is where he must oppose them. He moves to combine his forces, orders General Smith to march his brigade off immediately to join Stansbury. An hour later he follows as does most of the Cabinet, including the President. James Monroe, the Secretary of State, a one-time colonel in the Revolutionary army, dashes on ahead. It has always been his ambition to be commander-in-chief of the American forces in this war; now he has a chance to display his military acumen.

On the heights above the village, John Pendleton Kennedy of the crack United Company of the 5th Baltimore Light Dragoons – the "Baltimore 5th," as they are known – can hardly keep himself awake. He has actually had the novel experience of sleeping while on the march. What began as a glittering adventure – banners flying, bands playing, the populace huzzahing at every corner – has taken a darker turn. His comrades belong to the elite of Baltimore – barristers, professionals, wealthy merchants; he and his five friends have even brought along a black servant, Lige, to wait on them. But now the picnic is over. Routed out in the dark only hours after arriving, their kits in disarray, marched and countermarched in the night, they are used up. Kennedy has lost his boots in the midnight scramble to retire and is wearing dancing pumps on his swollen feet.

The British are only three miles away, but now another mix-up bedevils the Baltimore 5th. Having taken their position on the left of the forward line, supporting the riflemen and artillery, they are suddenly ordered back a quarter of a mile to an exposed position which leaves the forward guns and rifles without support. This is the work of Monroe, the Secretary of State, who has butted in, uninvited and without the knowledge of General Stansbury. By the time Winder arrives to inspect the lines, it is too late to make any change.

Stansbury's force is deployed in two ragged lines: the sharpshooters (most of whom have only muskets, not rifles) and cannons well forward, the three Maryland regiments some distance behind with the

368

crack 5th on the left, its field of fire impeded by an orchard. These will bear the brunt of the British attack. A mile to the rear, another line is hastily forming as the troops arrive – Smith's brigade from Washington and several hundred footsore militia from Annapolis, who have already marched sixteen miles. None, save a few regulars and the naval detachment, have had any recent training because, as the Secretary of War has told Winder, the best way to use the militia is on the spur of the occasion – to bring them to fight as soon as called out.

The Secretary of War is the last of the Cabinet to arrive on the heights above Bladensburg. The President is already here, a small, frail figure in black, two borrowed duelling pistols at his waist. He stands behind Stansbury's lines with the Attorney General and the Secretaries of State, War, and Treasury. This is a motley crew, their personal relations fraught with jealousies, hatreds, ambitions. Armstrong has no use for Winder, who was not his choice for commander-in-chief; he has pointedly ignored the General's letters pleading for reinforcements. Monroe and Madison have little liking for Armstrong, whom they see as a possible political rival. Armstrong for once has nothing to say; having made no effort to defend the capital, he must realize that his days in office are numbered.

Up rides William Simmons, another Armstrong-hater, recently fired from his job with the War Department. Now, however, he has buried his bitterness in the common cause. Spotting Monroe, he offers to ride into the village and scout out the enemy. He gets to Lownde's Hill, on the far side of town, and sees, in the near distance, a great cloud of dust. Back he gallops to discover that the presidential party is in front of its own lines, moving down toward the Bladensburg bridge. Simmons warns the President that the British advance has already reached the village.

"The enemy in Bladensburg!" Madison exclaims in surprise. His party wheels about as Simmons vainly calls after them:

"Mr. Madison, if you stop, I will show them to you...."

Only Richard Rush, the Attorney General, checks his horse. Simmons points out the redcoats entering the town, whereupon Rush too wheels about and gallops off, with Simmons riding after him, shouting that he has left his hat behind.

By 12:30, the battle is joined. Henry Fulford in the Baltimore 5th watches in amazement as the American cannons and sharpshooters pour a hail of fire onto the bridge. The British redcoats, dashing across, seem to take no notice; they move like clockwork: the instant a platoon is cut down it is filled up by men from the rear without the least confusion. George Gleig, on the bridge, has a different view: an entire company ahead of him is cut to pieces, and he has the grisly experience of trampling on his dead and dying comrades.

Without pausing for the rest of the British to come up, Colonel Thornton leads his men against the forward American skirmishers. Flinging aside their heavy packs, Gleig and the others drive the riflemen back into the woods, only to be faced with the main body of Marylanders. The Baltimore 5th surges forward, forcing the redcoats back to the river's edge. The carnage is dreadful. Almost every British officer is hit. Gleig's friend, Lieutenant Codd, falls dead beside him – the pair will never again forage for chickens. Not far away, crouching in the willows, Captain John Knox realizes he had never seen such fire. So many officers are down that he can expect promotion – if he lives. "By the time the action's over, the devil is in it if I am not a walking Major or a dead Captain," he tells himself. Harry Smith has been right; Thornton was too impetuous; he should have waited for the rest of the army.

Now, however, Major-General Ross has his Congreve rockets in position. Long tubes filled with powder, they operate on the same principle as a Fourth of July firework. They are hopelessly inaccurate but make a terrifying scream as they whoosh over the heads of the raw American troops, who have never before encountered anything like them. The Baltimore 5th, on the left of the line, stands fast, but the two regiments on the right break in panic. With its flanks exposed, the 5th also falls back. Officers dash about, vainly attempting to rally their fleeing men, but the retreat has become a rout.

John Kennedy, still in his dancing pumps, flings away his musket and joins the mob, carrying a wounded comrade to safety. Henry Fulford has only one idea in mind: to head for the woods, lie down, and sleep; instead, the musket balls and grape shot drive him into a swamp from which he later makes his way to a friendly farmhouse.

The rear line of Americans has only just formed when the fleeing Marylanders come dashing through. (Madison and his Cabinet have long since galloped off.) It stands briefly, then breaks. Only the naval veterans under Commodore Joshua Barney hold fast at their guns until out of ammunition. Barney, badly wounded in the thigh, cannot understand the rout.

"Damn them," he growls to his British captors, "there were enough of them to have eaten every one of you!"

The road to Washington and the city beyond is filled with fleeing militia. Winder, who has made no plans to gather his troops at a rallying point in case of retreat, decides to abandon the capital, an order that causes anguish among General Smith's brigade of Washington militia. Many vanish to their homes to look after their families. Those who can be collected are marched eighteen miles beyond the city to Montgomery Court House.

For the moment, the British are too exhausted to follow. George Gleig pursues the fleeing troops for a mile before he collapses and slakes his thirst in a muddy pool. He is lucky to be alive: a musket ball has torn the arm of his jacket, another has seared his thigh. He gathers what men he can and returns to join his battered regiment. It is dark before the scattered remains of his company can be collected. Then, tired or not, the light brigade marches triumphantly off toward the abandoned capital, the sky ahead bright with the glow of leaping flames.

●

DOLLEY MADISON waits in the President's house, listening to the rumble of cannon and seeing, in the distant sky, the flash of rockets She has no intention of leaving until she hears from her husband. Two pencilled messages have arrived, warning her to be ready to depart at a moment's notice. In the driveway stands her carriage loaded with trunks containing all the Cabinet papers. A wagon, recently procured, contains some silver plate and personal belongings.

Four artillerymen, posted at two cannons guarding the mansion, have deserted their posts. French John Siousa, her personal servant, offers to spike the guns and lay a trail of powder to the door, to destroy the house if necessary. Mrs. Madison will have none of it. At three, two messengers, grimy with dust, gallop up with orders from the President to leave immediately. She will not do so until she can rescue Gilbert Stuart's full-length portrait of George Washington. She and French John attack the frame with carving knife and axe. With the canvas rolled and placed in friendly hands, the First Lady of the United States climbs into her carriage and rolls through the streets of the capital, crowded with soldiers, senators, women and children, with carriages, horses, wagons and carts loaded with household furniture, all fleeing toward the wooden bridge on the west side of town.

Half an hour later, the President arrives with his party, exhausted and humiliated. All his theoretical ideas about the value of democratic volunteers have been shattered.

"I could never have believed that so great a difference existed between regular troops and a militia force if I had not witnessed the scenes of this day," he remarks. At dusk, he too leaves the city.

From his handsome four-storey house at the corner of First and A streets, Washington's leading physician, Dr. James Ewell, has been gloomily watching the retreat. He sees the Secretary of War in full flight, followed by crowds of riders, some of whom bawl out: "Fly, fly! The ruffians are at hand!...send off your wives and children!" In the distance a cloud of dust envelops the retreating army. Shaken with horror, the doctor turns to find his wife in convulsions, crying repeatedly, "Oh, what shall we do? What shall we do?" while his two daughters scream at her side. He decides to quit his own home and move his family to a neighbouring house. The owner, a Mrs. Orr, is so sick that Ewell is sure nobody will harm her or those she shelters.

General Ross and Rear-Admiral Cockburn enter the city at the head of the 3rd Brigade, which has escaped most of the fighting. From a large brick house on their right comes the crackle of musket fire, killing the General's horse and hitting four soldiers, one mortally. At once the Admiral's aide, James Scott, leads a party to the building and smashes down the door. The house, only recently occupied by Albert Gallatin, now treating for peace at Ghent, is empty. Up come the light companies of the 21st and demolish the building with Congreve rockets. At almost the same time, the retreating Americans blow up the navy yard. For the next forty-eight hours, Washington will be aglow.

The victors push into Capitol Square. Ahead lies the seat of government, a Greek temple, inviting destruction. It is not easy to fire the Capitol. In the lower storey only the frames, sashes, shutters, and doors will burn. The troops chop away with axes, tear open some rockets as tinder, and spread a trail of fire from room to room. In the House of Representatives there is better fodder for the incendiaries — galleries and stages of yellow pine, mahogany desks, tables, chairs. Piled in the centre of the great domed chamber, they make a gargantuan bonfire, the heat so intense that glass melts, stone cracks, columns are peeled of their skin, marble is burned to lime. So bright is this pyre that George Gleig, bivouacked outside the city, can see the faces of his men reflected in the glow. He recalls the burning of San Sebastian; except for that, he realizes, he has never in his life witnessed a scene more strikingly sublime. But to the people of Washington, so certain of victory that thousands made no preparation to flee, the spectacle is pure horror.

The Treasury building is next, then the President's Mansion. Here an advance party finds a table set for forty, apparently in anticipation of a victory dinner. Instead, the real victors toast the Prince Regent while Cockburn sardonically raises his glass to "Jemmy," as he calls the President. Looting precedes the flames. Everyone takes a souvenir. The Admiral urges a local bookseller to help himself – but not to anything expensive; the most luxurious items, he says, must feed the blaze. Ross helps pile furniture in the Oval Room while some of the seamen procure fire from a nearby beer house.

That done, the Admiral and the General enjoy dinner at Barbara Suter's boarding house. Cockburn blows out the candles, preferring, he says, the light cast by the burning buildings. An officer enters to ask if the War Department should be fired. Tomorrow, says the General, the men are exhausted.

Ross prepares to bed down in Dr. Ewell's empty house, then apologizes when its owner arrives, offers to go elsewhere. When Ewell insists, the General reassures him that his family is quite safe.

"I am myself a married man, have several sweet children and venerate the sanctities of conjugal and domestic relations," Ross declares – at least, that is the way the much-relieved physician remembers it.

Later Ross tells Ewell he regrets burning the Capitol library and says he would not have fired the President's Mansion had the First Lady remained. "I make war neither against letters nor ladies," he explains.

But the burning goes on the following day – private homes as well as public buildings to a value of more than a million dollars go up in smoke. Cockburn, riding a white mare with a black foal following, makes his way to the office of the violently anti-British newspaper, the *National Intelligencer*. Bowing to the entreaties of several women who fear the flames will spread to their homes, he spares the building but orders his men to destroy the contents. Out into the street go books, papers, type as the axes do their work.

"Be sure that all the C's are destroyed," says Cockburn, "so that the rascals can have no further means of abusing my name...."

Dolley Madison, meanwhile, arriving at a small tavern sixteen miles from town, finds herself excoriated by a group of women fugitives who blame the administration for all their troubles. Her escort forces open the door against their protests just as a violent storm breaks. It is the worst in living memory.

In Washington, the sky goes black, a torrent of rain sweeps through the blazing buildings, damping the flames, while a hurricane tears the roofs off houses, whirling them into the air like sheets of paper. George Gleig, camping on Capitol Hill with his company and used to the soft rains of the English countryside, has never experienced anything so terrifying. Only the jagged flashes of lightning relieve the darkness. His company is dispersed, the men fleeing for shelter or throwing themselves flat to the ground to prevent the tempest carrying them off. Several houses topple, burying thirty soldiers in the debris. The wind is so strong that two cannon are lifted from their mounts and hurled several yards.

For two hours the storm rages. When it is over, Ross decides it is time to move out. The withdrawal takes place at night and in secret, the populace ordered to remain indoors under pain of death. Fuel is added to the burning buildings and a handful of men detailed to leap about in the light of the flames to fool the enemy. The army moves out in silence. Four days later, unmolested, it is back at Benedict, embarking on the ships.

For the first time, the war has been carried to the heart of the United States. When Madison commenced hostilities two summers before, expecting an easy victory and, possibly, a new state in the Union, he could hardly have foreseen that he would one day be cowering in a hovel outside the capital, fearing imminent capture. Now, as the people of Washington return to their gutted city and Ross and Cockburn plan a new attack on Baltimore, another army of British regulars – the largest yet assembled – is preparing to cross the border and march on New York. What began as the invasion of Canada has now become the invasion of America, and in spite of the peace talks in Ghent, it is not yet over.

12

THE BATTLE OF
LAKE CHAMPLAIN
September, 1814

With thousands of Wellington's veterans shipped across the Atlantic to reinforce his thin army, Sir George Prevost can at last go on the offensive. He intends to march his troops — eleven thousand strong — down the Richelieu-Champlain corridor and take the war into New York State. To succeed he must seize Plattsburgh on Lake Champlain and destroy the newly built American fleet anchored in Plattsburgh Bay. All year, the two opposing navies on the lake have been engaged in a shipbuilding contest. As the British flotilla nears completion and Prevost's army marches south, the American commodore, Thomas Macdonough, awaits the coming attack.

ABOARD U.S. SARATOGA, Plattsburgh Bay, New York, September 4, 1814

Sunday dinner aboard the flagship of Commodore Thomas Macdonough, commander of the American fleet on Lake Champlain. The Commodore's gig arrives bringing a guest, a Yale student, John H. Dulles of Philadelphia. As the sun approaches the meridian, a predinner service is held on deck, and young Dulles notes that the three hundred members of the naval congregation are more than usually devout. He remarks on this to the Commodore, who replies, drily, "You must not be deceived by an inference that it is from pious feelings altogether." He smiles and adds, "There are other considerations controlling their conduct." There are indeed. Thomas Macdonough is totally in control of his fleet. Dulles, chatting with some junior officers, is "struck with the palpable evidence of the one pervading spirit of a master mind."

In spite of the stalemate on the Niagara peninsula, the war is far from over. On this Sunday afternoon, as Gordon Drummond continues to lob cannonballs at Fort Erie and the five Americans at Ghent begin, at last, to fence with their British counterparts, Sir George Prevost's vast army is marching down the western shore of Lake Champlain, virtually unopposed. A few miles to the north, a new British fleet is nearing completion. But here on Thomas Macdonough's flagship, all is calm.

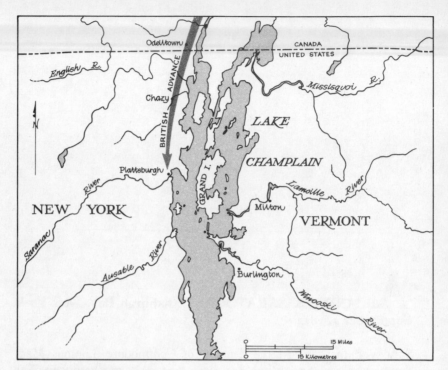

Lake Champlain, 1814

In his cabin, Macdonough quietly discusses the possibilities of the coming action. If the British destroy his fleet, he explains, Sir George Prevost can march his army, unobstructed, to the capital at Albany – even on to New York City, there to dictate an ignominious peace. The next few days will be decisive.

Dulles is impressed by Macdonough, who speaks "with the singular simplicity and with the dignity of a Christian gentleman." The Commodore looks younger than his thirty-one years. He has a light, agile frame and a bony face – all nose and jaw. His faith in a living God is unbounded. To Dulles he quotes from the epistle of St. James with its naval illustrations:

"He that wavereth is like a wave of the sea driven with the wind," and "Behold the ships, though so great, are turned about with a very small helm."

The chaplain offers a blessing before the midday meal. Halfway through a message arrives, which the Commodore relays to his officers:

378

"Gentlemen...I am just informed by the commander of the army that the signs of advance by the British forces will be signalled by two guns, and you will act accordingly."

He leaves the table and the conversation livens. One of the juniors makes so bold as to illustrate a remark with an oath, whereupon another turns to him and declares:

"Sir, I am astonished at your using such language. You know you would not do it if the Commodore was present."

Dead silence as the rebuke sinks in. What a curious company is this! Hardly the blasphemous and salty fraternity of song and story.

But then, no one would describe Thomas Macdonough as salty, though he has spent half his life in the navy. He is a devout Episcopalian, his religion so much a part of him that it cannot be separated from the rest of his personality. He does not flaunt his faith, for he has learned in fifteen years of naval service to keep himself under tight control, to curb a tendency toward impetuosity – even rashness. He is known as an amiable, even placid officer, not one to betray emotion.

And he is a survivor. One of Stephen Decatur's favourite midshipmen, he saw active service in the Mediterranean. He is brave and he is tough. Once, in hand-to-hand fighting on a Tripolitan gunboat when his cutlass broke, Macdonough wrested a pistol from his nearest assailant and shot him dead. Later he survived an epidemic of yellow fever that killed all but three of his shipmates. Two years of service on Lake Champlain, however, have worn him down, leaving him prey to the tuberculosis that will eventually kill him.

As on Erie and Ontario, the British and Americans on Lake Champlain have been engaged in a shipbuilding race. It has not been easy for Macdonough, who has had to compete with Chauncey for men and supplies. Yet, with the help of Noah Brown, the New York shipbuilding genius who worked on Perry's fleet, he has outdone Perry. In the spring, Brown launched the twenty-six-gun *Saratoga*, larger than any of Erie's vessels. Then, when Macdonough discovered that the British were building an even larger vessel, *Confiance*, he undertook to construct a second, the twenty-gun *Eagle*, launched in a record seventeen days after the keel was laid. Now he has outstripped the British, for *Eagle* has joined his squadron while the British flagship has yet to be rigged.

The creation of Macdonough's fleet has been a masterpiece of organization and ingenuity. One vessel, the seventeen-gun *Ticonderoga*, is a former steamer, transformed by Brown into a schooner.

Guns, cannon, shot, cables, and cordage have been hauled hundreds of miles to the shipyards at Otter Creek. Here, in the saw pits, green timber has been turned into planking while local blacksmiths have hammered out nails, bolts, fastenings, wire. Besides his two large vessels and *Ticonderoga*, Macdonough has three smaller sloops, six two-gun galleys, each manned by forty oarsmen, and four smaller galleys – sixteen vessels in all.

Now, with Prevost's army sweeping everything before it, Macdonough waits for the British fleet. He knows he cannot beat it in the open water, where the British long guns can savage his vessels at a comfortable distance. He must force them to come to him – to do battle within the confines of Plattsburgh Bay, where his powerful short-range carronades may hammer them to matchwood.

Will Downie, the British commander, hold his fleet outside the bay? Macdonough thinks not: at this season the possibility of a destructive gale is too great. But once they enter the bay, Macdonough can fight at a site of his own choosing.

The long narrow lake runs north and south, with the prevailing winds blowing from the north. Macdonough expects the British fleet will sweep up the lake toward its objective with the north wind behind it. Once the ships round Cumberland Head, however, they must turn into the wind in order to manoeuvre into the bay. They may, of course, drive directly across the mouth of the bay, but that is unlikely, for it would place them within range of the shore batteries on the far side.

With this in mind, Macdonough carefully places his fleet in a chain across the bay, stretching from the shallows near Crab Island on his right to Cumberland Head on his left. The chain runs almost north and south; that will force the British to attack bows on, a position that will allow Macdonough to rake their vessels from bow to stern. Nor can the British stand off out of range and batter the Americans with their long guns. Macdonough has so chosen his position in the cramped bay that there is not enough room.

He intends to fight at anchor, forcing the British to come to him, his vessels little more than floating batteries. It can be dangerous. He must be aware that Nelson destroyed two fleets at anchor – the French on the Nile, the Danes at Copenhagen. But Nelson had the wind behind him. By hitting the enemy line on the windward he was able to bear down on the opposing fleet and roll it up, ship by ship. Downie, the British commodore, cannot duplicate Nelson's feat from the lee-

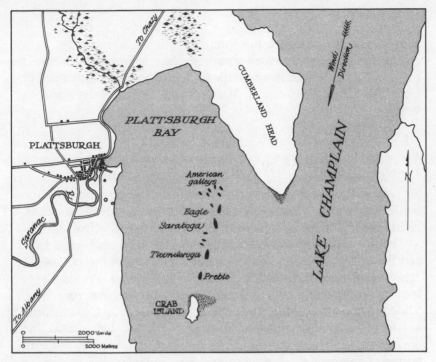

Macdonough at Anchor, Plattsburgh Bay, September, 1814

ward; the geography of Plattsburgh Bay makes that impossible. It is hard enough with lake vessels of shallow drafts and flat bottoms to beat up, close-hauled, against the wind.

Macdonough plans one further precaution. He must be able to manoeuvre quickly at anchor, without putting on sail. To do that, he equips his flagship, *Saratoga*, with a series of anchors and cables that will allow him to twist it about in any direction – through an arc of 180 degrees if necessary – in order to bring his guns to bear on targets of opportunity.

He cannot know what the British will do. He can only make an educated guess, based on his knowledge of the winds, the geography of the lake, his own capabilities, and the enemy's objectives.

The British are determined to seize Plattsburgh and destroy its defenders. To accomplish that and to continue on through the state, they must have naval support. That they cannot have without a naval victory. For once, the approaching winter is to the Americans' advantage. With the season far advanced, Macdonough is betting that

Prevost will not hazard a blockade but will opt immediately for a combined attack by Downie's squadron and his formidable army. If he does, and if the God in whom the Commodore so devoutly believes gives him favourable winds, Macdonough is calmly confident of victory.

•

PLATTSBURGH, NEW YORK, September 7, 1814

Sir George Prevost's mighty army – the greatest yet assembled on the border – pours into Plattsburgh's outskirts in two dense columns, brushing aside the weak American defenders like ineffectual insects.

These are Wellington's veterans. With Napoleon confined to Elba and the conflict in Europe at an end, sixteen thousand were brought across the Atlantic to finish the war in North America. Prevost has at least eleven thousand on this march through upper New York State. The logistics are awesome. To maintain its new army in Canada, Britain must ship daily supplies weighing forty-five tons across the ocean – a drain upon the British treasury which English property owners, facing new taxes, are beginning to deplore.

At eight in the morning, Major John E. Wool attempts to stem the scarlet tide. He has no chance. The heavy British column presses forward at a steady 108 paces to the minute, completely filling the roadway and routing the militia. An artillery captain tries to support Wool. His cannonballs tear heavy lanes through the British ranks, but the disciplined veterans march inexorably on, filling the gaps as they go. They disdain to deploy into line. Instead, as the bugles sound, the flanking companies toss aside their knapsacks, rush forward at a smart double, and disperse the fleeing Americans at bayonet point even as the main body marches on.

Prevost's brigades are under the direct control of Major-General De Rottenburg, who commands three battle-wise major-generals from Wellington's army – Manley Power, Thomas Makdougall Brisbane, and Frederick Philipse Robinson. They have been hand picked by the Iron Duke himself; he considers them the best he has. Not surprisingly, all three are sceptical of the colonial high command. Neither Prevost, De Rottenburg, nor the Adjutant-General, Colonel Baynes, now promoted to major-general, have much battle experience.

As the troops march into Plattsburgh against light resistance, Robinson has further cause to question Prevost's capabilities. He has already realized that the army is moving on its objective without any carefully thought-out plan. Now, as he approaches the Saranac River, the major obstacle between the American redoubts and the advancing British, his doubts are confirmed.

Prevost proposes an immediate attack. Is Robinson prepared to launch his demi-brigade in an assault on the heights across the river?

Robinson is always ready, but he has some questions:

Is the river fordable and, if so, where? What is the ground like on the other side? How far will the men have to march to reach the American redoubts? Are experienced guides available?

To his dismay, he is told that no one has the answers to any of these queries.

Robinson's men have been on the march since five in the morning. It is now three o'clock. He suggests to Prevost that the staff do its best to get all possible information and if it cannot be procured before dark, to defer the attack until daybreak. Guides, he says, are essential; they must be obtained at any price.

Undoubtedly his mind goes back to Wellington's crossing of the Bidassoa between Spain and France. There the Duke employed men disguised as fishermen to sound out the fords and the ground and to guide the attacking columns. But Prevost is no Wellington. It seems to Robinson that the high command is convinced that it is impossible to get reliable information and that it is simply wasting good money to try. Prevost is a penny-pincher; he has a secret service fund but withholds it from his generals.

It is clear now that no attempt will be made on the American redoubts until the following day. As Prevost camps his army on a ridge north of Plattsburgh, Robinson, the old campaigner, makes a personal reconnaissance of the village below: the scattered houses, perhaps eighty in number, four hotels, a few shops and public buildings; the river, spanned by two bridges, the planking of each removed by the retreating Americans; on the heights on the south side, three redoubts, two blockhouses, and, near the lake, a battery of big guns. He notes that the redoubts are not yet finished and that the guns are *en barbette* — not mounted. They can, he believes, easily be silenced during an assault.

He is an old hand at this, for he has been a soldier since the age of thirteen in Virginia, when he was commissioned an ensign at the outbreak of the American Revolution. At fifteen, he took a company into action at Horseneck. Since then his has been a life of action. Wounded three times – once fighting in America, twice in the Peninsular campaign – he is known as an officer of high and daring spirit, chosen to lead the advance in the successful assault on San Sebastian, mentioned several times in dispatches, noted for taking a village against a heavy artillery barrage without firing a shot. His lineage is distinguished, his family tree studded with clerics, jurists, and generals. John Beverley Robinson is his first cousin.

Robinson has urged that his assault force be called out and in position by first light, but dawn comes and no orders reach him. Sir George Prevost is having second thoughts.

Prevost is not Robinson's kind of general. The qualities that have made him a good administrator in the defence of Canada – prudence, conciliation, sober second thoughts, a tendency to delay – now work against him. He is essentially a diplomat; circumspection is his hallmark. He prefers to slide around a problem rather than meet it head on. He cannot bring himself even to write a harsh letter. His reproofs to subordinates are so delicately phrased that they seem almost like praise.

At forty-seven, he is in the prime of his career, his body supple, his face not unhandsome, though his official portrait cannot disguise the worried, hesitant cast of his eyes. These have not been easy years for George Prevost. His conciliation of the French Canadians, however admirable, has made him unpopular with the Anglophone elite in Quebec, who feel he is coddling a defeated race. His strategy, dictated by Great Britain, has been to remain strictly on the defensive, husbanding his inadequate forces. For more than two years his instincts have been to hold fast, to let the enemy come to him, to seek delay by armistice, to avoid costly mistakes. In this he has been spectacularly successful. Except for two small enclaves at Amherstburg and Fort Erie (the latter soon to be abandoned) and some foraging parties trampling their way up and down the Thames Valley, the Americans have failed to gain a foothold in Canada. The conquest of British North America is no closer to reality than it was in the summer of 1812. For this, Prevost can take much credit.

Now, however, events have taken an about-turn. For the first time, the Americans are outnumbered – and by the best troops in the world. An entire British division has penetrated deep into enemy territory. If Prevost is to succeed he must accommodate himself to a changed set of circumstances, put aside old habits, abandon the strategy of the previous twenty-seven months.

He cannot do it, cannot bring himself to launch an assault even against the weakly held entrenchments before him. The best American troops, four thousand in number, have already left to support Jacob Brown on the Niagara frontier – an incomprehensible decision by John Armstrong that galled their leader, Major-General Izard – but Prevost still hesitates. He remembers the three previous assaults on entrenched positions at Fort Meigs, Fort Stephenson, and Fort Erie, all abortive. The Americans, it seems, fight like demons behind their ditches and their abatis.

He cannot make up his mind. Robinson, fretting in his headquarters, receives an order to attend a meeting at six o'clock on the morning of the seventh. Before he can attend, it is countermanded. At eight, Sir George sends for him alone. He has decided that he cannot move on the Plattsburgh redoubts without the support of the fleet. It is just as well, for Robinson discovers, to his dismay, that in the midst of all this soul searching no one has thought to mount the British artillery to support the proposed assault.

At this point, a change comes over Sir George Prevost. In his impatience to bring the fleet down the lake at once, the sedulous diplomat becomes alarmingly shrill. Testy letters urging Captain Downie to get moving travel north by express rider. Prevost, who has been irritated by Sir James Yeo's vacillations, no doubt believes that the navy on Lake Champlain is dawdling. But Downie cannot move until his biggest ship, *Confiance*, is fitted; nor can he be blamed, since he has been in command for only three days. Yet Prevost knows he must attack soon. The fall season is far advanced. The maples that arch over the narrow roads are beginning to turn. Frost is in the air. The weather, which has halted every American advance into Canada, will soon be his enemy.

The notes to Downie grow more petulant, nettling the naval commander, forcing him to move before he is ready, goading him to fight on the enemy's terms and on the enemy's site, with a ship scarcely fitted and a crew yet untried.

•

MILTON, VERMONT, September 7, 1814

In spite of his governor's opposition to the war, Jonathan Blaisdell, a Milton house builder, has decided to answer the call of his country and cross the lake to Plattsburgh to help repulse the invading British.

Vermonters are undergoing a change of heart now that the war has been carried to their doorstep. Farmers who once sat out the war in opposition to the Hawks in Washington are abandoning their fields, heading for the lake by the hundreds, climbing aboard any vessel that will transport them quickly to Plattsburgh.

Jonathan Blaisdell is so eager to get at the British that he and two companions decide to ride their horses across a low sandbar to the island of South Hero in the lake. From there they plan to catch a boat to Plattsburgh. They are almost drowned in the attempt and end up, soaking wet, at Fox's Tavern on the Vermont shore.

More Vermonters crowd in, also intent on crossing. Two hours pass; the moon rises, encouraging another attempt. One hundred volunteers, strung out in a long line across the shallows, finally reach the island. The following day a sloop carries them to the scene of the action.

Until this week, Vermonters have cared so little about the war that they have not hesitated to continue the border smuggling that has been their livelihood – not just the usual livestock, cheese, fish, grain, tobacco, and potash but also the actual materials of war. Only the vigilance of Macdonough's fleet has prevented the British from equipping *Confiance* with spars, masts, naval stores, and caulking towed up the lake as recently as July by resourceful Vermont entrepreneurs.

Prevost's incursion has done what George Izard's troops could not accomplish: it has turned the Vermonters into patriots and war hawks. Within three days, twenty-five hundred volunteers flock to the colours to be greeted personally by the new commander at Plattsburgh, Brigadier-General Alexander Macomb. In an inspired gesture, he pins an evergreen bough in the hat of their leader, Samuel Strong – a symbol of the zeal of his Green Mountain Boys.

Macomb has need of these citizen soldiers. Since the unexpected departure of Major-General Izard and his four thousand regulars, the safety of the fort has depended on fewer than three thousand troops of whom about half are effective soldiers, the remainder either sick or untrained. On a man-to-man basis, the British outnumber the Americans more than three to one, but even that ratio is deceptive. Prevost has the cream of Wellington's army; Macomb's best soldier is no better than Prevost's worst.

The leading citizens of Plattsburgh have little faith in Macomb's ragtag army. They want him to retire gracefully to spare a wanton sacrifice of lives. Macomb has no such intention. If worst comes to worst, he intends to blow up the town. Most of the inhabitants have already fled.

Prevost's decision to wait for the fleet gives Macomb a week in which to strengthen his defences, gather reinforcements, and raise the morale of his small, largely untrained army. His three major redoubts are positioned in a triangle on the heights of a small peninsula that stretches like a fat thumb between the lake and the Saranac River. Each is protected by ditches, palisades, abatis.

Like Scott, Brown, and Izard, Macomb belongs to a younger generation of general officers, the new team thrown up by the war that will reshape the American army in the years to come. He is a chubby thirty-two, big chested, plump cheeked, blue eyed, bursting with health and good nature – the kind of man who will always seem younger than his years. The son of a Detroit fur merchant, raised in the shadow of an army camp, dandled on the knees of officers during his childhood, he is all soldier. Now he labours under extraordinary difficulties.

But Macomb intends to do his duty, and to that duty he brings an imaginative mind and a sensitive understanding of leadership. He is a strong believer in the military virtues of deception, intelligence, and morale. He may be short on manpower but he is long on acumen.

He makes it a point to issue arms and ammunition personally to the young volunteers crowding into the village, to address them in groups, thanking them for their *esprit*, and to advise them to act in small bands as partisans.

He goes out of his way to deceive Prevost. He never mounts a guard without parading all of his troops to give an impression of great numbers. He burns the buildings in front of the forts to clear the ground and reveal any potential assault force. In the glow of these fires, he marches platoons of reserves as if they were reinforcements. In spite of the rain he keeps a third of his regular force on the parapets each night.

Macomb is aware that spies are operating among his troops, passing as militia volunteers. He spreads the word that George Izard's army is within hailing distance and that he now has ten thousand militia under his command with an additional ten thousand on the way, then watches with satisfaction as the bogus soldiers steal across the Saranac bridge at night, carrying the news to Prevost.

He intends to get the most out of his small force. Even the sick are put to work manning two six-pounders at the makeshift hospital on Crab Island. Meanwhile, Macomb gives instructions to mask the roads leading to the river by planting pine trees on them and covering the bare areas with leaves, at the same time opening the entrances to old, unused roads. By these methods, he hopes the advancing British may lose their way.

The British, however, are confident of victory. On the tenth, Prevost again calls Major-General Robinson to his quarters to advise him that the fleet will be up with the first fair wind and that he must keep his brigade at the ready to ford the river and attack the three American redoubts. Robinson has only one request: he *must* be at the fords by daybreak, not a second later. To this the Governor General agrees.

At Putnam Lawrence's occupied house near the lake, a group of British officers are celebrating the morrow's victory. Soldiers roll up casks and barrels, stand them on end, lay boards across to make a table. The casks are brimming with wine and Jamaica rum. The table is laid with linen, china, glass, silver. The British toast the capture of Plattsburgh and victory over the American fleet.

Plattsburgh, someone is heard to say, will make quite a nice breakfast in the morning.

●

CHAZY, LAKE CHAMPLAIN, New York, September 10, 1814

Captain George Downie, commander of the British squadron, is irritated beyond measure by the persistent entreaties of Sir George Prevost. Since the British army reached Plattsburgh, the Governor General has been bombarding him with letters, each touchier than the last, urging him to move the fleet up the lake so that he can launch his assault on the American bastions.

"I need not dwell with you upon the Evils resulting to both services from delay," Prevost wrote on September 9, adding that he has directed an officer of the Provincial Cavalry to remain at Downie's headquarters until the fleet moves. Even though the fleet was not ready, Downie tried that very day to get under way, only to be forced back by adverse winds.

Now he holds a more insulting letter from Prevost. It seems to hint that Downie has been deceiving him about the weather:

I ascribe the disappointment I have experienced to the unfortunate change of wind, & shall rejoice to learn that my reasonable expectations have been frustrated by no other cause.

Reasonable expectations! Prevost's phrase stings Downie. All expectations have been unreasonable. He has been in charge of the fleet for no more than a week, does not know the lake, does not know the men, is unfamiliar with the strategic situation. His flagship, the frigate *Confiance*, is scarcely in fighting trim. Twenty-five carpenters are still on board fitting her with belaying pins, cleats, breaching blocks. There has been no time to scrape the green planks of her decks free of oozing tar. The firing mechanisms for her long cannon have not arrived; her gunners will have to make do with carronade locks. She is still taking on newly arrived marines and soldiers: there has been no time for the officers to be able to recognize, much less know, the men who will serve under them.

This last-minute scramble means that there will be no time for a shakedown cruise. The big frigate will go into action with a strange crew who have scarcely had a chance to fire her guns or hoist her sails. Yet it could all have been avoided if Sir James Yeo – or Prevost – had not been obsessed with the shipbuilding war on Lake Ontario. Not until Macdonough's *Saratoga* appeared on the lake in late May did the British commanders wake up to their peril. Now they are paying for their inattention.

Downie shares his disgust over Prevost's letter with his second-in-command, Captain Daniel Pring, whom he has just replaced as senior commander on the lake.

"I will not write any more letters," he declares to Pring. "This letter does not deserve an answer but I will convince him that the naval force will not be backward in their share of the attack."

In short, goaded by Prevost, he will not wait for the enemy to emerge from the safe harbour at Plattsburgh to meet him on the open lake. He will chance a direct bows-on attack against Macdonough's anchored fleet.

Downie is prepared to attempt this dangerous action only because Prevost has told him that he will launch his land assault at the same time. Once the shore batteries have been stormed and taken, Downie believes, Macdonough will be in peril. With the captured guns turned on him he will have to quit his anchorage and, during the confusion, the British will have the advantage.

At midnight, the wind switches to the northeast. Downie weighs anchor, and the fleet slips southward toward Plattsburgh Bay carrying one thousand men, including the riggers and outfitters still straining to complete their work.

At five, the fleet reaches Cumberland Head. Here Downie scales his guns – clears out the bores, which have never been fired, with blank cartridges. This is the signal, pre-arranged with Prevost, to announce his arrival and to co-ordinate a simultaneous attack by the land forces.

In the hazy dawn, Downie boards his gig, nudges it around the point, and examines the American fleet through his glass.

Macdonough's four large vessels are strung out in line across the bay, with the gunboats in support – the twenty-gun brig *Eagle* at the northernmost end, followed by the larger *Saratoga*, twenty-six guns, the schooner *Ticonderoga*, seven guns, and the sloop *Preble*, seven guns, at the rear. With twenty-seven long cannon and ten heavy carronades, Downie's *Confiance* is more than a match for Macdonough's flagship. On the other hand, the combined batteries of *Saratoga* and *Eagle* can hurl a heavier weight of metal than can Downie's two largest vessels, *Confiance* and *Linnet*, the latter a brig of sixteen guns under Captain Pring.

With this in mind, Downie plans his attack. *Confiance* will take on the American flagship *Saratoga*, first passing *Eagle* and delivering a broadside, then turning hard a-port to anchor directly across the bows of Macdonough's ship. *Linnet*, supported by the sloop *Chubb*, will engage *Eagle*. In this way the two largest American vessels will be under fire from three of the British. The fourth and smallest British vessel, the sloop *Finch*, and eleven gunboats will hit the American rear, boarding the former steamer *Ticonderoga* and at the same time attacking the little *Preble*.

Back on his flagship, Downie calls his officers to a conference, outlines his strategy, and speaks a few words of encouragement to the ship's company:

"Now, my lads, there are the American ships and batteries. At the same moment we attack the ships our army are to storm the batteries. And, mind, don't let us be behind."

They answer with a cheer.

At almost the same time, Macdonough's men kneel on the deck of *Saratoga* as their commander reads a short prayer:

"Thou givest not always the battle to the strong, but canst save by many or by few – hear us, Thy poor servants, imploring Thy help that Thou wouldst be a defence unto us against the face of the enemy. Make it clear that Thou art our Saviour and Mighty Deliverer, through Jesus Christ, our Lord."

From the mast of the flagship, Macdonough's signal reminds his men why they are fighting:

Impressed seamen call on every man to do his duty.

In that message there is unconscious irony. It is well that Macdonough is not a party to the peace talks at Ghent where both the British and American negotiators have already decided to toss the whole bitter matter of impressment into the dustbin.

As the British fleet turns into line abreast, a silence falls over the bay. It is not broken until the ships come within range. *Eagle* hurls the first shot at Downie's *Confiance*, which has moved into the van. The ball splashes well short of its objective. *Linnet*, passing the American flagship en route to its target, fires a broadside that does little damage except to shatter a crate containing a fighting gamecock. The rooster flies into the rigging, crowing wildly, a touch of bravado that raises a cheer from *Saratoga*'s crew.

Downie, gazing anxiously at the headland, wonders to James Robertson, his First Officer, why Prevost has not commenced his attack. On *Saratoga*, Macdonough personally sights a long twenty-four and fires the first shot at his opponent's flagship. The heavy ball strikes the tall frigate near the hawse hole and tears its way the full length of the deck, killing and wounding several of Downie's crew and demolishing the wheel.

Now the action becomes general. Grey smoke pours from the guns, cannonballs ricochet across the glassy waters of the bay, chain-shot tears through the rigging. Through this maelstrom, *Confiance* sails toward her objective, sheets tattered, hawsers shredded, two anchors shot away. But the wind is erratic, and Downie realizes he cannot cross the head of the American line as he had hoped. He is forced to anchor more than three hundred yards from Macdonough's *Saratoga* – a manoeuvre he executes with great coolness under the other's hammering fire – but in doing so he loses two port anchors and fouls the kedge anchors at his stern. That will cost *Confiance* dear.

Downie's guns have not yet fired. His long twenty-fours have been carefully wedged with quoins for point-blank fire and double-shotted for maximum effect. Now, at a signal, a sheet of flame erupts from the British flagship, and more than seven hundred pounds of cast iron

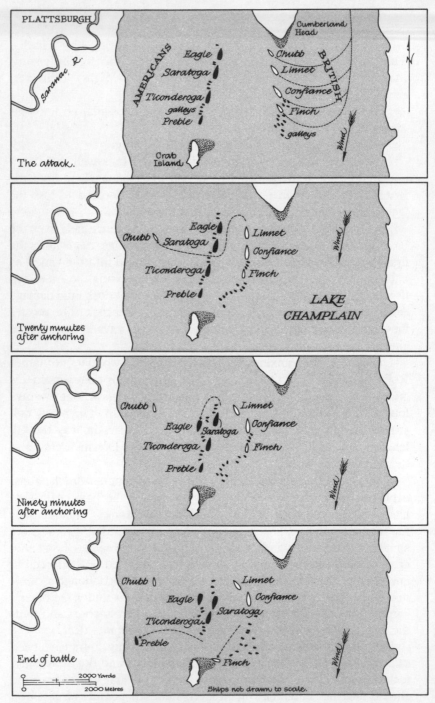

The Battle of Lake Champlain

392

strike *Saratoga*. The effect is terrible. The American frigate shivers from round top to hull, as if from a violent attack of ague. Macdonough sees half his crew hurled flat on the deck. Forty are killed or wounded; the scuppers are running with blood. The Commodore's right-hand man, Lieutenant Peter Gamble, is among the dead, killed instantly while on his knees, sighting the bow gun.

Saratoga replies to *Confiance*, broadside for broadside. As George Downie stands behind one of his long twenty-fours, commanding the action, an enemy ball strikes the muzzle, knocking the gun off its carriage and thrusting it back into the commander's midriff. Downie falls dead, his watch flattened, his skin unbroken. For the British, it is a critical loss.

Linnet and *Chubb* have moved up to support *Confiance* in her battle with the two big American vessels. But a series of withering broadsides from *Eagle* so badly cripples *Chubb* that with half her crew casualties, her sails in tatters, her boom shaft and halyards wrecked, her hammock netting ablaze, her commander wounded, and only six men left on deck, she drifts helplessly and finally strikes her colours.

At the end of the line, *Finch* and the British gunboats are attacking the schooner *Ticonderoga* and the little sloop *Preble*. The latter wilts under the onslaught, cuts her cable, and drifts out of action. But only four of the British gunboats remain to do battle. The rest flee the action, their militia crews cowering in the bottoms under a shower of grape and musket fire, while the commander of the flotilla bolts to the hospital tender, remaining there until the end of the battle, eventually evading court martial only by escaping while en route to trial.

Ticonderoga wards off *Finch*, which is raking her from the stern, but is herself in trouble, taking water, her pumps struggling to keep up with the inflow. *Finch*'s commander, Lieutenant William Hicks, brandishing a cutlass to bring the terrified pilot into line, tries to wear the British sloop in the light erratic wind and finds himself stuck fast on a reef near Crab Island, where he fights a brief engagement with the invalids manning their six-pounders. He, too, is out of action.

The four remaining British gunboats, sweeps thrashing the water, come within a boathook of *Ticonderoga*. Her commander, Lieutenant Stephen Cassin, a commodore's son, coolly walks the taffrail amid a shower of shot, directing his men to ward off the boarders. His second-in-command is cut in two by a cannonball and hurled into the lake. A sixteen-year-old midshipman, Hiram Paulding – a future rear-admiral – mans the guns, finds the slow match useless, and repeats

Barclay's action on Erie by discharging his pistol into the powder holes. In between the cannon blasts he continues to fire the pistol at the British, still vainly trying to scramble aboard.

But the main battle is at the head of the line between the American *Saratoga* and *Eagle* and the British *Confiance* and *Linnet*. *Eagle*, with most of her starboard guns rendered useless, cuts her cable and changes position to bring her port broadside into action. In doing so she positions herself to threaten *Confiance* but leaves Macdonough's flagship exposed to *Linnet*'s raking broadsides.

Linnet's cannons batter *Saratoga*'s long guns into silence. All but one of Macdonough's carronades have been dismounted in the action or wrecked by overzealous crews who overload in the absence of experienced officers. Hardly a man on either flagship has escaped injury. Macdonough is lucky. As he bends over a gun to sight it, a spanker boom, sliced in two by cannon fire, knocks him briefly insensible. A little later he suffers a grislier mishap: the head of his gun captain, torn off by British round-shot, comes hurtling across the deck, strikes him in the midriff, knocking him into the scuppers. He is winded but unharmed.

Now the naval bolt on *Saratoga*'s last carronade breaks, throwing the heavy gun off its carriage and hurling it down the hatch. Macdonough is in trouble. He has no guns left on the starboard side and only one officer. In most situations this would be enough to force him to strike his colours, but Macdonough has prepared for such an emergency. He turns to the complicated series of spring cables, hawsers, and kedge anchors that will allow him to wind his ship: to swing it end for end so that he can bring the seventeen guns on his port side – none of which has been fired – to bear upon his opponent.

It is a difficult and awkward manoeuvre, requiring careful timing and skill – a knowledge of when to raise one anchor, when to drop another. Now it must be done under the hazard of enemy fire.

Fortunately that fire has slackened, for the British ships too are in a bad way, and the guns of *Confiance* are firing too high. The seamen, new to the frigate, to each other, and to their officers, have had no gun drill. The cannon have been set for point-blank range, but at each blast they leap up on their carriages. The quoins, which are supposed to wedge them in place, are loosened, causing the muzzles to edge up. As a result, more damage is done to hammocks, halyards, spars, and pine trees on the shore than to the opposing vessels.

Macdonough manages to wind his ship half-way round until she is at right angles to her former position. There she sticks, stern facing *Linnet*'s broadside. The British brig rakes the battered American flagship and the line of sweating seamen straining at the hawser. A splinter strikes the Commodore's sailing master, Peter Brum, as he runs forward to oversee the manoeuvre. It slices through his uniform, barely touching the skin but stripping him of his clothing. Naked, he continues his task.

Slowly, Brum and Macdonough get the ship turning again until the first of her portside carronades comes into play against *Confiance*. The gun crews go to work as the frigate continues her half circle and, one by one, the heavy guns open fire.

On *Confiance*, Downie's young successor, James Robertson, is attempting the same manoeuvre but with less success. His frigate is in terrible shape, her masts like bunches of matches, her sails like bundles of rags, her rigging, spars, and hull shattered. Almost half her crew are out of action. The wife of the flagship's steward, in the act of binding a wounded seaman's leg, is struck by a ball that tears through the side of the ship, carries away her breasts, and flings her corpse across the vessel. One of Nelson's veterans aboard *Confiance* is heard to remark that compared to this action, Trafalgar was a mere fleabite. The ship's carpenter has already plugged sixteen holes below the waterline, but a great seven-foot gash in her hull, where a plank has been torn away, cannot be mended. To keep her from sinking it has been necessary to run in all the guns on the port side – most are useless anyway – and double shot those on the starboard to keep the holes above the water.

Because her anchors have been torn away it is almost impossible for Robertson to duplicate Macdonough's manoeuvre, but he is trying, swinging the frigate by putting a new spring on the bow cable – a daring feat under fire. Half-way round, she sticks fast at right angles to her enemy, *Saratoga*, whose newly freed guns can rake her from bowsprit to taffrail. At this point, Robertson's crewmen refuse to do more. Why should they? they ask. Most of the British gunboats have not entered the battle. And where is the promised army support? Not a musket, not a cannon has been heard on the land side. Reluctantly, Robertson hauls down his colours.

Linnet, under Daniel Pring, fights on for fifteen minutes more – the water rising so quickly in her lower deck that the wounded must be lifted onto chests and tables – then she, too, surrenders. Hicks, aboard *Finch*, stuck on a shoal, sees the flags go down and follows suit. Only the gunboats escape. The battle, which has lasted for two hours and twenty minutes, is over.

The senior British officers join Robertson and proceed to *Saratoga* to surrender their swords. As they step aboard, Macdonough meets them, bows. Holding their caps in their left hands and their swords by the blades, they advance, bowing, and present their weapons. Macdonough bows once more.

"Gentlemen, return your swords into your scabbards and wear them," he says. "You are worthy of them." He takes Robertson by the arm and walks the deck with his prisoners.

A twenty-one-year old Vermont farmboy, Samuel Shether Phelps, seeing the engagement has ended, takes a rowboat, pulls for *Saratoga*, climbs onto the deck, almost slips in the blood, picks his way between the wounded and dead. Years later, when he is a state senator, he will be able to tell his children that the man he saw walking the deck, cap pulled low over his eyes, face and hands black with powder and smoke, was Commodore Thomas Macdonough, the legendary hero of the Battle of Plattsburgh Bay.

●

PLATTSBURGH, LAKE CHAMPLAIN, New York, September 11, 1814

Major-General Frederick Philipse Robinson has been up since before dawn, fidgeting over the tardiness of his commander-in-chief. His task is to lead two brigades across the Saranac and then to assault the heights with artillery support. His men should have been at the ford by daybreak; Prevost has promised him that. But the order has not come and now it is almost eight. Why the delay?

Prevost heard from Downie as early as 3:30 A.M. that the fleet was on its way, but the men are not yet in motion; instead, they have been told to cook breakfast. Something else troubles Robinson: the heaviest artillery has not yet arrived, nor are there batteries in place to receive the big guns. They cannot possibly be put in action before late morning.

From Cumberland Head Robinson hears the distant boom of cannon: Downie is scaling his guns, the signal that he is about to attack. An order comes from Prevost to attend at headquarters. The meeting takes an hour as Prevost reviews his plans. As Robinson turns to leave, the Governor General looks at his watch.

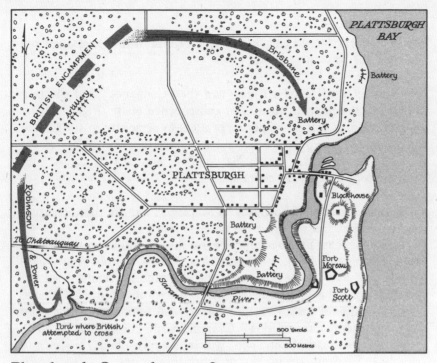

Plattsburgh, September 11, 1814

"It is now nine o'clock," he says. "March off at ten."

Clearly, Prevost expects the sea battle to go on all day. But as the two brigades move off in full view of the contest, *Preble, Finch*, and *Chubb* are already out of action. On Robinson's left, Major-General Brisbane leads his brigade against the lower bridge, his flank protected by the water. Robinson's force heads for Pike's ford.

After a mile and a half, the troops are faced by a bewildering pattern of cart tracks leading into a thick wood. The army halts as the guides argue over the route. Finally the force retraces its steps and after an hour's delay arrives at the river. Macomb's deception has paid dividends.

From the bay comes the sound of cheering. A victory? By whom? Robinson dispatches an aide to find out. Meanwhile, he orders his men to rush the Saranac. They race down the bank and splash across the shallow ford in the face of heavy fire from four hundred American riflemen concealed on the far shore. The defenders scatter as the brigades form on the far side in perfect order. As Robinson rides forward to give orders for the attack, his aide returns with a message from Baynes, the adjutant-general:

I am directed to inform you that the "Confiance" and the brig having struck their colours in consequence of the frigate having grounded, it will no longer be prudent to persevere in the service committed to your charge, and it is therefore the orders of the Commander of the Forces that you will immediately return with the troops under your command.

Robinson and his fellow general Manley Power are thunderstruck and chagrined, but they give the order to retire.

Major-General Brisbane tells Prevost that he will carry the forts in twenty minutes if given permission, but Prevost will not grant it. He knows that even if he does seize the redoubts he cannot hold the ground while the lake remains under American control. With the American militia rushing to the colours and reinforcements on the way, the enemy can sail down Champlain and cut off his rear. The roads are in dreadful condition, winter is approaching, his lines of supply and communication are stretched thin.

Prevost has also intercepted a letter from a Vermont colonel to Macomb announcing that the recalcitrant governor of that state, Martin Chittenden, is marching from St. Alban's with ten thousand volunteers, that five thousand more are on their way from St. Lawrence County, New York, and four thousand from Washington County. Almost twenty thousand men! Prevost sees himself surrounded by a guerrilla army of aroused civilians lurking in the woods, blocking the roads, stealing into his camp under cover of night, demoralizing his men, scorching the earth, murdering stragglers. What he does not know is that the letter is a fake. Macomb has outwitted him by an old ruse. Has Prevost forgotten that Brock used an identical forgery to convince Hull, at Detroit, that he was surrounded by thousands of Indians?

The Governor General moves his army back so swiftly that it reaches Chazy before Macomb realizes his adversaries have departed. He cannot know it, but even at this moment the British are facing another setback at Baltimore. Here, in a vain attack, Ross meets his death and a poetic young lawyer named Francis Scott Key, watching the rockets' red glare over the embattled Fort McHenry, is moved to compose a national anthem for his country to celebrate the sight of the

Stars and Stripes flying bravely in the dawn's early light to signal British defeat.

Robinson is sick at heart over Prevost's "precipitate and disgraceful" move back to Canada. "Everything I see and hear is discouraging," he writes to a friend. "This is no field for a military man above the rank of a colonel of riflemen.... This country can never again afford such an opportunity, nothing but a defensive war can or ought to be attempted here, and you will find that the expectations of His Majesty's ministers and the people of England will be utterly destroyed in this quarter."

And, he might add, across the channel in the Belgian city of Ghent, where the news from Lake Champlain will have its own effect on the long-drawn-out negotiations for peace.

13

GHENT
August – December, 1814

GHENT, BELGIUM, August 7, 1814

Down the cobbled streets of the ancient Flemish town this Sunday morning, past greasy canals and spiky guild houses, comes a minor diplomat with a very English name – Anthony St. John Baker, secretary to the British peace mission. He crosses the Place d'Armes, enters the Hôtel des Pays-Bas, asks for the American commission, is met by James Bayard's secretary, George Milligan, who points him in the direction of the Hôtel d'Alcantara, a three-storey building, cracked and weatherbeaten, on the Rue des Champs. It is said to be haunted – so spooky that servants are hard to hire – but if so, the ghosts have fled the arrival of the five American plenipotentiaries who have leased it for the peace talks and who have given it the wry title of "Bachelor's Hall."

Bayard, the handsome Federalist senator from Delaware, is alone when Baker calls to invite the Americans to meet the following day with the British at his temporary lodgings in the Hôtel du Lion d'Or. Why not meet here? Bayard asks innocently: an excellent room is available. But the Englishman will have none of it, refuses with exquisite politeness even to look at the room. The American, with equal civility, tells him that an answer will be forthcoming later in the day.

Thus are fired the opening shots in the long, weary diplomatic war that will be waged here in this ancient clothmakers' town, to parallel the real war being fought four thousand miles away on the Canadian border. On this very Sunday morning, as the two diplomats spar over the choice of a meeting place, Gordon Drummond unmasks his cannon before Fort Erie and begins his futile week-long bombardment.

The four American negotiators (Jonathan Russell is out of town) meet at noon to discuss what John Quincy Adams calls "an offensive pretension to superiority" on the part of the British. By every rule of diplomatic etiquette, the British should come to *them*! Adams hauls out a heavy tome by Georg Friedrich von Martens, the German expert on international law, to prove this point. Bayard finds a case in Ward's *History of the Law of Nations* where the British themselves had resisted a similar overture. Henry Clay urges that this assumption of superiority be resisted, but Albert Gallatin is not so sure; the Swiss-born ex-cabinet minister is not inclined to slow the negotiations with questions of ceremony.

The discussion drags on for two hours until dinner. Adams proposes that they agree to meet the British "at any place other than their own lodgings." Gallatin suggests softening the phrase to "any place that may mutually be agreed upon." It is the first of many occasions when the former secretary of the treasury will curb his colleagues' irritability.

Thus the stage is set for five months of frustrating bargaining and much hair-splitting. The Americans have already spent a month in Ghent attending functions in their honour, bartering for lodgings, traipsing up and down the narrow streets sightseeing, gazing at the canals and the oils of the Van Eycks, lingering over wine and cigars (to Adams's great displeasure), and, in the absence of the British, sounding each other out on the peace terms. Surprisingly, the disharmony that existed in the last days in St. Petersburg has vanished. Adams, who once hoped never to deal with Bayard again, now finds him the best of companions.

The following day, at one, the Americans take the measure of the three British negotiators. Vice-Admiral Lord Gambier, the titular chairman, is pompous but genial, the epitome of the desk admiral who has seldom been to sea, a big man with an enormous glistening bald head surrounded by a frizzle of greying hair. He is vice-president of the British Bible Society, a fact that sits well with John Quincy Adams.

Dr. William Adams (no kin to John Quincy) is an Admiralty lawyer and, though he prides himself on his wit and humour, is a garrulous bore, his mind stuffed with legalisms, his tongue more cutting than witty. He is such a nonentity that it is said that Lord Liverpool, when questioned about him, could not remember his name.

Henry Goulburn, the youngest of the trio, is of different mettle. A confirmed Yankee-phobe who can scarcely conceal his dislike of everything American, he will struggle in the days ahead to curb his natural irritability in the interests of diplomacy. This thirty-year-old public servant is the real chairman of the British mission and the closest of the three to the British government.

After the usual professions of a sincere and ardent desire for peace (which neither side believes of the other), the meeting gets down to business. Goulburn, for the British, suggests four topics for discussion:

First, the question of impressment, the only stated reason for the war.

Second, the absolute necessity of pacifying the Indians by drawing a boundary line for their territory.

Third, a revision of the border between Canada and the United States.

Fourth, no renewal of a former agreement allowing the Americans certain fishing privileges on Canadian waters and shores "without an equivalent."

From this and from the two days of discussion that follow, two things become clear:

First, neither side is much interested in discussing impressment. The issue, which has inflamed American public opinion since the *Chesapeake* crisis of 1807, which perhaps more than anything else brought on the war and on which both sides have refused to budge an inch, is now dead. The need has passed; the war in Europe is over. In the bitter exchanges that follow, nobody will bother to mention the forcible seizure of British deserters from American ships. Yet thousands have died or been maimed or rendered homeless because of the emotion it engendered.

Second, the British are determined to stick on the question of Indian rights. It is, they insist, a *sine qua non* – an indispensable condition. Without it there can be no peace. Behind their determined stand lie years of promises to the native peoples on both sides of the border: the cultivation of Tecumseh and his federation, the pledges of Brock,

Elliott, Dickson, and others that the Great White Father will never forsake his tribal allies.

At this first meeting, the British intentions toward the Indians are so vague that in the days that follow the Americans press for more details. The request seems to irritate Goulburn and his colleagues, but finally they blurt it out: Great Britain wants an Indian buffer state separating the United States from Canada, an area in which neither Canadians nor Americans can purchase land. Though the British decline to go into more detail – they have said too much already – the Americans wake up to the fact that they are being asked to cede a great chunk of their country to people who have been massacring and scalping their soldiers. To this they cannot agree. And, since the British trio in Ghent are mere messenger-boys for a more formidable trio of peers in London – Liverpool, Castlereagh, and Bathurst – negotiations cease until London is heard from.

Nine days pass. During the hiatus, Lord Gambier and Dr. Adams attend a cosy little dinner party given by the Americans; Goulburn stays away, pleading laryngitis. It is August 13, the eve of Drummond's costly attack on Fort Erie, but there is no talk of war. Innocuous pleasantries are batted about the table like shuttlecocks. Gambier tells of meeting Adams's distinguished father and discusses the British Bible Society. Dr. Adams and his namesake discuss their common heritage and conclude they are not cousins.

An entire week from the eleventh to the eighteenth is taken up preparing a report of the negotiations for the American Secretary of State, James Monroe, each of the five taking it upon himself to revise and amend the phraseology of the others. The following day the British announce that they have heard at last from their government. At a meeting that afternoon, they spell out their new demands:

First, the Indian buffer state must extend to the line settled upon at the Treaty of Greenville in 1795. That means that most of Ohio and the future states of Indiana, Illinois, Wisconsin, and Michigan will become Indian territory. Unless the Americans immediately sign a provisional article, subject to ratification by their government, the conference will be suspended.

Second, since the United States has clearly intended to conquer Canada and since Canada is the weaker of the two nations, the British – but not the Americans – must be allowed to keep naval vessels on the Great Lakes and to build forts along their shores for their security.

Third, in order to link her Atlantic colonies with Canada, Britain requires a corner of the state of Maine for a connecting road.

In addition, she wants to perpetuate her right to navigate the Mississippi, as agreed upon in an earlier treaty. This, it develops, is in exchange for American fishing rights in Canadian territory.

The Americans are stunned. Gallatin, in his courteous way, asks what is to be done with the hundred thousand white settlers who now occupy the proposed Indian buffer state. Why, replies the Admiralty lawyer Dr. Adams, they must shift for themselves.

In John Quincy Adams's opinion, the tone of the British is peremptory, their language even more overbearing than before. A confirmed pessimist, he is convinced that the talks are at an end, an opinion shared by the others except Clay. They ask that the British proposals be put in writing and, on August 21, sit down to respond. That takes four days. Adams's first draft is considered too offensive by Gallatin, too flowery by Clay, too ungrammatical by Russell. At eleven o'clock on the evening of the twenty-fourth – two hours past Adams's bedtime – they are still at it, altering, erasing, patching, until no more than a fifth of Adams's original document remains. Finally, on the twenty-fifth – the night of the burning of Washington – the note to the British is signed. Simply put, it rejects the idea of an Indian state and of British military sovereignty over the Great Lakes.

Each side now expects the other to break off negotiations and go home, yet neither wants to be blamed for shattering the hopes of peace. The Americans are convinced that the British tactics are to delay negotiations in the hope of strengthening their hand with victories on the other side of the Atlantic. But they cannot believe the British will back down in the face of this latest rejection.

The days drag by with no official word from the British, although there is a good deal of unofficial socializing, much of it tight-lipped, in which each side tries to sound out the other. On September 1, John Quincy Adams drops in on Henry Goulburn and is convinced from the conversation that the British are holding up an answer to the American note only "to give a greater appearance of deliberation and solemnity to the rupture." It appears to Adams that Goulburn is inflexible, that behind the bland mask of diplomacy there smoulders an abiding hatred of everything American.

Goulburn talks continually of the need to secure Canada from the threat of American annexation. This is the real reason for the Indian buffer state.

"The Indians are but a secondary object," he declares, in a moment of callous candour. "As the Allies of Great Britain she must include them in the peace.... But when the boundary is once defined it is immaterial whether the Indians are upon it or not. Let it be a desert. But we shall know that you cannot come upon us to attack us without crossing it."

So much, then, for the moral commitment to Britain's native supporters. The security of Canada has been substituted. But the great and real object, Adams is convinced, is "a profound and rankling jealousy at the rapid increase of population and of settlements in the United States, an impotent longing to thwart their progress and to stunt their growth."

Goulburn is equally convinced that the United States does not want peace and is negotiating only to find some means of reconciling the American public to a continuation of the war. He believes they will find that excuse in the Indian boundary question. He is certain that negotiations are at an end, and that does not entirely displease him. Like so many of his class he still regards the Americans as colonial upstarts – vulgar republicans who must be taught a lesson.

On September 5, the British negotiators bounce the ball back to the Americans. With only a slight modification (a suggestion to discuss any counter-proposal or modification to the Indian question), the note, though longer, does not depart from the original British stand. It is up to the Americans, the British say, to decide whether to continue the peace talks, to refer to Washington for instructions, or to "take upon themselves the responsibility of breaking off the negotiation altogether."

Four of the American commissioners – all but Henry Clay – are convinced that this is the end, and Clay is half convinced. But Clay is a consummate card player and knows the value of a poker face. He has a gut feeling that if the Americans stand firm, the British may back off. He is partial to a game called Brag, in which both sides attempt to out-bluff one another. On September 5, Clay decides to out-Brag the British. He writes to Henry Goulburn, asks him to arrange for his passport: he plans, he says, to return home immediately. Goulburn himself may not be averse to this, but there are others more senior in Whitehall who, faced with the mounting war costs and the growing war weariness, may take a different view.

•

WALMER CASTLE, KENT, ENGLAND, September 11, 1814

In the murky confines of Henry VIII's grotesque, turreted fortress – as sombre and heavy as its occupant – the second Earl of Liverpool is harbouring some gloomy second thoughts about the depth of his country's moral commitment to her Indian allies.

The question of the Indians, the Prime Minister tells his colonial secretary, Lord Bathurst, is "one of growing embarrassment." Of course, they must be included in the peace treaty. *But...*(one can almost see the cold eyes narrow, the heavy jaw grow firmer), is it really necessary to insist on the *sine qua non* of an Indian buffer state, a kind of sylvan Utopia between the Ohio and the Great Lakes where the natives can gambol, knocking off deer and wild turkey, and cultivating their fields of maize? The Prime Minister hardly thinks so, in fact has never really believed the *sine qua non* would stick. Of course, if a *specific* promise has been made, then honour requires it be kept. But has it been made? Clearly, Lord Liverpool believes that nothing specific has ever been promised the Indians beyond the vague pledge that their Father across the water would never desert them. Now their Father proposes to desert them by watering down British demands, once declared irrevocable, to a simple stipulation that the Indians shall be restored to all the rights and privileges they enjoyed before the war – a promise subject to many interpretations.

Liverpool wants to set the Indian question aside in order to get on to more important matters. He is perfectly prepared to yield on the exclusive military occupation of the Great Lakes. What he really wants is to hold what the British have gained by conquest, specifically, Michilimackinac and Fort Niagara. If he can get these, and Sackets Harbor into the bargain, then he will waive all claims to a chunk of Maine. If the Americans stick on Sackets Harbor because the British do not occupy it, he proposes to delay negotiations in the hope that Sir George Prevost will seize it, as well as Plattsburgh, or some other piece of American territory. The American suspicions are well founded: it has long been British strategy to stretch out negotiations until further military successes in North America strengthen their hand. Wellington's troops have been pouring into Canada since July. If only Prevost would move! Gazing over the misty headland toward the Strait of Dover, Liverpool, the titular Lord Warden of the Cinque Ports, cannot know that Prevost *is* moving – but backwards, toward Chazy and the border.

Henry Clay is right. The last thing the British prime minister wants is a sudden break at Ghent. He blames his commissioners for taking "a very erroneous view of our policy," and has taken steps to make sure that Goulburn, now quite baffled by the twists and turns of British manoeuvring, understands it. If the peace talks founder on the absurd question of an Indian state and British control of the lakes, Liverpool is certain that the war will become very popular in America.

The British press is howling for revenge, crying that the Americans must be chastised for daring to make war on the world's most powerful nation. But the Prime Minister is a realist. The ten-year struggle with Napoleon has imposed a crushing financial burden on his country. The powerful English landowners are aroused over the increase in the property tax, which must be continued if the war in North America goes on. The commercial and maritime interests want to return to business as usual. Liverpool must rid himself of this nuisance war as soon as practicable – but on the best possible terms.

In Ghent, Goulburn has reported, a little gleefully, that the American government does not want peace, but Lord Liverpool believes otherwise. He is well aware that the United States is teetering on the edge of bankruptcy; that it is having difficulty obtaining further loans to finance the war; and that if the war does continue for another year, financial disaster will certainly result. He also recognizes that there is danger in this, for "the war would then be rendered a war of despair, in which all private rights and interests would be sacrificed to the public cause."

Goulburn must be made to understand this. Next morning, Lord Bathurst undertakes to do just that. Four days later, the chagrined young diplomat receives Bathurst's instructions and, in his dismay, pens a sarcastic answer:

I...cannot sufficiently thank you for so clearly explaining what are the views and objects of the government with respect to negotiations with America. Before I received it, I confess that I was impressed with the idea that the government did not wish negotiation to be protracted unless there was a prospect of a successful issue....

"I do not deem it possible to conclude a *good peace* now," Goulburn adds, a little bitterly, "as I cannot consider that a good peace which would leave the Indians to a dependence on the *liberal policy* of the United States."

Goulburn is not seduced by the proposed new clause in the treaty. High-flown phrases about restoring the natives to their pre-war privileges cannot obscure the fact that the Great White Father *is* abandoning his children to an uncertain future. The whole history of the United States has been one of merciless exploitation of the Indians. Can the tribes south of the border expect anything different from the established policy of grabbing their lands and moving them farther and farther beyond the frontier? Later in the month, Goulburn raises a second, more practical objection to the new British policy. Will not post-war America attempt to exclude the British from "that trade which we carried on previous to the war with those Indians as independent nations?" The Americans have already made that clear.

But the British prime minister has all but put the Indians out of his mind in the interests of ending the conflict:

"Goulburn and our other commissioners evidently do not feel the inconvenience of the continuance of the war. I feel it strongly, but I feel it as nothing now compared with what it may be a twelve-month hence, and I am particularly anxious, therefore, that we should avoid anything, as far as may be in our power, which may increase our difficulties in concluding it."

In the international game of Brag, it seems, Henry Clay, the loose-limbed Kentucky gambler, holds all the cards.

●

BRUSSELS, BELGIUM, October 3, 1814

Henry Clay, after three days of sightseeing among the Gothic spires and cobbled squares of the Flemish capital, is surprised on this autumn Monday to receive from Henry Goulburn a graceful, if uncharacteristic, little note accompanying a packet of newspapers from the United States.

"If you find Brussels as little interesting as I have done," Goulburn writes sweetly, "you will not be sorry to have the occupation of reading the latest Newspapers which I have received, I therefore inclose them to you and shall be glad to have them back by tomorrow evening. I take this opportunity of mentioning that I do not propose leaving this late [sic] Tuesday morning in case you should be desirous of extending your excursion...."

But Clay's excursion as well as his disposition is ruined as soon as he opens the papers, which Goulburn, on specific instructions from Lord Bathurst, has so charitably sent him. *Washington in flames!* In the days that follow, Clay's normal optimism gives way to despair. He trembles whenever he picks up a late newspaper. Everything seems to be going wrong: Chauncey's refusal to co-operate with Jacob Brown at Fort George; Drummond (whom he believed captured) threatening Gaines's army and consequently Chauncey's fleet; and now this!

It is not the destruction of public property that wounds him "to the very soul"; it is his country's disgrace – "that a set of pirates and incendiaries should have been permitted to pollute our soil, conflagrate our Capital, and return unpunished to their ships."

Adams is equally downcast. "We must drink the cup of bitterness to the dregs," he writes to his wife, Louisa. Bayard is wrought up to such a pitch of fury that, he declares to Adams, the desecration of Washington should "make every American take his children to the altar and swear them to eternal hatred of England."

In this heated atmosphere the negotiations continue at Ghent, never face to face, always by diplomatic note, both sides giving a little, the British still "arrogant, overbearing and offensive," in Adams's view, and the Americans never as bold or spirited as he thinks they ought to be. The British send off their draft notes to be re-drafted by the real negotiators in England; the Americans spend days arguing over grammar, phraseology, style, tone, length, punctuation. When Adams tries to moralize, peppering each missive with references to God, Providence, and Heaven, Clay cries "Cant!" and Russell, who is in Clay's shadow, laughs openly. Gallatin, the conciliator, ends up writing most of the final drafts.

Not being faced with such wrangles, the English messenger-boys find time heavy on their hands. They have taken up headquarters in the former convent of Chartreux on the outskirts of the town, and here, in John Quincy Adams's observation, they live "as secluded as if they were monks." Lord Gambier, whom Adams quite likes (he appears "an excellent and well meaning man") asks if the Americans have made many acquaintances. Indeed they have, attending a continual round of theatres and dinner parties. The old admiral, who is not much of a mixer, has made only one – the Intendant and his family. Goulburn, who has brought over his wife and small son (the latter recovering from "infantile fever") spends his time with his family. Both he and Dr. Adams are, to the Americans, typical snobbish Britishers who dislike everything that is not English and make no secret of their tastes. The latter, whom Bayard considers "a man of no breeding," boasts that he has not been to the theatre in ten years and reveals that his real enthusiasm is for Indian jugglers. The Americans greet this with a slight sneer; they, too, are not immune to snobbishness.

By late October, the exchange of paper and the instructions from London and Washington serve to clarify and pare down the real issues between the two countries. The backing and filling is accompanied, as always, by long ideological arguments, legalese, appeals to morality, and charges, both imagined and real, of perfidy, greed, lack of principle. But all that is for the public record. The real differences between the antagonists can be described by two Latin phrases: *status quo ante bellum* and *uti possidetis*. The Americans are prepared now to settle for the same conditions that existed before the war – to act, in short, as if the war had never taken place. The British, flushed with success and expecting momentary news of the fall of Sackets Harbor and Plattsburgh, want to keep what they have conquered by right of possession.

The news of Prevost's defeat and the failure of the British attack on Baltimore's Fort McHenry, coming at the end of October, puts a new complexion on the negotiations. Liverpool is furious over Prevost's incompetence. The war in North America has cost ten million pounds, and now this! Stalemate! Is there no end to it? Liverpool grasps at a straw: why not send the Duke of Wellington to Canada to take charge of the army? Such a gesture might easily speed up negotiations; the Duke is known to be anxious for peace with America if the terms are honourable. "Honour" has become a key word. *Peace with honour.* Both sides are more interested in saving face than they are in clinging to bits of real estate or keeping promises to obscure native chieftains. If honour can be satisfied, blood will cease to flow on the morrow. Financially, the Americans are more desperate than the British. Gallatin has just informed Monroe that not a dollar can be obtained in Europe to finance the war. Nonetheless, among the spires of Ghent the rival commissions must continue their diplomatic ritual dance. It has seven more weeks to go.

Three months have passed since the two teams first faced each other. Since that date, Mackinac Island has been relieved, *Tigress* and *Scorpion* captured, Fort Erie attacked, defended, and abandoned, Washington burned with all of Jefferson's papers, Baltimore and Plattsburgh besieged. Francis Scott Key has written "The Star Spangled Banner," John Armstrong has been fired as Secretary of War, and Duncan McArthur's mounted Kentuckians have laid waste the valley of the Thames. Thousands have been killed including William Drummond, Hercules Scott, George Downie, Joseph Willcocks, Robert Ross, and an innocent old Loyalist farmer, William Francis, murdered for no good reason in his bed at Long Point by American partisans.

Along the thousand miles of embattled border, from Montreal to the western margins of Lake Huron, everything is as it was when the year began. The Americans hold Amherstburg. The British occupy Michilimackinac and Fort Niagara. In Ghent there is progress of a sort. The American mission, with British agreement, is actually composing the outline of a peace treaty.

Shortly after five on these raw November mornings, John Quincy Adams pulls himself out of bed, lights a tallow candle, stokes the fire in the grate, warms his numbed fingers, and starts to work on a draft of the document, knowing from bitter experience that his colleagues are waiting to tear it to pieces.

Almost immediately he runs into a confrontation with Henry Clay. Since the Peace of 1783, New Englanders have enjoyed the right to catch and dry their fish in British territory in return for free access, by the British, to the Mississippi. Adams, the New Englander, wants to retain that right; Clay, the Southerner, is opposed.

It would be difficult to find two statesmen more unlike in temperament, habit, or conviction than John Quincy Adams and Henry Clay. By an ironic coincidence, their rooms adjoin one another so that as Adams rises at daybreak, he can often hear Clay preparing to go to bed. Clay loves to linger over dinner, drawing on strong cigars and fortifying himself with table wine before his customary late night card game. Adams bitterly begrudges these wasted moments; at one point he even decided to take dinner by himself, only to be dissuaded by a surprisingly persuasive Clay. Adams is a sour pessimist devoid of humour; Clay has a gambler's optimism. Adams's features are so arranged that he seems to be perpetually scowling. Clay's high cheek bones, long face, and winsome mouth make him appear forever good humoured.

Adams finds it difficult to curb his anger when Clay dismisses the fisheries question as trifling. The Kentuckian will on no account permit the Mississippi to be turned into a British waterway. If that means giving up New England's fishing rights, so be it. In the end, however, Clay proposes an ingenious way out of the impasse: the matter of the fisheries, he says, is linked irretrievably to the recognition of American independence; it does not require negotiation. Adams does not demur.

As usual, John Quincy discovers, to his chagrin, that three-quarters of his draft is struck out by the others. One paragraph, however, he is determined to include. Monroe has instructed the commission that peace can be concluded if both sides will agree to return to the pre-war situation – *status quo ante bellum* – leaving the sticky points about boundaries and commerce to future negotiation. Adams believes that the time has come to face the British with this proposal.

It is now November 10. What Henry Clay and his colleagues do not know is that only the previous day the Duke of Wellington put a damper on Lord Liverpool's hopes. What is the point of his going to Canada, he asks Castlereagh, until the British control the lakes? There is worse: the Duke does not believe that Britain has a right to demand any cession of territory from the United States. The war has been successful: the Americans have not succeeded in their plan to seize Canada. But neither have the British been able to carry the war to the enemy's territory.

"Why stipulate for the *uti possidetis?*" Wellington asks. "You can get no territory; indeed, the state of your military operations, however creditable, does not entitle you to demand any: and you only afford the Americans a popular and creditable ground, which I believe their Government are looking for, not to break off the negotiations, but to avoid to make peace."

That does it. Goulburn, blissfully unaware of this turn of affairs, is prepared to break off negotiations in Ghent because of the American insistence on a return to pre-war status. As far as he is concerned it is only a matter of tactics. But Liverpool knows the game is up. France is in a turmoil; the preparations over the coming Congress of Vienna are unsatisfactory from a British point of view; the revolt in England against continuing the property tax is becoming alarming; rents are depressed. Great Britain has larger concerns – the balance of power in Europe being one – than the border war in North America. It is "desirable to bring the American war if possible to a conclusion," Liverpool tells Castlereagh. Parliament would violently oppose its continuance "upon what is called a new principle."

On November 26, the British commissioners inform the Americans in a series of marginal notes to the draft treaty that *uti possidetis* has been abandoned and that the "new principle," *status quo ante bellum*, is accepted. The original questions – impressment, blockade – are tossed aside, although the British still want access to the Mississippi and assurance that the Indians will be restored to their pre-war privileges.

It is a difficult document for Henry Goulburn to swallow. He does not like giving way to the Americans and is especially reluctant to do so now since almost everything he originally demanded on behalf of his government has been abandoned. But orders are orders. His conscience pricks him on the matter of the Indians: "I had till I came here no idea of the fixed determination which prevails in the breast of every American to extirpate the Indians and appropriate their territory," he tells Bathurst, "but I am now sure that there is nothing which the people of America would so reluctantly abandon as what they are pleased to call their natural right to do so."

It is all over but the wrangling. "We have everything but peace in our hands," Adams reports to his wife. The remaining obstacles are so trifling that neither nation would tolerate a war over them. Yet these obstacles, which Adams calls insignificant, occupy another month.

On December 1, the two commissions meet officially face to face for the first time since August 18, talk for three hours, settle little. The talks go on, the notes fly back and forth, hairs are split, words stricken, phrases expunged, concessions made, until by December 10 only two points of contention remain: the whole matter of the Mississippi River and the American fisheries, together with British insistence on hanging on to Moose Island, an obscure pinpoint in Passamaquoddy Bay.

The real argument is not with the British. It is, again, between Clay and Adams. Adams is convinced that the British are sticking in order to cause a split in the Union. If New England loses its fishing rights in Newfoundland, Massachusetts will be at loggerheads with Kentucky.

But Clay stalks back and forth across the room shouting over and over again:

"I will never sign a treaty upon the *status quo ante bellum* with the Indian article, so help me God!"

This acrimony spills over the next morning at the old Chartreux convent, when Adams, on behalf of his colleagues, rejects any British right to Moose Island. At that Goulburn loses control, and for two hours the verbal battle seesaws to no solution. Yet both sides are fully aware that neither country will continue the war over these minor debating points.

It is this awareness and the sheer weariness induced by the long bitter arguments that, in the end, produce a peace treaty. Like the exhausted troops stalemated along the Niagara frontier, the negotiating teams are worn out, dispirited, ready to agree to almost anything. In the end, all five agree to say nothing at all about the fisheries or the Mississippi or anything else; all these disputed points can be settled by others after peace is proclaimed. The British agree to everything, with some minor reservations, but even that does not satisfy Clay, who suggests breaking off negotiations then and there. At that, Albert Gallatin, whose clear mind, good humour, and calm mien have guided the five-man ship through some rough shoals, becomes uncharacteristically impatient. He has no objection, he says, to Mr. Clay amusing himself as long as he thinks proper, but as soon as he chooses to be serious he will propose a conference with the British tomorrow.

Adams has come to admire Gallatin, in whose character he sees "one of the most extraordinary combinations of stubbornness and flexibility that I ever met within man."

Indeed, Adams has come to respect the members of the commission with whom he has been closeted since July. He admires the once-despised Bayard for "the most perfect control of his temper... real self command" and has a good word for Russell, who has taken a lesser part in the negotiations. And Clay? Well, he understands Clay, in spite of their differences of belief and inclination. Both suffer from fits of temper, and Adams is nothing if not ruthlessly honest with himself. In Clay he sees his emotional mirror image. "There is the same dogmatical, overbearing manner, the same harshness of look and expression, and the same forgetfulness of the courtesies of society in both." But "nothing of this weakness has been shown in our conferences with the British plenipotentiaries. From two of them, and particularly from Mr. Goulburn, we have endured much; but I do not recollect that one expression has escaped the lips of any one of us that we would wish to be recalled."

It is all but over. Ghent, which has been their home for six months, will soon recede into memory. Adams's long solitary walks by the canal, Clay's all night card parties, the brittle social repartee with their antagonists, the long, lazy dinners, the manoeuvring, the wrangling, the casuistry, Goulburn's frustrations, Gambier's pontifications, Gallatin's mediation – all this is part of history.

On the morning of December 24, most of the plenipotentiaries on both sides are occupied by scribbling – they must prepare fair copies of the new treaty, six in all. The ceremony of signing is set for three o'clock, but the Americans are not ready and cannot meet for another hour. At four, their carriage draws up before the big, grey convent of Chartreux and, with their secretary, Hughes, the five men in long dark coats embroidered in gold enter the long dark room for their final duties.

A few small errors remain to be altered. Then with pen and ink, sand and sealing wax, the documents are rendered official, subject to ratification in Washington and London. Lord Gambier hands the three British copies to John Quincy Adams, whereupon the future president of the United States turns his over to the Admiral, remarking, as he does so, that he hopes this will be the last treaty of peace between Great Britain and the United States. It is half-past six on Christmas Eve – an appropriate anniversary for a peace treaty.

And what does the treaty say? In eleven articles and more than three thousand words it says very little. Nothing about impressment or blockade, those bitter bones of contention that caused tempers to flare, swords to be unbuckled, and war to explode. Nothing about fishing rights, captured territory, boundaries, control of the lakes, or any of the other fractious issues over which the representatives of two countries have broiled and bickered. And so little about the Indians that this question too amounts to nothing.

It is as if no war had been fought or, to put it more bluntly, as if the war that was fought was fought for no good reason. For nothing has changed; everything is as it was in the beginning save for the graves of those who, it now appears, have fought for a trifle:

Porter Hanks, late of Michilimackinac, torn in two by a British cannonball; Isaac Brock, dead with a rifle bullet in his heart on the slippery slopes of Queenston; Henry Clay's brother-in-law, vainly pleading for his life at the River Raisin, slaughtered and scalped; Zebulon Pike, pillowed on a British standard, gasping out his last moments; young Cecil Bisshopp, expiring from gangrene after the débâcle at Black Rock; Robert Barclay's shoulder mangled, Shadrach Byfield's arm sliced off, John McClay's skull cracked open – all for eleven pages of paper that change nothing.

And more: a seven-year-old child, Jervis Gillette, slain on the streets of Lewiston in December, 1813; a bewildered immigrant, Jacob Overholzer, rotting in a Kingston jail; Métoss's small son shot dead before Fort Meigs; Sally Lovejoy, killed in her front parlour at Buffalo; and a nameless, sixty-year-old farmer dying in his wife's arms in a makeshift tent near Lundy's Lane – for what?

History will ignore all but a handful of these victims. In the official statements, and the unofficial ones, too, the war will be described as if it were a football game, with much emphasis on strategy and tactics, on valour and "honour," but much less on cowardice, shame, horror, and confusion. Lake Erie and Fort McHenry will go into the American history books, Queenston Heights and Crysler's Farm into the Canadian, but without the gore, the stench, the disease, the terror, the conniving, and the imbecilities that march with every army.

Men will write that the War of 1812 was the making of the United States: for the first time she was taken seriously in Europe; that it was also the making of Canada: her people were taught pride through a common resistance to the invaders; that bloody and insane though it may have been, Lundy's Lane and Stoney Creek produced the famous undefended border between the two nations.

True. But in terms of human misery and human waste – the tall ships shattered by cannonball and grape; the barns and mills gutted by fire; villages put to the torch, grain fields ravaged, homes looted, breadwinners shackled and imprisoned; and thousands dead from cannon shot and musket fire, gangrene, typhus, ague, fever, or simple exposure, can anyone truly say on this crisp Christmas Eve that the game was ever worth the candle?

AFTERVIEW
The Legacy

LIKE A RUNAWAY MACHINE, the war, which ended officially at the close of 1814, continued on its own momentum into the new year. It is entirely characteristic of this bloody and senseless conflict that its bloodiest and most senseless battle should have been fought a fortnight after the peace treaty was signed. The secretary of the commission, Christopher Hughes, was still on the high seas on January 8, the document in his dispatch case, when Wellington's brother-in-law, Sir Edward Pakenham, led eight thousand troops in an ill-timed and badly planned frontal attack against Andrew Jackson's army near New Orleans. In half an hour, Jackson's collection of American regulars, Kentucky sharpshooters, and bayou pirates, secure behind their bulwarks of cotton bales, smashed the assault, killing or wounding some two thousand British soldiers. Pakenham himself was slain.

The foray against New Orleans had been ordered by the British government weeks before, even as the commissioners bickered in Ghent. Its purpose was to hasten the peace negotiations and, with a victory, to force better terms from the Americans. Ironically, the final document was signed almost at the moment when the doomed Pakenham took up his new command.

But no one on the swampy shores of the shallow Pontchartrain knew that the war was over; nor would they know for another month. The Battle of New Orleans, renowned in song and story, had no military significance, was fought to no purpose. In Andrew Jackson, however, the Union had a future president and in the victory a cause for rejoicing after the shame of Washington.

The news of the battle reached the capital early on February 4. Six days later, Christopher Hughes arrived with the treaty. The American commissioners had been nervous about its reception, but now, with the bells pealing and the bonfires blazing, there was no cause for worry. The country entered into a paroxysm of joy. Nobody cared about the details; few ever inquired. The words on everybody's lips were VICTORY and PEACE.

Having won the last battle, the Americans were convinced that they won the War of 1812. Having stemmed the tide of invasion and kept the Americans out of their country, Canadians believed that *they* won the war. Having ceded nothing they considered important, the British were serene in the conviction that *they* won it. But war is not a cricket match. The three nations that celebrated peace were beggared by the conflict, their people bereaved, their treasuries emptied, their graveyards crowded. In North America, the charred houses, the untended farms, the ravaged fields along the border left a legacy of bitterness and distrust.

But the real losers were the Indians. When Black Hawk of the Sauks heard the details of the Peace of Ghent, he wept like a child. A few weeks before he had delivered a prophetic speech: "I have fought the Big Knives and will continue to fight them, until they retire from our lands." And fight them he did. In 1832, the Black Hawk War rekindled Tecumseh's dream of an Indian confederacy. It was a war doomed, as all Indian revolts were doomed, to failure.

The news of the peace did not reach Mackinac Island until May. Lieutenant-Colonel McDouall, still in command, was "prostrated with grief." For three years the British had held the key to the Northwest; now they were giving it up. Clearly the British negotiators, "egregiously duped," in McDouall's bitter phrase, had no comprehension of Mackinac's significance. The Peace of Ghent meant the end of British influence and British fur trade in the Upper Mississippi.

The Indians knew betrayal when they saw it. "*Father!*" Sausamauee of the Winnebago cried out to McDouall in his anguish, "you prom-

424

ised us repeatedly that this place would not be given up...it would be better that you had killed at once, rather than expose us to a lingering death.... The peace made between you and the Big Knives *may* be a lasting one; but it cannot be for us, for we hate them; they have so often deceived us that we cannot put any faith in them."

The tribes realized that the British had deceived them, too. Three summers before, Brock and Tecumseh had ridden proudly together into the defeated fort at Detroit, symbols of mutual respect between the British and the natives. What price now the pledges of the Great White Father to his children? What meaning the long years of sacrifice by Robert Dickson, starving with his adopted people in the land of the Sioux and Winnebago? Like the Indians, Dickson was ruined by the war. Unable to return to the Upper Mississippi, he moved west to the Red River settlement and ended his days in obscurity.

For the Indians, the conflict was waged for real goals, not empty phrases. Political and military leaders constantly used the clichés of warfare to justify bloodshed and rampage. Words like *honour... liberty...independence...freedom* were dragged out to rally the troops, most of whom, struggling to save their skins, knew them to be empty. But for Tecumseh, Roundhead, Métoss, Black Hawk, and all the native statesmen for whom this war meant tribal survival, these words were real. Honour stood for personal bravery, not a carefully ambiguous document announcing peace. Liberty meant freedom to roam the plains and forests, not the right to be independent of Great Britain. Of the thousands who fell in battle – reluctant Canadian farmers, drafted American militia, career British regulars, foreign mercenaries – few fought for an ideal. But the Indians did.

It is true that the young braves, like so many of their white counterparts, were also in the war for loot and drink, for adventure and glory, for escape from routine. But when the war ended, the white soldiers knew that if they lived they could go home. Where was home for the Indians?

All three English-speaking nations could be sure that when peace was declared, business would continue as before. But not the Indians. The British gave back Mackinac and Fort Niagara; the Americans returned Amherstburg to Canada. Boundary disputes were resolved by commission; a treaty ended the shipbuilding war on the Lakes; the Undefended Border was proclaimed with pride. But the Indians did not get back their hunting grounds.

In the summer of 1815, the United States signed fifteen treaties with the tribes, guaranteeing their status as of 1811. But it did not return an acre of land. The dream of an Indian state never came true. Did the British ever believe it would? The war that bolstered national feeling on both sides of the border crippled the pride of the native peoples. As civilization marched westward, the Indians retreated. Tecumseh's tribe, the Shawnee, found themselves drifting from reservation to reservation in Kansas and Oklahoma. The Winnebago of Green Bay, ravaged by war and disease, moved to Iowa, then Minnesota, and finally Nebraska. The Miami ended on reservations in Kansas, the Potawatomi in Oklahoma.

By that time, the War of 1812 was remembered only in terms of catch-phrases: *Don't give up the ship... We have met the enemy and they are ours... Push on, brave York Volunteers.* History gave the conflict short shrift; and yet, for all its bunglings and idiocies, it helped determine the shape and nature of Canada. Like the Battle of Waterloo, it was, to use Wellington's phrase, "a near run thing." The balance might have been tipped another way had the leadership on either side been more incisive, the weather less captious, or the Gods of War less perverse. A change of wind on Lake Champlain could have led to the capture of upper New York State. The sniper's bullet that killed Isaac Brock undoubtedly helped prolong the struggle.

Events, not individuals, it is said, control the course of history. The War of 1812 suggests the opposite. Canada's destiny, for better or for worse, was in the hands of human beings, subject to human caprices, strengths, and emotions. If the ambitious Winfield Scott had waited for the army at Lundy's Lane, if the haughty Commodore Chauncey had deigned to support Jacob Brown at Fort George, could Upper Canada have held out? Tecumseh was unique. If he had not been born, would another have risen in his place?

Human failings frustrated American strategy. If Kingston or Montreal had fallen, Ontario would be an American state today. But Dearborn and Wilkinson were flawed commanders. An American Brock might have pierced the heartland of the nation and cut the jugular between the two provinces. But the invaders were reduced to hacking vainly at the country's extremities.

The war helped set the two countries on different courses. National characteristics were evolving: American ebullience, Canadian reserve. The Americans went wild over minor triumphs, the Canadians remained phlegmatic over major ones. Brock was knighted for Detroit, but there were no gold medals struck, no ceremonial swords, banquets, or fireworks to mark Châteauguay, Crysler's Farm, Stoney Creek, or Beaver Dams. By contrast, Croghan's defence of Fort Stephenson was the signal for a paroxysm of rejoicing that made him an overnight hero in the United States.

American hero worship filled the Congress, the Senate, and the state legislatures with dozens of war veterans. Three soldiers – Harrison, Jackson, and Zachary Taylor – became president. But there were no Canadian Jacksons because there was no high political office to which a Canadian could aspire. The major victories were won by men from another land who did their job and went home. Brock and de Salaberry were Canada's only heroes, Laura Secord her sole heroine. And Brock was not a Canadian.

The quality of boundless enthusiasm, which convinces every American school child that the United States won the war, is not a Canadian trait. We do not venerate winners. Who remembers Billy Green, John Norton, Robert Dickson, or even William Hamilton Merritt? The quintessential Canadian hero was a clergyman, not a soldier, a transplanted Scot, a supporter of entrenched values, a Tory of Tories. Dour, earnest, implacable, John Strachan acquired a reputation for courage and leadership that made him a power in Upper Canada and helped freeze its political pattern.

Strachan's thrust was elitist. He believed implicitly in everything the Americans had rejected: an established church, a limited franchise, a ruling oligarchy. He despised Americans, loathed Americanisms. "Democracy" and "republicanism" were hateful words. The York elite, linked by intermarriage and soon to be dubbed the Family Compact, wanted no truck with elected judges or policemen, let alone universal male suffrage.

The war helped entrench certain words in the national lexicon and certain attitudes in the national consciousness. Three words – *loyalty, security*, and *order* – took on a Canadian connotation. *Freedom*, tossed about like a cricket ball by all sides, had a special meaning, too: it meant freedom from the United States. *Liberty* was exclusively American, never used north of the border, perhaps because it was too close to *libertine* for the pious Canadians. Radicalism was the opposite of loyalty, democracy the opposite of order.

Loyalty meant loyalty to Britain and to British values. Long after Confederation, John A. Macdonald could bring an audience to its feet by crying: "A British subject I was born; a British subject I will die" – meaning that he would never die an American. On this curiously negative principle, uttered by the first prime minister of an emerging nation, did the seeds of nationalism sprout.

At the start of the war, Upper Canada was largely American, though its leaders were not. But by 1815, the Americans had become The Enemy. They had ravaged the Thames Valley, burned every house along the Niagara, and laid waste the St. Lawrence. It was no longer prudent to espouse American ideas: in 1813 farmers had been jailed in York for that crime. The example of Willcocks, Markle, and Mallory, the three turncoats, could not go unremarked. Before the war, as elected members of the lower house, they had opposed the established order. Now they stood convicted, *in absentia*, of high treason.

British colonial rule meant orderly government, not the democracy of the uneducated mob. The war enshrined national stereotypes: the British redcoats were seen as a regimented force, the Kentucky militia as an unmannerly horde. The pejorative was "Yankee." In the Canadian vernacular, Yankees were everything the York and Montreal elite were not: vulgar, tobacco-chewing upstarts in loud suits, who had no breeding and spoke with an offensive twang. Tiger Dunlop, the British surgeon, captured this attitude when he described how a servant told Red George Macdonell that a Yankee officer was waiting to sell him some smuggled beef. He knew he was a Yankee, he said, "for he wore his hat in the parlour and spit on the carpet." The stereotype persisted into the next century as the political cartoons of the post-war years demonstrate.

The Invasion of Canada did not initiate that snobbery: it had been part of the English attitude toward the upstart colony since the days of the Revolution. But the bitterness of war made it acceptable, even desirable, in Canada.

Angered by the strident boastings of American generals that this was "a war of extermination" (Hull) or "a war of conquest" (Smythe); hardened in the crucible of fire that destroyed old loyalties and encouraged new hatreds; goaded by those who had a vested interest in maintaining the *status quo*; and inspired by a new nationalism springing from the embers of conflict, few Canadians found it possible to consider, at least openly, the American way as a political choice for the future.

The alternative was already in place – the British colonial way: comfortable, orderly, secure, paternalistic. From that, for better or worse, we have never entirely detached ourselves. The flames of war have long since died; the agony has been forgotten, the justification long obscured. But the legacy of that bitter, inconclusive, half-forgotten conflict still remains.

Aftermath

John Quincy Adams became Secretary of State in 1817 under President James Monroe and, with Henry Clay's help, defeated Andrew Jackson for the presidency in 1824. He did not serve a second term but was a congressional representative from 1831 to 1848, the year of his death.

William Allan became a member of the Legislative Council of Upper Canada in 1825 and served on the Executive Council from 1836 to 1840. A pillar of the Family Compact, he died in 1840.

John Armstrong's political career ended with the burning of Washington. Failing in an attempt to be elected to the Senate, he spent his remaining days in farming and writing. In his *Notices of the War of 1812* he attempted to vindicate his record. He died in 1843.

Robert Barclay waited eleven years after the Battle of Lake Erie before he achieved post rank. He was made a captain in 1824, fathered eight children, died in 1837.

James Bayard died in June, 1815, six months after the conclusion of the peace talks at Ghent.

Alexander Bourne helped found a town on the Maumee, named it Perrysburg, became canal commissioner for Ohio, and laid down most of the waterways in that state. He died in 1848.

John Boyd was discharged from the army in 1815. Toward the end of his life he was naval officer for the Port of Boston. He died in 1830.

Jacob Brown became commander of the U.S. Army in 1821, continuing until his death in 1828.

Cyrenius Chapin continued his medical practice in Buffalo until his death in 1838.

Isaac Chauncey continued his naval career, helped negotiate a treaty with Algiers, and ended his years as president of the Board of Navy Commissioners, charged with the administration of the service. He died in 1840.

Henry Clay again became Speaker of the House of Representatives, entered the Senate in 1831, ran unsuccessfully against Andrew Jackson for the presidency in 1832. He remained in public life until his death in 1852.

George Croghan married a member of the powerful Livingston family of New York, served as postmaster in New Orleans in 1824 and inspector general of the regular army, and fought in the Mexican War. Drink clouded his last years. He died of cholera in New Orleans in 1849.

Henry Dearborn left the army in 1815 after being turned down for the post of Secretary of War. In 1822 he was made Minister to Portugal. He died in 1829.

Robert Dickson helped Lord Selkirk establish his colony on the Red River. He died in 1823.

David Bates Douglass returned to West Point as an instructor and later taught civil engineering and architecture at New York University. From 1834 to 1836 he was engineer in charge of New York City's water supply.

Gordon Drummond succeeded Sir George Prevost as Governor General. He returned to England in 1816, was promoted to full general. He died in London in 1854.

Dominique Ducharme was appointed Indian agent at Lake of Two Mountains, Quebec, a post he held until his death in 1853.

William "Tiger" Dunlop became a journalist in England, returned to Canada with John Galt, in the service of the latter's Canada Company, and represented Huron Riding in the Legislative Assembly from 1841 to 1846. He died in 1848.

Jesse Elliott remained in the navy, becoming commander-in-chief of the Mediterranean Fleet in 1835. Disgruntled officers preferred thirteen charges against him, and he was suspended from the navy for four years. A new administration in Washington remitted part of the suspension and he was given, in 1844, command of the Philadelphia Navy Yard. He died in 1845.

James FitzGibbon rose to become a full colonel and acting adjutant-general. He was leader of the loyalist forces at Montgomery's Tavern who helped suppress William Lyon Mackenzie's rebellion in 1837. He returned to England in 1846, was appointed military knight of Windsor, and died in 1860.

Edmund Gaines took part in several Indian wars, quarrelled openly with Winfield Scott, successfully defended himself at a court martial for insubordination during the Mexican War, and was a constant thorn in the War Department's side. He died, unrepentant, in 1849.

Albert Gallatin became U.S. Minister to France and later to Great Britain. In 1831 he became president of the National Bank in New York. He died in 1849.

George Gleig fought at Waterloo then studied at Oxford, took orders, was named chaplain general of the British forces in 1844. A prolific writer, he produced biographies of Wellington and Clive. He died in 1888.

Henry Goulburn became a member of the Privy Council in 1821 and chief secretary to the Lord-Lieutenant of Ireland. For most of his parliamentary career after 1828 he held cabinet posts, notably that of Chancellor of the Exchequer. He died in 1856.

Billy Green lived all his life in Saltfleet township. He ran a sawmill on the original Green land and died in his eighty-fourth year in 1877.

Wade Hampton was reputed to be the wealthiest planter in the United States at the time of his death in 1835.

Jarvis Hanks had a long career as a teacher, signpainter, silhouette artist, and portraitist; he studied medicine, exhibited with the National Academy of Design in New York, fathered ten children, and died in Cleveland in 1853.

William Henry Harrison entered Congress in 1816 and became a Senator in 1825. In 1840 he nudged out Henry Clay as Whig presidential candidate. His military record and his slogan "Tippecanoe and Tyler, too" won him a landslide victory. One month after his inauguration, he died of pneumonia.

John Harvey became successively Lieutenant-Governor of New Brunswick, Governor of Newfoundland, and Lieutenant-Governor of Nova Scotia. He was knighted in 1834 and at the time of his death, in 1852, was a lieutenant-general.

Thomas Jesup rose to be Quartermaster General of the American army. His distinguished forty-two-year service in that post has never been equalled. He died in 1860.

Richard Johnson ran for vice-president in 1837 using the slogan "Rumpsey, Dumpsey, Colonel Johnson killed Tecumseh." His four years in office were undistinguished. He died in 1850.

Morgan Lewis became president of the New York Historical Society and a founder of New York University. He lived to be ninety, dying in 1844.

Thomas Macdonough was promoted to captain immediately after the naval battle on Lake Champlain. He died at sea of tuberculosis in 1825 at the age of forty-two.

Alexander Macomb rose to become commanding general of the U.S. Army, a post he held from 1828 until his death in 1841.

Benajah Mallory was outlawed and his Canadian property forfeited. He lived in Rochester after the war, but his subsequent career is not known.

Abraham Markle also forfeited his lands. After the war he moved to the Wabash and died in obscurity. His family remained at Newark.

William Hamilton Merritt became an enthusiastic promoter of the first Welland canal and one of the great figures in canal transportation in Canada. He entered politics in 1832, served as president of the Executive Council of the Province of Canada from 1848 to 1851, was Chief Commissioner of Public Works, and later a member of the Legislative Council of Canada. He died in 1862.

Joseph Morrison served in Ireland, India, and Burma, was promoted to brigadier-general, and died at sea in 1826.

Usher Parsons enjoyed a distinguished academic and medical career after leaving the navy. He helped organize the American Medical Association and published fifty-six books and articles. He died in 1868.

Oliver Hazard Perry died in Venezuela of yellow fever while descending the Orinoco River six years after his great victory.

Peter B. Porter ran unsuccessfully for Governor of New York in 1817, served on the boundary commission that followed the Treaty of Ghent, and was briefly Secretary of War in 1828–29. He died at Niagara Falls in 1844.

Sir George Prevost, recalled to face a court martial in connection with his defeat at Plattsburgh, died in 1816, one week before the hearing.

Henry Procter, suspended as a result of his defeat on the Thames, died in 1822.

The Prophet, Tecumseh's mystic brother, was given a small pension by the British government and died in Kansas in the mid-1830s.

Phineas Riall was named governor of Grenada in 1816, was knighted in 1833, and died in Paris, a full general, in 1850.

John Richardson's works include his long poem *Tecumseh, Warrior of the West*, his novel *Wacousta*, his personal history of the war, and a number of novels, the best-known being *The Canadian Brothers*. His military career included three years of service with the British Auxiliary Legion in Spain from 1834 to 1837. In the early 1840s he edited two periodicals from Brockville. He moved to Montreal and later to New York, where he died in poverty at the age of sixty.

Eleazar Ripley demanded a court martial to vindicate his character after Jacob Brown blamed him for losing the guns at Lundy's Lane. But President Madison held that Congress's gold medal was vindication enough. Ripley left the army in 1820 and became a politician. He died in 1839.

Frederick Philipse Robinson was briefly Lieutenant-Governor of Upper Canada in the summer of 1815. He died, a full general and a Knight Commander of the Bath, in 1852, in his eighty-eighth year.

John Beverley Robinson rose to become Chief Justice of Upper Canada, Speaker of the Legislative Council, and president of the Executive Council. He was one of the guiding spirits of the Family Compact, was created a baronet in 1854, and died in 1863.

Jonathan Russell continued as U.S. Minister to Sweden and Stockholm until 1819. In 1822 he became embroiled in a bitter controversy with his former colleague, John Quincy Adams, arising from a dispute between Clay and Adams at the time of the Ghent negotiations. Adams successfully accused Russell of treachery and the resultant controversy is said to have caused Russell's retirement from public life. He died in 1832.

Charles-Michel de Salaberry, created a Commander of the Bath in 1817 for his victory at Châteauguay, was appointed to the Legislative Council of Lower Canada the following year. He died in 1829.

Winfield Scott became general-in-chief of the U.S. Army in 1841. Victorious in the war with Mexico in 1847, he ran for the presidency in 1852 but was badly beaten by Franklin Pierce. He retired in 1861 on the eve of the Civil War and died five years later at the age of eighty.

Sir Roger Hale Sheaffe rose to become a full general. He died at Edinburgh at the age of eighty-two.

John Strachan, one of the pillars of the Family Compact, was a member of the Executive Council of Upper Canada from 1818 to 1836. In 1839 he became Bishop of Toronto. He was the first president of King's College – the future University of Toronto – and also the founder of Trinity College. He died in 1867, in his ninetieth year.

John Vincent achieved the rank of full general. He died in London in 1848 at the age of eighty-three.

James Wilkinson talked himself into an acquittal before a court martial of his juniors – much to President Madison's disgust – and spent his declining years justifying his career in three carefully edited volumes of documents, *Memoirs of My Own Times*. He died in Mexico in 1825.

Sir James Yeo died on a voyage home from Africa in 1818, aged thirty-five.

Author's Note and Acknowledgements

This book is the second of two dealing with the War of 1812 as it affected Canada and Canadians. Except for a short account of the burning of Washington, I have confined the narrative to the border struggle. Other events, such as the siege of Baltimore, the Battle of New Orleans, and the naval encounters along the Atlantic seaboard have already been dealt with capably by British and American writers.

My own work, which looks at the war from a Canadian point of view, is not intended primarily as a military or political history. These exist. Thus, I have not thought it necessary to list every military unit that fought along the border between 1812 and 1815. Nor have I attempted to go into minuscule detail on minor tactical points. Some lesser skirmishes – Prevost's attack on Sackets Harbor in 1813, Wilkinson's abortive attempt against the Lacolle Mill in 1814, to name two – have been omitted.

This is, rather, a *social* history of the war, the first to be written by a Canadian. I have tried to tell not only what happened but also *what it was like*; to look at the struggle not as a witness gazing down from a mountaintop but as a combatant struggling in the mud of the battlefield; to picture the war from the viewpoints of private soldiers and civilians as well as from those of generals and politicians; to see it through the eyes of ordinary people on both sides – farmer and housewife, traitor and spy, drummer boy and Indian brave, volunteer, regular, and conscript.

For this reason, both books have been based largely on primary sources – letters, military dispatches, documents, reports, diaries, journals and memoirs. I have invented nothing. Dialogue is reproduced exactly as reported by those who were present. If I have on occasion entered the minds of the participants it is because they themselves reported their own thoughts and feelings. This raw material, scattered over two continents, was gathered by my assistant, the indispensable Barbara Sears. I find it difficult to express properly my admiration for her industry and tenacity.

She and I would like to thank the various people and institutions who helped search out the documents which form the underpinnings of these books:

From the Metropolitan Toronto Central Library, Edith Firth and the staff of the Canadian History Department; Michael Pearson and the staff of the History Department; and Norma Dainard, Keith Alcock, and the staff of the newspaper section. From the Public Archives of Canada, Patricia Kennedy, Gordon Dodds, Bruce Wilson, Brian Driscoll, Glenn T. Wright, and Grace Campbell. From the *Dictionary of Canadian Biography*, Robert Fraser. From Parks Canada, Robert Allen of Ottawa and the staffs at Fort George and Fort Malden. And these individuals: Peter Burroughs, Esther Summers, Bob Green, Paul Roney, and Patrick Brode.

Also: the Public Archives of Ontario; the Library of Congress, Manuscript Division, Washington; the U.S. National Archives; the Public Record Office, London; the Filson Club, Louisville, Kentucky; the National Library of Scotland; the William L. Clements Library, University of Michigan; the Indiana State Library; and the historical societies of Vermont, New York, Rhode Island, Buffalo and Erie County, Delaware, Maryland, Kentucky, and Pennsylvania; and the Lundy's Lane and the Niagara Falls Historical Societies.

I am again grateful to those friends and professionals who read the manuscript in draft form and made so many useful suggestions, especially to Janice Tyrwhitt, Charles Templeton, Jack McClelland, Maggie Dowling, and Elsa Franklin. My wife, Janet, the best proofreader I know, again prevented me from grammatical embarrassment, and my editor, Janet Craig, rescued me once more from inconsistency. Research notes were organized under the supervision of my secretary, Ennis Armstrong, who also typed much of the manuscript in its various stages. To all these I say thank you. There will be errors; I hope they are minor; they are all mine.

Kleinburg, Ontario
March, 1981

Notes

Abbreviations used:
ASPFR   American State Papers, Foreign Relations
ASPMA   American State Papers, Military Affairs
ASPNA   American State Papers, Naval Affairs
BHS   Buffalo Historical Society
DAB   *Dictionary of American Biography*
DNB   *Dictionary of National Biography*
LC   Library of Congress
OBA   Ontario Bureau of Archives
PAC   Public Archives of Canada
PAO   Public Archives of Ontario
PRO   Public Record Office
RIHS   Rhode Island Historical Society
SBD   *Select British Documents*
SN   Secretary of the Navy
SW   Secretary of War
UCS   Upper Canada Sundries
USNA   United States National Archives

Prelude: New Brunswick Goes to War

page *line*

17 14 Le Couteur, pp. 490–500, *passim*; Squires, pp. 118–36, *passim*.

Overview

25 26 Cruikshank, *Documentary History*, V: 151, regulations; Sheaffe, "Letterbook," p. 346, Sheaffe to Prevost, 13 March 1813.
26 6 Dunlop, p. 40.
26 10 Scott, p. 31.
26 16 Ibid., p. 35.
26 28 Jackson, *Black Hawk*, p. 71.
27 3 Ibid.
30 2 Cruikshank, *Documentary History*, V: 87, Dearborn to SW, 3 March 1813.

The Capture of Little York

37 8 PAO, Strachan Papers, Strachan to Brown, 26 April 1813.
37 17 Ibid.
38 5 Ibid.

page *line*

38 15 Strachan, *Letterbook*, p. 18, Strachan to McGillivray, n.d.
38 24 Ibid.
38 38 PAO, Strachan Papers, Strachan to Brown, 20 Oct. 1807.
38 39 Ibid., Strachan to Brown, 21 Oct. 1809.
39 7 Ibid., Strachan to Brown, 13 July 1806.
39 28 Strachan, *Sermon*.
40 6 *Niles Register*, 28 Oct. 1815.
40 13 Hollon, pp. 205–6.
40 17 Quoted in Lossing, p. 586.
40 18 Ibid.
40 22 Terrell, pp. 130–31.
40 31 Ibid., pp. 27–28.
41 3 Quoted in Hollon, p. 202.
41 25 Cruikshank, *Documentary History*, V: 162–63, Brigade orders, 25 April 1813.
41 31 Cumberland, pp. 14–15.
42 2 Ibid.
42 3 Humphries, p. 7.
42 9 Cruikshank, *Documentary History*, V: 147, Sheaffe to Bathurst, 5 April 1813; W. Wood,

page line

SBD, II: 89, Sheaffe to Prevost, 5 May 1813.

42 11 W. Wood, SBD, II: 92, Sheaffe to Prevost, 5 May 1813.

42 18 Firth, p. 279, Ely Playter Diary, 26 April 1813.

42 20 Magill, *passim*.

42 26 PAC, UCS, RG 5, A1, vol. 17, no. 116, McGill to Sheaffe, 17 May 1813.

42 36 PAC, UCS, State Books, vol. F, report on Mrs. Derenzy's application; Derenzy to De Rottenburg, 5 July 1813; deposition signed by Leah Allan, S. Heward, W. Loe, 23 July 1813.

43 9 Firth, p. 292, Wilson to Wilson, 5 Dec. 1813.

43 14 Ibid., p. 279, Ely Playter Diary, 26 April 1813.

43 19 *The Yankee* (Boston), 2 July 1813.

43 25 Firth, p. 279, Ely Playter Diary, 26 April 1813.

43 28 Ibid., p. 294, Strachan to Brown, 26–27 April 1813.

44 2 PAO, Strachan Papers, Strachan to Brown, 9 Oct. 1808.

44 16 Ibid.

44 21 Firth, p. 294, Strachan to Brown, 26 and 27 April 1813.

44 34 Ibid., pp. 279–80, Ely Playter Diary, 27 April 1813.

45 8 PAC, RG 8, vol. 923, pp. 12–16, Brock to Lt.-Col. Green, 8 Feb. 1804.

45 17 C. Elliott, *Scott*, p. 73.

45 24 W. Wood, SBD, II: 89–91, Sheaffe to Prevost, 5 May 1813.

45 26 Ibid., p. 89.

46 5 Ibid., pp. 89–90.

46 7 Cruikshank, *Documentary History*, V: 193, Chewett, Strachan, et al. to ?, 8 May 1813.

46 15 W. Wood, SBD, II: 89–90, Sheaffe to Prevost, 5 May 1813.

47 4 Firth, pp. 304–5, Pearce account.

47 6 Cumberland, p. 17.

47 12 Cruikshank, *Documentary History*, V: 179–80, Fraser to ?, May 1813.

47 19 Firth, p. 304, Pearce account.

page line

48 8 Cruikshank, *Documentary History*, V: 180–81, Fraser to ?, May 1813; ibid., p. 207, Finan journal; W. Wood, SBD, II: 90, Sheaffe to Prevost, 5 May 1813; Loyal and Patriotic Society, p. 229.

48 21 *Anglo-American Magazine*, December 1853, p. 565.

48 28 Firth, p. 304, Pearce account.

48 32 Cruikshank, *Documentary History*, V: 181, Fraser to ?, May 1813; Lossing, p. 588.

48 35 Firth, p. 280, Ely Playter Diary, 27 April 1813.

49 4 W. Wood, SBD, II: 90–91, Sheaffe to Prevost, 5 May 1813; Firth, p. 280, Ely Playter Diary, 27 April 1813; Cruikshank, *Documentary History*, V: 193–94, Chewett, Strachan, et al. to ?, 8 May 1813; Cruikshank, "Contest for...Lake Ontario in 1812 and 1813," p. 176.

49 6 Cruikshank, *Documentary History*, V: 181, Fraser to ?, May 1813.

49 13 Cruikshank, "Contest for...Lake Ontario in 1812 and 1813," p. 176; *Documentary History*, V: 194, Chewett, Strachan, et al. to ?, 8 May 1813.

49 21 Cruikshank, *Documentary History*, V: 208, Finan journal.

49 29 Firth, p. 294, Strachan to Brown, 26 and 27 April 1813.

49 34 W. Wood, SBD, II: 91, Sheaffe to Prevost, 5 May 1813.

49 38 Firth, pp. 304–5, Pearce account.

50 7 Ibid., p. 280, Ely Playter Diary, 27 April 1813.

50 15 Ibid.; W. Wood, SBD, II: 86, Sheaffe to Prevost, 30 April 1813; ibid., p. 91, Sheaffe to Prevost, 5 May 1813.

50 22 Firth, p. 280, Ely Playter Diary, 27 April 1813; PAC, RG 5, A1, vol. 19, no. 49, Saunders petition.

50 26 Cruikshank, *Documentary History*, V: 182, Fraser to ?, May 1813.

page	line	
50	*39*	Ibid.
51	*8*	Ibid., p. 183, statement of killed and wounded.
51	*17*	Firth, p. 280, Ely Playter Diary, 27 April 1813; PAC, RG 5, A1, vol. 26, petition, Gugins to Gore.
51	*19*	Cumberland, p. 27; Cruikshank, *Documentary History*, V: 183, statement of killed and wounded.
51	*22*	Cruikshank, *Documentary History*, V: 182, Fraser to ?, May 1813.
51	*27*	*Niles Register*, 5 June 1813.
51	*31*	Cruikshank, *Documentary History*, V: 182, Fraser to ?, May 1813.
51	*36*	Ibid., p. 170, Chauncey to SN, 28 April 1813.
52	*1*	*Niles Register*, 5 June 1813.
52	*10*	Firth, pp. 294–95, Strachan to Brown, 26–27 April 1813.
52	*29*	Cruikshank, *Documentary History*, V: 210–11, Finan journal.
52	*37*	Firth, p. 295, Strachan to Brown, 26–27 April 1813.
53	*9*	Ibid., p. 280, Ely Playter Diary, 27 April 1813.
53	*21*	Ibid., pp. 280–81.
53	*28*	Ibid., p. 295, Strachan to Brown, 26–27 April 1813.
53	*31*	Cruikshank, *Documentary History*, V: 196, Chewett, Strachan, et al. to ?, 8 May 1813.
54	*3*	Ibid.; Firth, p. 295, Strachan to Brown, 26–27 April 1813.
54	*11*	Cruikshank, *Documentary History*, V: 196, Chewett, Strachan, et al. to ?, 8 May 1813.
54	*14*	Firth, p. 295, Strachan to Brown, 26–27 April 1813.
54	*24*	Cruikshank, *Documentary History*, V: 196, Chewett, Strachan, et al. to ?, 8 May 1813.
54	*27*	OBA, 9th Report, p. 143.
54	*34*	Firth, pp. 301–2, statement of Major Givins's losses; p. 296, Strachan to Brown, 26–30 April 1813.
55	*9*	Kerr, p. 14.
55	*28*	Firth, p. 307, Beaumont Diary, 27 April 1813.
55	*31*	Ibid., p. 295, Strachan to Brown, 26–28 April 1813.
56	*38*	Ibid.
56	*40*	Cruikshank, *Documentary History*, V: 224, memo, Thomas Ridout, 5 May 1813.
57	*8*	Selby, pp. 20–21.
57	*21*	Firth, p. 281, Ely Playter Diary, 28–30 April 1813.
57	*24*	Ibid., p. 282.
57	*34*	T. Palmer, *Historical Register*, Chauncey to Jones, 4 June 1813.
57	*35*	Firth, p. 308, Beaumont Diary, 1 May 1813.
58	*8*	Cruikshank, *Documentary History*, V: 172, *New York Statesman*, 29 May 1813.
58	*17*	PAC, RG 5, A1, vol. 16, Cutter information against John Lyon et al., 16 Aug. 1813; Cutter information against James Mulat et al., 16 Aug. 1813.
58	*23*	PAC, RG 5, A1, vol. 16, Palmer information against Elijah Bentley, 23 Aug. 1813.
58	*35*	PAC, RG 5, A1, vol. 16, Mulholland information against Finch, 24 Aug. 1813.
58	*40*	Firth, p. 293, Wilson to Wilson, 5 Dec. 1813.
59	*2*	*Niles Register*, 4 Nov. 1815, p. 160.
59	*12*	PAC, MG 24, F13, Chauncey to SN, 7 May 1813.
59	*23*	Cruikshank, *Documentary History*, V: 199–200, Chewett, Strachan, et al. to ?, 8 May 1813; *The Yankee* (Boston), 2 July 1813.
59	*27*	Cruikshank, *Documentary History*, V: 199–200, Chewett, Strachan, et al. to ?, 8 May 1813.
59	*31*	Kerr, p. 19.
59	*37*	PAC, MG 24, F13, Chauncey to SN, 7 May 1813.
60	*3*	Ibid., Chauncey to SN, 11 May 1813.
60	*11*	Armstrong, *Notices*, I: 227.
60	*27*	Cruikshank, *Documentary History*, V: 201, Chewett, Strachan, et al. to ?, 8 May 1813.
60	*30*	Ibid.
60	*35*	Ibid.
60	*38*	Ibid., p. 200.

page line

60 41 Firth, p. 312, Powell to Powell, 6 June 1813.

Stalemate on the Niagara Peninsula

65 8   W. Wood, SBD, III, pt. 2: 574, Merritt narrative; Cruikshank, *Documentary History*, V: 250, Vincent to Prevost, 28 May 1813.

65 13 Cruikshank, *Documentary History*, V: 250, Vincent to Prevost, 28 May 1813.

65 21 Cruikshank, "Battle of Fort George," p. 23.

66 2   Ibid., p. 24.

66 4   PAO, Ely Playter Diary, 27 May 1813.

66 9   "Reminiscences of American Occupation," p. 25.

66 12 Cruikshank, "Battle of Fort George," p. 24.

66 13 Ibid.

66 20 Ibid.

66 27 Mackenzie, *Perry*, pp. 107–9.

67 4   Ibid., p. 108.

68 12 Ibid., p. 109.

68 19 Cruikshank, "Battle of Fort George," p. 25.

68 24 Boyd, p. 16, Miller to a general, n.d.

68 31 C. Elliott, *Scott*, p. 97.

68 34 Lossing, p. 599.

68 39 Mackenzie, *Perry*, p. 109.

69 3   Scott, p. 88.

69 6   Boyd, pp. 4–5.

69 10 W. Wood, SBD, II: 103–7, Vincent to Prevost, 28 May 1813; Boyd, p. 5; Cruikshank, "Battle of Fort George," p. 26.

69 12 Cruikshank, "Battle of Fort George," p. 29.

69 17 W. Wood, SBD, II: 103–7, Vincent to Prevost, 28 May 1813.

69 24 Cruikshank, "Battle of Fort George," p. 26.

69 29 W. Wood, SBD, II: 106, Vincent to Prevost, 28 May 1813; Cruikshank, *Documentary History*, VI: 180, Hamilton to Henderson, 4 July 1813; ibid., V:

page line

246, Clegg to Claus, 27 May 1813.

69 34 Cruikshank, *Documentary History*, V: 304, diary of Col. Claus.

70 10 Scott, pp. 89–90.

70 14 C. Elliott, *Scott*, p. 99.

70 17 Cruikshank, "Battle of Fort George," p. 27.

70 22 Scott, p. 90.

70 31 Ibid., pp. 90–91; C. Elliott, *Scott*, p. 100.

71 5   Cruikshank, "Battle of Fort George," p. 27.

71 14 C. Elliott, *Scott*, p. 100.

71 17 Scott, p. 91.

71 33 Quoted in H. Adams, VII: 188.

72 29 M. Thompson, "Billy Green," p. 175.

73 6   W. Wood, SBD, III, pt. 2: 576, Merritt narrative.

73 18 M. Thompson, "Billy Green," p. 175.

74 31 Ibid., pp. 175–76.

75 6   Morgan, p. 219.

75 8   Ibid.

75 14 FitzGibbon, p. 69.

75 18 W. Wood, SBD, II: 142–45, Vincent to Prevost, 6 June 1813; ibid., pp. 139–41, Harvey to Baynes, 6 June 1813.

75 27 M. Thompson, "Billy Green," p. 176.

75 36 Ibid., p. 177.

75 40 Ibid., p. 176.

76 7   Ibid.

76 9   Biggar, p. 387.

76 20 Cruikshank, *Documentary History*, VI: 33–34, *Niles Register*, 19 Oct. 1816, Chandler narrative.

76 23 Ibid., p. 13, FitzGibbon to Somerville, 7 June 1813; W. Wood, SBD, II: 139–41, Harvey to Baynes, 6 June 1813.

76 25 Biggar, p. 387.

76 32 Cruikshank, *Documentary History*, VI: 13–14, FitzGibbon to Somerville, 7 June 1813.

77 6   Ibid., pp. 16–17, FitzGibbon memo, 1 Jan. 1854.

77 13 Quoted in Cruikshank, "Stoney Creek," p. 10.

442

77 19 Cruikshank, *Documentary History*, VI: 27, Chandler to Dearborn, 18 June 1813.

77 21 Ibid., p. 50, letter from a U.S. officer, 22 June 1813.

78 3 Ibid., p. 27, Chandler to Dearborn, 18 June 1813; Cruikshank, "Stoney Creek," p. 11.

78 10 Cruikshank, *Documentary History*, VI: 14, FitzGibbon to Somerville, 7 June 1813; ibid., p. 17, FitzGibbon memo, 1 Jan. 1854.

78 16 Cruikshank, "Stoney Creek," p. 16.

78 20 W. Wood, SBD, III, pt. 2: 580, Merritt narrative.

78 26 Ibid., II: 140–41, Harvey to Baynes, 6 June 1813.

78 35 Ibid., III, pt. 2: 580, Merritt narrative.

78 40 Ibid., II: 139–41, Harvey to Baynes, 6 June 1813; Lossing, p. 604.

79 3 Cruikshank, *Documentary History*, VI: 56, Evans to Vincent, 8 June 1813.

79 7 Ibid., pp. 116–19, *Niles Register*, 19 Oct. 1816, Chandler narrative; Cruikshank, "Battle of Fort George," p. 16.

79 10 W. Wood, SBD, II: 139–41, Harvey to Baynes, 6 June 1813.

79 13 Cruikshank, "Battle of Fort George," p. 16.

79 20 Ibid., pp. 16–17.

79 24 Ibid., p. 17.

79 27 Cruikshank, *Documentary History*, VI: 62, Evans to Harvey, 10 June 1813.

79 30 Ibid., pp. 77–78, no. 7, Dearborn to Lewis.

79 36 Ibid., p. 63, return, 10 June 1813.

81 8 FitzGibbon, pp. 76–77; Cruikshank, *Documentary History*, VI: 116–17, *Montreal Gazette*, 6 July 1813; ibid., pp. 202–4, Askin to Askin, 8 July 1813.

82 9 Morgan, p. 194.

82 10 FitzGibbon, p. 56.

82 13 Morgan, p. 194.

82 15 FitzGibbon, p. 64.

82 31 Cruikshank, *Documentary History*, VI: 150–51, report of court of inquiry; W. Wood, SBD, III, pt. 2: 584–85, Merritt narrative.

83 18 Cruikshank, *Documentary History*, VI: 127–28, Laura Secord narrative.

83 22 Moir, pp. 107–8, certificate of James FitzGibbon, 11 May 1827.

84 3 Ibid.; PAO, Misc. coll., Story of Laura Ingersoll Secord as related by Laura Secord Clark, 1933.

84 9 Cruikshank, *Documentary History*, VI: 130–31, Boerstler narrative.

84 14 Chapin, p. 10.

84 34 Cruikshank, *Documentary History*, VI: 95–96, Dearborn to Armstrong, 20 June 1813.

85 3 Cruikshank, *Documentary History*, VI: 126, Ducharme to ?, 5 June 1826.

85 6 Ibid., p. 95, SW to Dearborn, 19 June 1813; ibid., p. 6, Dearborn to SW, 6 June 1813.

85 12 Chapin, p. 10.

85 32 Ibid., p. 40, Chapin to Armstrong, 26 April 1838.

85 33 Cruikshank, *Documentary History*, VI: 132, Boerstler narrative.

86 5 Ibid., p. 136; Chapin, p. 10.

86 7 Chapin, p. 10.

86 11 Cruikshank, *Documentary History*, VI: 151, report of court of inquiry, 17 Feb. 1815.

86 14 Ibid., p. 146, Roach journal.

86 17 Ibid., p. 131, Boerstler narrative.

86 23 Ibid., p. 148, Roach journal.

86 26 Ibid.

86 29 Ibid., p. 131, Boerstler narrative.

86 35 Ibid., p. 126, Ducharme to ?, 5 June 1826.

87 19 Ibid., pp. 126–27.

88 16 Ibid., pp. 130–37, Boerstler narrative.

88 27 Chapin, pp. 9–15.

page	line	
88	38	Cruikshank, *Documentary History*, VI: 133–34, Boerstler narrative; FitzGibbon, p. 87.
89	18	FitzGibbon, p. 87.
89	29	Ibid.
89	38	Chapin, p. 14.
91	1	FitzGibbon, pp. 89–91.
91	8	Cruikshank, *Documentary History*, VI: 151, Roach journal; ibid., pp. 120–21, FitzGibbon to Kerr, 30 March 1818; ibid., p. 127, Ducharme to ?, 5 June 1826; W. Wood, SBD, III, pt. 2: 585, Merritt narrative.
91	12	Cruikshank, *Documentary History*, VI: 141, Boerstler to Dearborn, 25 June 1813; ibid., p. 114, return of prisoners, 24 June 1813.
91	14	Ibid., pp. 142–44, *Buffalo Gazette*, 29 July 1813.
91	22	Quoted in Cruikshank, "Fight in the Beechwoods," p. 22.
91	26	Ibid., p. 21.
91	28	Cruikshank, *Documentary History*, VI: 187, SW to Dearborn, 6 July 1813.
92	4	Ibid., p. 228, statement by FitzGibbon.
92	7	PAC, MG 24, F4, Bisshopp Papers, Hackett to Bisshopp, 20 July 1813; PAC, RG 8, vol. 679, pp. 108–9, Fulton to Prevost, 18 June 1813.
92	17	Cruikshank, *Documentary History*, VI: 228, statement by FitzGibbon.
92	30	Ibid., p. 228.
92	38	Ibid.
93	2	Ibid.
93	10	Cruikshank, *Documentary History*, VI: 223–24, Porter to Dearborn, 13 July 1813; "Burning of Buffalo," p. 263; "Village of Buffalo," pp. 92, 193.
94	22	Cruikshank, *Documentary History*, VI: 228–30, Sloan recollection.
94	31	PAC, MG 24, F4, Bisshopp Papers, Bisshopp to sister, 21 March 1813.
94	33	Ibid.
94	35	FitzGibbon, p. 111.
94	37	Ibid.
95	5	PAC, MG 24, F4, Bisshopp Papers, Hackett to Bisshopp, 20 July 1813.
95	18	Cruikshank, *Documentary History*, VI: 224, Porter to Dearborn, 13 July 1813.
95	21	Ibid., pp. 224–25.
95	33	PAC, MG 24, F4, Bisshopp Papers, Hackett to Bisshopp, 20 July 1813.
95	40	Ibid.
96	5	Ibid.
96	8	Cruikshank, *Documentary History*, VI: 230, Sloan recollection; FitzGibbon, p. 110.
96	9	PAC, MG 24, F4, Bisshopp Papers, Hackett to Bisshopp, 20 July 1813.
96	18	Ibid.
96	23	Firth, p. 316, *Kingston Gazette*, 10 Aug. 1813.
96	35	Ibid., p. 319, Allan to Baynes, 3 Aug. 1813.
97	3	Cruikshank, *Documentary History*, VI: 302, Powell and Strachan to Freer, 2 Aug. 1813.
97	22	Ibid., pp. 302–3.
97	28	Ibid., p. 303.
97	34	Firth, p. 319, Allan to Baynes, 3 Aug. 1813.
98	4	Ibid.; Cruikshank, *Documentary History*, VI: 303, Powell and Strachan to Freer, 2 Aug. 1813.
98	8	PAC, RG 5, A1, vol. 16, information of George Cullen, 16 Aug. 1813.
98	11	Ibid.; also Wm. Huff information, 7 Sept. 1813.
98	19	Firth, pp. 282–83, Ely Playter Diary.
98	22	Cruikshank, *Documentary History*, VI: 308–9, Chauncey to SN, 4 Aug. 1813.
99	3	PAC, RG 5, A1, vol. 16, Wm. Forrest information, 16 Aug. 1813; Jacob Anderson information, 18 Aug. 1813.
99	13	Ibid., Robinson to De Rottenburg, 16 Aug. 1813.

page line

The Siege of Fort Meigs

103   11   Harrison, II: 417, Harrison to SW, 15 April [?] 1813; E. Wood, "Journal," p. 371.

103   22   E. Wood, "Journal," pp. 378–79.

104   6   Harrison, II: 427, Harrison to SW, 21 April 1813.

104   10   Bourne, p. 41.

104   25   USNA, M221/57/S126, Shelby to SW, 20 March 1813; Harrison, II: 428, SW to Harrison, 27 April 1813.

104   27   Lossing, p. 475.

104   30   E. Wood, "Journal," p. 383; Harrison, II: 430.

105   2   Harrison, II: 416, Harrison to Shelby, 9 April 1813; E. Wood, "Journal," p. 377; USNA, M221/57/S126, Shelby to SW, 20 March 1813.

105   14   E. Wood, "Journal," p. 384.

105   17   Harrison, II: 416, Harrison to SW, 9 April 1813.

105   25   E. Wood, "Journal," p. 385.

106   1   Harrison, II: 430, Harrison to SW, 28 April 1813.

108   2   Richardson, *Richardson's War*, pp. 155–58.

108   14   Lossing, p. 478.

108   33   Ibid., p. 482.

109   23   Ibid.

109   24   Averill, p. 23.

109   38   E. Wood, "Journal," pp. 387–90.

110   7   Winter, pp. 122–23.

110   18   Richardson, *Eight Years*, p. 135.

110   34   Randall, p. 486.

111   32   Bourne, pp. 139–40, 148–49.

112   6   Ibid., pp. 148–49.

112   17   E. Wood, "Journal," pp. 389–90.

112   23   Lossing, p. 483.

112   35   Richardson, *Eight Years*, p. 136.

113   3   "Siege of Fort Meigs," p. 59.

113   6   McAfee, *History*, p. 262.

113   14   Howe, p. 865.

113   26   Ibid., p. 868, Lorraine's narrative.

113   37   Ibid., p. 869, Lorraine's narrative.

114   6   Ibid.

115   9   Bourne, pp. 151–53.

115   17   Howe, p. 869.

115   24   Harrison, II: 431, Harrison to SW, 5 May 1813; "Siege of Fort Meigs," p. 60; E. Wood, "Journal," p. 392.

115   29   E. Wood, "Journal," p. 393.

116   19   Howe, p. 865.

116   35   E. Wood, "Journal," p. 394; Harrison, II: 432, Harrison to SW, 5 May 1813; Lossing, p. 485.

117   12   Harrison, II: 432, Harrison to SW, 5 May 1813; McAfee, *History*, p. 265.

117   30   Howe, p. 869, Underwood narrative; Draper MSS, Tecumseh Papers, 6YY23, Underwood narrative.

117   36   Lossing, p. 480.

118   9   Draper MSS, Tecumseh Papers, 6YY23, Underwood narrative.

119   13   Brannan, pp. 158–59, Clay to Harrison, 13 May 1813.

119   17   Ibid.

119   18   Ibid.

119   21   Harrison, II: 443, Harrison to SW, 13 May 1813.

119   23   E. Wood, "Journal," p. 394.

119   30   Draper MSS, Tecumseh Papers, 6YY23, Underwood narrative.

120   6   Howe, p. 870, Underwood narrative.

120   10   Lossing, p. 485.

120   17   Richardson, *Eight Years*, p. 138.

120   25   Howe, p. 870; "General Orders," p. 11, General Order, 6 May 1813.

120   36   Bourne, p. 39.

121   36   Richardson, *Eight Years*, pp. 137–38; *Richardson's War*, pp. 150–51.

122   10   Howe, p. 870, Underwood narrative.

122   30   Ibid.

122   40   Draper MSS, Tecumseh Papers, 6YY22, Combs to Laughlin; Howe, p. 871, Underwood narrative.

123   5   Draper MSS, Tecumseh Papers, 6YY22, Combs to Laughlin.

123   8   *New Monthly Magazine*, December 1826.

123　17　Howe, p. 871, Underwood narrative.

123　35　Draper MSS, Tecumseh Papers, 6YY23, Underwood narrative.

124　3　Ibid., 6YY22, Combs to Laughlin.

125　3　Howe, p. 873, Underwood narrative.

125　11　Richardson, "Canadian Campaign," p. 169; *Richardson's War*, pp. 158–59.

125　25　Ibid.

126　7　Lossing, p. 480.

126　18　Ibid., pp. 487–88; Richardson, *Richardson's War*, pp. 152–53; Brannan, pp. 152–54, Harrison to Armstrong, 9 May 1813; E. Wood, "Journal," p. 401.

126　30　W. Wood, SBD, II: 35, Procter to Prevost, 14 May 1813.

126　35　Ibid.; Richardson, *Richardson's War*, p. 160.

126　40　Richardson, *Richardson's War*, pp. 160–61.

127　8　W. Wood, SBD, II: 35, Procter to Prevost, 14 May 1813.

127　11　Brannan, p. 156, Harrison to SW, 13 May 1813.

127　16　W. Wood, SBD, II: 39, General Order, 21 May 1813.

127　21　"General Orders," p. 13, General Order, 9 May 1813.

127　28　Ibid., pp. 15–16.

The Contest for Lake Erie

132　20　Metcalf, p. 95, Elliott to Chauncey, 11 Oct. 1812.

132　24　Rosenberg, pp. 55–56.

133　3　Parsons, *Battle*, p. 33.

133　11　Dutton, p. 209.

133　15　Snow, p. 13.

133　22　RIHS, Parsons Diary, 13–15 June 1813.

134　2　W. Dobbins, *History*, p. 322.

134　5　Ibid.; W. Wood, SBD, II: 246, Barclay to Vincent, 17 June 1813.

135　1　Rosenberg, p. 38.

135　4　Ibid., pp. 38–41.

135　5　Ibid., pp. 39–40.

135　18　Ibid., p. 24.

136　10　PAC, RG 8, vol. 679, p. 177, Procter to McDouall, 4 July 1813; ibid., pp. 181–86, Procter to Prevost, 4 July 1813.

136　15　W. Wood, SBD, II: 245–46, Barclay to Vincent, 17 June 1813.

136　27　PAC, RG 8, vol. 679, p. 177, Procter to McDouall, 4 July 1813; ibid., p. 181, Procter to Prevost, 4 July 1813.

136　32　W. Wood, SBD, II: 248–49, Barclay to Procter, 29 June 1813; ibid., p. 259, Barclay to Prevost, 16 July 1813.

136　36　Ibid., p. 253, Procter to Prevost, 11 July 1813.

137　8　Ibid.

137　13　Ibid.

137　32　Cruikshank, *Documentary History*, VI: 256, Prevost to Bathurst, 20 July 1813; PAC, MG 24, F13, Chauncey Papers, Chauncey to SN, 7 May 1813.

137　35　W. Wood, SBD, II: 251, Prevost to Procter, 11 July 1813.

137　37　PAC, RG 8, vol. 679, p. 177, Procter to McDouall, 4 July 1813.

138　1　W. Wood, SBD, II: 255, Prevost to Procter, 12 July 1813.

138　9　Ibid., p. 44, Procter to Prevost, 9 Aug. 1813.

138　16　Ibid.

138　25　Richardson, *Eight Years*, p. 140.

138　35　Harrison, II: 474, Clay to Harrison, 20 June 1813; "General Orders," pp. 21–22, General Order, 21 July 1813; Howe, p. 878.

139　3　Harrison, II: 494, Harrison to SW, 23 July 1813.

139　12　Richardson, *Eight Years*, pp. 140–41; Averill, p. 31.

139　19　Richardson, *Eight Years*, pp. 140–41; *Richardson's War*, p. 178.

139　30　Howe, p. 878; Harrison, II: 499, Clay to Harrison, 26 July 1813.

139　34　W. Wood, SBD, II: 44–45, Procter to Prevost, 9 Aug. 1813; Richardson, *Richardson's War*, pp. 178–79.

140　5　McAfee, *History*, p. 322.

page line
140   9   Ibid.
140   13   Harrison, II: 502, Harrison to Croghan, 29 July 1813.
140   19   McAfee, *History*, pp. 322–23.
140   21   Charles Williams, "George Croghan," p. 388.
140   29   Harrison, II: 503, Croghan to Harrison, 30 July 1813.
141   2   Filson Club, Scrapbook MSS B1/F489, Wright to Duncan, 7 May 1869.
141   19   McAfee, *History*, pp. 323–24.
141   32   LC, Eustis Papers, Harrison to Eustis, 6 Jan. 1812.
141   38   Harrison, II: 528, Croghan to editor of *Liberty Hall*, 27 Aug. 1813.
142   10   Ibid., p. 528; Charles Williams, "George Croghan," p. 387.
142   16   Harrison, II: 510, Harrison to SW, 4 Aug. 1813.
142   17   McAfee, *History*, p. 324.
142   23   Harrison, II: 512, Harrison to SW, 4 Aug. 1813.
142   24   Ibid., p. 514, Croghan to Harrison, 5 Aug. 1813; ibid., p. 528, Croghan to editor of *Liberty Hall*, 27 Aug. 1813.
142   27   W. Wood, SBD, II: 45, Procter to Prevost, 9 Aug. 1813.
142   34   Ibid.
143   7   Ibid.
143   15   Harrison, II: 512–13, Harrison to SW, 4 Aug. 1813.
143   19   Lossing, p. 501.
143   22   Harrison, II: 513, Harrison to SW, 4 Aug. 1813.
143   24   Lossing, p. 501.
143   31   *Niles Register*, 4 Sept. 1813.
143   40   McAfee, *History*, pp. 325–26.
144   8   Harrison, II: 515, Croghan to Harrison, 5 Aug. 1813; Filson Club, Scrapbook MSS B1/F489, Wright to Duncan, 7 May 1869.
144   16   *Niles Register*, 4 Sept. 1813.
144   20   Richardson, *Richardson's War*, pp. 179–80.
144   37   *Niles Register*, 4 Sept. 1813.
145   1   Byfield, p. 365.
145   9   Lossing, p. 503.
145   12   Ibid.
145   15   Richardson, *Richardson's War*, p. 180.

page line
145   20   Byfield, p. 365.
145   23   *Niles Register*, 4 Sept. 1813.
145   24   Filson Club, Scrapbook MSS B1/F489, Wright to Duncan, 7 May 1869.
146   13   Byfield, pp. 365–66.
146   37   Beasley, pp. 23–24.
146   40   *Niles Register*, 4 Sept. 1813.
147   7   Harrison, II: 512, Harrison to SW, 4 Aug. 1813.
148   17   Quoted in Mackenzie, *Perry*, p. 122.
148   19   Ibid., pp. 125–26.
148   21   Ibid., p. 126.
148   24   Ibid., pp. 126–27; Dodge, p. 18; Brown, p. 93.
148   30   Dutton, p. 100.
148   37   Quoted in Snow, p. 19.
149   1   W. Dobbins, *History*, p. 390, Champlin narrative.
149   10   Rosenberg, pp. 50–51.
149   15   W. Dobbins, *History*, p. 329.
149   24   Rosenberg, p. 51.
149   31   Ibid., pp. 51–52; W. Dobbins, *History*, p. 390, Champlin narrative.
149   39   Lossing, p. 515.
150   5   W. Dobbins, *History*, p. 331.
150   13   Parsons, "Brief Sketches," p. 176.
150   20   Mackenzie, *Perry*, pp. 139–40.
150   28   Quoted in Mackenzie, *Perry*, p. 142.
151   3   Ibid., pp. 142–43.
151   7   Ibid., p. 146.
151   15   Ibid., pp. 139–40.
151   22   *Documents in Relation to the Differences*, p. 33, Wm. Taylor's affidavit.
151   28   Dutton, p. 115.
151   36   Harrison, II: 525, Harrison to SW, 22 Aug. 1813; Dutton, p. 119.
152   2   Dutton, p. 123; Parsons, *Battle*, pp. 7–8.
152   11   Mackenzie, *Perry*, pp. 155–56.
152   16   Ibid., pp. 157–58.
152   18   W. Dobbins, *History*, pp. 340–41.
152   27   Dutton, p. 140.
152   31   Ibid., p. 142; W. Dobbins, *History*, p. 342.
152   39   Dutton, p. 142.

page	line	
153	16	Mackenzie, *Perry*, p. 169; W. Dobbins, *History*, p. 342.
153	29	W. Dobbins, *History*, p. 342.
153	32	Dutton, p. 143.
154	1	W. Wood, SBD, II: 274, Barclay to Yeo, 12 Sept. 1813.
154	4	Ibid., pp. 303–4, Barclay narrative.
154	8	Ibid., p. 274, Barclay to Yeo, 12 Sept. 1813.
154	15	Cruikshank, *Documentary History*, VII: 95–96, Procter to Freer, 3 Sept. 1813.
154	17	W. Wood, SBD, II: 266, Procter to Prevost, 29 Aug. 1813.
154	20	Ibid., pp. 268–69, Barclay to Yeo, 1 Sept. 1813.
154	30	Cruikshank, *Documentary History*, VII: 49, Prevost to Procter, 22 Aug. 1813.
154	34	W. Wood, SBD, II: 264, Procter to Prevost, 26 Aug. 1813.
154	37	Ibid., p. 265.
155	5	Cruikshank, "Contest for...Lake Erie," p. 377.
155	11	Ibid.
156	3	Dodge, pp. 15–19.
156	7	Ibid., p. 17.
156	11	Ibid., p. 8.
156	32	A.B. Burt, "Barclay," p. 170.
156	35	Ibid.
157	11	W. Wood, SBD, II: 298, Barclay narrative.
157	17	W. Dobbins, *History*, p. 343.
157	30	Maclay, I: 504.
158	5	Parsons, *Battle*, p. 13.
158	14	Burges, pp. 121–22, Parsons to Perry.
158	18	Dodge, p. 20.
158	27	Cooper, *History of the Navy*, II: 453–54; Lossing, pp. 521–22; *Documents in Relation to the Differences*, pp. 31–32, Wm. Taylor's affidavit.
158	33	J. Elliott, *Speech*, p. 6.
159	3	Ibid.; Mackenzie, *Perry*, pp. 173–74.
159	8	Lossing, p. 520.
159	20	Mackenzie, *Perry*, p. 175.
160	7	Bunnell, p. 133.
160	11	Burges, p. 122, Parsons to Perry.
160	17	Mackenzie, *Perry*, p. 176.
160	26	Ibid.; Burges, p. 122, Parsons to Perry.
160	29	Mackenzie, *Perry*, p. 177.
160	30	Lossing, p. 522.
160	31	Parsons, *Battle*, p. 13.
160	40	Paullin, p. 180, Yarnell testimony.
161	12	W. Wood, SBD, II: 275, Barclay to Yeo, 12 Sept. 1813; *Documents in Relation to the Differences*, pp. 31–32, Wm. Taylor's affidavit; Mackenzie, *Perry*, p. 178.
161	31	W. Wood, SBD, II: 275, Barclay to Yeo, 12 Sept. 1813.
162	10	Mackenzie, *Perry*, pp. 185–86; Parsons, "Brief Sketches," pp. 173–74; Parsons, *Battle*, p. 12.
162	19	Parsons, *Battle*, p. 13.
162	28	Lossing, pp. 524–25.
162	31	Ibid.
163	5	Parsons, "Brief Sketches," pp. 173–74, 176.
163	10	Parsons, "Surgical Account," p. 314.
163	18	Ibid.
163	22	Ibid.
163	34	Bunnell, p. 117.
163	37	Ibid.
164	2	Parsons, *Battle*, p. 12.
164	5	Dutton, pp. 154–55.
164	16	Maclay, p. 516; Cruikshank, "Contest for...Lake Erie," p. 383.
164	23	Paullin, pp. 180–81, Yarnell testimony; *Documents in Relation to the Differences*, p. 17, Lt. Turner's affidavit; ibid., p. 18, Parsons's affidavit; ibid., p. 25, Lt. Stevens's affidavit.
165	8	Dutton, p. 156.
165	21	Bunnell, pp. 114–15; Brown, p. 90.
165	22	Paullin, pp. 84–85, list of killed and wounded; Emerson, pp. 233–35, muster roll of fleet.
165	29	*Documents in Relation to the Differences*, p. 27, Lt. Champlin's affidavit.
165	37	Dutton, p. 169; W. Wood, SBD, II: 318, George Young testimony.

page	line	
_166_	_15_	Paullin, p. 181, Yarnell testimony; Cleveland City Council, _Inauguration_, p. 84, Chapman narrative; _Documents in Relation to the Differences_, p. 26, Forrest to ?, 29 Jan. 1821; BHS, A.C. Goodyear Collection, box 1, Fairchild to Lossing, 12 Oct. 1853.
_166_	_18_	Parsons, "Surgical Account," p. 314.
_166_	_21_	Paullin, p. 80, Perry to Jones, 13 Sept. 1813.
_166_	_31_	Dutton, pp. 160–61.
_166_	_40_	Dutton, p. 161; _Documents in Relation to the Differences_, p. 26, Lt. Stevens's affidavit; ibid., p. 28, Lt. Champlin's affidavit.
_167_	_16_	W. Wood, SBD, II: 276, Barclay to Yeo, 12 Sept. 1813; Mackenzie, _Perry_, p. 195.
_168_	_5_	Mackenzie, _Perry_, pp. 192–93; J. Elliott, _Speech_, p. 8; W. Wood, SBD, II: 276, Barclay to Yeo, 12 Sept. 1813.
_168_	_9_	Bunnell, p. 115.
_168_	_17_	W. Wood, SBD, II: 276, Barclay to Yeo, 12 Sept. 1813.
_168_	_22_	Lossing, p. 528.
_168_	_29_	J. Elliott, _Speech_, p. 8.
_168_	_31_	Parsons, _Battle_, p. 13.
_169_	_2_	J. Elliott, _Speech_, p. 8.
_169_	_4_	Cooper, _History of the Navy_, II: 467n.
_169_	_14_	Paullin, p. 43, Perry to Harrison, 10 Sept. 1813.
_170_	_4_	Ibid., p. 49, Perry to Jones, 10 Sept. 1813.
_170_	_8_	W. Wood, SBD, II: 272, Procter to de Rottenberg, 12 Sept. 1813.
_170_	_14_	Lossing, p. 533.
_170_	_16_	Brown, p. 88.
_170_	_26_	Parsons, _Battle_, p. 14; W. Dobbins, _History_, p. 352.
_171_	_5_	Parsons, _Battle_, p. 14; Parsons, "Surgical Account," p. 315.
_171_	_11_	Dutton, p. 177.
_171_	_16_	Mackenzie, _Perry_, p. 280.
_171_	_22_	A.B. Burt, "Barclay," p. 177.
_171_	_24_	Ibid.
_171_	_33_	Mackenzie, _Perry_, p. 220.
_171_	_37_	Parsons, _Battle_, p. 18.
_172_	_7_	Paullin, pp. 80–82, Perry to Jones, 13 Sept. 1813.
_172_	_11_	_Documents in Relation to the Differences_, p. 10, charges against Perry.
_172_	_13_	Parsons, _Battle_, p. 17.
_172_	_16_	_Documents in Relation to the Differences_, p. 22, Perry to Elliott, 18 June 1818.
_172_	_19_	Mackenzie, _Perry_, p. 218, Elliott to Perry, 19 Sept. 1813.
_172_	_29_	Ibid., pp. 218–19, Perry to Elliott, 19 Sept. 1813.
_173_	_3_	_Documents in Relation to the Differences_, pp. 17–18, Lt. Turner's affidavit.
_173_	_12_	ASPNA, I: 566, 570, 572.

Retreat on the Thames

page	line	
_177_	_3_	PRO, WO71/243, Procter court martial, Warburton testimony.
_177_	_9_	Drake, p. 187.
_178_	_17_	Ibid., p. 186.
_178_	_40_	PRO, WO71/243, Procter court martial, Wm. Jones testimony.
_179_	_2_	Ibid.; ibid., Hall testimony.
_179_	_27_	Drake, p. 187.
_180_	_11_	PRO, WO71/243, Procter court martial, appendix 7, Tecumseh's speech, 15 Sept. 1813.
_180_	_14_	Ibid.
_180_	_27_	Ibid.
_180_	_34_	Ibid.
_180_	_38_	Ibid., Hall testimony.
_181_	_14_	Hatch, p. 116.
_181_	_33_	PRO, WO71/243, Procter court martial, Warburton testimony.
_182_	_9_	Ibid., App. 26, Baynes to Procter, 18 Sept. 1813.
_182_	_12_	W. Wood, SBD, II: 282, Harvey to Procter, 17 Sept. 1813.
_182_	_34_	Richardson, "Canadian Campaign," p. 252.
_183_	_3_	PRO, WO71/243, Procter court martial, Hall testimony.
_183_	_6_	Ibid., Warburton testimony.
_183_	_10_	Ibid., Hall testimony.
_183_	_13_	Ibid., Warburton testimony.
_183_	_15_	Drake, p. 191.
_183_	_20_	PRO, WO71/243, Procter court martial, Evans testimony.

page	line	
183	22	Horsman, *Matthew Elliott*, p. 212.
183	26	PRO, WO71/243, Procter court martial, Dixon testimony.
184	6	Ibid., Warburton testimony, Evans testimony.
184	12	Quaife, *War on the Detroit*, p. 141.
184	27	Ibid., pp. 141–42.
184	33	Harrison, II: 555, Harrison to SW, 30 Sept. 1813.
185	1	PRO, WO71/243, Procter court martial, Chambers testimony, Hall testimony.
185	5	Ibid., Warburton testimony.
185	10	Ibid.
185	17	W. Wood, SBD, II: 283, Harvey to Procter, 17 Sept. 1813.
185	21	Ibid., p. 285, Prevost to Procter, 6 Oct. 1813.
186	17	PRO, WO71/243, Procter court martial, Dixon testimony.
186	21	Ibid.
187	13	McAfee, "Papers," 27 and 28 Sept. 1813.
187	28	Ibid., 19 May 1813.
188	5	Meyer, p. 81.
188	8	Ibid.
188	9	USNA, M221/54/J148, Johnson to SW, 16 April 1813.
188	14	"Visit," p. 202.
188	18	McAfee, "Papers," 26 July 1813.
188	26	Ibid., *passim*.
188	28	"Visit," p. 202.
188	35	McAfee, "Papers," 30 Sept. 1813; Sholes, pp. 523–24.
189	2	Harrison, II: 550–51, Harrison to SW, 27 Sept. 1813; ibid., p. 550, Harrison to Meigs, 27 Sept. 1813.
189	5	Ibid., p. 555, Harrison to SW, 30 Sept. 1813.
189	15	Ibid., p. 493, Harrison to Shelby, 20 July 1813.
189	20	Ibid.
189	33	McAfee, *History*, pp. 380–81.
189	38	Harrison, II: 558, Harrison to SW, 9 Oct. 1813.
190	2	McAfee, *History*, p. 364.
190	9	Ibid., p. 382.
190	20	"Visit," p. 203.
190	26	McAfee, "Papers," 2 Oct. 1813.
190	34	McAfee, *History*, p. 383; Harrison, II: 558, Harrison to SW, 9 Oct. 1813.
190	39	Harrison, II: 558, Harrison to SW, 9 Oct. 1813.
191	2	Ibid.
191	17	PRO, WO71/243, Procter court martial, Crowther testimony.
191	25	Ibid., Warburton testimony.
191	33	Ibid.; ibid., Caldwell and Chambers testimony.
192	16	Ibid., Chambers testimony.
192	18	Ibid., Warburton testimony.
192	20	Tucker, *Tecumseh*, p. 307.
192	28	Richardson, *Richardson's War*, p. 226.
192	33	PRO, WO71/243, Procter court martial, Warburton testimony.
193	4	Ibid.; ibid., Evans, Chambers, Crowther testimony; Appendix 6, Procter defence.
193	11	Ibid., Evans testimony.
193	34	Holmes, p. 8.
194	2	Lauriston, p. 89.
194	9	Holmes, p. 8.
194	18	Arnold, p. 3.
194	25	Lossing, p. 560.
194	32	Tucker, *Tecumseh*, p. 309.
195	23	Richardson, *Richardson's War*, p. 232, Bullock to friend, 6 Dec. 1813; PRO, WO71/243, Procter court martial, Gilmore and Crowther testimony.
195	27	Ibid., Evans and Hall testimony; Richardson, *Richardson's War*, p. 230, Bullock to friend, 6 Dec. 1813; W. Wood, SBD, II: 323–27, Procter to De Rottenburg, 23 Oct. 1813.
195	31	PRO, WO71/243, Procter court martial, Warburton testimony.
196	4	W. Wood, SBD, II: 323–27, Procter to De Rottenberg, 23 Oct. 1813.
196	22	Richardson, *Richardson's War*, p. 232.
196	27	Ibid., pp. 232–33.
197	4	PRO, WO71/243, Procter court martial, Evans testimony.
197	6	Ibid., Hall testimony.

The Assault on Montreal

page	line	
229	25	Wilkinson, III, Thorn, Ross, and Eustis testimony; ASPMA, I: 474, Wilkinson to Armstrong, 1 Nov. 1813.
229	31	BHS, Hanks Memoir, p. 12.
229	36	Cruikshank, *Documentary History*, IV: 104, Chauncey to SN, 30 Oct. 1813.
230	4	ASPMA, I: 477, Wilkinson journal.
230	8	Cruikshank, *Documentary History*, IV: 105, Chauncey to SN, 30 Oct. 1813.
230	14	Ibid., p. 123, Mulcaster to Yeo, 2 Nov. 1813.
230	16	Ibid., p. 155, Chauncey to SN, 11 Nov. 1813.
231	3	ASPMA, I: 477, Wilkinson journal, 6 Nov. 1813.
231	7	W. Wood, SBD, II: 441, Wilkinson proclamation, 6 Nov. 1813.
231	20	Wilkinson, III: 129, Lewis testimony.
232	7	ASPMA, I: 477, Wilkinson journal, 6 Nov. 1813; Lossing, p. 550.
232	15	Scott, p. 107.
232	28	Swift, *Memoirs*, 6 Nov. 1813; Wilkinson, III, Pinkney testimony.
232	40	Wilkinson, III: 211–12, App. 13; Swift, *Memoirs*, 6 Nov. 1813.
233	5	ASPMA, I: 477, Wilkinson journal, 7 Nov. 1813.
233	20	Ibid., 8 Nov. 1813; Sellar, *U.S. Campaign*, p. 17; Wilkinson, III, App. 24, council of war, 8 Nov. 1813.
233	25	Wilkinson, III, App. 24, council of war, 8 Nov. 1813.
233	31	ASPMA, I: 477–78, Wilkinson journal, 8–9 Nov. 1813; ibid., General Order, 10 Nov. 1813.
234	5	ASPMA, I: 475, Wilkinson to SW, 16 Nov. 1813; ibid., p. 478, Wilkinson Journal, 10 Nov. 1813; Wilkinson, III, Lee testimony; BHS, Hanks Memoir, p. 13.
234	15	Way, p. 203.
234	22	Smart, Sewell narrative, 11 Nov. 1860.
237	2	USNA, M221/54/L162, Lewis to SW, 14 Nov. 1813; Wilkinson, III, Bull and Pinkney testimony; Delafield, p. 99.
237	10	ASPMA, I: 475, Wilkinson to SW, 16 Nov. 1813.
237	18	Wilkinson, III, Boyd testimony.
237	29	DAB.
237	39	Salisbury, n.p.
238	3	Smart, Sewell narrative, 11 Nov. 1860.
239	9	Way, p. 213.
239	17	Cruikshank, *Documentary History*, IV: 166, memo on Plenderleath, 1 Jan. 1854.
239	21	Ibid.
239	33	Sellar, *U.S. Campaign*, p. 23.
239	38	W. Wood, SBD, II: 442, Morrison to De Rottenburg, 12 Nov. 1813.
240	17	Smart, Sewell narrative, 11 Nov. 1860.
240	22	Sellar, *U.S. Campaign*, p. 24.
240	29	Wilkinson, III, Pinkney testimony.
241	10	Brannan, p. 268, Boyd to Wilkinson, 12 Nov. 1813.
241	15	Cruikshank, *Documentary History*, IV: 194, Wilkinson to SW, 18 Nov. 1813.
241	19	ASPMA, I: 475–76, Wilkinson to SW, 16 Nov. 1813.
241	28	Ibid., p. 462, Hampton to Wilkinson, 8 Nov. 1813.
241	36	Ibid., p. 476, Wilkinson to SW, 16 Nov. 1813.
242	2	Ibid., p. 479, General Order, 13 Nov. 1813.
242	8	Ibid., p. 478, Wilkinson to SW, 17 Nov. 1813; Wilkinson, III, Wilkinson to SW, 24 Nov. 1813.
242	15	Wilkinson, III, App. 9, Ross to Inspector General.
242	17	BHS, Hanks Memoir, p. 14.
242	20	Wilkinson, III, App. 9, note by Ross.
242	22	Ibid.
242	24	Brannan, p. 286, Izard to Wilkinson, 6 Dec. 1813.
242	27	Sellar, *U.S. Campaign*, p. 28.

page	*line*	
243	*10*	PAC, RG 19 E5A, claims Numbers 380, 390, 396, 397, 400, 409, 430, 437, 459.
243	*16*	Dunlop, p. 23.

The Niagara in Flames

247	*8*	Unless otherwise noted, source for this section is W. Wood, SBD, III, pt. 2, Merritt narrative.
250	*5*	McClure, p. 16.
250	*9*	Cruikshank, "Drummond's Campaign," p. 10.
250	*19*	McClure, p. 16.
251	*28*	Kirby, p. 4.
252	*5*	Cruikshank, *Documentary History*, IV: 264, McClure to Tompkins, 10 Dec. 1813; ibid., IX: 49, McClure to public.
252	*8*	Ibid., IV: 264, McClure to Tompkins, 10 Dec. 1813.
252	*12*	Ibid.
252	*14*	McClure, pp. 17, 18.
252	*21*	ASPMA, I: 484, Armstrong to McClure, 4 Oct. 1813.
252	*38*	Chapin, pp. 22–23; Cruikshank, *Documentary History*, IX: 122, Chapin to public.
255	*20*	"Reminiscences of American Occupation," p. 20.
255	*35*	Ibid., pp. 21–22.
255	*40*	Ibid., p. 21.
256	*10*	Ibid., p. 20; PAC, RG 19 E5A, vol. 3740, Dickson claim.
256	*18*	W. Wood, SBD, III, pt. 3: 607–8, Merritt narrative.
256	*20*	Ibid., p. 607.
256	*29*	Cruikshank, *Documentary History*, IV: 270, Murray to Vincent, 12 Dec. 1813; ibid., p. 275, Murray to Vincent, 13 Dec. 1813.
256	*37*	W. Wood, SBD, III, pt. 2: 607, Merritt narrative; "Reminiscences of American Occupation," pp. 21, 24.
257	*16*	Kirby, p. 6.
257	*22*	Mather, p. 272.
257	*29*	W. Wood, SBD, III, pt. 2: 608–9, Merritt narrative.
258	*10*	Cruikshank, *Documentary History*, IX: 3, Harvey to Murray, 17 Dec. 1813; Kirby, p. 7.
258	*18*	Mather, p. 272.
258	*23*	Cruikshank, *Documentary History*, IX: 19, Driscoll narrative.
258	*34*	Ibid., VI: 270–71, General Order, 12 Dec. 1813.
259	*4*	Ibid., IX: 45, McClure to SW, 25 Dec. 1813.
259	*19*	Ibid., pp. 19–20, Driscoll narrative.
259	*28*	Ibid., p. 20.
259	*37*	Cruikshank, *Documentary History 1814*, pp. 298–99, Murray to Baynes, 17 April 1814.
259	*41*	Cruikshank, *Documentary History*, IX: 20, Driscoll narrative.
260	*8*	Ibid., p. 13, return of enemy's losses, 19 Dec. 1813; ibid., p. 14, General Order, 19 Dec. 1813.
260	*11*	W. Wood, SBD, II: 499, General Order, 24 Sept. 1814.
260	*16*	Ibid., p. 492, Drummond to Prevost, 20 Dec. 1813.
260	*31*	Cruikshank, *Documentary History*, IX: 14, Riall to Drummond, 19 Dec. 1813; "Military Service of 1813/14," pp. 102–3.
261	*20*	Clara Williams, pp. 315–22.
261	*31*	Cruikshank, *Documentary History*, IX: 31, *New York Evening Post*, 11 Jan. 1814.
261	*33*	Ibid., p. 46, McClure to Granger, 25 Dec. 1813.
261	*35*	Ibid., pp. 45–46, McClure to SW, 25 Dec. 1813; ibid., pp. 52–53, Spencer to Tompkins, 26 Dec. 1813.
261	*40*	Ibid., p. 53, Spencer to Tompkins, 26 Dec. 1813; ibid., p. 61, McClure to Granger, 28 Dec. 1813.
262	*28*	Byfield, pp. 373–74.
263	*30*	Lossing, p. 637.
264	*15*	"Village of Buffalo," p. 198; "Burning of Buffalo," p. 342.
264	*29*	"Burning of Buffalo," p. 338; Ketchum, p. 303; Johnson, p. 260.
264	*36*	Johnson, p. 251.
265	*3*	Wilner, I: 248.
265	*14*	"Burning of Buffalo," p. 335; "Village of Buffalo," p. 197.

284 37 Ibid., p. 910, Crawford to Clay, 15 May 1814.

285 3 Ibid., p. 914, Hughes to Clay, 16 May 1814.

285 32 Ibid., p. 925, Clay to Russell, 27 May 1814; ibid., p. 913, Hughes to Clay, 16 May 1814.

286 5 Ibid., p. 921, Russell to Clay, 22 May 1814.

287 4 Cruikshank, "Contest for...Lake Ontario in 1814," p. 125.

288 7 Ibid., passim.

288 36 Hanks, p. 55.

290 38 Ibid.

291 4 C. Elliott, Scott, p. 108.

291 6 Ibid., p. 147.

291 10 Scott, p. 19.

291 24 USNA, M221/57/S489, Scott to SW, 17 May 1814.

292 2 Cruikshank, "John Beverley Robinson," pp. 211–12.

292 5 Cruikshank, Documentary History 1814, pp. 330–31, return of property destroyed; ibid., p. 331, Talbot to Loyal and Patriotic Society.

292 16 Ibid., pp. 414–15, Cochrane to Croker, 18 July 1814.

292 26 Richardson, "Canadian Campaign," pp. 538–51, passim.

295 25 PAC, RG 5, A1, vol. 16, p. 6845, Robinson to Loring, 18 June 1814.

296 28 PAO, Robinson Papers, Strachan to Robinson, 2 June 1814.

296 33 PAC, RG 5, A1, vol. 16, p. 6846, Robinson to Loring, 18 June 1814.

296 37 Robinson, Life, p. 56, J.B. Robinson narrative.

297 4 PAC, RG 5, A1, vol. 16, p. 6852, Robinson to Loring, 18 June 1814.

297 22 Ibid., p. 6851.

297 27 Ibid., p. 6847.

297 30 PAC, RG 5, A1, vol. 16, pp. 6872–73, Warren to Loring, 20 June 1814.

298 18 PAO, RG 22/05/12a, Criminal Assize Minute Book B, 21 June 1814.

298 22 PAC, RG 5, A1, vol. 16, Scott to Drummond, 14 July 1814.

298 24 Riddell, "Ancaster 'Bloody Assize,'" p. 214, Scott to Drummond, 28 June 1814.

298 29 PAC, RG 5, A1, vol. 16, Scott to Drummond, 5 July 1814.

298 31 Ibid., Scott to Drummond, 8 July 1814.

The Struggle for the Fur Country

303 8 "Copies of Papers," pp. 575–76, 583–85.

303 20 PAC, CO42/157/7–10, Prevost to Bathurst, 10 July 1814.

304 13 W. Wood, SBD, III, pt. 1: 269, Bullock to Loring, 26 Feb. 1814.

304 31 Cruikshank, "Nancy," p. 79.

304 34 Tohill, p. 110.

305 20 PAC, RG 8, vol. 257, p. 45, Prevost to Bathurst, 26 Jan. 1814.

306 9 Tohill, p. 108.

306 24 PAC, CO42/157/7–10, Prevost to Bathurst, encl. McDouall speech to Indians.

306 27 PAC, RG 8, vol. 257, p. 287, Dickson to Freer, 18 June 1814.

307 15 W. Wood, SBD, III, pt. 1: 254, McDouall to Drummond, 16 July 1814.

307 27 Ibid., p. 255.

307 32 Grignon, p. 272.

308 16 Niles Register, 10 Sept. 1814, Croghan to SW, 9 Aug. 1814.

308 19 Ibid.

308 25 Van Fleet, pp. 108–9.

308 29 W. Wood, SBD, III, pt. 1: 278, McDouall to Prevost, 14 Aug. 1814.

308 37 Ibid.

308 38 Ibid., p. 275.

308 40 Cruikshank, "Nancy," p. 96, McDouall to Drummond, 17 July 1814.

309 10 May, p. 34; Van Fleet, p. 112.

309 15 Niles Register, 10 Sept. 1814, Croghan to SW, 9 Aug. 1814.

309 22 Ibid.

309 32 Van Fleet, p. 221.

309 36 Niles Register, 10 Sept. 1814, Croghan to SW, 9 Aug. 1814.

page line

310 *19* W. Wood, SBD, III, pt. 1:
274–75, McDouall to Prevost,
14 Aug. 1814.

310 *29* May, pp. 36–37.

310 *40* Ibid.

311 *9* *Niles Register*, 10 Sept. 1814,
Croghan to SW, 9 Aug. 1814.

311 *10* Cruikshank, "Nancy," p. 105,
return of killed and wounded, 11
Aug. 1814.

311 *17* Ibid., pp. 101–3, Sinclair to SN,
9 Aug. 1814; Van Fleet, p. 58;
May, p. 38.

311 *20* Cruikshank, "Nancy," pp.
101–3, Sinclair to SN, 9 Aug.
1814.

311 *29* Ibid.

312 *7* Cruikshank, "Battle of Fort
George," p. 60.

312 *15* Cruikshank, "Nancy," p. 84.

312 *26* *Niles Register*, 24 Sept. 1814,
Croghan to McArthur, 23 Aug.
1814.

312 *36* Ibid., 12 Nov. 1814, Sinclair to
SN, 15 Aug. 1815.

313 *12* Cruikshank, "Nancy," pp.
120–21, Worsley to Yeo, 15
Sept. 1814.

313 *17* Ibid.; May, p. 39.

314 *5* W. Wood, SBD, III, pt. 1:
277–78, McDouall to Drum-
mond, 9 Sept. 1814.

314 *36* Cruikshank, "Nancy," pp.
120–23, Worsley to Yeo, 15
Sept. 1814; W. Wood, SBD, III,
pt. 1: 279, Bulger to McDouall,
7 Sept. 1814.

The Last Invasion

317 *10* Scott, pp. 122–23.

317 *18* Cruikshank, *Documentary History 1814*, p. 403, SW to Brown,
10 June 1814.

317 *23* Scott, pp. 121–22.

318 *3* Cruikshank, *Documents Relating
to the Invasion...1814*, p. 78,
Brown memo, 9 July 1814.

318 *10* Ibid., pp. 72, 77; Elliott, *Scott*,
p. 56.

318 *15* Cruikshank, *Documentary History
1814*, p. 26, Porter to Tompkins,
3 July 1814; Scott, p. 123.

page line

318 *18* BHS, Hanks Memoir, p. 40.

318 *28* Scott, pp. 125–26.

319 *19* Cruikshank, *Documentary History 1814*, p. 408, monthly
return, Gen. Brown's division,
1 July 1814.

319 *29* Treat, p. 45, Everett testimony.

320 *3* Ibid., pp. 10, 19, 20.

320 *21* Ibid., p. 20.

320 *25* Ibid., p. 20 and *passim*; Cruikshank, *Documentary History
1814*, p. 39, Brown to SW, 7
July 1814.

321 *2* J.L. Babcock, "Campaign of
1814," p. 126, Porter to Stone,
26 May 1840.

321 *5* Ibid.

321 *14* Cruikshank, *Documentary History 1814*, p. 473, Jesup narrative; ibid., p. 372, McMullen
narrative.

321 *19* J.L. Babcock, "Campaign of
1814," p. 126, Porter to Stone,
26 May 1840.

321 *32* White, pp. 14, 15.

321 *39* W. Wood, SBD, III, pt. 1:
115–16, Riall to Drummond,
6 July 1814.

322 *5* Ibid., III, pt. 2: 613, Merritt
narrative.

322 *12* Ibid., III, pt. 1: 115, Riall to
Drummond, 6 July 1814; ibid.,
part 2, p. 615, Merritt narrative.

322 *26* Hay, p. 70.

322 *35* Ibid., pp. 72–73.

323 *4* J.L. Babcock, "Campaign of
1814," p. 127, Porter to Stone,
26 May 1840.

323 *8* Ibid., p. 129.

324 *4* White, pp. 17, 18.

324 *13* Scott, pp. 127–28; Cruikshank,
*Documents Relating to the Inva-
sion...1814*, p. 75, Brown memo.

324 *16* Ibid., p. 128.

324 *19* Hanks, p. 56.

324 *28* Scott, pp. 128–29.

324 *32* Ibid.

324 *36* Ibid., p. 127.

325 *5* Hanks, p. 56.

325 *9* C. Elliott, *Scott*, p. 161.

325 *14* Ibid., pp. 161–62.

page	line	
325	19	Cruikshank, *Documents Relating to the Invasion...1814*, p. 75, Brown memo; Treat, p. 13.
325	25	Cruikshank, *Documentary History 1814*, p. 45, Scott to Adj. Gen., 15 July 1814.
326	4	Hay, pp. 73, 74.
326	9	Scott, p. 134.
326	18	W. Wood, SBD, III, pt. 1, Riall to Drummond, 6 July 1814; ibid., p. 119, return of killed and wounded, 5 July 1814; Cruikshank, "Lundy's Lane," p. 19.
326	24	W. Wood, SBD, III, pt. 1: 119, return of killed and wounded, 5 July 1814; Cruikshank, *Documentary History 1814*, p. 43, return of killed and wounded.
327	18	White, pp. 20–23.
327	40	Ibid., pp. 23–27.
328	3	W. Wood, SBD, III, pt. 1: 126, Riall to Drummond, 9 July 1814; ibid., p. 128, Drummond to Prevost, 13 July 1814.
328	9	Ibid., pp. 127–28.
328	24	White, pp. 27–28.
329	8	Douglass, pp. 1, 5.
329	13	Hanks, p. 56.
329	24	Cruikshank, *Documents Relating to the Invasion...1814*, p. 77, Brown memo; *Documentary History 1814*, p. 475, Jesup narrative.
329	36	Cruikshank, *Documentary History 1814*, p. 64, Brown to Chauncey, 13 July 1814.
330	6	Cruikshank, *Documents Relating to the Invasion...1814*, Brown to Armstrong, 25 July 1814; "Lundy's Lane," p. 22; *Documentary History 1814*, p. 126, Chauncey to SN, 10 Aug. 1814.
330	24	Cruikshank, *Documents Relating to the Invasion...1814*, pp. 72–73, memorial of David Secord; ibid., p. 74, Stone to Tompkins, 25 July 1814.
330	29	Davis, p. 143.
330	36	Hanks, p. 57.
331	3	Cruikshank, *Documentary History 1814*, p. 87, Brown to SW, 25 July 1814.
331	5	Cruikshank, "Lundy's Lane," p. 29.
331	10	W. Wood, SBD, III, pt. 1: 144–45, Drummond to Prevost, 27 July 1814.
331	18	Cruikshank, *Documentary History 1814*, p. 466, Brown diary.
331	34	Douglass, p. 13.
332	1	Cruikshank, *Documentary History 1814*, p. 477, Jesup narrative.
332	8	W. Wood, SBD, III, pt. 1: 145, Drummond to Prevost, 27 July 1814.
332	20	Cruikshank, *Documentary History 1814*, p. 477, Jesup narrative.
332	39	Douglass, pp. 13–15.
333	18	W. Wood, SBD, III, pt. 1: 145–46, Drummond to Prevost, 27 July 1814.
333	27	Scott, pp. 140–41.
333	32	Ibid., p. 140.
333	40	Cruikshank, *Documentary History 1814*, p. 478, Jesup narrative.
335	2	Douglass, p. 21.
335	5	Cruikshank, *Documentary History 1814*, p. 478, Jesup narrative.
335	9	Ibid., p. 356, evidence at trial of Lt. Blake.
335	11	Ibid., pp. 335–37, Leavenworth to ?, 15 Jan. 1815.
335	13	W. Wood, SBD, III, pt. 1: 144, Drummond to Prevost, 27 July 1814.
335	36	Douglass, pp. 15–16.
336	3	Cruikshank, *Documentary History 1814*, p. 468, Brown diary.
336	12	Douglass, p. 16.
336	18	Cruikshank, *Documentary History 1814*, p. 98, Brown to SW, 7 Aug. 1814.
336	29	Ibid., p. 105, Miller to ?, 28 July 1814.
336	32	Ibid., p. 106, Allen to brother, 26 July 1814.
336	35	Ibid., p. 347, evidence of Capt. MacDonald.
336	37	Cruikshank, "Lundy's Lane," p. 38.

page	line	
336	40	Cruikshank, *Documentary History 1814*, p. 347, evidence of Capt. MacDonald.
337	21	Douglass, p. 21.
337	31	Byfield, p. 378.
337	38	Cruikshank, *Documentary History 1814*, pp. 469–70, Brown diary.
338	3	James, *Military Occurrences*.
338	12	Cruikshank, *Documentary History 1814*, p. 470, Brown diary.
339	3	Ibid., p. 375, McMullen narrative.
339	12	Ibid.
339	19	Ibid.
339	25	Cruikshank, *Documents Relating to the Invasion...1814*, p. 60, Brown to SW, 7 Aug. 1814.
339	36	Cruikshank, *Documentary History 1814*, p. 339, Leavenworth to ?, 15 Jan. 1815.
340	22	Cruikshank, "Lundy's Lane," p. 39.
340	30	Scott, p. 145.
340	36	Cruikshank, *Documentary History 1814*, p. 471, Brown diary.
341	5	Ibid., p. 348, Leavenworth to ?, 15 Jan. 1815.
341	12	Ibid., p. 376, McMullen narrative.
341	15	Ibid., p. 352, Col. Hindman statement.
341	18	Ibid., pp. 348–49, evidence of Capt. MacDonald.
341	21	Ibid., p. 352, Col. Hindman statement.
341	25	Ibid.
341	35	W. Wood, SBD, III, pt. 1: 157, District General Order, 26 July 1814; Cruikshank, *Documentary History 1814*, pp. 420–21, report of killed and wounded.
341	40	W. Wood, SBD, III, pt. 1: 152, District General Order, 26 July 1814.
342	3	Cruikshank, *Documentary History 1814*, Austin to SW, 29 July 1814.
342	7	Ibid., pp. 420–21, report of killed and wounded.
342	10	LC, Jesup MSS, Scott to Jesup, 5 Sept. 1814.
342	30	Cruikshank, *Documents Relating to the Invasion...1814*, p. 61, Brown to SW, 7 Aug. 1814.
342	34	Cruikshank, *Documentary History 1814*, p. 472, Brown diary.
343	4	Ibid., p. 353, Lt. Tappan statement.
343	10	Ibid., pp. 353–54.
343	31	LC, Jesup MSS, Scott to Jesup, 5 Sept. 1814.
343	37	Cruikshank, *Documentary History 1814*, pp. 102–3, Porter to Tompkins, 29 July 1814.
344	19	Ibid., pp. 376–77, McMullen narrative.
344	24	Douglass, p. 23.
344	25	Cruikshank, *Documentary History 1814*, p. 378, McMullen narrative.
345	15	Dunlop, pp. 33–35.
345	26	Cruikshank, *Documentary History 1814*, pp. 118–19, Harvey to Conran, 2 Aug. 1814.
346	6	Byfield, pp. 378–79.
346	25	Ketchum, pp. 201–2; Cruikshank, *Documentary History 1814*, p. 120, Tucker to Conran, 4 Aug. 1814.
346	32	Byfield, p. 379.
347	2	Cruikshank, *Documentary History 1814*, p. 427, District General Order, 5 Aug. 1814.
348	5	Byfield, pp. 379–83.
348	9	Douglass, p. 26; W. Wood, SBD, III, pt. 1: 178, Drummond to Prevost, 15 Aug. 1814.
348	22	Douglass, pp. 26, 27; Cruikshank, *Documentary History 1814*, p. 157, Ripley to Gaines, 17 Aug. 1814.
349	2	W. Wood, SBD, III, pt. 1: 178–82, Drummond to Prevost, 15 Aug. 1814; Douglass, pp. 24–27.
349	11	Cruikshank, *Documentary History 1814*, pp. 139–40, General Order, 14 Aug. 1814.
350	6	Yaple, pp. 24–25; Cruikshank, *Documentary History 1814*, p. 138, General Order, 14 Aug. 1814; *Journal of the Society for*

page line

Army Historical Research, vol. 22 (1943–44), pp. 318–19.

350 13 Douglass, p. 26.

350 22 Cruikshank, *Documentary History 1814*, pp. 138–39, General Order, 14 Aug. 1814.

350 29 Cruikshank, "Siege," p. 13.

350 40 Cruikshank, *Documentary History 1814*, pp. 169–70, Young to Scott, 20 Dec. 1814.

351 12 Dunlop, p. 51.

351 16 Ibid., p. 52.

351 27 Cruikshank, *Documentary History 1814*, pp. 156–57, Ripley to Gaines, 17 Aug. 1814; Douglass, p. 27.

351 40 Cruikshank, *Documentary History 1814*, p. 153, Gaines to SW, 23 Aug. 1814; ibid., pp. 144–45, Fischer to Harvey, 15 Aug. 1814; ibid., pp. 156–57, Ripley to Gaines, 17 Aug. 1814.

352 7 W. Wood, SBD, III, pt. 1: 188–89, Fischer to Harvey, 15 Aug. 1814; ibid., pp. 189–94, Drummond to Prevost, 16 Aug. 1814; Cruikshank, *Documentary History 1814*, pp. 156–57, Ripley to Gaines, 17 Aug. 1814.

352 16 Cruikshank, "Siege," p. 20.

353 9 Douglass, p. 27.

353 34 Ibid., pp. 27–28.

353 39 Cruikshank, "Siege," p. 22.

354 4 Dunlop, p. 52.

354 9 Cruikshank, *Documentary History 1814*, pp. 153–54, Gaines to SW, 23 Aug. 1814.

354 15 Ibid., p. 154.

354 26 Douglass, p. 29.

354 32 W. Wood, SBD, III, pt. 1: 179–80, Drummond to Prevost, 15 Aug. 1814.

355 15 Cruikshank, *Documentary History 1814*, pp. 168–69, Couteur to Couteur, 29 July 1814.

355 28 W. Wood, SBD, III, pt. 1: 192–93, return of killed and wounded, 15 Aug. 1814.

355 36 BHS, Hanks Memoir, pp. 27–28.

356 3 Wood, SBD, III, pt. 1: 189, Drummond to Prevost, 16 Aug. 1814.

356 10 Cruikshank, *Documentary History 1814*, pp. 174–76, Prevost to Drummond, 26 Aug. 1814.

356 18 Douglass, p. 33.

357 10 Dunlop, pp. 48–49.

357 13 Cruikshank, *Documentary History 1814*, p. 214, report of killed and wounded; W. Wood, SBD, III, pt. 1: 197–99, return of killed and wounded, 17 Sept. 1814.

357 21 Cruikshank, *Documentary History 1814*, p. 225, Drummond to Prevost, 21 Sept. 1814.

357 30 Ibid., p. 233, Izard to SW, 28 Sept. 1814.

357 32 W. Wood, SBD, III, pt. 1: 211, Drummond to Prevost, 11 Oct. 1814; ibid., p. 217, Drummond to Prevost, 15 Oct. 1814.

357 38 Ibid., pp. 217–18, Drummond to Prevost, 15 Oct. 1814.

358 7 Cruikshank, *Documentary History 1814*, p. 256, Izard to SW, 16 Oct. 1814.

358 13 Ibid., p. 243, Prevost to Drummond, 11 Oct. 1814; W. Wood, SBD, III, pt. 1: 223, Drummond to Prevost, 20 Oct. 1814.

358 17 W. Wood, SBD, III, pt. 1: 231, Drummond to Prevost, 23 Oct. 1814.

358 18 Cruikshank, *Documentary History 1814*, p. 284, Izard to SW, 2 Nov. 1814.

358 24 Ibid., p. 286.

358 30 Ibid.

358 39 W. Wood, SBD, III, pt. 1: 243, Drummond to Prevost, 5 Nov. 1814.

The Burning of Washington

363 8 Barrett, pp. 117–32.

363 15 Ibid., pp. 131–33.

364 16 Ibid., p. 134.

364 32 Lord, p. 98.

365 6 Barrett, p. 138.

366 3 Ibid., p. 138; Lord, p. 119.

366 12 Sir H. Smith, pp. 158–59.

366 14 C. Ingersoll, p. 175.

366 19 Barrett, p. 138.

366 27 ASPMA, I: 556–57, Winder narrative.

The Battle of Lake Champlain

page line

388 32 W. Wood, SBD, III, pt. 1: 381, Prevost to Downie, 9 Sept. 1814.

389 3 Ibid., p. 383, Prevost to Downie, 10 Sept. 1814.

389 8 Ibid., p. 461, Pring statement.

389 9 Ibid., p. 421, Cox testimony.

389 15 Ibid., pp. 411–12, Brydon testimony.

389 29 Ibid., p. 442, Pring testimony.

389 39 Ibid., p. 437.

390 9 Ibid., p. 414, Brydon testimony.

390 30 Mahan, II: 377.

390 36 W. Wood, SBD, III, pt. 1: 471, Robertson statement; ibid., p. 414, Brydon testimony.

391 4 Folsom, p. 253.

391 7 Macdonough, p. 176.

391 19 Lossing, p. 867.

391 26 Ibid., pp. 866–67.

391 36 Macdonough, p. 178; Folsom, p. 253.

393 6 Macdonough, pp. 179–80; Roosevelt, p. 392.

393 11 Roosevelt, p. 393.

393 18 W. Wood, SBD, III, pt. 1: 422–23, Bodell testimony.

393 33 Macdonough, p. 180; W. Wood, SBD, III, pt. 1: 430, Lt. Bell testimony; ibid., pp. 484, 490, Hicks testimony.

394 3 Macdonough, p. 181.

394 9 Niles Register, supplement, vol. 7, p. 135, Henley to SN, 12 Sept. 1814.

394 19 Folsom, p. 254; P. Palmer, Lake Champlain, p. 204.

394 28 Clark, p. 83, Macdonough to SN, 11 Sept. 1814.

395 7 Lossing, pp. 871–72.

395 26 W. Wood, SBD, III, pt. 1: 383–84, Robertson to Pring, 15 Sept. 1814; ibid., pp. 418–19, Brydon testimony; P. Palmer, Lake Champlain, p. 205.

395 36 W. Wood, SBD, III, pt. 1: 373–77, Robertson to Pring, 12 Sept. 1814.

396 1 Ibid., pp. 490–91, Hicks testimony.

396 10 Macdonough, p. 185.

396 18 Ibid., p. 188.

397 1 Robinson, "Expedition to Plattsburgh," p. 510.

page line

398 8 Ibid., pp. 511–12.

398 12 Lossing, p. 874.

398 24 Ibid., p. 875.

398 33 W. Wood, SBD, III, pt. 1: 360, Macomb to SW, 15 Sept. 1814.

399 9 Bathurst, pp. 292–93, Robinson to Merry, 22 Sept. 1814.

Ghent

403 20 J.Q. Adams, Memoirs, III: 3–4, 7 Aug. 1814.

404 14 Ibid.; Clay, I: 963, Clay to Monroe, 18 Aug. 1814.

404 18 Ibid.

405 21 J.Q. Adams, Memoirs, III: 5–6.

406 8 Ibid., p. 9.

406 23 Ibid., p. 15.

407 7 Ibid., pp. 17–19; Clay, I: 968–70, journal, 19 Aug. 1814.

407 11 J.Q. Adams, Memoirs, III: 19.

407 15 Ibid., p. 20.

407 23 Ibid., pp. 20–23.

407 25 ASPFR, III: 711–13, U.S. to British Commissioners, 24 Aug. 1814.

408 2 J.Q. Adams, Memoirs, III: 25; Writings, V: 112, Adams to Monroe, 5 Sept. 1814.

408 11 J.Q. Adams, Writings, V: 112, Adams to Monroe, 5 Sept. 1814.

408 17 Ibid., p. 119.

408 22 Wellington, IX: 221, Goulburn to Bathurst, 5 Sept. 1814.

408 32 Ibid., p. 249, draft note, 1 Sept. 1814.

408 34 Clay, I: 972, Clay to Crawford, 22 Aug. 1814.

409 2 Clay, I: 973, Clay to Goulburn, 5 Sept. 1814.

409 25 Bathurst, pp. 286–87, Liverpool to Bathurst, 14 Sept. 1814; Wellington, IX: 240, Liverpool to Bathurst, 11 Sept. 1814.

409 35 Bathurst, p. 287, Liverpool to Bathurst, 14 Sept. 1814.

410 14 Wellington, IX: 214, Liverpool to Castlereagh, 2 Sept. 1814.

410 32 Ibid., p. 240, Liverpool to Bathurst, 11 Sept. 1814.

411 3 Ibid., p. 265, Goulburn to Bathurst, 16 Sept. 1814.

411 7 Ibid., p. 266.

page *line*

411   19   Ibid., p. 287, Goulburn to
              Bathurst, 26 Sept. 1814.
411   27   Bathurst, p. 289, Liverpool to
              Bathurst, 15 Sept. 1814.
412   6   Clay, I: 982, Goulburn to Clay,
              3 Oct. [?] 1814.
412   18   Ibid., pp. 988–89, Clay to
              Crawford, 17 Oct. 1814.
412   20   J.Q. Adams, *Writings*, V: 161,
              Adams to Louisa Adams, 18
              Oct. 1814.
412   23   Ibid.
412   28   J.Q. Adams, *Memoirs*, III: 51.
412   39   J.Q. Adams, *Writings*, V: 174,
              Adams to Louisa Adams, 28
              Oct. 1814.
413   9   Ibid., p. 175.
413   11   Ibid., p. 108, Adams to Louisa
              Adams, 30 Aug. 1814; ibid., p.
              205, Adams to Louisa Adams,
              22 Nov. 1814.
413   29   Wellington, IX: 367, Liverpool
              to Castlereagh, 21 Oct. 1814.
413   30   Ibid., p. 383, Liverpool to
              Castlereagh, 28 Oct. 1814.
413   32   Ibid., p. 405, Liverpool to
              Castlereagh, 4 Nov. 1814.
414   1   Gallatin, I: 642, Gallatin to
              Monroe, 26 Oct. 1814.
415   19   J.Q. Adams, *Memoirs*, III:
              60–66.

page *line*

415   34   Castlereagh, pp. 186–89, Wel-
              lington to Liverpool, 9 Nov.
              1814.
415   38   Wellington, IX: 432, Goulburn
              to Bathurst, 14 Nov. 1814.
416   5   Ibid., p. 438, Liverpool to
              Castlereagh, 18 Nov. 1814.
416   6   Ibid.
416   12   Clay, I: 1001, British to U.S.
              Commissioners, 26 Nov. 1814.
416   22   Wellington, IX: 452–54, Goul-
              burn to Bathurst, 25 Nov. 1814.
416   25   J.Q. Adams, *Writings*, V: 219,
              Adams to Louisa Adams, 29
              Nov. 1814.
417   2   J.Q. Adams, *Memoirs*, III:
              101–3.
417   6   Ibid., p. 108.
417   22   Ibid., p. 120.
417   25   J.Q. Adams, *Writings*, V: 238,
              Adams to Louisa Adams, 16
              Dec. 1814.
417   40   Ibid., pp. 237–39.
418   22   J.Q. Adams, *Memoirs*, III: 126.

Afterview

424   25   Bulger, p. 132, Bulger Report,
              18 April 1815.
424   32   Ibid., p. 143, McDouall to
              Bulger, 2 May 1815.
428   35   Dunlop, p. 22.

Select Bibliography

Unpublished manuscript material

Public Archives of Canada:
RG 8, "C" series *passim*, British Military Records
CO 42, vols. 143–163 (Lower Canada); vols. 351–355 (Upper Canada). Colonial
Office, original correspondence, Secretary of State.
RG 19 E5(a), Department of Finance, War of 1812 Losses, vols. 3728–3768
passim
Upper Canada Sundries RG 5 A1, vols. 16, 19, 26
Upper Canada Sundries, state books, vol. F
MG 24 F4 Bisshopp Papers
MG 24 F13 Chauncey Papers

Public Archives of Ontario:
Ely Playter Diary
Strachan Papers
Robinson Papers

U.S. National Archives:
RG 107 Records of the office of the Secretary of War
  M6, reels 5–7, Letters sent by the Secretary of War
  M221, reels 42–67, Letters received by the Secretary of War

Library of Congress:
William Eustis Papers
Thomas Jesup Papers

Wisconsin Historical Society:
Draper MSS, Tecumseh Papers

Rhode Island Historical Society:
Usher Parsons Diary

Buffalo Historical Society:
A.C. Goodyear Collection
Jarvis Hanks Memoir

Public Record Office, London:
WO 71/243, Court martial of Henry Procter

Filson Club:
Scrapbook MSS B1/F489

Published primary sources

[Adams, John Quincy.] *Memoirs of John Quincy Adams, Comprising Portions of His Diary from 1795 to 1848*, vols. III and IV, edited by Charles Francis Adams. Philadelphia: J.B. Lippincott, 1874.

——— *The Writings of John Quincy Adams*, vol. IV, *1811–1813*, edited by Worthington Chauncey Ford. New York: Macmillan, 1914.

Armstrong, John. *Hints to Young Generals. By an Old Soldier.* Kingston, N.Y.: 1812.

——— *Notices of the War of 1812*, 2 vols., vol. I, George Dearborn, 1836; vol. II, Wiley & Putnam, 1840.

Babcock, James L. (ed.). "The Campaign of 1814 on the Niagara Frontier," *Niagara Frontier*, vol. 10 (1963).

Barrett, Charles Raymond Booth. *The 85th King's Light Infantry.* London: Spottiswoode, 1913.

[Bathurst, Henry.] *Report on the Manuscripts of Earl Bathurst Preserved at Cirencester Park*, prepared by Francis Bickley. London: Historical Manuscripts Commission, vol. 76, 1923.

Bayard, James. "Letters of James Asheton Bayard," *Delaware Historical Society Papers*, vol. 31 (1901).

——— "Papers of James Bayard," edited by Elizabeth Donnan, in *Annual Report of the American Historical Association for the year 1913*, vol. II. Washington: 1915.

Booth, Mordecai. "The Capture of Washington in 1814 As Described by Mordecai Booth," *Americana*, vol. 28 (1934).

Bourne, Alexander. "The Siege of Fort Meigs, year 1813. An eyewitness account," *Northwest Ohio Quarterly*, vols. 17 and 18 (1945 and 1946).

Boyd, John P. *Documents and Facts Relative to the Military Events during the Late War.* Boston, 1816.

Brannan, John (ed.). *Official Letters of the Military and Naval Officers of the United States, during the War with Great Britain in the Years 1812, 13, 14 & 15.* Washington: Way & Gideon, 1823.

[Brenton, E.B.] *Some Account of the Public Life of the Late Lieutenant-General Sir George Prevost, Bart., Particularly of His Services in the Canadas....* London: Cadell, 1823.

Brown, Samuel. *Views of the Campaigns of the Northwest Army & c....* Burlington, Vt., 1814.

Bulger, Alfred (ed.). "The Bulger Papers," *State Historical Society of Wisconsin Collections*, vol. 13 (1895).

Bunnell, David C. *The Travels and Adventures of David C. Bunnell....* Palmyra, N.Y.: J.H. Bortles, 1831.

"The Burning of Buffalo," *Buffalo Historical Society Publications*, vol. 9 (1906).

Byfield, Shadrach. "Narrative," *Magazine of History*, extra no. 11, 1910.

[Castlereagh, Viscount.] *Correspondence, Despatches and Other Papers of Viscount Castlereagh*, edited by C.W. Vane, vol. IX. London, 1848–53.

[Chandler, John.] "General John Chandler of Monmouth, Maine, with Extracts from His Autobiography," edited by George Foster Talbot, *Maine Historical Collections*, vol. 9 (1887).

Chapin, Cyrenius. *Chapin's Review of Armstrong's Notices of the War of 1812.* Black Rock, N.Y.: D.P. Adams, 1836.

Clark, Byron N. "Accounts of the Battle of Plattsburgh from Contemporaneous Sources," *Vermont Antiquarian,* vol. 1 (1903).

[Clay, Henry.] *The Papers of Henry Clay,* vols. I and II, edited by James Hopkins. Lexington, Ky.: University of Kentucky Press, 1959 and 1961.

"Copies of Papers on File in the Dominion Archives at Ottawa, Canada, Pertaining to Michigan As Found in the Colonial Office Records," *Michigan Pioneer and Historical Collections,* vol. 25 (1896).

Combs, Leslie. "Account of Fort Meigs," *American Historical Record,* vol. I, 1872.

"Correspondence between Hon. William Dickson Prisoner of War and Gen. Dearborn, 1813," *Niagara Historical Society Papers,* no. 28.

Cruikshank, E.A. (ed.). *The Documentary History of the Campaign upon the Niagara Frontier 1812–1814.* 9 vols. Welland: Lundy's Lane Historical Society, 1896–1908.

———— (ed.). *Documents Relating to the Invasion of the Niagara Peninsula by the United States Army Commanded by General Jacob Brown in July and August 1814.* Niagara-on-the-Lake: Niagara Historical Society Publications, no. 33, 1920.

Delafield, Julia. *Biographies of Francis Lewis and Morgan Lewis.* New York: A.D.F. Randolph, 1877.

Dobbins, Daniel and Dobbins, William. "The Dobbins Papers," *Buffalo Historical Society Publications,* vol. 8 (1905).

Documents in Relation to the Differences Which Subsisted between the Late Commodore O.H. Perry and Captain J.D. Elliott. Boston, 1834.

Douglas, John. *Medical Topography of Upper Canada.* London: Burgess and Hill, 1819.

[Douglass, David Bates.] "An Original Narrative of the Niagara Campaign of 1814," edited by John T. Horton, *Niagara Frontier,* vol. 11 (1964).

Dunlop, William. *Tiger Dunlop's Upper Canada....* Toronto: McClelland and Stewart, 1967.

Edgar, Matilda. *Ten Years of Upper Canada in Peace and War, 1805–1815; Being the Ridout Letters....* Toronto: W. Briggs, 1890.

Elliott, Jesse D. *Speech...delivered in Hagerstown, Md., on 14th Nov. 1843.* Philadelphia: G.B. Zeiber & Co., 1844.

Ewell, James. "Unwelcome Visitors to Early Washington," *Records of the Columbia Historical Society,* vol. 1 (1897).

Finan, Patrick. *Journal of a Voyage to Quebec in the Year 1825.* Newry, Ireland: Alexander Peacock, 1828.

Firth, Edith (ed.). *The Town of York, 1793–1815.* Toronto: Champlain Society for the Government of Ontario, University of Toronto Press, 1962.

[Gallatin, Albert.] *The Writings of Albert Gallatin,* vol. I, edited by Henry Adams. Philadelphia: J.B. Lippincott, 1879.

"General Orders. Fort Meigs to Put-in-Bay April–September 1813," *Register of the Kentucky Historical Society,* vol. 60 (1962).

Grignon, Augustin. "Seventy-two Years' Recollections of Wisconsin," *State Historical Society of Wisconsin Collections,* vol. 3 (1856).

[Hanks, Jarvis.] "A Drummer Boy in the War of 1812: The Memoir of Jarvis Frary Hanks," edited by Lester Smith, *Niagara Frontier,* vol. 7 (1960).

[Harrison, William Henry.] *Messages and Letters*, 2 vols., edited by Logan Esarey. Indiana Historical Collections, vols. 8 and 9. Indianapolis: Indiana Historical Commission, 1922.

Hatch, William S. *A Chapter in the History of the War of 1812 in the Northwest....* Cincinnati: Miami Printing & Publishing, 1872.

Hay, George. "Recollections of the War of 1812," *American Historical Review*, vol. 32 (1926).

Howe, Henry. *Historical Collections of Ohio*, vol. II. Cincinnati, 1902.

Izard, George. *Official Correspondence....* Philadelphia, 1816.

Jackson, Donald (ed.). *Black Hawk, an Autobiography*. Urbana, Ill.: University of Illinois Press, 1964 [reprint].

Kentucky Gazette.

Klinck, Carl F. (ed.). *Tecumseh: Fact and Fiction in Early Records*. Englewood Cliffs, N.J.: Prentice-Hall, 1961.

Lajeunesse, Ernest J. (ed.). *The Windsor Border Region*. Toronto: University of Toronto Press, 1960.

"Lawe and Grignon Papers," *Reports and Collections of the State Historical Society of Wisconsin*, vol. 10 (1883).

[Le Couteur, John.] "The March of the 104th Foot from Fredericton to Quebec, 1813," edited by Maj. M.A. Pope, *Canadian Defence Quarterly*, vol. 7 (1930).

"List of Losses Claimed on Houses Burned in Niagara Dec. 13th, 1813," *Niagara Historical Society Publications*, no. 27 (n.d.).

Loyal and Patriotic Society of Upper Canada. *The Report of the...Society...with an Appendix, and a List of Subscribers and Benefactors*. Montreal: W. Gray, 1817.

McAfee, Robert. "The McAfee Papers," *Register of the Kentucky Historical Society*, vol. 26 (1928).

McClure, George. *Causes of the Destruction of the American Towns on the Niagara Frontier and Failure of the Campaign of the Fall of 1813*. Bath, N.Y., 1817.

Macdonough, Rodney. *The Life of Commodore Thomas Macdonough, U.S. Navy*. Boston: Fort Hill Press, 1909.

McKenney, Thomas L. *Memoirs....* New York: Paine & Burgess, 1846.

[Madison, Dolley.] *Memoirs and Letters of Dolly Madison*, edited by her grandniece. Port Washington, N.Y.: Kennikat Press, 1971 [reprint].

[Madison, James.] *The Writings of James Madison*, vol. VIII, *1808–1819*, edited by Gaillard Hunt. New York, London: G.P. Putnam's Sons, 1908.

Mann, James. *Medical Sketches of the Campaigns of 1812, 13, 14*. Dedham, Mass., 1816.

Manning, William R. (ed.). *Diplomatic Correspondence of the United States: Canadian Relations, 1784–1860*, vol. I. Washington: Carnegie Endowment, 1940.

"Military Service of 1813/14 As Shown by the Correspondence of Major General Amos Hall," *Buffalo Historical Society Publications*, vol. 5 (1902).

[Monroe, James.] *The Writings of James Monroe*, vol. V, *1807–1816*, edited by Stanislaus Murray Hamilton. New York, London: G.P. Putnam's Sons, 1901.

New Monthly Magazine, 1826.

Niles Weekly Register, 1812–15.

[Norton, Jacob Porter.] "Jacob Porter Norton, a Yankee on the Niagara frontier in 1814," edited by Daniel R. Porter, *Niagara Frontier*, vol. 12 (1965).

"Old Sub," *United Service Journal*, 1840, part I.

Ontario, Bureau of Archives. *Report of the Bureau of Archives for the Province of Ontario, 1st–15th, 1903–1918/19*, no. 7 (1910) and no. 9 (1912). Toronto: King's Printer, 1904–20.

Padover, Saul (ed.). *Thomas Jefferson and the National Capital....* Washington: U.S. Government Printing Office, 1946.

Palmer, T.H. (ed.). *The Historical Register of the United States*, 4 vols. Philadelphia, 1814–16.

Parsons, Usher. *The Battle of Lake Erie*. Providence, R.I.: Rhode Island Historical Society, 1854.

——— "Brief Sketches of the Officers Who Were in the Battle of Lake Erie," *Inland Seas*, vol. 19 (1963).

——— "A Surgical Account of the Battle of Lake Erie," *New England Journal of Surgery and Medicine*, October, 1818.

Paullin, Charles O. (ed.). *The Battle of Lake Erie: A Collection of Documents, Chiefly by Commodore Perry....* Cleveland: Rowfant Club, 1918.

[Pike, Zebulon Montgomery.] *The Journals of Zebulon Montgomery Pike*, edited by Donald Jackson. Norman, Okla.: University of Oklahoma Press, 1966.

Quaife, Milo M. (ed.). *War on the Detroit: The Chronicles of Thomas Verchères de Boucherville, and The Capitulation by an Ohio Volunteer*. Chicago: Lakeside Press, 1940.

"Reminiscences of American Occupation of Niagara from 27th May to 10th Dec. 1813," *Niagara Historical Society Publications*, no. 11 (n.d.).

Richardson, John. "A Canadian Campaign," *New Monthly Magazine*, London, 1827.

——— *Eight Years in Canada*. Montreal: H.H. Cunningham, 1847.

[Richardson, John.] *The Letters of Veritas....* Montreal: W. Gray, 1815.

[Richardson, John.] *Richardson's War of 1812...*, edited by Alexander C. Casselman. Toronto: Historical Publishing, 1902.

Roach, Isaac. "Journal of Major Isaac Roach, 1812–1824," *Pennsylvania Magazine of History and Biography*, vol. 17 (1893).

Robinson, C.W. "The Expedition to Plattsburgh upon Lake Champlain, Canada 1814," *Journal of the Royal United Service Institute*, vol. 61 (1916).

Scott, Winfield. *Memoirs of Lieut.-General Scott, Written by Himself*, 2 vols., vol. I. New York: Sheldon, 1864.

[Sheaffe, Roger Hale.] "Documents Relating to the War of 1812: the Letterbook of Gen. Sir Roger Hale Sheaffe," *Buffalo Historical Society Publications*, vol. 17 (1913).

[Sholes, Stanton.] "A Narrative of the Northwestern Campaign of 1813," edited by Milo M. Quaife. *Mississippi Valley Historical Review*, vol. 15 (1929).

"The Siege of Fort Meigs," *Register of the Kentucky Historical Society*, vol. 19 (1921).

Slater, D. "An Old Diary," *Journal and Transactions of the Wentworth Historical Society*, vol. 5 (1908).

Smart, James. "The St. Lawrence Project...." Unpublished paper in Queen's University Library, Kingston, Ont.

Smith, Sir Harry. *The Autobiography of Lt. General Sir Harry Smith...*, vol. I. London: John Murray, 1901.

[Smith, Margaret Bayard.] *Forty Years of Washington Society...*, edited by Gaillard Hunt. London: T. Fisher Unwin, 1906.

[Strachan, John.] *John Strachan: Documents and Opinions*, edited by J.L.H. Henderson. Toronto: McClelland and Stewart, 1969.

[Strachan, John.] *The John Strachan Letterbook, 1812–1834*, edited by George Spragge. Toronto: Ontario Historical Society, 1946.

Strachan, John. *A Sermon Preached at York...August 2nd, 1812*. York, 1812.

Swift, Joseph Gardner. *Memoirs of General Joseph Gardner Swift*. Worcester, Mass., 1890.

Treat, Joseph. *The Vindication of Captain Joseph Treat....* Philadelphia, 1815.

United States Congress, *American State Papers: Foreign Relations*, vol. III. Washington: Gales & Seaton, 1832.

———— *American State Papers: Indian Affairs*, vol. I. Washington: Gales & Seaton, 1832.

———— *American State Papers: Military Affairs*, vol. I. Washington: Gales & Seaton, 1832.

———— *American State Papers: Naval Affairs*, vol. I. Washington: Gales & Seaton, 1832.

"The Village of Buffalo in the War of 1812," *Buffalo Historical Society Publications*, vol. 1 (1897).

"Visit of Col. R.M. Johnson to Springfield 18–20 May 1843. Report from State Register 26 May 1843," *Journal of the Illinois State Historical Society*, vol. 13 (1921).

Wellington, Duke of. *Supplementary Despatches: Correspondence and Memoranda of Field Marshal Arthur Duke of Wellington*, vol. IX. London, 1862.

White, Samuel. *History of the American Troops during the Late War....* Baltimore, 1829.

Wilkinson, James. *Memoirs of My Own Times*, 3 vols. Philadelphia, 1816.

Wood, Eleazer. "Eleazer D. Wood's Journal of the Northwestern Campaign," in George Cullum, ed., *Campaigns of the War of 1812–15....* New York: J. Miller, 1879.

Wood, William C.H. (ed.). *Select British Documents of the Canadian War of 1812*, Champlain Society, vols. 13–15, 17. Toronto: The Society, 1920–28.

York [Upper Canada] *Gazette*: 1812–13.

Secondary Sources

Adams, Henry. *A History of the United States of America during the Administrations of Thomas Jefferson and James Madison*. New York: Charles Scribner's Sons, 1889–91.

Allen, Robert S. "The British Indian Department and the Frontier in North America, 1755–1830," *Canadian Historic Sites: Occasional Papers in Archeology and History*, no. 14 (1975).

Anderson, David. "The Battle of Fort Stephenson," *Northwest Ohio Quarterly*, vol. 33 (1961).

Anglo American Magazine, December, 1853.

Arnold, Thaddeus. "The Battle of the Thames and Death of Tecumseh," unpublished manuscript, Chatham and Kent Historical Society.

Averill, James P. *Fort Meigs: A Condensed History....* Toledo, O., 1886.

Babcock, Louis L. "The Siege of Fort Erie," *New York State Historical Association Proceedings*, vol. 8 (1909).

———— *The War of 1812 on the Niagara Frontier*. Buffalo: Buffalo Historical Society, 1927.

Bailey, John R. *Mackinac, Formerly Michilimackinac*. Lansing, Mich.: 1895.

Bannister, J.A. "The Burning of Dover," *Western Ontario Historical Notes*, vol. 21 (1965).

Bayles, G.H. "Tecumseh and the Bayles Family Tradition," *Register of the Kentucky Historical Society*, vol. 46 (1948).

Baylies, Nicholas. *Eleazer Wheelock Ripley of the War of 1812*. Des Moines, Ia.: Brewster, 1890.

Beasley, David R. *The Canadian Don Quixote: The Life and Works of Major John Richardson, Canada's First Novelist*. Erin, Ont.: Porcupine's Quill, 1977.

Beirne, Francis F. *The War of 1812*. New York: Dutton, 1949.

Berger, Carl. *The Sense of Power: Studies in the Ideas of Canadian Imperialism, 1867–1914*. Toronto: University of Toronto Press, 1970.

Bethune, Alexander N. *Memoir of the Right Reverend John Strachan D.D., LL.D., First Bishop of Toronto*. Toronto: Henry Rowsell, 1870.

Biggar, E.B. "The Battle of Stony Creek," *Canadian Magazine*, vol. 1 (1893).

Blanco, Richard L. "The Development of British Military Medicine, 1793–1814," *Military Affairs*, February, 1974.

Boissonnault, Charles-Marie. *Histoire politico-militaire des Canadiens-Français*. Trois Rivières: Editions du Bien Public, 1967.

Brett-James, Anthony. *Life in Wellington's Army*. London: Allen and Unwin, 1972.

Buell, W.S. "Military Movements in Eastern Ontario during the War of 1812," *Ontario Historical Society Papers and Records*, vol. 10 (1913).

Burges, Tristam. *The Battle of Lake Erie*. Philadelphia: William Marshall, 1839.

Burns, R.J. "God's Chosen People: The Origins of Toronto Society, 1793–1818," *Canadian Historical Association, Historical Papers*, Toronto, 1973.

Burt, Alfred L. *The United States, Great Britain and British North America from the Revolution to the Establishment of Peace after the War of 1812*. New Haven: Yale University Press, 1940.

Burt, A. Blanche. "Captain Robert Heriot Barclay, R.N.," *Ontario Historical Society Papers and Records*, vol. 14 (1916).

Butler, Mann. *A History of the Commonwealth of Kentucky....* Cincinnati: J.A. James, 1836.

Caffrey, Kate *The Twilight's Last Gleaming: The British Against America, 1812–1815*. New York: Stein and Day, 1977.

Chalou, George C. "The Red Pawns Go to War: British-American Indian Relations, 1810–1815." Ph.D. dissertation, University of Indiana, 1971.

Cleaves, Freeman. *Old Tippecanoe: William Henry Harrison and his Time*. New York: Charles Scribner's Sons, 1939; reprinted, New York: Kennikat Press, 1969.

Cleveland City Council. *Inauguration of the Perry Statue at Cleveland*. Cleveland: Cleveland, Fairbanks, Benedict, 1861.

Coffin, William F. *1812: The War and Its Moral: A Canadian Chronicle*. Montreal: J. Lovell, 1864.

Coles, Harry L. *The War of 1812*. Chicago: University of Chicago Press, 1965.

Colquhoun, A.H.U. "The Career of Joseph Willcocks," *Canadian Historical Review*, vol. 7 (1926).

Cook, Samuel F. *Mackinaw in History*. Lansing, Mich.: R. Smith, 1895.

Cooper, James Fenimore. *The Battle of Lake Erie....* Cooperstown, N.Y.: H. & E. Phinney, 1843.

———— *The History of the Navy of the United States of America*, vol. II. London, 1839.

———— "Oliver Hazard Perry," *Graham's Magazine*, vol. 22 (1843).

Coutts, Katharine B. "Thamesville and the Battle of the Thames," *Ontario Historical Society Papers and Records*, vol. 9 (1908).

Craig, G.M. *Upper Canada: The Formative Years, 1784–1841*. Toronto: McClelland and Stewart, 1963.

Cramer, C.H. "Duncan McArthur: The Military Phase," *Ohio State Archaeological and Historical Quarterly*, vol. 46 (1937).

Cruickshank, David A. "The Plattsburgh Campaign, September 1814." M.A. thesis, Queen's University, 1971.

Cruikshank, E.A. "The Battle of Fort George," *Niagara Historical Society Publications*, no. 1 (1896).

———— "The Battle of Lundy's Lane," *Lundy's Lane Historical Society Publications*, vol. 1, part 7 (1893).

———— "The Battle of Stoney Creek and the Blockade of Fort George," *Niagara Historical Society Publications*, no. 3.

———— "The Contest for the Command of Lake Erie in 1812–13," *Royal Canadian Institute Transactions*, vol. 6 (1899).

———— "The Contest for the Command of Lake Ontario in 1812 and 1813," *Royal Society of Canada Transactions*, ser. 3, sect. 2, vol. 10 (1916).

———— "The Contest for the Command of Lake Ontario in 1814," *Ontario Historical Society Papers and Records*, vol. 21 (1924).

———— "The County of Norfolk in the War of 1812," *Ontario Historical Society Papers and Records*, vol. 20 (1923).

———— "Drummond's Winter Campaign," *Lundy's Lane Historical Society Publications*, vol. 1, part 3 (n.d.).

———— "An Episode of the War of 1812: The Story of the Schooner 'Nancy,'" *Ontario Historical Society Papers and Records* vol. 9 (1910).

———— "The Fight in the Beechwoods," *Lundy's Lane Historical Society Publications*, vol. 1, part 6 (1895).

———— "From Isle aux Noix to Chateauguay," *Royal Society of Canada Transactions*, ser. 3, sect. 2, vol. 7 (1913).

———— "Harrison and Procter," *Royal Society of Canada Proceedings*, ser. 3, sect. 2, vol. 4 (1910).

———— "John Beverley Robinson and the Trials for Treason," *Ontario Historical Society Papers and Records*, vol. 25 (1929).

——— "Laura Secord's Walk to Warn Fitzgibbon," *Niagara Historical Society Publications*, no. 36 (1924).

——— "Robert Dickson, the Indian Trader," *State Historical Society of Wisconsin Collections*, vol. 12 (1892).

——— "The Siege of Fort Erie," *Lundy's Lane Historical Society Publications*, vol. 1, part 14 (1905).

——— "A Study of Disaffection in Upper Canada," *Royal Society of Canada Transactions*, ser. 3, sect. 2, vol. 6 (1912).

Cumberland, Barlow. *The Battle of York*. Toronto: Wm. Briggs, 1913.

——— "The Navies on Lake Ontario in the War of 1812," *Ontario Historical Society Papers and Records*, vol. 8 (1907).

Currie, Emma. *The Story of Laura Secord and Canadian Reminiscences*. St. Catharines, 1913.

Curzon, S.A. "The Story of Laura Secord," *Lundy's Lane Historical Society Publications*, vol. 1, part 9 (1891).

Dale, Allan. "Chateauguay," *Canadian Geographical Journal*, vol. 11 (1935).

Dangerfield, George. "Lord Liverpool and the United States," *American Heritage*, vol. 6 (1955).

David, Laurent Oliver. *Le Héros de Châteauguay*. Montreal: Cadieux et Jerome, 1883.

Davis, P.M. "The Four Principal Battles of the Late War," *Magazine of History*, extra no. 55 (1917).

Dawson, Moses. *A Historical Narrative of the Civil and Military Services of Major-General William H. Harrison*.... Cincinnati, 1824.

Dictionary of American Biography, 22 vols. New York: Charles Scribner's Sons, 1928–58.

Dictionary of Canadian Biography, vol. IX: *1861–1870*. Toronto: University of Toronto Press, 1976.

Dictionary of National Biography, 22 vols. Oxford: Oxford University Press, 1885–1900.

Dobbins, William. *History of the Battle of Lake Erie*. Erie, Pa.: Ashby Printing Co., 1913.

Dodge, Robert. *The Battle of Lake Erie*. Fostoria, O.: 1967.

Douglas, R. Alan. "Weapons of the War of 1812," *Michigan History*, vol. 47 (1963).

Drake, Benjamin. *Life of Tecumseh, and of His Brother the Prophet, with a Historical Sketch of the Shawanoe Indians*. Cincinnati: E. Morgan, 1841.

Dutton, Charles Judson. *Oliver Hazard Perry*. New York: Longmans, Green, 1935.

Eaton, Clement. *Henry Clay and the Art of American Politics*. Boston: Little, Brown, 1957.

Elliott, Charles W. *Winfield Scott: The Soldier and the Man*. New York: Macmillan, 1937.

Emerson, George D. *The Perry's Victory Centenary. Report of the Perry's Victory Centennial Commission, State of New York*. Albany: J.B. Lyon, 1916.

Engelman, Fred L. *The Peace of Christmas Eve*. New York: Harcourt, Brace and World, 1962.

Ermatinger, C.O. "The Retreat of Procter and Tecumseh," *Ontario Historical Society Papers and Records*, vol. 17 (1919).

Erney, Richard A. "The Public Life of Henry Dearborn." Ph.D. dissertation, Columbia University, 1957.

Everest, Allan S. "Alexander Macomb at Plattsburg, 1814," *New York History*, vol. 44 (1963).

FitzGibbon, Mary Agnes. *A Veteran of 1812: The Life of James FitzGibbon*. Toronto: W. Briggs, 1894.

Folsom, William R. "The Battle of Plattsburg," *Vermont Quarterly*, vol. 20 (1950).

Forester, C.S. *The Age of Fighting Sail: The Story of the Naval War of 1812*. Garden City, N.Y.: Doubleday, 1956.

—— "Victory at New Orleans," *American Heritage*, vol. 8 (1957).

—— "Victory on Lake Champlain," *American Heritage*, vol. 15 (1963).

Fortescue, Sir John. *A History of the British Army*, 13 vols., vols. VIII and IX. London: Macmillan, 1917.

Fraser, John. *Canadian Pen and Ink Sketches*. Montreal, 1890.

Gilpin, Alec. *The War of 1812 in the Old Northwest*. Toronto: Ryerson Press; East Lansing, Mich.: Michigan State University Press, 1958.

Goltz, Charles H. "Tecumseh and the Northwest Indian Confederacy." Ph.D. dissertation, University of Western Ontario, 1973.

Gosling, D.C.L. "The Battle at Lacolle Mill, 1814," *Journal of the Society for Army Historical Research*, vol. 47 (1969).

Graves, Donald E. "The Canadian Volunteers, 1813–1815," *Military Collector and Historian*, vol. 31 (1979).

Green, Ernest. *Lincoln at Bay: A Sketch of 1814*. Welland, 1923.

—— "New Light on the Battle of Chippewa," *Welland County Historical Society Papers and Records*, vol. 3 (1927).

Gurd, Norman S. *The Story of Tecumseh*. Toronto: W. Briggs, 1912.

Hamil, Fred Coyne. *The Valley of the Lower Thames, 1640–1850*. Toronto: University of Toronto Press, 1951.

Hamilton, Edward P. "The Battle of Plattsburgh," *Vermont History*, vol. 31 (1963).

Hammack, James W., Jr. *Kentucky and the Second American Revolution: The War of 1812*. Lexington, Ky.: University of Kentucky Press, 1976.

Hare, John S. "Military Punishments in the War of 1812," *Journal of the American Military Institute*, vol. 4 (1940).

Havighurst, Walter. *Three Flags at the Straits: The Forts of Mackinac*. Englewood Cliffs, N.J.: Prentice-Hall, 1966.

Henderson, J.L.H. *John Strachan*. Toronto: University of Toronto Press, 1969.

Hill, Ralph Nading. *Lake Champlain, Key to Liberty*. Taftsville, Vt.: Countryman Press, 1977.

Hitsman, J. Mackay. *The Incredible War of 1812: A Military History*. Toronto: University of Toronto Press, 1965.

—— "Sir George Prevost's Conduct of the Canadian War of 1812," *Canadian Historical Association Report*, 1962.

Hodge, Frederick, W. (ed.). *Handbook of American Indians North of Mexico*, 2 vols. Washington: Smithsonian Institution, Bureau of American Ethnology, Bulletin no. 30, 1906; reprinted, New York: Pageant Books, 1959.

Hollon, William E. *The Lost Pathfinder: Zebulon Montgomery Pike*. Norman, Okla.: University of Oklahoma Press, 1949.

Holmes, T.K. "Pioneer Life in Kent County," *Kent Historical Society Papers and Addresses*, vol. 1 (1914).

Horsman, Reginald. *Matthew Elliott, British Indian Agent*. Detroit: Wayne State University Press, 1964.

————— *The War of 1812*. New York: Knopf, 1969.

Hough, Franklin B. *A History of St. Lawrence and Franklin Counties, New York....* Albany: Little & Co., 1853.

Humphries, Charles. "The Capture of York," *Ontario History*, vol. 51 (1959).

Hurd, Duane H. *History of Clinton and Franklin Counties, New York*. Philadelphia: J.W. Lewis, 1880.

Ingersoll, Charles J. *Historical Sketch of the Second War between the United States of America and Great Britain....* Philadelphia: Lea and Blanchard, 1845–49.

Ingersoll, James H. "The Ancestry of Laura Secord," *Ontario Historical Society Papers and Records*, vol. 23 (1926).

Ingraham, Edward. *A Sketch of the Events Which Preceded the Capture of Washington by the British*. Philadelphia, 1849.

Ingram, George. "The Story of Laura Secord Revisited," *Ontario History*, vol. 57 (1965).

Irving, L. Homfray. *Officers of the British Forces in Canada during the War of 1812–15*. Welland: Tribune Print. for Canadian Military Institute, 1908.

Jackson, Donald. "How Lost Was Zebulon Pike?" *American Heritage*, vol. 16 (1965).

Jacobs, James R. *Tarnished Warrior: Major-General James Wilkinson*. New York: Macmillan, 1938.

James, William. *A Full and Correct Account of the Military Occurrences of the Late War between Great Britain and the United States of America*, 2 vols. London, 1818.

Jarvis, Russell. *A Biographical Notice of Commodore Jesse D. Elliott....* Philadelphia, 1835.

Johnson, Crisfield. *A Centennial History of Erie County, New York....* Buffalo: Matthew and Warren, 1876.

Kelton, Dwight H. *Annals of Fort Mackinac*. Detroit: Detroit Free Press, 1888.

Kerr, W.B. "The Occupation of York," *Canadian Historical Review*, vol. 5 (1924).

Ketchum, William. *An Authentic and Comprehensive History of Buffalo...*, vol. II. Buffalo: Rockwell, Baker & Hill, 1864–65.

Kirby, William. *Annals of Niagara*. Welland: Lundy's Lane Historical Society, 1896.

Koke, Richard J. "The Britons Who Fought on the Canadian Frontier: Uniforms of the War of 1812," *New York Historical Society Quarterly*, vol. 45 (1961).

Land, J.H. "The Battle of Stoney Creek," *Journal and Transactions of the Wentworth Historical Society*, vol. 1 (1892).

Lauriston, Victor. *Romantic Kent, the Story of a County*. Chatham: Shepherd Printing, 1952.

Lighthall, William Douw. *An Account of the Battle of Chateauguay....* Montreal: W. Drysdale, 1889.

Lord, Walter. *The Dawn's Early Light*. New York: W.W. Norton, 1972.

Lossing, Benson J. *The Pictorial Field-book of the War of 1812....* New York: Harper and Brothers, 1868.

Lower, Arthur R.M. *Canadians in the Making: A Social History of Canada*. Toronto: Longmans, Green, 1958.

Lyman, Olin. *Commodore Oliver Hazard Perry and the War on the Lakes*. New York: New Amsterdam Book Co., 1905.

McAfee, Robert. *History of the Late War in the Western Country....* Lexington, Ky.: Worsley and Smith, 1816.

Mackenzie, Alexander S. *Commodore Oliver Hazard Perry...His Life and Achievements*. Akron, O.: J.K. Richardson, 1910 [first published 1840].

McKenzie, Ruth. *Laura Secord: The Legend and the Lady*. Toronto: McClelland and Stewart, 1971.

Maclay, Edgar Stanton. *A History of the United States Navy from 1775 to 1901*. New York: D. Appleton, 1901.

Macmillan Dictionary of Canadian Biography, 4th ed., edited by W. Stewart Wallace and W.A. McKay. Toronto: Macmillan, 1978.

Magill, M.L. "William Allan and the War of 1812," *Ontario History*, vol. 64 (1972).

Mahan, Alfred T. *Sea Power in Its Relations to the War of 1812*, 2 vols. Boston: Little, Brown, 1905.

Mahon, John K. *The War of 1812*. Gainesville: University of Florida Press, 1972.

Marine, William M. *The British Invasion of Maryland, 1812–15*. Baltimore, 1913.

Mason, Philip P. (ed.). *After Tippecanoe: Some Aspects of the War of 1812*. Toronto: Ryerson Press; East Lansing, Mich.: Michigan State University Press, 1963.

Mather, J.D. "The Capture of Fort Niagara, 19th December 1813," *Canadian Defence Quarterly*, vol. 3 (1926).

May, George S. *War, 1812* [Lansing?]: Mackinac Island State Park Commission, 1962.

Mayo, Bernard. *Henry Clay, Spokesman of the New West*. Boston: Houghton Mifflin, 1937.

———— "The Man Who Killed Tecumseh," *American Mercury*, 1930.

Metcalf, Clarence S. "Daniel Dobbins, Sailing Master, U.S.N....." *Inland Seas*, vol. 14 (1958).

Meyer, Leland Winfield. *The Life and Times of Colonel Richard M. Johnson of Kentucky*. New York: Columbia University Press, 1932.

Moir, John S. "An Early Record of Laura Secord's Walk," *Ontario History*, vol. 51 (1959).

Morgan, Henry J. *Sketches of Celebrated Canadians....* Quebec: Hunter, Rose, 1862.

Muir, R.C. "Burford's First Settler, Politician and Military Man – Benajah Mallory," *Ontario Historical Society Papers and Records*, vol. 26 (1930).

Mullaly, Frank B. "The Battle of Baltimore," *Maryland Historical Magazine*, vol. 54 (1959).

Muller, Charles G. *The Proudest Day: Macdonough on Lake Champlain*. New York: John Day, 1960.

———— "Commodore & Mrs. Thomas Macdonough, Some Light on Their Family," *Delaware History*, vol. 9 (1960).

Muller, H.N. "A 'Traitorous and Diabolic Traffic': The Commerce of the Champlain-Richelieu Corridor during the War of 1812," *Vermont History*, vol. 44 (1976).

———— "Smuggling into Canada: How the Champlain Valley Defied Jefferson's Embargo," *Vermont History*, vol. 38 (1970).

Oman, Sir Charles. *Wellington's Army, 1809–1814*. London: Arnold, 1913.

Palmer, Peter. *History of Lake Champlain, from...1609...to...1814*, 3rd ed. New York: Frank F. Lovell, 1885[?].

Perkins, Bradford. *Castlereagh and Adams: England and the United States, 1812–1823*. Berkeley: University of California Press, 1964.

Quaife, Milo M. "Governor Shelby's Army in the River Thames Campaign," *Filson Club History Quarterly*, vol. 10 (1936).

———— *The Yankees Capture York*. Detroit: Wayne University Press, 1955.

Quisenberry, A.C. "Colonel George Croghan," *Register of the Kentucky Historical Society*, vol. 10 (1912).

———— "Kentuckians in the Battle of Lake Erie," *Register of the Kentucky Historical Society*, vol. 9 (1911).

Randall, E.O. "Tecumseh, the Shawnee Chief," *Ohio Archaeological and Historical Society Publications*, vol. 15 (1906).

Raudzens, George. "'Red George' Macdonell, Military Saviour of Upper Canada?" *Ontario History*, vol. 62 (1970).

Richards, George H. *Memoir of Alexander Macomb, the Major-General Commanding the Army of the United States....* New York: McElrath, Bangs, 1833.

Riddell, William R. "Benajah Mallory, Traitor," *Ontario Historical Society Papers and Records*, vol. 26 (1930).

———— "An Echo of the War of 1812," *Ontario Historical Society Papers and Records*, vol. 23 (1926).

———— "The Ancaster 'Bloody Assize' of 1814," *Ontario Historical Society Papers and Records*, vol. 20 (1923).

———— "The First Canadian War-time Prohibition Measure," *Canadian Historical Review*, vol. 1 (1920).

———— "Joseph Willcocks, Sheriff, Member of Parliament, Traitor," *Ontario Historical Society Papers and Records*, vol. 24 (1927).

Robinson, Sir Charles W. *Life of Sir John Beverley Robinson, Bart., C.B., D.C.L....* Toronto: Morang, 1904.

Roosevelt, Theodore. *The Naval War of 1812....* New York: G.P. Putnam's Sons, 1883.

Rosenberg, Max. *The Building of Perry's Fleet on Lake Erie, 1812–13*. [Harrisburg?]: Pennsylvania Historical and Museums Commission, 1968.

Roske, Ralph J. and Donely, Richard W. "The Perry-Elliott Controversy: A Bitter Footnote to the Battle of Lake Erie," *Northwest Ohio Quarterly*, vol. 34 (1962).

Ryerson, Adolphus Egerton. *The Loyalists of America and Their Times, from 1620 to 1816*, 2 vols, 2nd ed. Toronto: W. Briggs, 1880.

Salisbury, George. *Battle of Crysler's Farm* [pamphlet], n.d.

Selby, Charlotte, "Memoirs," unpublished, courtesy Joyce Douglas.

Sellar, Robert. *The Histories of the County of Huntingdon and of the Seigniories of Chateaugay and Beauharnois....* Huntingdon, Que.: Canadian Gleaner, 1888.

———— *The U.S. Campaign of 1813 to Capture Montreal....* Huntingdon, Que., 1914.

Skeen, C. Edward. "Mr. Madison's Secretary of War," *Pennsylvania Magazine of History and Biography*, vol. 100 (1976).

———— "Monroe and Armstrong, a Study in Political Rivalry," *New-York Historical Society Quarterly*, vol. 57 (1973).

Smelser, Marshall. "Tecumseh, Harrison and the War of 1812," *Indiana Magazine of History*, vol. 65 (1969).

Smith, Alison. "John Strachan and Early Upper Canada, 1799–1814," *Ontario History*, vol. 52 (1960).

Smith, J.H. "The Battle of Stoney Creek," *Journal and Proceedings of the Hamilton Association*, 1896–97.

———— "Historical Sketch of the County of Wentworth," *Wentworth Historical Society Papers and Records*, vol. 10 (1922) [first published 1897].

Snow, Richard. "The Battle of Lake Erie," *American Heritage*, vol. 27 (1976).

Squires, William Austin. *The 104th Regiment of Foot (the New Brunswick Regiment), 1803–1817*. Fredericton: Brunswick Press, c. 1962.

Stacey, C.P. "Another Look at the Battle of Lake Erie," *Canadian Historical Review*, vol. 39 (1958).

———— *The Battle of Little York*. Toronto: Toronto Historical Board, 1963.

———— "The Ships of the British Squadron on Lake Ontario, 1812–14," *Canadian Historical Review*, vol. 34 (1953).

Stanley, George F.G. "British Operations in the American Northwest, 1812–15," *Journal of the Society for Army Historical Research*, vol. 22 (1943–44).

———— "The Indians in the War of 1812," *Canadian Historical Review*, vol. 31 (1950).

———— "The New Brunswick Fencibles," *Canadian Defence Quarterly*, vol. 16 (1938).

Stone, William. *The Life and Times of Sa-Go-Ye-Wat-Ha or Red Jacket*, 2nd rev. ed. Albany, 1866.

Sulte, Benjamin. *La Bataille de Châteauguay*. Quebec: R. Renault, 1899.

Suthren, Victor. "The Battle of Châteauguay," *Canadian Historic Sites: Occasional Papers in Archeology and History*, no. 11 (1974).

Terrell, John Upton. *Zebulon Pike: The Life and Times of an Adventurer*. New York: Weybright and Talley, 1968.

Thompson, E.J. "Laura Ingersoll Secord," *Niagara Historical Society Publications*, no. 25 (1913).

Thompson, Mabel W. "Billy Green, the Scout," *Ontario History*, vol. 44 (1952).

Tohill, Louis A. "Robert Dickson, Fur Trader on the Upper Mississippi," *North Dakota Historical Quarterly*, vol. 3 (1928).

Tucker, Glenn. *Poltroons and Patriots: A Popular Account of the War of 1812*, 2 vols. Indianapolis: Bobbs-Merrill, 1954.

——— *Tecumseh: Vision of Glory*. Indianapolis: Bobbs-Merrill, 1956.

Upton, Emory. *The Military Policy of the United States*. Washington: Government Printing Office, 1907.

Van de Water, Frederic F. *Lake Champlain and Lake George*. Indianapolis: Bobbs-Merrill, 1946.

Van Fleet, James A. *Old and New Mackinac....* Ann Arbor, 1870.

Wallace, W.S. *The Story of Laura Secord: A Study in Historical Evidence*. Toronto: Macmillan, 1932.

Warner, Mabel V. "Memorials at Lundy's Lane," *Ontario Historical Society Papers and Records*, vol. 51 (1959).

Watson, O.K. "Moraviantown," *Ontario Historical Society Papers and Records*, vol. 28 (1932).

Way, Ronald. "The Day of Crysler's Farm," *Canadian Geographical Journal*, vol. 62 (1961).

Wickliffe, Charles A. "Tecumseh and the Battle of the Thames," *Register of the Kentucky Historical Society*, vol. 60 (1962).

Wilkinson-Latham, Robert. *British Artillery on Land and Sea, 1790–1820*. Newton Abbot: David and Charles, 1973.

Williams, Charles. "George Croghan," *Ohio Archaeological and Historical Society Publications*, vol. 12 (1903).

Williams, Clara S. "An Experience of 1813," *Buffalo Historical Society Publications*, vol. 26 (1922).

Williams, John S. *History of the Invasion and Capture of Washington and of the Events Which Preceded and Followed*. New York: Harper & Brothers, 1857.

Wilner, Merton. *Niagara Frontier: A Narrative and Documentary History*, 4 vols. Chicago: S.J. Clarke, 1931.

Winter, Nevin O. *A History of Northwest Ohio....* Chicago: Lewis Publishing, 1917.

Wise, S.F. and Brown, R. Craig. *Canada Views the United States: Nineteenth-Century Political Attitudes*. Toronto: Macmillan, 1967.

Yaple, R.L. "The Auxiliaries: Foreign and Miscellaneous Regiments in the British Army, 1802–1817," *Journal of the Society for Army Historical Research*, vol. 50 (1972).

Young, Bennett H. "The Battle of the Thames," *Filson Club Publication* no. 18 (1903).

Zaslow, Morris and Turner, Wesley B. (eds.). *The Defended Border: Upper Canada and the War of 1812*. Toronto: Macmillan, 1964.

Index

McKay, William, 307
McKee, Alexander, 192
McKee, Mrs. Alex, 255
McKee, Thomas, 305
McKenney, Cornet Amos, 248-49
Mackinac Island, *see* Michilimackinac Island
McLean, Donald, 42, 48, 54, 57
McMullen, Alexander, 338-39, 341, 343-44
MacNab, Allan, 42, 257, 258
McNeale, Capt. Neal, 46, 48
Macomb, Brig.-Gen. Alexander, 386-88, 398, 434; described, 387
McRee, Col. William, 335-36
Madawaska River, 15
Madison, Dolley, 371, 373
Madison, Maj. George, 294, 295
Madison, President James, 24, 212, 282, 369, 370, 372, 374
Madison, 41, 46, 51, 58, 66, 68, 69
Mallory, Benajah, 81, 253, 261, 262, 280, 281, 434
Manchester, N.Y., 261
Mann, James, 69
Manning, David, 215-18, 221
Manning, Jacob, 215-18
Markle, Abraham, 253, 281, 291-92, 298, 434
Mascotopah, *see* Dickson, Robert
May, Wilson, 164
Menominee Indians, 111, 125, 142, 307, 310
Merritt, Capt. William Hamilton, 65, 73, 78, 247-51, 256, 257, 260, 341, 434
Methodism, 39
Métoss, 106-8
Miami Indians, 184, 426
Michilimackinac Island, 23, 207, 303-4, 306, 313, 314, 409, 414, 424, 425; American attack on, 307-11
Militia, Canadian: 25, 38, 43, 45-46, 49-50, 60, 72-73, 83, 278, 321, 330; Beauharnois, 218, 223, 226; Canadian Voltigeurs, 25, 218-19, at battle of Châteauguay, 221, 224, 226, at Crysler's Farm, 234, 236, 237-

38; Châteauguay Chasseurs, 224; Essex and Kent, 126; Green Bay Fencibles, 307; Incorporated (Upper Canada), 25; Lincoln, 92, 257; Niagara Light Dragoons, 249; Norfolk, 280; Oxford, 280; Provincial Dragoons, 65, 82, 234, 247-49; Sedentary, 25; Select Embodied (Lower Canada), 25, 220, 223-24, 5th Battalion, 218; York Volunteers, 38; Sedentary and Select Embodied at battle of Châteauguay, 218-28
Militia, U.S.: 23, 25, 103-4, 181-82, 251-52, 358; Baltimore 5th, 368-69, 370; Canadian Volunteers, 81, 252, 261, 339; District of Columbia, 367, 371; Kentucky, 24, 25, 144, 152, 186-88, 189-90, 293, at Fort Meigs, 104-5, 117, 120-22, 127, at battle of Thames, 198-204; Maryland, 367-70; New York, 23; Pennsylvania, 23, 104, 148, 190, 319, 320, 321, 335, 338-39, 367; Vermont, 386; Virginia, 103, 221, 367
Miller, Col. James, 336, 343
Milligan, George, 403
Mississauga Indians, 43
Mississippi River Valley, 306-7, 308
Mitchell, Col. George, 53, 54
Mohawk Indians, 66, 82, 83, 87, 91, 111, 321
Monroe, James, 212, 274, 368, 369, 415; quoted, 282
Montreal, 213-14, 215, 217, 218, 221, 229, 230, 241
Moose Island, 416, 417
Moraviantown, U.C., 186, 191, 192, 196, 205, 208
Morrison, Capt. John, 120, 122
Morrison, Lt.-Col. Joseph, 234-36, 238-39, 339, 434
Morristown, N.Y., 230
Morton, Simeon, 58
Muir, Maj. Adam, 125, 184, 193
Mulcaster, Capt. William, 157, 230, 233, 237
Mulholland, Henry, 58

488

Procter, Maj.-Gen. Henry, 24, 105, 136, 137, 140, 148, 154, 177, 179, 180-87, 189, 190, 191, 192, 435; at Fort Meigs, 111-27 *passim*, 138-39; at Fort Stephenson, 142-47; and Indians, 142-43, 184-86; and battle of Thames, 195-205, 207-8

Prophet, the, 110, 138, 177, 178, 192, 435

Prophetstown, Indiana Terr., 193

Provincial Corps of Light Infantry, *see* Militia, Canadian: Canadian Voltigeurs

Prussia, 22

Purdy, Col. Robert, 221-27

Put-in Bay, O., 151, 170, 206, 280

Queen Charlotte, 158-61, 164, 167-68

Queenston, U.C., 84, 86, 322, 328-29, 330, 331; battle of, 22, 44, 255, 289

Riall, Maj.-Gen. Phineas, 260, 266, 279, 318-19, 328, 330, 332, 435; at Chippawa, 321, 324, 327; described, 322; at Lundy's Lane, 333-35

Richardson, John, 197, 292-95, 435; at Fort Meigs, 112, 121, 125, 139; at Fort Stephenson, 146; at battle of Thames, 201, 204, 205, 206

Richardson, Dr. Robert, 206

Ridout, Thomas, 99

Ripley, Lt.-Col. Eleazar W. (later Brig.-Gen.), 237, 289, 318, 319, 329, 332, 333, 342-43, 356, 358, 435; at Chippawa, 325; at Lundy's Lane, 335, 336, 339, 340

River aux Canards, 182

River Raisin, battle of, 89, 116, 117, 144, 181, 293; *see also* Frenchtown

Roach, Capt. Isaac, 86

Roberts, Benjamin, farm, 215

Robertson, James, 391, 395, 396

Robinson, Maj.-Gen. Frederick Philipse, 382, 385, 388, 396-98, 435; described, 383-84; quoted, 399

Robinson, John Beverley, 44, 99, 280-81, 384, 435; and Ancaster trials, 295-99

Robinson, Capt. Peter, 99

Roe, Billy, 57

Rogers, John, 255

Rogers, Pte. Reuben, 15-17

Rolette, Joseph, 307

Romanzoff, Count, 275, 276, 277

Ross, Maj.-Gen. Robert, 363-66, 370, 372, 373, 374, 398

Ross, Dr. William, 214

Rush, Richard, 369

Russell, Jonathan, 435; at Gothenburg, 281, 282, 283, 285, 286; at Ghent, 404, 412, 417

Russell, Peter, 253

Sacjaquady Creek, 346

Sackets Harbor, N.Y., 17, 29, 30, 31, 72, 97, 133, 211-12, 214, 242, 280, 289, 409; and shipbuilding contest, 286-88

St. André, L.C., 16

St. Catharines, U.C., *see* Shipman's Corners

St. Clair, Maj.-Gen. Arthur, 179

St. Davids, U.C., 86, 257, 330

St. John, Margaret, 262, 263, 265, 266, 267-68

St. John, Margaret (the younger), 267

St. John, Maria, 266

St. John, Martha, 265, 267

St. John, Parnell, 267

St. John, Sarah, 266

St. John family, 266, 267, 268

St. Joseph's Island, 308, 311

St. Lawrence River, 217, 218, 221, 228, 230, 242, 243, 289

St. Lawrence, 287, 288, 357, 358

St. Petersburg, Russia, 155, 271-72

St. Regis, N.Y., 241

Sandwich, U.C., 183, 184

San Sebastian, Spain, 372, 384

Saranac River, 383, 397

Saratoga, 379, 381, 389, 390, 391-96

Sauk Indians, 111

Saunders, Matthias, 50, 51

Sausamauee, quoted, 424-25

Schnall, Mrs., 205

Scorpion, 158, 160, 308, 311, 312, 313, 314